Joseph 665-8524

The Revolution of 1905 and Russia's Jews

The Revolution of 1905 and Russia's Jews

EDITED BY STEFANI HOFFMAN
AND EZRA MENDELSOHN

PENN

University of Pennsylvania Press

Philadelphia

האוניברסיטה העברית בירושלים
The Hebrew University of Jerusalem

Publication of this volume was aided by a grant from the Leonid Nevzlin Research Center for Russian and East European Jewry at the Hebrew University of Jerusalem.

Published by
University of Pennsylvania Press
Philadelphia, Pennsylvania 19104–4112

Printed in the United States of America on acid-free paper

10   9   8   7   6   5   4   3   2   1

A Cataloging-in-Publication record is available from the Library of Congress
ISBN 978-0-8122-4064-1

To Jonathan Frankel, from his colleagues, students, and friends

Contents

Introduction

Benjamin Nathans

Like so much else that occurred in tsarist Russia, the Revolution of 1905 occupies a controversial and much-visited site in the landscape of modern Jewish history. Debates over its significance began even before the revolutionary heat had dissipated, as participants sought to make sense out of a staggering chain of events that, in the space of less than a year, gave rise to Russia's first democratically elected parliament as well as to campaigns of murderous anti-Jewish violence on a scale hitherto unknown under tsarist rule. For each of the dozen Jews elected by their fellow citizens to the Duma, as the new parliament was known, more than two hundred and fifty paid with their lives in pogroms across the Pale of Settlement. Why, asked an eyewitness in Vilna, had "popular spontaneity destroyed what had been achieved by revolutionary reason and conscious will?"[1] Should the Russian Empire's Jews—the majority of the world's Jewish population—join hands with the revolutionary cause? To what end, in what manner—and at what cost?

Historians, in search of the long view, have elaborated these debates in a variety of directions. Some have understood 1905 as the final collapse of hopes for Jewish emancipation under tsarist rule, a generation-defining transition to militant mass politics on the Jewish street. Others, by contrast, have regarded 1905 as a lethal blow to the hothouse of socialist and nationalist ideologies, turning Jewish youth (like their Russian counterparts) inward to the self, to aesthetics, and other manifestations of so-called decadence. And still others have found in it the catalyst of the record-setting exodus of Jews to North America, or by contrast, of a smaller group destined for—and destined to transform radically— Palestine and the Land of Israel. The Revolution of 1905, in short, has served as a nodal point in the history of Jewish Eastern Europe and a crucible for ideas and practices that would shape Jewish life in Europe and beyond.

The Bolshevik leader Vladimir Lenin famously described 1905 as a "dress rehearsal" for the ultimate revolutionary drama of 1917. There is much truth to this assessment. All the principal elements of 1905 resurfaced, as if on cue, twelve years later. Once again a disastrous war (this time against Germany and Austria-Hungary rather than Japan) eroded popular support for Tsar Nicholas II. Once again the revolutionary dynamic was reflected in the successive appearance on stage of liberal and socialist groups and their putative popular constituencies. And once again, political upheavals triggered waves of ethnic violence. But Lenin also—though less famously—described the Paris Commune of 1870 and the February 1917 Revolution in Petrograd as dress rehearsals for the events of October, suggesting that, for him at least, actual historical lineages were less important than the inexorable forward march of revolution itself.[2]

The present volume seeks to loosen the bonds that tie 1905 to its alleged world-historical antecedents and consequences, to bring the reader face-to-face with participants and eyewitnesses, and to confront a revolutionary process whose hallmark, as Abraham Ascher puts it in the opening chapter, lay precisely in the ambiguity of its outcome. This very ambiguity invites us to explore not only the transformative impact of 1905 but also the ways in which the revolution failed to deflect certain continuities of Russian Jewish life, while steering others in unanticipated directions that do not comfortably align with conventional notions of revolutionary radicalism or cultural decadence. It further invites us to consider whether, for Russia's Jews, the turning points of the 1905 epoch were not only such empire-wide events as the general strike, the creation of a parliament, and the explosions of pogrom violence but also less visible changes in communal organization, print culture, and patterns of migration. The authors of the essays in this volume insist on viewing 1905 not as a dress rehearsal (whether for the Russian Revolution of 1917 or, at a greater distance, the achievement of Jewish political sovereignty in 1948) but as a performance in its own right. The volume's contributors have resisted classifying the revolutionary drama as triumph or tragedy, seeking instead to offer fresh reassessments of key actors (individual and collective), crucial scenes, and the shape of the plot as a whole.

The theatrical metaphor is not accidental. Over the course of the last two decades, historians of modern Russian and East European Jewry have broadened the scope of their investigations from political parties and ideologies to more diffuse—and often culturally mediated—forms of power and representation.[3] This trend can be understood partly as a belated joining of the "cultural turn" that reoriented much of the humanities in the 1970s and 1980s and partly as a more local recognition that the highly combustible mixture of socialist and nationalist ideologies that defined so much of twentieth-century Jewish life is now "history"—and has thereby lost its near monopoly on our historical imagination.

The widening of the study of Russian Jewry to include not just politics but political culture, not just ideologies but identities, and, most important, the shift from analytic categories defined by historical actors to those selected by historians themselves found expression in a pathbreaking work of scholarship by the man in whose honor the present volume appears. Whatever the ambiguities of 1905 as a turning point in modern Jewish history, there can be little doubt that Jonathan Frankel's *Prophecy and Politics: Socialism, Nationalism, and the Russian Jews, 1862–1917*, first published in 1981, marked a turning point in modern Jewish historiography. More than a quarter-century later (and now reissued for a new generation of readers), it remains the preeminent study of the formation of a Jewish political culture, a virtual encyclopedia of the enormously influential Russian Jewish radical milieu.[4]

Prophecy and Politics liberated Russian Jewish history from the inherited, largely Marxian paradigms fashioned by fin de siècle Jewish political parties. It did so most dramatically in the case of the Bund, the Jewish labor movement whose turn to Yiddish and Jewish nationalism—in spite of its ideological commitment to internationalism—had long been understood as a natural concession to the linguistic and existential needs of Jewish workers, the movement's "base." Frankel demonstrated that, on the contrary, the turn to Yiddish and Jewish nationalism was neither natural nor inevitable and, in fact, stemmed from the existential needs of the Bund's intelligentsia leaders in the context of their tangled relations with their Russian revolutionary counterparts on the one hand and the specter of linguistic "self-russification" by Jewish workers on the other. It was Frankel's close attention to what he called "the problem of self-definition, the unending search for identity" on the part of the Russian Jewish intelligentsia that made possible this self-emancipation from the received wisdom.[5] As one reviewer put it, the book's "true subject" was "the tension between personal inclinations and general interests, between the individual's subjective truth and the historical progress of the nation."[6]

The analytic ambition of *Prophecy and Politics*, however, reached far beyond its volte-face regarding the relationship between individual and party genealogies. One of its signal achievements, in fact, was to show that rival parties, movements, and ideologies (socialist, Zionist, territorialist, autonomist, etc.) could most fruitfully be understood as parts of a single Jewish intelligentsia milieu whose internal affinities ran deep below the surface of incessant sectarian rivalries and antagonisms. Those affinities, Frankel argued, were nourished by a shared apocalyptic mood, a potent blend of religious and secular (ideological) messianism.[7] Yet another breakthrough consisted in Frankel's insistence that radical Jewish politics evolved in a complex dialectic of emulation and estrangement vis-à-vis analogous Russian and Polish movements—which is to say, that Jewish politics could be fully apprehended only within a multiethnic, imperial framework. And as if that were not a sufficiently broad canvas, *Prophecy and Politics* pioneered a genuinely transcontinental Jewish history, following the radical Russian Jewish milieu as it transplanted itself onto the alien soil of the American labor movement and the Jewish settlements of Ottoman Palestine.

Across this wide-ranging narrative, Frankel's famously "thick" descriptions rendered his restless revolutionaries in their full complexity as human beings. While anchored in a conception of modern Jewish history that privileges moments of collective crisis as engines of change, *Prophecy and Politics* resisted the kinds of schematic models of historical development so dear to its protagonists, instead restoring a vital sense of contingency to their fate in tsarist Russia and beyond. The liberation from teleological models of development, it seems to me, helps account for the enduring influence of *Prophecy and Politics*. As the diverse essays in the present volume amply illustrate, it is virtually impossible to write about Jews, power, and culture in late imperial Russia—not to mention a host of related topics—without engaging the questions and arguments raised by Frankel over the course of his scholarly career.

Among those questions and arguments, of course, are some that touch directly on the subject of the present volume. The Revolution of 1905, Frankel has written, "did not represent a major turning point, a basic reevaluation of values, the creation of fundamentally new political movements." "What it did do was to make broader circles than ever before conscious of the urgency of the Jewish problem; to stimulate the creation of additional parties and organizations dedicated to its solution; and to bring them together into a complicated shifting system of alliances and rivalries."[8] The effect of 1905, in other words, was additive rather than transformative. Frankel's assessment was grounded in a comparative framework: for him, 1905 was suspended between two historically more significant moments, namely, the pogroms of 1881–82 and the general crisis they produced in Russian Jewry and the nexus of world war and revolution in 1917, in the course of which the three empires crucial to the Jews' fate—the Russian, the Austrian, and the Ottoman—disintegrated.

And yet, the passage quoted above begs several questions: How did 1905 change the way the "urgency of the Jewish problem" was construed? What were those "additional parties and organizations" that arose during and after the revolution? And how did the "alliances and rivalries" they engendered differ from those that preceded 1905? The

third and final part of *Prophecy and Politics*, "Ideology and Émigré Realities," shifts the mise-en-scène of the Jewish intelligentsia after 1907 (the
effective end date of the first revolutionary epoch) from Russia to
America and Palestine. While there is no denying the historical significance of these offshoots, the effect is a kind of optical illusion whereby
the curtain drops on Jewish history *in Russia* until another revolutionary
crisis erupts in 1917, as if, in the words of a Bundist newspaper in 1908,
"Only ruins remain."[9]

The present volume suggests that far more than ruins remained.
Inspired by Frankel's self-emancipation from the Jewish intelligentsia's
own master narrative and by his legendary generosity to students and
colleagues around the world, its authors offer a fresh look at the revolutionary dynamic as well as new analyses of Russian Jewry's post-1905 fortunes. As Brian Horowitz points out in his chapter on the Society for the
Promotion of Enlightenment among the Jews of Russia, "as with so
much of Jewish history, one has to be sensitive as much to potentialities
as to realities." The postrevolutionary era, after all, lasted scarcely a decade, until the incursion of German and Austrian troops into the Pale of
Settlement during World War I, transforming Jewish life far more radically than had the upheavals of 1905. During that decade, however, ideas
and practices came to the fore that suggest an important shift in the
political culture of Russian Jewry, a weakening of the "prophetic" mode
of the previous era and of the messianic expectations that fueled it. It
was this partial erosion of the apocalyptic that opened the field for the
host of alternatives explored in the chapters that follow.

Part I of the present volume, "Reassessing the 1905 Revolution,"
introduces readers to the shaping forces of the revolutionary era as a
whole, understood as extending from the semi-legal public gatherings
of 1904 to the reassertion of monarchical authority in 1907. In "Interpreting 1905," Abraham Ascher, the doyen of Western historians of Russia's first revolution, emphasizes the extraordinary complexity of the
revolutionary drama, its many unpredictable twists and turns, not least
among them the unexpected outcome of Russia's first democratic elections. While pressure from below failed to transfer political power from
one social class to another, the massive "assault on authority" was effective enough to make the toppling of the old regime suddenly more than
credible. Hence the ambiguous outcome of 1905: tsarism was left intact,
but the revolution weakened its foundations far more profoundly than
had decades of attempted assassinations, terrorist attacks, and local
uprisings.

The tsar, however, insisted on regarding the revolution as an unambiguous failure. In his essay "Nicholas II and the Revolution," Richard
Wortman, the leading authority on the political culture of the Russian

monarchy, argues that well before 1905 Nicholas had adopted a "national myth" prescribing that Russia be governed according to an imagined premodern ideal of autocratic rule, an "organic union" of tsar and people. Based on a shared religious faith and spiritual destiny, the "national myth" left little room for Jews and other non-Orthodox groups. If anything, Nicholas viewed the events of 1905 as confirmation of the threat to Russia posed by Jews and other outsiders, and they strengthened his own resolve to rescue Russia in the manner of his medieval ancestor from the Time of Troubles, the founder of the Romanov dynasty, Tsar Mikhail Fedorovich.

Some of the practical implications of the "national myth" in the revolutionary era are explored in Part II, "The Old Regime Confronts Its 'Jewish Question.'" As Semion Goldin demonstrates in his chapter "The 'Jewish Question' in the Tsarist Army in the Early Twentieth Century," in the empire's largest and most multiethnic institution—the army—there was broad support, at least at the elite level, for ending the military conscription of Jews and thereby reversing the limited integration that had begun three-quarters of a century earlier under Tsar Nicholas I. In the wake of the 1905 Revolution, a majority of military commanders came to regard Jews not just as poor soldiers but also as politically subversive. This was a view graphically reinforced by the increasingly virulent depiction of Jews in the right-wing press, a phenomenon analyzed by Robert Weinberg in his chapter "The Russian Right Responds to 1905: Visual Depictions of Jews in Postrevolutionary Russia." Here it was not so much the army as the Duma, the revolution's most visible success, that was cast as a tool of behind-the-scenes Jewish subversion.

It is important to note, however, that on the whole, the revolutionary era did not witness a retrenchment in the Russian state's Jewish policies. Jews were not expelled from the army (though their chances of promotion to officer status continued to be severely limited and, with the outbreak of war in 1914, were virtually eliminated). Although still restricted in their civil rights, Jews were granted equal political rights as voters and candidates in the Duma elections of 1906 and 1907. Dmitrii Elyashevich's analysis of state control of the printed word, "A Note on the Jewish Press and Censorship during the First Russian Revolution," shows that in 1905 government censorship ceased to apply distinct criteria to Jewish publications as opposed to those of other ethnic and religious minorities, including the largest minority of all, ethnic Russians. Thus Jewish publishing houses benefited equally from the lifting of prepublication censorship, with enormous consequences for the burgeoning Jewish public sphere.

That public sphere is the leading subject of Part III, "1905 as a Crossroads for the Empire's Jews." A freer press reduced the incentive to operate underground and thereby shifted the balance of power between legal and illegal political parties in the Jewish world. Similarly, the Duma privileged electoral politics over clandestine agitation, and radical Jewish parties that had boycotted the first elections (in 1906) quickly changed their minds and decided to join the fray a year later. The broadening of legally sanctioned public activities transformed the work of Jewish organizations across the political-cultural spectrum. In his chapter "Victory from Defeat: 1905 and the Society for the Promotion of Enlightenment among the Jews of Russia," Brian Horowitz explores the empire's oldest public Jewish organization as it shifted from educational philanthropy aimed at increasing Jewish enrollment in Russian schools to the creation of separate Jewish educational institutions such as primary schools, libraries, a rabbinical seminary, and a teachers' institute. His description of attempts to make the society itself more democratic— more like a Jewish parliament, in fact—suggests the complex mix of integrative and separatist forces at work, as a quintessentially liberal organization came to pursue an agenda of de facto cultural autonomy.

The post-1905 prominence of voluntary associations, as Vladimir Levin and Jeffrey Veidlinger show, was characteristic of both the Jewish and Russian worlds. Bundists and Zionists—like their Social Democratic and Socialist Revolutionary counterparts—found themselves on unfamiliar terrain, often disappointed that amateur theaters, orchestras, choirs, and literary discussion groups were uninterested in serving as legal covers for underground political work. Such associations threatened, moreover, to expose Jewish workers to the "bourgeois" influence of traditional Jewish society. And yet, Levin argues in his "The Jewish Socialist Parties in Russia in the Period of Reaction," voluntary associations quietly fostered a kind of internal Jewish revolution in the wake of the larger Revolution of 1905. Threatened with a loss of influence among the Jewish masses, Jewish socialists of all stripes were forced not only to cooperate with nonsocialist (i.e., "bourgeois") activists but also to work within traditional Jewish communal structures that many had previously criticized or shunned altogether.

The effect of such *Gegenwartsarbeit*—the Zionist term for "working in the here-and-now"—was, on the one hand, a tempering (one is tempted, following the historian Gershom Scholem, to say "neutralizing") of messianic instincts through an injection of pragmatism into Jewish political culture and, on the other, a potential revitalization of communal institutions whose authority had been eroding for over a century. Indeed, in his essay "Jewish Cultural Associations in the Aftermath of 1905," Veidlinger argues that such associations gradually usurped the leadership roles previously played by traditional religious and communal authorities. Institutions such as public libraries, moreover, served as "social equalizers," spaces where people of different classes and genders could mix in ways considered taboo by traditional Jewish society. Thus in contrast to Nicholas II's attempt to return to what he imagined to be Russia's medieval heritage of paternal rule through an unmediated spiritual bond between tsar and (Russian Orthodox) people, Jewish efforts focused on the local level, on modernizing the *heder* (the Jewish primary school), opening its doors to girls, forming a variety of mutual aid and cultural societies, and democratizing the governing structure of local Jewish communities.

However, as Scott Ury shows in "The Generation of 1905 and the Politics of Despair: Alienation, Friendship, Community," 1905 by no means extinguished the instinct for radical change. Ury looks closely at some of the young Jewish men who flocked to the empire's cities in the years leading up to and during the revolution, including David Yosef Green (later Ben-Gurion) and other future Zionist leaders. Before they made their name (literally, in Green's case) as a generation defined by the violent upheavals of 1905 and the subsequent exodus to Palestine, Ury contends, Green and others were united by a profound sense of dislocation from family, birthplace, and tradition, a "lost generation" hungry for new forms of community. These tormented figures were forged in Frankel's Russian Jewish radical milieu, desperately searching for "total solutions" (as Green put it in 1905) and often torn between personal and what were construed as "national" or "historical" needs. An exquisite example of the apocalyptic mood prevalent in such circles appears in a private letter by the nineteen-year-old Hebrew writer Uri Nissan Gnessin:

We must consecrate ourselves, purify ourselves. . . . Because all of these doubts and questions are nothing more than the result of our own profanity. Once our souls are purified, these [matters] will also disappear. . . . For the time being, dedicate your energies to the needs of the local community so that you can later be of use to the entire people of Israel. . . . Work, Work, Work![10]

Whatever its ultimate purpose, work in the here-and-now—including the newly legalized electoral politics—produced its own problems in the here-and-now. In "1905 as a Watershed in Polish-Jewish Relations," Theodore R. Weeks explores the parting of the ways between Poles and Jews that was accelerated by the revolutionary experience. If the anti–Russian Polish uprising of 1863 marked a moment of interethnic cooperation (partly mythic, to be sure) between Jews and Poles, in 1905 the winds were blowing in a very different direction. Minorities on both sides that had previously endorsed the idea of Jewish assimilation (or integration) all but evaporated in the wake of the revolution, as the volatile mix of democracy and nationalism in a multiethnic empire cast the divergence of Polish and Jewish interests into stark relief. Indeed, it was the refusal of Jewish voters to support the election of a Polish nationalist to the Duma in 1912, as Weeks notes, that triggered the infamous anti-Jewish boycott of that year in Warsaw and other cities of Russian Poland—an event that, along with the trial of Mendel Beilis in Kiev on charges of ritual murder, marked the low point of Jewish-gentile relations in the post-1905 era.

Part IV, "Cultural Reflections of Revolution," moves the discussion beyond political culture to the tension between political and aesthetic commitments. Several essays in this section explore efforts to represent the revolution in literary form; others analyze the revolution's impact on cultural production and the idea of culture itself.

As Jonathan Frankel has recently observed, 1905 became the subject of "instant fictionalization" in multiple literatures of the Russian Empire.[11] In her survey, "Polish Literature's Portrayal of Jewish Involvement in 1905," Agnieszka Friedrich extends Theodore Weeks's analysis of the Polish case, exploring over a dozen contemporary Polish-language fictional depictions of revolutionary Jews. Within the relatively formulaic genre of the revolutionary novel, she finds a variety of authorial stances, none of them particularly favorable to the idea of Polish-Jewish cooperation. Hannan Hever presents a very different critique of Jewish revolutionary activity in his essay "Rebellion in Writing: Yosef Haim Brenner and the 1905 Revolution." In Brenner, himself a veteran of the Zionist, Bundist (Jewish socialist), and Socialist Revolutionary movements, Hever finds a resurgence of the apocalyptic instinct, now however deliberately shorn of any political dimension, indeed cast as a revolt against Jewish politics itself. Sickened by explanations of anti-Jewish violence designed to confirm the ideological stance of this or that party, Brenner fashioned his own version of what was by then an established genre—the post-pogrom jeremiad. Unlike Lev Pinsker's 1882 pamphlet *Automancipation!* and Haim Nahman Bialik's 1903 epic poem *In the City of Slaughter,* however, Brenner reserved his deepest venom for the endless talk ("filthy nonsense") generated by Jewish political movements, "any contact or dealing with which," argues the hero of Brenner's 1906 Hebrew story "From A. to M.," "is [an] ineradicable disgrace."[12] Instead, Hever shows, Brenner turned inward, to a "sublime, holy pessimism"—precisely the sort of "decadent" retreat deplored by his erstwhile comrades.

The conflict between aesthetic autonomy and revolutionary or national legitimation lies at the heart of Kenneth Moss's "1905 as a Jewish Cultural Revolution? Revolutionary and Evolutionary Dynamics in the East European Jewish Cultural Sphere, 1900–1914." Addressing the central theme of the present volume, Moss offers a key revisionist argument regarding the controversial role of 1905 as a turning point in modern Jewish cultural history. The revolution's ambiguous outcome, he suggests, did not so much *introduce* the tension between aesthetics and politics as *catalyze* a trend already well under way at the turn of the century, a trend best characterized as evolutionary rather than revolutionary. Dissatisfied with explanations of Jewish modernism (such as Brenner's) as a form of psychic compensation for failed revolution, Moss argues that the main function of 1905 was to force the tension between art and ideology to the surface of Jewish cultural life and, indeed, to transform it into "the central organizing conflict of the Yiddish cultural sphere for the rest of its pre-Holocaust history." Thus Moss subtly recasts Jonathan Frankel's own reading of 1905, concurring in Frankel's assessment of 1905's essentially additive rather than transformative impact on the Jewish world but shifting the frame of analysis from political culture to the relationship *between* politics and culture.

Like Moss, Barry Trachtenberg traces the emergence of new forms of Jewish cultural expression in Eastern Europe, in this case the development of literary criticism, folklore studies, philology, and linguistics, all centered on the Yiddish language. The ambiguity of its title notwithstanding, Trachtenberg's "The Revolutionary Origins of Yiddish Scholarship, 1903–17" suggests that the origins of Jewish *visnshaft* (scholarship aspiring to scientific objectivity) lie in the *pre*revolutionary period. As in the case of Jewish literary modernism, one can discern in East European Jewish scholarship a tension between aspirations for intellectual autonomy and a desire to serve the cause of revolution or nation building (or both). Like Moss, Trachtenberg notes continuities in the development of Yiddish-language scholarship that extend well into the 1920s, with the founding of research centers such as the YIVO Institute for Jewish Research in Vilna (Wilno) and Soviet-sponsored Institutes for Jewish Culture in Kiev and Minsk.

Mikhail Krutikov, too, looks to the interwar period for the legacy of 1905. In his chapter "Writing between the Lines: 1905 in the Soviet-Yiddish Novel of the Stalinist Age," Krutikov extends Agnieszka Friedrich's investigation of literary representations to the early Soviet decades, examining works by two Soviet Yiddish writers, Lipman Levin (who wrote under the pen name Lipman-Levin) and Pinkhas Kahanovich ("Der Nister"). Like Friedrich, Krutikov finds a high degree of formulaic consistency in literary depictions of the 1905 Revolution. The dominant scheme, a narrative triptych of war, revolution, and pogroms, conveniently reinforced the Bolshevik version of 1905 as a dress rehearsal for 1917, the three-part sequence appearing to fit both revolutions perfectly. Krutikov is able to show, however, that although this nar-

rative became part of Bolshevik orthodoxy, it originated in late tsarist-
era works by Sholem Aleichem and Sholem Asch, neither of whom was
associated with the Bolsheviks. Furthermore, Krutikov argues, both
Lipman-Levin and Der Nister subtly—and subversively—altered the
officially approved narrative in ways meant to suggest the distinctively
Jewish qualities of their revolutionary protagonists.

The final section of the book, "Overseas Ripples:1905 and American
Jewry," moves the story not only forward in time but also—as pioneered
by *Prophecy and Politics*—beyond the borders of the Russian Empire.
Whether or not the revolution fashioned a "generation" (a term usually
applied to the Second Aliyah, the tens of thousands of Jewish emigrants
who made their way to Palestine after 1905, rather than to the hundreds
of thousands who journeyed to North America and other points west of
Russia), there is little doubt that the revolution's political tremors and
ethnic violence set off some of the largest waves of Jewish emigration in
modern history.

In her essay, "The 1905 Revolution Abroad: Mass Migration, Russian
Jewish Liberalism, and American Jewry, 1903–14," Rebecca Kobrin proposes that migrants bound for the New World, like their counterparts in
the Second Aliyah, formed a distinct cohort. Their exodus constituted a
kind of social revolution—for those who left as well as for those who
stayed behind. In part this was a consequence of their unprecedented
numbers, which in turn reflected new commercial technologies of
steamship transport and mass advertising. But Kobrin suggests that Jewish immigrants to the United States in the period of 1905 were also qualitatively distinct. Tapping the rich collection of autobiographical essays
solicited from East European Jewish immigrants by the New York branch
of YIVO in 1942, she finds a strong current of attitudes and aspirations
best understood under the rubric of liberalism: respect for individual
financial success, educational achievement, and social integration. In
contrast to Zionism and Jewish socialism, liberalism in this sense hardly
qualified as ideology, if by that term one means a program designed to
transform the world. Most intriguingly, Kobrin proposes that these qualities were less an effect of migration to the United States than its cause,
or to put it differently, that the American variety of Russian Jewish liberalism was born in Russia itself.

The persistence of Russia in the minds and collective action of Russian Jewish immigrants in America is the main theme of Eli Lederhendler's essay, "Democracy and Assimilation: The Jews, America, and the
Russian Crisis from Kishinev to the End of World War I." The revolutionary era, and particularly the pogroms, were crucial to the narrative
of persecution in the Old World and, by implication, redemption in the
New. As Lederhendler puts it, the revolutionary crisis "lent the act of

immigration the character of destiny or fate." Thus for Russian Jewish immigrants in America, and for their offspring, there could be little doubt as to whether 1905 constituted a turning point; it became, in the most literal sense, their point of departure.

Most works honoring distinguished scholars consist of essays and articles by former students of the honoree. It seems no exaggeration to say that virtually everyone who works on the history of Jews in Eastern Europe, or on the origins of modern Jewish politics, is a student of Jonathan Frankel. The authors represented in this volume include doctoral students and colleagues from Frankel's long and illustrious career at the Hebrew University of Jerusalem, but the lion's share are historians and literary scholars from other universities, indeed from other continents, for whom Frankel's influence—personal as well as intellectual—has been formative. I am grateful to count myself among them. In Jonathan Frankel we honor a man whose exceptional kindness and generosity to younger scholars, like his pioneering scholarship, continue to make an indelible impression.

Part I
Reassessing the 1905 Revolution

Chapter 1
Interpreting 1905

Abraham Ascher

Although it has long been acknowledged that the Revolution of 1905 was an important event in Russian history, there has been much disagreement about why it was important. It might be useful to review the major interpretations of 1905—by my count five altogether—and to offer what I consider to be not only the most plausible but also the one that I think throws light on the revolution's significance for Jewish history. Not surprisingly, a persistent bone of contention has been the duration of the upheaval, an issue that touches on all the questions in dispute. In my view, the name of the turbulence should actually be "The Revolution of 1904–1907," which is, perhaps, too cumbersome. But it is arguable that the revolution began late in 1904 with the widespread agitation by liberals against tsarism and ended in June 1907 with the dissolution of the Second Duma. Of course, the ideological predispositions of historians account in part for the diversity of opinion on this issue as on all others, but there are two additional factors that help explain the wide range of interpretation: the incredible complexity of the events that composed the upheaval and the ambiguity of the outcome of 1905.

Until the collapse of the Soviet Union in 1991, the interpretation with the largest number of adherents was the one advanced by Lenin, who in 1920 referred to Russia's first revolution as a "dress rehearsal," by which he meant that without it, the "victory of the October Revolution of 1917 would have been impossible." However, Lenin's characterization of 1905 was also meant to suggest the inevitability of 1917 because after a dress rehearsal comes the first performance. In the Leninist scheme, the revolution began with Bloody Sunday on January 9, 1905, when, on orders of the tsarist authorities, troops fired on thousands of unarmed marchers seeking extensive reforms from the government, killing 130 and seriously wounding 299. In a lecture in 1915, Lenin affirmed that both the general strike in October 1905 and the armed uprising in December, which was led by the Bolsheviks, "marked the highest point in the rising tide of the Russian revolution"; on other occasions, he declared that the uprising alone merited that designation. In his view, "one of the fundamental reasons" for the revolution's defeat was the peasantry's inadequate organization and insufficient aggressiveness. At the same time, he contended that the intransigence of the ruling class precluded any outcome other than the one that occurred. Nevertheless, Lenin attached worldwide significance to 1905 because the events in Russia had aroused the revolutionary fervor of masses of people in Western Europe and "throughout the whole of Asia."

In addition, he claimed that although the upheaval was a bourgeois-democratic revolution "in its social content," in its methods of struggle it was proletarian because the strike was the chief weapon in the endeavors to overthrow the existing order. Hence, the working class constituted the "leading force, the vanguard" of the entire oppositional movement. Both by example and through agitation, Lenin asserted, the striking workers had stirred up a large number of peasants, thus confirming his belief that the revolution in Russia would be effected by the proletariat in alliance with the peasantry rather than with the middle class, whom he dismissed as weak and politically untrustworthy.[1]

Lenin's views became the standard interpretation of 1905 in the Soviet Union and guided the work of historians there for some seventy years. The literature on the subject was vast: a scholarly bibliography on 1905 published as early as 1930 ran to 715 pages.[2] The intense Soviet interest in the events of 1905 clearly reflected the political leadership's desire to enhance the legitimacy of communism. If it could be demonstrated that Leninist policies were unimpeachable even in 1905, when the Bolsheviks suffered a major political and military defeat, the Communist Party's claim to preeminence in Soviet society and in the world-wide struggle for socialism would be that much stronger.

But it would be misleading to suggest that Soviet scholarship on 1905 was monolithic. There were, in fact, four phases in that scholarship, corresponding to broader political and cultural trends in the country. In the years from 1921 to 1930, which may be designated as the period of pluralistic Marxism, the publications on 1905 were notably partisan but historians still respected the canons of historical scholarship.[3]

The dean of Soviet historians at the time, Mikhail Pokrovskii, published three volumes of monographs and documents with the express purpose of replacing the four-volume Menshevik study[4] that appeared between 1909 and 1914 and remains to this day the most exhaustive study of the revolutionary upheaval. The Mensheviks had emphasized the contribution of the working class to the undermining of the old order, but they did not claim that the proletariat had exercised hegemony over the oppositional movement throughout that year. Indeed, they had devoted a great deal of space to the agitation against tsarism of other social groups, such as the bourgeoisie, the intelligentsia, the peasantry, as well as various national minorities. In general, the Menshevik historians were less interested in glorifying the proletariat than in understanding what had happened, why the revolution had gone awry. Characteristically, D. Koltsov (pseud. of Boris Abramovich Ginzburg) posed the following question on the very first page of his study of the working class in the years from 1905 to 1907: "Why was the proletariat in the end isolated and forced to repel the blows of reaction on its own?"[5] Only a detailed examination of developments in Russia, Koltsov held, could provide the answer to this difficult question.

Pokrovskii was not troubled by such questions. His point of departure in analyzing 1905 was the Bolshevik seizure of power in 1917. He looked upon 1905 as merely a precursor to 1917 and consequently went to great lengths to justify and magnify the role of the Bolsheviks, who, in fact, were a relatively small group within the opposition in 1905. He dogmatically insisted that the Moscow uprising late in 1905 was "objectively necessary" and the culmination of the revolutionary process, even though it was crushed by the government, an outcome that greatly enhanced the tsar's ability to reassert his political preeminence. In Pokrovskii's mind, the insurrection was psychologically of the utmost importance because it marked the first occasion when ordinary people took it upon themselves to shoot at the authorities. This action broke the "magic spell" that had surrounded the tsar and his armed forces.[6] "If there had been no December uprising," he concluded, "there would have been neither a February nor an October 1917. This was the first blow, which was entirely necessary."[7]

Pokrovskii also leveled serious charges at the Mensheviks without, however, belittling all their tactics. He contended that they had not been "entirely revolutionary" in 1905 and had lacked "sympathy for revolutionary methods," although he thought that they had become "antirevolutionary" only in 1906. But some of their actions evoked praise from Pokrovskii. He thought that they had been right to form the St. Petersburg Soviet and that they had shown good judgment in rejecting the demands of workers right after Bloody Sunday for "armed action" against the government, which "could only have led to another massacre."[8] Nor did Pokrovskii blame the leaders of the Menshevik or other non-Bolshevik parties for the failure of the revolution. In his view, the masses "were not entirely revolutionary" and that had its effect on the revolutionary leadership.[9]

Pokrovskii's analysis of 1905 was the most authoritative in the 1920s, but it was not uncommon for Bolshevik writers to advance their own interpretations, sometimes at variance with the official line. Mikhail I.

Vasil'ev-Iuzhin, for example, contended that political miscalculations by Bolshevik leaders had been a major factor in the defeat of the December uprising and, therefore, of the entire revolution. They had erred in failing to make greater efforts to win the peasants over to the political struggle against the government.[10] And the journal *Istorik-Marksist*, founded specifically to promote Bolshevik historiography, published criticism of some of the most sacred tenets of Bolshevik scholars. In 1926 it printed a long, and in part quite amusing, attack by a certain Comrade Skabysh on scholars who claimed that the proletariat was in a thoroughly militant mood in 1905. It was not true, Skabysh insisted, that workers constituted a disciplined social force committed to a radical social program and to armed action against the authorities. To drive home his point about the workers' lack of zeal, Skabysh recalled the following incident: "On January 9 [1905] a group of us were at the house of a worker who regarded himself as a revolutionary. . . . His wife baked some pancakes and said to us: 'First eat some pancakes and then go see the tsar.' And having eaten the pancakes we went to see the tsar." On a more serious note, Skabysh recalled that in October 1905 workers were prepared to stay out on strike for only a short period of time regardless of whether or not they were going to be paid. But after three or four days they began to indicate that they would return to work unless they were assured of pay for the days they missed. "Now tell me, please," Skabysh asked, "was this a genuinely revolutionary movement?" He, for one, could not but be "extremely dubious" about the existence in October 1905 of a "revolutionary spirit among the Petersburg proletariat." It is true that Skabysh was not a professional historian, but the appearance of his comments in *Istorik-Marksist* cast doubt on the romantic version of working-class conduct in 1905 that had become the stock in trade of most Soviet scholars.[11]

During the second phase of Soviet historical writing on 1905, which lasted from about 1930 to 1955, scholars increasingly came under the direct control of the Communist Party, and their work declined dramatically in quality and quantity. Rigid orthodoxy, polemical attacks on opponents of Bolshevism, and even grotesque distortions of well-established facts were the hallmarks of this scholarship. The liberal bourgeoisie was accused of "perfidious conduct," Stalin's role in the events leading up to the revolution was vastly exaggerated and glorified, the Bolsheviks were credited with having organized the general strike of October 1905 and with having played a preeminent role in the movement to create soviets, and the Mensheviks as well as the Socialist Revolutionaries were accused of "treachery" during the Moscow insurrection in December 1905.[12]

That these crude interpretations and distortions of the history of 1905 were not shared by all Soviet scholars became evident in 1955, two years after Stalin's death. On the fiftieth anniversary of the upheaval, a number of scholarly and balanced studies appeared, initiating the third phase of scholarship. The editorial article in the January issue of *Voprosy istorii*, the leading journal of the historical profession, began by denouncing bourgeois and Menshevik interpretations of the first revolution but then sharply criticized a number of Soviet historians for claiming that already in the first days following Bloody Sunday the working class acted as a well-organized and politically conscious force. In fact, according to the editors of the journal, the massive strikes and demonstrations at that early stage of the upheaval were spontaneous occurrences and the Social Democrats still exerted very little influence over the proletariat. Indeed, a fundamental task for historians was to examine *how* the working class *gradually* gained political consciousness. Throughout 1955 and 1956, *Voprosy istorii* criticized the quality of historical scholarship in general over the preceding twenty-five years and called on scholars to remember that the task of historians was "to explain, not hush up, historical facts."[13]

The third phase came to an abrupt end in March 1957 with the dismissal of eight of the eleven editors of *Voprosy istorii*. The new editorial board agreed to toe the party line once again. "Historical scholarship," the journal now proclaimed, "is one of the most important participants in the ideological battlefront," and scholars must take every precaution to avoid "toning down" the struggle against the "ideological opponents of Marxism-Leninism." All the revisionist interpretations of 1905 that had appeared in 1955 and 1956 were repudiated and several hard-line Stalinist historians were rehabilitated. It seemed as if scholarship on 1905 would return to Stalinist orthodoxies.

In actual fact, the fourth phase of Soviet historiography on 1905, beginning in 1957 and continuing until the Gorbachev era, turned out to be far more diversified and interesting than anyone could have anticipated. The pluralistic Marxism of the 1920s once again became the guiding principle for the historical profession. To be sure, historians revived the dogmatic interpretations of 1905 dominant in the 1930s and 1940s, but they generally avoided blatant crudities and falsifications. They also sought to buttress the officially sanctioned interpretations with studies based on extensive research, and some of these works are quite sophisticated and informative.[14] Perhaps most important, some comprehensive and reliable collections of archival material were published.[15] And on one occasion the authorities permitted the publication of a challenge to one of the most hallowed interpretations of 1905—that the proletariat exercised hegemony over the oppositional movement throughout the revolutionary period. The challenge quickly came under attack, but it is noteworthy that the critique consisted of more than polemics; it was, in fact, a far-reaching scholarly rebuttal. The controversy marked the final breakdown in the scholarly consensus on 1905, and to this day diversity continues to characterize historical discussions of the revolution.[16]

In the West, there has also been great interest in the revolution, especially during the past four decades or so, and although the interpretations have been diverse and nuanced, it is fair to say that social historians have been dominant. They also tend to focus on the masses, and in particular the working class, in the conviction that they were the driving force of the revolution. Moreover, many of them also consider Bloody Sunday to have been the starting point of the upheaval and view the armed uprising in Moscow as its high point. Finally, these historians tend to dismiss the government's concessions as totally inadequate, and they are highly skeptical about the notion that there was any possibility of imperial Russia's peaceful transformation into a constitutional monarchy with political institutions comparable to those in Western Europe.[17]

By contrast, more traditional or, if you will, conservative commentators on 1905—and they would include some Russian émigré intellectuals, former government officials as well as scholars—argue that it was the legitimate fears of the authorities that the opposition would never be satisfied with moderate reforms that precluded a peaceful solution to the crisis. Only a monarchical order with a powerful tsar could prevent the disintegration of Russian society and maintain the Russian Empire as a viable state.

The most unqualified statement of the conservative position can be found in S. S. Oldenburg's detailed and quite fanciful biography of Tsar Nicholas II, published in Belgrade in 1939. Oldenburg lauded Nicholas as an intelligent, strong-minded, decent, and charming man whose only concern was the well-being of Russia. True, Nicholas favored a "homogeneous empire," but he disliked the "systematic persecution of Jews, heretics, and schismatics." He was certain that "the government could crush the revolution by force, but he wanted to reconstruct Russian life by eliminating the discord that separated the government from the majority of society if not also from the vast majority of the people." Hence, he adopted a series of reforms, "a program of renovation," but his efforts were stymied by "those who clung to the treacherous and illusory idea of 'the people,'" that is, the opponents of autocracy, who were never satisfied with any of the concessions granted by the authorities.[18]

In a more recent and much more nuanced biography of Nicholas, Dominic Lieven notes that the tsar's political views were very similar to those of his grandfather, Alexander II, who ruled from 1855 to 1881. In a conversation with Otto von Bismarck in 1861, Alexander had granted that "greater participation by respectable notables in official business could only be advantageous. The difficulty, if not impossibility, of putting this principle into effect lay only in the experience of history that it had never been possible to stop a country's liberal development at the point beyond which it should not go. . . . Above all, God knows what would become of relations between the peasants and the lords if the authority of the Emperor was not still sufficiently intact to exercise the dominating influence." Nicholas II, according to Lieven, agreed with Bismarck's reply that if the crown's absolute power were undermined "the risk of a murderous peasant war would become very great."[19] Both Oldenburg and Lieven strongly suggested that Nicholas had no choice but to act more or less as he did.

In his excellent book on the rise of Social Democracy in Russia, John Keep suggested—and this is the fourth interpretation—that although the term "The Russian Revolution of 1905" is "too well established and convenient to be discarded," a "purist would be justified in arguing that there was no such thing."[20] Certainly, an orthodox Marxist might dispute the designation of revolution for the events of 1905, for political power was not transferred from one social class to another. Non-Marxists, who define a revolution as a fundamental change in the system of legality, might also hesitate to use the term "revolution" because the tsar's authority remained paramount even though it was clearly reduced.

Yet there are good reasons for contemporaries' adoption of the term and for its retention by political activists as well as historians. From late 1904 until late in 1905, the assault on authority from below was so massive, potent, and successful that the old regime appeared to be disintegrating. The challenge to the established order came from mass movements representing four different social groups: liberals among the middle class and nobility, industrial workers, peasants, and some of the national minorities. The ultimate aims of these groups differed in fundamental ways, but they were united in their determination to end autocratic rule in Russia, which they all held responsible for the country's economic stagnation and archaic social and political institutions. There was considerable unrest, as well as numerous mutinies in the army and navy. Virtually no geographical region remained unaffected by the turbulence. Moreover, the currents of rebellion were so diverse that at times it seemed as though Russia was undergoing not one revolution but a whole series of parallel revolutions. Civil order broke down, and for several months the government seemed capable of little more than biding its time until the outbursts of defiance, generally unplanned and unorganized, had spent themselves. So effective a challenge to the state's monopoly of power, even though temporary, may justifiably be characterized as a revolution.

The last interpretation I want to consider might be termed, for want of a better term, "broadly liberal."[21] It depicts the revolution not as an event that made any one path of development inevitable but rather as a critical juncture that opened up several paths. Under intense pressure, initially from liberals for political change and then from other social groups also interested in economic and social change, the autocracy appeared to suffer a loss of nerve. For an entire year, beginning in the fall of 1904, the government oscillated between accommodation and repression, but neither policy succeeded in ending the unrest. On the contrary, taking the government's inconsistency as a sign of weakness, the various groups within the opposition were encouraged to step up their agitation. Indeed, had the opposition groups been able to collabo- rate fully and throughout the turbulence, the outcome might well have been quite different.

During the general strike in October 1905—the high point of the rev- olution in the "liberal" interpretation—the pressure from mass move- ments became so acute that it drove the autocracy to the verge of collapse, impelling the tsar to promise civil liberties and to declare that henceforth no law would be enacted without the approval of an elected legislature. By conceding that he was no longer the sole repository of political power, Nicholas did what he had vowed never to do: he aban- doned the principle of autocracy although he did not acknowledge that this was what he was doing. Realizing that Russian politics had entered a new phase, the liberal press hailed the manifesto as a "great historical event," the "first step toward a Russian constitution," the beginning of a "new order," the triumph of a "peaceful national revolution."[22] The editors of the highly regarded legal journal *Pravo* claimed that Russia "since October 17 has theoretically been a constitutional monarchy" and that "no contrivance or vacillations by the authorities" could stop the forward movement of the democratic idea.[23]

It seemed that the old order had no choice but to retreat and that nothing could stop the political transformation of Russia along Western lines. Even though that prospect did not materialize and even though some important concessions granted during the revolutionary upsurge were subsequently repealed amid a torrent of ruthless repression, some institutional changes introduced during the period of unrest survived what is generally considered to have been a failed revolution. Most nota- bly, Russia retained an elected legislature as well as political parties speaking for various social and economic interests. Moreover, there was considerably more freedom of expression and more freedom to assem- ble and organize after 1905 than had prevailed before that year. There can be no doubt that, although the autocrat continued to exercise ulti- mate power, the Russia of 1907 was not the Russia of 1904.

A few examples illustrate what was probably the most dramatic change in Russia—the profound politicization of many sectors of society. Under the law of December 11, 1905, which specified the electoral procedures for the selection of the First Duma (parliament), somewhere between twenty and twenty-five million people were enfranchised. Of these between 30 and 40 percent actually went to the polls, a rather impressive achievement for a country holding its first-ever elections, in which a large percentage of the people was still illiterate. The comment of a sick, elderly general after he had voted reflected the thinking of many Russians. "You know," he said, "all my life I dreamed of this day, dreamed of living until then."[24]

The results of the election came as a shock to the authorities, who had expected the poorly educated peasants to vote en masse for conservative candidates. Of the 478 deputies (out of a projected total of 524) chosen by the time the Duma met, only about thirteen could be considered *somewhat* sympathetic to the prevailing order. The staunch supporters of autocracy did not elect a single deputy. Slightly more than one-fifth of the deputies (108) belonged to one or another of the intelligentsia professions, and this group, not surprisingly, came to play a major role in the Duma's debates and parliamentary maneuvers. Wags, fearing that the intelligentsia's penchant for taking doctrinaire positions would paralyze the new legislature, recalled Heinrich Heine's quip about the Frankfurt Assembly in 1848: "140 Professoren—armes Vaterland, Du bist verloren [140 professors—wretched fatherland, you are lost]."[25] Those fears proved unfounded, but the differences between the legislature and the government were so deep that the Duma accomplished little, and it was dissolved by the tsar in July 1906.

The Second Duma, chosen early in 1907, was even more hostile to the old order than the First, and once again the authorities and the legislature failed to cooperate, leading to another dissolution (in June 1907), this time involving what amounted to a coup d'état initiated by Prime Minister Petr Stolypin. The government now peremptorily changed the electoral law and made the suffrage far more restrictive, which led to the election of a conservative Duma (the Third). By this time, however, many Russians had had a taste of participation in the political process that would not be forgotten. Indeed, the crisis of the old regime in 1916 and 1917 forcefully demonstrated that the Duma remained a vibrant institution despite the restrictive electoral law enacted in 1907. The significant majority in the legislature that fiercely criticized the autocracy spoke for large sectors of the population. The Provisional Government that took control after the tsar's abdication in February 1917 was the Duma's creation. Without the reforms introduced during the Revolution of 1905, such developments would have been inconceivable.[26]

No less important, several political parties or movements emerged during the revolution and remained active until they were outlawed by the communists. Indeed, it is no exaggeration to say that the political landscape was transformed by the general strike in October 1905 and the issuance of the manifesto on the seventeenth of that month. Initially, the strongest new party was the Constitutional Democratic Party (generally known as the Kadets), essentially a movement of professionals and liberal landowners who wished to convert Russia into a constitutional monarchy on the British model. Although never given legal status, the Kadets created a formidable organization that dominated the first two Dumas and played a diminished, though not insignificant, role in the last two. To the right of the Kadets stood the Union of October 17, which relied for its support on commercial and industrial interests in the cities and the moderately conservative nobility in the provinces. The Octobrists were strong supporters of the monarchy, both as a symbol of national unity and as a center of political authority. Basically, as their name indicates, they were content with the settlement reached under the October Manifesto: the tsar was to retain considerable authority, but the Duma, representing significant strata in society, would play a vital role in determining national policies.

Even right-wing extremists, who on principle opposed the creation of parties because this ran counter to their belief in the untrammeled authority of the autocrat, established numerous organizations that took part in the rough and tumble of politics. The largest one, the Union of the Russian People, made antisemitism the centerpiece of its program; although this was a cause that had considerable support in the empire, the Union never became a mass movement.[27] But it could count on the beneficence of Tsar Nicholas II, who never gave up his preference for autocracy. Nicholas was, in fact, by far the greatest obstacle preventing the liberalization of Russia.

The press changed in fundamental ways during the revolution. By the time of the so-called Days of Liberty late in 1905, which lasted for some ten weeks after the issuance of the October Manifesto, the country enjoyed such a remarkable degree of freedom of expression and association that some foreign observers were actually alarmed lest extremists would now increase their following among the masses. To the German ambassador in St. Petersburg, it almost seemed as though "the government wants to facilitate the work of revolutionaries." The criticism in the press of the government was fierce. Some caricatures were beyond the comprehension of the Minister of Internal Affairs, Petr N. Durnovo, who relied on Aleksandr. V. Gerasimov, chief of the St. Petersburg Okhrana (special secret police force), for enlightenment. "This is Count Witte and here (represented as a pig or toad) is you, Your Excellency." Durnovo asked what could be done to "restore order." "If I were permitted to close down all revolutionary presses and to arrest 700 to 800 people," Gerasimov replied, "then I guarantee that I could bring calm to St. Petersburg." Durnovo, however, refused to authorize such harsh measures on the ground that the new constitutional order forbade it.[28] In fact, within a few weeks, and especially after the dissolution of the Second Duma, the police cracked down on the press and closed many newspapers. But quite a few managed somehow to survive and continued to publish articles that in one way or another exposed the flaws in the prevailing social and political order.

During the general strike in October 1905, the working class, though numerically small, emerged as an organized group capable of exerting decisive influence on public affairs. Briefly in late 1905, the St. Petersburg Soviet (council) was so influential that the conservative newspaper *Novoe vremia* complained that there were really two governments, one led by Count Witte and one by Georgii S. Khrustalev-Nosar (chairman of the Petersburg Soviet), and that no one knew who would arrest whom first. The soviet did not last very long, but working-class organizations, especially trade unions, continued to function.

Workers took advantage of the law of March 4, 1906, which, for all its limitations, legalized a range of union activities. During the next fifteen months, 59 unions were legally recognized in St. Petersburg, and another 17 remained unregistered; in Moscow, 64 were officially sanctioned, and 11 remained unregistered. At their peak, the 42 unions in the capital for which figures are available attained a membership of 55,000; in Moscow (also for 42 unions) there were 52,000. True, the union movement incorporated only a small share of the workforce—9 percent in St. Petersburg and 10 percent in Moscow—but these are nevertheless impressive statistics. In Germany in 1907, only about 22 percent of all industrial laborers belonged to unions. In the Russian Empire as a whole, the membership of the 273 registered unions in 1907 came to over 106,000 people. There is no hard information on the size of the remaining 631, but it is likely that by early 1907 the membership of all the unions exceeded 300,000. Despite the harassment of unions by the government in the years from 1907 onward, the "preceding two and a half years," according to the leading authority on the subject, "had left an imprint on the workers' movement that could not be erased. Trade unions declined but they did not vanish."[29]

Large numbers of peasants, who in their totality constituted over 80 percent of the population, also became politically active during the Revolution of 1905. This refers not only to the various waves of unrest, during which peasants pillaged estates, felled trees and seized lumber, took possession of meadows and pastures, and engaged in strikes, but also to the peasants' participation in the so-called petitions campaign in the spring of 1905, which was probably more important than the unrest because it reflected a quite sophisticated politicization of the peasantry. The bureaucracy did its best to prevent the Imperial Manifesto of February 18, 1905, which called on "private persons and institutions" to offer suggestions on how to improve the government and the "people's existence," from being disseminated in the villages, but many peasants learned of it anyway and within a few months they sent some one hundred petitions to St. Petersburg. In them peasants called not only for the transfer of all state and landlords' land to them but also for the introduction of democracy. By and large, the peasants still expressed loyalty to the tsar, but often they indicated that their allegiance to the throne was conditional: the tsar would retain their support only if he embarked on a program of far-reaching reform. As one historian, Francois-Xavier Coquin, put it, the petition campaign revealed that "the peasant world . . . was revolutionary despite itself."[30] And the formation in the summer of 1905 of the "All-Peasant Russian Peasants' Union" signified that the villagers had turned to politics on a national scale. As I indicated earlier, in the elections to the first two dumas, the peasants voted overwhelmingly for candidates opposed to the old order.

There is one other area, minority rights, in which some modest changes took place. Although it is not easy to separate the national from the social and political factors in assessing their relative importance in stimulating unrest in 1905, there is no doubt that national sentiment was strong among a growing number of the more than one hundred ethnic groups that together constituted slightly over one half of the empire's population. All previous efforts at russification of the minorities had failed to stifle their aspirations for autonomy or independence. Soon after unrest erupted in St. Petersburg early in 1905, particularly ferocious disorder broke out in several outlying regions, most notably in the former Kingdom of Poland, the Caucasus, and the Baltic provinces (Estland, Livland, and Kurland). In Finland, large numbers of people demonstrated against the tsarist policy of russification that had been imposed on the country during the preceding five years. The "national factor," as Andreas Kappeler rightly noted, "certainly exacerbated the social and political conflicts" in the empire.[31]

For the authorities in St. Petersburg, this unrest posed a dual danger because the minorities, who were concentrated in the borderlands, were looked upon as potential supporters of the enemy in time of war. In addition, the government feared that if autonomy were widely extended, the empire would cease to be a "unitary state," to use the parlance of the time, and the autocrat's power would then inevitably be sharply curtailed. But the authorities were also motivated by sheer prejudice. They considered the minorities to be culturally inferior, and they were especially antagonistic toward the Jews, who numbered about five million. The tsarist government had long imposed economic, legal, and social restrictions on the Jews that were more extensive and demeaning than the measures taken against any other group. Forced, with few exceptions, to live in one region of the empire, the Pale of Settlement, Jews also had to pay special taxes, could not attain the rank of officer in the army, and were almost completely excluded from employment in the bureaucracy. Moreover, their attendance at secondary schools and universities had been constrained since 1887 by rigid quotas. At bottom, the hostility toward the Jews derived from the belief that they were marked by "innate vices" that made their integration into Russian society impossible. The prominence of Jews in all the radical movements and, to a somewhat lesser extent, in the liberal movement, was in large measure the fruit of the government's discriminatory policies.

In an endeavor to blunt the opposition, in November 1905 the government revoked the decree of 1901 that had abolished the autonomy of the Finnish army, and the authorities accepted the principle of the irremovability of local judges in Finland. In addition, administrative decrees that placed special burdens on Old Believers were revoked, and on April 17 the tsar issued a decree granting religious toleration.[32] The position of the Jews improved in one important respect. They were granted the suffrage in national elections, and twelve of their number were elected to the First Duma, where they spoke out against official misconduct toward their coreligionists.

This was but one aspect of a larger trend within the Jewish community during the period of the upheaval—its politicization. For the first time, Jews in Russia became active in national politics. Already in late 1904, six thousand activists issued a "Declaration of Jewish Citizens" calling for civic equality for Jews. In February 1905, religious communities in thirty-two cities sent a petition with a similar demand to the authorities in St. Petersburg. A few weeks later, sixty-seven activists formed the Union for the Attainment of Full Rights for the Jewish People of Russia, which in short order established branches in fourteen provinces. The new organization called not only for equal rights for Jews but also for cultural autonomy, that is, for the right of Jews to maintain their own schools and their own language, namely, Yiddish.

By 1906, three new socialist parties emerged, all of which adopted militant positions on nationalist and working-class issues. Finally, the Bund, the largest Social Democratic organization in the empire, played a major role in the revolution. It urged workers to go out on strike, to obtain weapons, and to learn the art of street fighting. About 1,100 Jews joined the "fighting units" (*boevy otriady*) that became skilled at protecting meetings and at defending Jewish communities against the pogroms that erupted with special ferocity in October 1905 and June 1906. The tenacity of the fighting units in defending Jewish interests evoked the admiration of non-Jews, who tended to have a low opinion of the Jews' physical courage.[33]

But the overall status of Jews as an oppressed minority did not improve significantly, despite efforts late in 1906 by Prime Minister Stolypin to lift some of the restrictions imposed on them. Motivated both by a desire to wean Jews away from radicalism and by the belief that it was morally indefensible to maintain the status quo, Stolypin persuaded the cabinet to support a series of modest measures to lighten the burden on the Jews, only to be rebuffed by the tsar, who claimed that "an inner voice" prevented him from giving his approval.[34]

Nonetheless, important changes had taken place in Russia during the Revolution of 1905. Slowly, painfully, against all odds, some associations relatively free from government control had been created in the years from 1904 to 1907, and these amounted to first steps in the formation of a civil society, a prerequisite for a genuine constitutional order. True, the men and women who had initiated the struggle against the old order in 1904 had hoped for much more; but in view of the obstacles they encountered—a stubborn monarch, a hostile bureaucracy, and a ruthless army—their achievement was not negligible. As a revolution, 1905 was a failure, but it was a failure that nonetheless brought about important changes in Russia.

The overall picture that emerges from a study of the Revolution of 1905 is one of great complexity. Clearly, the men in positions of leadership in society and in the state were guided by their wish to defend their own interests and those of the social groups they claimed to represent. Yet by itself this does not adequately explain their behavior. No side in the revolutionary conflict was monolithic; policy disagreements existed within each camp. Some leaders, fearing the abyss, advocated flexibility and compromise. Even more to the point, both statesmen and leaders of the opposition occasionally took positions out of keeping with their predilections. It was not uncommon for archconservatives to favor far-reaching concessions and for militants on the left to oppose bellicose tactics. And on three occasions—in October 1905, in June, and then again in July 1906—very senior government officials conducted extensive meetings with leading liberals with the aim of bringing members of the opposition into the government. True, nothing came of the discussions, but if thoughtful people at the time believed that an agreement might be reached, on what basis can historians claim that failure was a foregone conclusion? A student of 1905 encounters many surprises, which is why the revolution makes so complicated and fascinating a story.

*No, it makes one
Hungrier,*

An approach to the study of 1905 that stresses complexity and ambiguity might seem to deprive the revolution of some of its excitement by not linking it directly to the more momentous Revolution of 1917 and thus undermining the thesis that it was a dress rehearsal for 1917. Such an approach, however, yields better—and ultimately more exciting—history: it is closer to what actually happened. The individuals who participated in the mass movements of 1905 did not believe that they were merely preparing the way for the real event at some future date, and my sense is that this was also true of many Jewish activists in 1905. They were trying to bring about far-reaching changes then and there. And those attempts were not necessarily doomed to fail. At least during the first fifteen months of the upheaval, the authorities considered some daring reforms that would have satisfied enough of the opposition's demands to have brought the unrest to an end. It was, in many ways, a period of missed opportunities. And some of the reforms, as we have seen, were not derisory.

This is not to say that the changes that remained in effect in 1907 were irreversible or that the struggle between the two major political camps—one favoring the status quo and the other a dismantling of the autocracy—had ended. Nor is this surprising. After all, most countries undergoing transitions from absolutism to constitutionalism endured long periods of conflict; the path to what is generally referred to as modernity has rarely been smooth, almost never without many zigzags and major catastrophes. In France, the Revolution of 1789 initiated a transition that ended only in 1905, when republican institutions finally seemed firmly established. In those 116 years, France underwent at least three revolutions and several periods of political turmoil that threatened the foundations of the state. In Germany, or, initially, in the German states, the process took about a century, from 1848 to 1945, during which there were two revolutions, a National Socialist regime, and two terrible world wars, and even then the establishment of a constitutional order and representative government owes much to the policies of the Western powers that occupied the country after 1945. Great Britain is often held up as an example of a country with a long history of constitutionalism and political stability. But Britain, too, experienced a period of political turbulence and revolution that included the execution of a king.

If one takes such a long-range view of Russian history, then the Revolution of 1905 can be seen not simply as a failure or as an event that was important, allegedly, because it led inexorably to 1917. On the contrary, 1905 should be viewed as an upheaval that opened up new possibilities for the country that were suppressed by the Bolshevik Revolution of 1917. Seventy-four years later, in 1991, it turned out that even that cataclysmic event did not introduce a political system of very long duration. In the nearly two decades since then, the country has been in the throes of yet another upheaval, including a struggle on behalf of the same ideals that had animated much of the opposition in 1905: the rule of law; government by the people; individual rights; and respect for ethnic and religious minorities. Though aborted, the Revolution of 1905 left an enduring legacy: it initiated a process of political, economic, and social change that even now has not run its full course.

Chapter 2

Nicholas II and the Revolution

RICHARD WORTMAN

Most accounts of 1905 place Nicholas II at the periphery of the revolution, portraying him as a figure buffeted by events, reacting in a defensive, inconsistent manner and exacerbating critical situations by vacillating between indecisiveness and obstinacy. Undoubtedly, Nicholas was a weak authority figure who was nonplussed by the turmoil that confronted him. Recent research has shown, however, that the characterization of him as a passive defender of the status quo, a ruler reacting unwittingly to social and political developments beyond his control, does not reflect his true part in the unfolding of the revolution and its ultimate defeat. This chapter aims to clarify his role, to show how Nicholas II understood the future of Russian society within the framework of a myth that both legitimized and exalted his authority, even as it was subject to its greatest challenge.

Nicholas II viewed the world through a prism that presented him as a national ruler who would restore a regime of personal patriarchal rule. The national myth justifying Russian autocracy arose in the 1880s to counter the Western principles of legality and openness that had been used to justify reform policies during the reign of Alexander II. Alexander III held westernized educated society and reformist officials in the state administration responsible for the laxity that had allowed the revolutionary movement to flourish and culminate in the assassination of Alexander II in 1881. As I have argued in *Scenarios of Power*, the national myth heralded a break with the entire Petrine tradition of emulating the West.[1] In the manifestoes and ceremonies that followed the accession of Alexander III in 1881, the national myth evoked a religious and ethnic bond between the tsar and the Russian people, which had, presumably, withstood the processes of westernization and safeguarded the basic foundations of the Russian monarchy and state. The Russian tsar now strove to embody not the existing state, contaminated by westernized accretions, the reformed courts, and the zemstva (organs of local self-government established in 1864), but an idealized vision of pre-Petrine Russian institutions as an organic union of tsar and people, along the lines evoked in the writings of the Slavophiles.

The reign of Alexander III marks the beginning of an effort to separate the image of the monarch from that of the institutions of the existing state structure and to identify him more closely with the Orthodox Church and the Russian people, the *narod*, or, more specifically, the Russian peasantry. The ideal autocratic national state was evoked as an extension of the monarch's personal power, which was centered in the Ministry of Interior, obedient to his will and unencumbered by rule and law. For Alexander, as for his mentor and advisor Konstantin Pobedonostsev, "a true Russian" (*istinnyi russkii chelovek*) meant a person who believed in a strong centralized authority capable of enforcing the union between tsar and people. "Russian" (*russkii*) as an adjective justified both the counterreforms and the russification campaigns of Alexander III's reign. Neither policy achieved its goal of fundamentally transforming the government, but the myth introduced a vision of change, prompting further efforts to strengthen monarchical authority and to delegitimate the post-reform state with its concerns for legality and autonomy.

The ideological turn of the 1880s held great significance for the Jewish population of the empire. From the reign of Peter the Great, the Russian monarchs had presented themselves as European in culture, ideology, and political institutions, which I have described as the European myth. The Jews had been treated as one of the subordinate nationalities of the empire governed by their own communities and laws. Later, under Nicholas I and Alexander II, the government sought to assimilate them into a Russian culture that was European in its values and manners. Under the national myth, however, the Jews represented an alien element, scattered among Russian populations and intruding on the union of tsar and people. The Jews lacked their own territory. They had taken advantage of the liberal measures of the reform era to move to cities such as Moscow and St. Petersburg, attend the universities, and gain admittance to the Russian bar. The national myth's appeal to ethnic identity and its rejection of the Western character of the autocracy encouraged the exclusionist image of the Jew not only as alien but also as an enemy of the Russian nation. The pogroms of 1881, though not encouraged by the monarchy, were taken as signs of an antagonism shared by the Russian people. The government introduced limits on Jewish residence and restricted admissions to the universities and the bar. [2] The monarchy endeavored to cleanse Moscow, the symbolic center of the national autocracy, of Jews.[3] When Grand Duke Sergei Aleksandrovich assumed the office of governor-general of Moscow in 1891, he requested, with the tsar's support, that the Jews be removed, leading to brutal expulsions of two-thirds of the city's thirty thousand Jewish residents, many of whom were living in the city legally. Sergei was the uncle whose views Nicholas II found most congenial.

Nicholas, like Alexander III, accepted the pre-Petrine imagery of the national myth, including the belief that the Orthodox religion and the Russian people's adherence to it expressed the true spirit of Russia. But his attitude toward the state apparatus and his religious faith were quite different from his father's. He distrusted government officials, bound by formality and administrative rule, in general, and he was especially wary of those who were dynamic and gifted, as threatening to his personal authority. He did not surround himself with a group of like-minded officials or friends who could give him counsel. He believed that the national sanction for his power entitled him to exert authority as he wished, blinding him to constraints, both of institutions and reality. Likewise, he distrusted the Orthodox hierarchy. His religious faith was personal, not the mediated religion of the Orthodox Church, ministered through prayer and sacrament, but a direct, unmediated bond with God, which he and Alexandra felt they shared with holy men from the people. He envisioned his rule in terms of a neo-Slavophile image of a patriarchal tsar, ruling through ministers like his minister of interior Dmitrii Sipiagin, who believed that Russia should be governed by landlords advancing the well-being of the peasantry. Sipiagin proposed the introduction of a new system of petitioning the tsar as a way of overcoming the obstructions of the administration and establishing a patriarchal form of justice.

Nicholas felt a powerful emotional bond with the Russian people that he described in his decrees, diary, and personal correspondence. He wrote about his feelings during his coronation in 1896 and the trips he made to Moscow to celebrate Easter in 1900 and 1903: he was the first Russian emperor to celebrate Easter in Moscow since Nicholas I in 1849. In 1900, Nicholas issued a rescript to Grand Duke Sergei, expressing thanks for the attainment of his "intense wish" to spend Holy Week in Moscow "among the greatest national shrines, under the canopy of the centuries-old Kremlin." He declared that he had found his communion with his people, "with the true children of our beloved Church, pouring into the temples," and a "quiet joy" filled his soul. Sharing the Easter holiday with the worshipers gave him a spiritual mandate. "In the unity in prayer with My people, I draw new strength for serving Russia, for her well-being and glory." He wrote to his mother, the dowager Maria Fedorovna, after the services, "I never knew that I was able to attain such *religious ecstasy* as I experienced during this Passion Week. This feeling is now much stronger than it was in 1896. . . . This time my soul is so calm, everything here makes for the peace of prayer and the spirit."[4]

The peasant uprisings of the first years of the twentieth century, rather than shaking Nicholas's trust in the unity of people with the tsar, prompted him to find confirmation of it in public meetings with peasants and in visions of Muscovite assemblies of the land. Encouraged by the minister of interior, Viacheslav Plehve, he visited Kursk, which was near an area that had witnessed unrest, and held meetings with peasant elders from Kursk and six other provinces. When Nicholas arrived, a delegation of eighty-seven volost' elders greeted him with bread and salt. With Plehve at his side, the tsar threatened punishment for those who disobeyed but promised his own attention to the peasants' well-being.[5] Nicholas understood these meetings in terms of his scenario, as expressions of his particular personal and spiritual bond with the peasants. In a letter to Alexandra of September 1, 1902, he wrote that the speech to the peasants went off well "because it is much easier to talk to simple people." On October 20, he wrote to Prince Vladimir Meshcherskii that he had returned from Kursk "in a very elevated and cheerful frame of mind." "We ourselves have constantly wanted to go to the interior of our Native Land but circumstances have prevented it. In the future, I hope that such trips will follow one after another."[6]

Nicholas's sense of his national-religious mission grew stronger during the next year. In April 1903, he made another Easter visit to Moscow, where he again felt a great spiritual uplift. In July, he traveled to Sarov for the highly publicized canonization of Serafim of Sarov. Serafim, the abbot of the Monastery at Sarov in Tambov Province, was an early nineteenth-century elder (*starets*), known for his holy life, his visions, and his powers of curing and prophecy. Thousands of worshipers gathered for the event. Nicholas and the grand dukes carried the remains of Serafim around the Assumption Cathedral before a large crowd of worshipers. "During the entire procession," Nicholas wrote in his diary, "we carried the coffin on a stretcher. It created a tremendous impression to see how the people, and especially the sick, cripples, and the unfortunate, regarded the procession of the cross. The moment when the beatification began and then the kissing of the remains were most solemn." The next day he wrote, "How touching [*umilitelen*] the procession of the cross was yesterday, but with the coffin open. The elevation of the spirit [*pod"em dukha*] was enormous."[7]

After Sarov, A. A. Mosolov recalled, the words "tsar" and "people" followed each other directly in many of the tsar's statements and Nicholas increasingly looked upon the people as "half-grown youths." He felt a desire to come close to them, to "show physical affection to the people he loved," but he was prevented by the size of the crowds and fears of another Khodynka—the tragic stampede at the time of his coronation.[8] Nicholas regarded the relationship between himself and the peasantry as a spiritual bonding between likes, rather than an attraction of opposites. The mutual veneration of Serafim exemplified a shared faith.

Instead of rehearsing the complex discussions, concessions, and repressions that ensued during the revolution itself, I shall focus on Nicholas's views of the new system and how he reconciled it with his conception of autocracy. Throughout the revolution he clearly demonstrated his belief that he had not forsaken his office as sovereign. This was evident in the pre-Petrine imagery invoked by him and his advisors that derived sovereignty from God and the wishes of the Russian people. It was also manifest in his close watch over his ministers, who fulfilled his dictates, even while they shielded him from open responsibility.

The myth defied and excluded contradictory evidence. Neither military defeat nor almost universal opposition could shake his conviction— quite the contrary. He attributed the widespread violence and demands for social and political change to the influence of foreigners, revolutionaries, and the Jews. The *ustoi*, the foundations of Russia, remained impermeable and needed only ruthless retribution to be saved.

In his first meeting with the tsar on August 25, 1904, Petr Sviatopolk-Mirskii aptly described the situation: "The condition of things has become so aggravated that one may consider the government to be in a state of enmity with Russia. It is necessary to make peace." Mirskii accepted the position of minister of interior on condition that the tsar announce a program of reforms, including civil liberties and a limited degree of participation in the enactment of legislation. He argued for the need to win the support of society (*obshchestvo*). He tried to show that the participation of elective representatives from the zemstvo and major city dumas in governmental decisions was compatible with autocracy. The tsar would retain the right to change administrative institutions. The representatives would help the government formulate plans to increase legality in the Senate and other state institutions and to reform and democratize the zemstva.[9]

Although Nicholas promised him full support, he conceived political reform in the context of his vision of seventeenth-century Rus'. He proposed an assembly of the land, which would express his direct bond with the people and circumvent "society." This remained Nicholas's idée fixe during and after 1905. His image of a *zemskii sobor*, an assembly of the land, allowed him to retain absolute power while presumably heeding the wishes of the people. He would remain sovereign regardless of institutional changes.[10]

Under the blows of Bloody Sunday, the concern about foreign loans, and the lack of confidence in the loyalty of the army, Nicholas relented once more and accepted the principle of popular participation, but cast in the form of an assembly of the land. This would be a national assembly that represented the people without imposing institutional limitations or elevating the leaders of society. On January 31, 1905, Minister of Agriculture Alexei Ermolov presented a report, written in old-style Russian rhetoric, calling for a zemskii sobor. Nicholas had to hearken to the people's voice "before Rus' loses faith in its God-given Tsar, in his force and his might." He would summon elective representatives, "from all estates of the Russian land."[11]

In a rescript of February 18, 1905, to the new minister of interior, Aleksandr Bulygin, who replaced Sviatopolk-Mirskii, the tsar announced his wish to assemble "the worthiest people" to head a commission to draft plans for a representative institution. He stated his views before a delegation of fourteen zemstvo officials that he received at Peterhof on June 6. Nicholas declared, "Let there be, as there was of old, that unity between Tsar and all Rus', the meeting between me and the people of the land that forms the basis of the system resting on unique [*samobyt-nye*] Russian principles."[12] In the complex formulation of an election law, Nicholas, the Grand Duke Vladimir, and even Pobedonostsev worked to ensure a substantial representation of the peasantry. The conference introduced a provision guaranteeing the peasants at least fifty-one among the 412 deputies. For the same reason another provision eliminated a literacy requirement for Duma deputies. This part of the Bulygin project would be carried over to the law of December 11, 1905, which governed elections to the State Duma. Most of the urban population, including almost the entire working class, was left without franchise. Furthermore, the Duma would have only a consultative voice. It would pass on all legislation but the government could issue laws without its approval if it gained the consent of the State Council, which remained an entirely appointive body.

Nicholas considered that the new institutions, which would make known the needs of the people, did not conflict with the principle of autocratic power. In the manifesto of August 3, Nicholas expressed the hope that the deputies would justify his confidence and that they would "render to Us useful and zealous assistance in Our toils for the sake of Our common Mother Russia, to uphold the unity, security, and greatness of the State as well as national order and prosperity."[13] He clearly felt confident that the project did not jeopardize his absolute power. When several officers of the Preobrazhenkii Guards asked whether military men could serve as deputies, Nicholas replied, "Military men, members of the Duma? On the contrary, they must dissolve the Duma if this is required."[14]

The plan convinced the leaders of the liberation movement that they could no longer hope that personal appeals to the tsar would bring about major reforms. They increasingly sought democratic support among the urban workers and the peasants. The strike movement continued, culminating in the great general strike of October 1905. On October 17, 1905, Nicholas II issued the October Manifesto, drafted under the guidance of Sergei Witte, which promised the establishment of a State Duma elected by all classes of the population, without whose agreement no law could take effect. The manifesto also granted the basic civil liberties—personal inviolability, and freedom of religion, speech, assembly, and association. On the same day, Nicholas appointed a cabinet headed by Witte, Russia's first prime minister, who was responsible to the tsar.

The manifesto elicited widespread rejoicing at what society regarded as the end of absolute monarchy. It brought a loosening of previous restrictions on Jews, who again began to flow into the universities and again were admitted to the bar in significant numbers. It is clear, however, that Nicholas believed that the very fact that he had issued the manifesto was a confirmation of autocratic authority. His reasoning came out in a disagreement over the form in which the concessions would be announced. Witte had urged Nicholas merely to declare that the tsar had asked him as prime minister to formulate the projects for the new institutions and to leave the details for him to work out. In this way, he argued, the tsar would not bind himself with promises. But, Andrew Verner has persuasively argued, such a measure would make it seem that the reform came from state officials, representing a break from the old system of the tsar's personal rule. Nicholas insisted on a manifesto, which made it clear that the reform was the tsar's grant for the benefit of the people. In this way, he denied a break between the autocracy and the new order. He appeared as the founder of the new system and, having founded it, clearly felt himself entitled to change it when he saw fit.[15]

In April 1906, shortly before the elections, deliberations began on new Fundamental Laws to formalize the reforms in the state system introduced since October. The question arose as to whether the monarch's power in Article One of the Fundamental Laws should be defined as "autocratic and unlimited" (*samoderzhavnyi i neogranichennyi*). Both adjectives had been removed in the draft of the Duma charter of February 20, 1906, but Nicholas had then insisted on restoring the word "autocratic." By the April conference, Nicholas wanted the word "unlimited" reinstated as well. He had been convinced by the ebbing of the revolution and the campaign of letters and telegrams organized by those opposed to the October Manifesto in the government and the far-right parties. He described "the touching feelings of loyal subjects, together with the plea not to limit My power." Reproach, Nicholas declared at the conference, would come from "the so-called educated element, the proletarians, and the third element [the professionals who staffed the zemstvos' administration]. But I am certain that eighty percent of the Russian people will be with me."[16]

Nicholas found additional confirmation for this belief in the ardent entreaties of members of the extreme right-wing Union of the Russian People, who presented him and the tsarevich with membership badges. At the presentation, Nicholas accepted the badges with thanks and then declared, "The burden of power placed on Me in the Moscow Kremlin I will bear Myself, and I am certain that the Russian people will help Me. I will be accountable for My authority before God." A member of the delegation delivered a speech declaring that the tsar should not trust those men put forward by Masons and others "who depend on aliens." The Russian word was *inorodtsy*, a legal category that included Jews at the time. The Russian people had crossed themselves before the tsar, and the tsar should rely on "Russian people." "No gates of hell will overcome the Russian Tsar, surrounded by his people." The tsar replied, "Yes, I believe that with your help, I and the Russian people will succeed in defeating the enemies of Russia."[17]

Nicholas could insist on the old definition of "unlimited and autocratic" power because he believed that the new representative institutions in no way constrained his right to dispense with them if he so wished. But the officials at the special conference thought otherwise, observing that the new institutions did limit the tsar's power in some ways. Nicholas relented on the term "unlimited'" but "autocratic" remained in the Fundamental Laws issued on April 23, 1906. However, "autocratic" had one meaning for the leading state officials, another for the tsar. For them, it meant that the tsar received his power from God and his forbears. For him it meant that he remained sovereign, that he retained the primary legislative authority that had allowed him to issue the October Manifesto, that he was the creator of the new institutions, and that he alone could change them.[18] The Fundamental Laws of 1906 sought to ensure that the acts of the new state institutions would be governed by law. But the contradiction between autocratic and representative government persisted, and liberal jurists agreed that the new institutions left the basic principle of autocracy untouched. The Fundamental Laws could be changed only at the tsar's initiative; laws would be enacted by the tsar with the participation of the Duma. In this sense the tsar remained sovereign, and the new Fundamental Laws sustained Nicholas's belief in his autocratic power, while seeming to introduce a limited principle of the rule of law.[19]

The election law of December 11, 1905, worked out by Witte and

Sergei Kryzhanovskii, an official in the Ministry of Interior, extended the system of curiae, proposed for the Bulygin Duma, to the workers and urban population. The workers received their own curia (a discrete group of voters entitled to elect a given number of representatives), but no minimum of seats as did the peasants.[20] Although the peasants were underrepresented in terms of their numerical weight in the population, their deputies would determine the mood of the next Duma. Many officials, including Witte himself and those close to Nicholas, thought this a good thing, because they believed that the peasants remained devoted to the tsar. Grand Duke Konstantin Konstantinovich also placed his hopes on the peasants. He wrote in his diary on October 26, 1905, "My companions and I all maintain our support for autocratic government and nurture the hope that if many peasant deputies are elected to the State Duma, then it may be possible to return to the autocratic model of government, which undoubtedly has the support of our peasant masses."[21] In February 1906 a new State Council was created, half to be elected by estates and institutions and half to be appointed by the tsar to act as a counterweight to the Duma.

But the results of the elections to the first State Duma immediately dispelled the illusions of a conservative, monarchist peasantry. The peasants voted heavily for the opposition parties—the Constitutional Democrats (or Kadets) and the Laborers' (*Trudoviki*) Party—that promised expropriation of the noble' estates. Nicholas used the official reception of Duma deputies to make clear that he remained the sovereign and autocrat. His moderate advisors urged him to appear at the Tauride Palace, where the Duma was to meet, as a gesture of conciliation. He chose instead to follow the German example for the opening of the Reichstag, that is, to address the deputies in sovereign precincts amid the symbols of imperial sovereignty. The reception took place in the throne room of the Winter Palace.

The ceremony impressed the deputies and the world with the distance between the autocracy—comprising the emperor, the imperial family, the members of the court, and the officials in the State Council—and the elected deputies of the Duma. On the right side of the hall stood the members of the State Council, courtiers, and generals wearing braided uniforms decorated with medals, and the ladies of the court in the decolleté "Russian dress" and *kokoshnik* tiaras worn at the highest state occasions. Assistant Minister of Interior V. I. Gurko wrote, "Naively believing that the people's representatives, many of whom were peasants, would be awed by the splendor of the Imperial court, the women of the imperial family were bedecked in jewels."[22]

While the right side was harmonious in its uniformity, the Duma deputies standing on the left presented a motley picture of the political and national diversity of the empire. Some of the liberal deputies dressed simply to make clear their identification with the common people. The English journalist Henry Nevinson described a microcosm of the empire: "Sturdy peasants in homespun cloth, one Little Russian in brilliant purple with broad blue breeches, one Lithuanian Catholic bishop in violet robes, three Tatar mullahs with turbans and long gray cassocks, a Balkan peasant in white embroidered coat, four Orthodox monks with shaggy hair, a few ordinary gentlemen in evening dress, and the vast body of the elected in the clothes of every day."[23]

The tsar set himself apart from both groups by entering in a formal imperial procession to the strains of "God Save the Tsar." Masters of Ceremony led with their maces; behind them court officials carried the imperial regalia. Following them came twelve Palace Grenadiers, then the emperor, flanked by the two empresses and followed by the members of the imperial family. After entering, the tsar kissed the metropolitan of St. Petersburg, who then held a brief prayer service. He ascended the steps and sat upon the throne, which, it was said, had been draped with the imperial mantle by the empress herself, in artistic folds. The imperial crown and other items of regalia were visible on stools at his side. The scene was caught in photographs published in newspapers and leading periodicals and a large painting that was publicly exhibited.

The reception was staged to place the regalia at the focal point of the hall. Brought from Moscow for the occasion, the regalia confirmed the sacred sources of the tsar's authority. Nicholas's speech to the Duma expressed his conviction that the assembly was an extension of the autocratic will and that its deputies were obliged to earn his confidence. Speaking down to the Duma representatives from the steps of the throne, he declared that Providence had moved him "to summon elected deputies from the people to help in legislation." He expressed his trust in them both to clarify the needs of the peasantry and to advance the education and prosperity of the people. He admonished them that for these goals, "not only freedom is necessary but also order on the basis of law is necessary." He declared his "intense desire to see My people happy and to bequeath My son a legacy of a strong, well-ordered and enlightened State." He called upon God to bless his labors, "in union with the State Council and State Duma," and asked that the day mark "the renewal of the moral make-up of the Russian Land, the day of the rebirth of its best forces." Nicholas concluded by exhorting the deputies to turn to their work with "reverence" (*blagogovenie*) and asked them to justify the trust of tsar and people.[24]

The speech received loud applause from the right of the hall and hostile silence from the left. Not only had Nicholas continued to speak of "his" people but he had also failed to make a gesture of conciliation by issuing an amnesty for political prisoners. The deputies returned to the Tauride Palace, where they drafted an indignant response. Later that day Nicholas wrote in his diary that he had worked for a long time, "but with a light heart after the successful completion of the ceremony."[25]

Meanwhile, Nicholas made sure that the ministers took brutal and effective measures of retribution. Under his close supervision, the minister of interior, Petr Durnovo, reorganized the local administration and sent out governors-general to respond to the insurrections. The tsar exulted at the obliteration of insurgent groups and the execution of insurrectionary workers. In a letter to his mother about the bloody suppression of the Bolshevik armed uprising in December 1905, Nicholas expressed his relief and his expectation that the same tactic would be used elsewhere. "Terror must be answered by terror. Now, Witte himself has realized this." He instructed commanders not to negotiate or make concessions but to retaliate and punish, that is, to annihilate on the spot.

At the same time, he continued to believe that the majority of the people remained personally loyal to him. Although he played no role in sponsoring the pogroms against the Jews, he regarded them approvingly as demonstrations that he and the common people shared the same antipathy. He wrote to his mother on October 25, 1905, that "nine-tenths of the trouble makers are Jews" and that the people had turned against them violently for that reason. "But not only the kikes [*zhidy*] suffered; so did the Russian agitators, engineers, lawyers, and all kinds of other bad people."[26] For him, the pogroms represented another sign of the unity of tsar and people. He sympathized, as already noted, with the extreme right-wing antisemitic organization, the Union of the Russian People, which had helped to foment the pogroms, and he approved all petitions for pardon submitted by members convicted for participation in these disturbances.[27]

Nicholas also pressed his new prime minister, Petr Stolypin, to employ the most ruthless and least legal expedients against the oppositional movements. Abraham Ascher has shown the tsar's dominant role in the establishment of the field court-martials and the coup d'état of June 3, 1907, both of which have carried Stolypin's name. On August 12, 1906, a bomb went off in Stolypin's suburban villa, leaving twenty-five dead and Stolypin's son and daughter seriously injured. Nicholas instructed the prime minister to find ways to realize his "inexorable desire to eradicate sedition and restore order." Fearing that the tsar might choose to establish a dictatorship, Stolypin submitted a proposal for field court-martials to counter terrorism. It was issued on August 19, 1906, as an emergency decree, under Article 87 of the Fundamental Laws. The "Stolypin court-martials" were, in fact, an effort to satisfy the tsar's demand for violent retribution.

The decree assigned governors-general the power to bring revolutionaries before military courts that could issue summary sentences, including death. While court-martials had been included in the emergency provisions governing most of Russia during the revolution, those tribunals did not forgo rules of legal procedure and their verdicts could be appealed. The law of August 19, 1906, dispensed even with an investigation when guilt was "so obvious" that one was not necessary. Only Stolypin and the minister of justice, Ivan Shcheglovitov, opposed it. The decree turned the countryside into a battlefield. Between 1906 and 1909, the field court-martials sentenced nearly 2,700 people to execution. In those three years, more people lost their lives for political crimes than during the entire nineteenth century. In addition, over 22,000 were sent into administrative exile.

While Stolypin defended and supported the field court-martials, his goal was the creation of a new political nation made up of property owners who would have a stake in defending the state and the monarchy. This conception grew out of the view embraced by Witte and others in the bureaucracy that the government could lead society. But it also involved plans to transform the peasantry by dissolving the commune and creating a new class of independent peasant proprietors. Provinces with communal land tenure were the sites of the most frequent and violent insurrections, convincing many officials and noblemen that the commune, rather than constituting a bulwark of order, had become a hotbed of peasant rage. The landed nobility supported Stolypin's program to protect property and to dissolve the peasant commune, while calling for a narrowing of the electorate for the Duma.

In November 1906, under Article 87 of the Fundamental Laws, Stolypin began issuing the laws that would permit the breakup of peasant communes and the establishment of separate farms, which would be held with individual property rights. Article 87 required that such decrees had to be confirmed by the Duma when it next resumed sessions. But the elections to the Second Duma, which convened in March 1907, increased the strength of the left. The majority of deputies continued to demand expropriation of land and refused to approve the laws. On June 3, 1907, Nicholas issued a manifesto announcing the dissolution of the Second Duma. A new electoral law was introduced under Article 87. This violated the Fundamental Laws, which specifically barred the use of the emergency provisions to change the electoral law.

The manifesto of June 3, 1907, is usually termed the Stolypin "coup d'état." But, as Ascher has made clear, the prime minister once more had acted only under the insistent prodding of the emperor. On June 2, when Nicholas signed the law, he wrote to Stolypin that delay in dissolving the Duma was "intolerable." "It is necessary to display decisiveness and firmness to Russia. . . . There must be no delay, not one minute of hesitation! God favors the bold!" In the decree of June 3, announcing the dissolution of the Duma, Nicholas declared that he would continue to honor the rights granted by the October Manifesto and would change only "the means of summoning deputies from the people" to the Duma. He insisted that the Duma, "created for the strengthening of the Russian State [*Gosudarstvo Rossiiskoe*], must be Russian [*russkii*] in spirit as well" and whereas other nationalities should have deputies, they should not be allowed to decide "purely Russian" questions. These problems could not be decided by legislative means but only by the authority giving the first law, "the historical Power of the Russian Tsar." He emphasized, "It is from the Lord, God, that imperial power over our people is entrusted to us. Before His throne we shall answer for the fate of the Russian state."[28]

The call for a legislature that was "Russian in spirit" meant, in practice, the sharp reduction in the representation of other nationalities such as Poles, Tatars, and Armenians and the exclusion of deputies from eastern borderlands such as the steppe and Turkestan regions. The change also gave substance to a central thrust of the national myth—identifying all those who resisted the monarch's power as not truly Russian, as enemies of the state. Nicholas's telegram to the Union of the Russian People, which had campaigned for the Duma's dissolution and for a restoration of true autocracy, gives a sense of the future he envisioned for Russia. "I am confident that now all the truly faithful and affectionate sons of the Russian homeland will unite still more closely, and as they continually increase their numbers, they will assist Me in bringing about a peaceful renewal of our great and holy Russia and in improving the goodly way of life of her people."[29]

Stolypin also desired a legislature that was "Russian in spirit," but his concept of the Russian nation differed sharply from Nicholas's belief in a unity between tsar and people. Stolypin strove to make the state the focus of national unity. The state would unite landholders of all classes, including peasant proprietors, and merchant and industrial capitalists. Property would ensure a stake in the regime and break down estate barriers; it would inspire a state spirit, *gosudarstvennost'*, among all groups in Russia that would find in it a champion of Russian domination in the empire and abroad.

The new electoral law attained Stolypin's goal of strengthening the conservative and nationalist forces in the Third Duma, which served its full term from 1907 to 1912. The Octobrist party, the party of landholders and industrialists, held a plurality, and, at least for a while, the prime minister was able to develop a working relationship with their leader, the Old Believer industrialist Alexander Guchkov. The Duma approved

of Stolypin's land laws providing for the dissolution of the peasant commune. The Octobrist leadership cooperated with Stolypin to introduce
reforms of the army and navy and laws for the development of universal
primary education.

But Stolypin was hobbled by the loss of support from the tsar, whose
trust in him diminished as the revolutionary threat passed. Stolypin's
state nationalism presumed the development of a cultural and historical
sense that would unite the nation apart from the tsar, a view that could
hardly win the latter's sympathy. In Nicholas's eyes, his bonds with the
people were personal, to be displayed in fervent expressions of spiritual
kinship and mutual devotion, giving him almost mystical feelings of exal-
tation. Tsarskoe Selo, where he carried on his family life, became the
principal site of his communion with the people. There he gathered
around him those who shared his views, his symbolic elite, now shrunk
to those hostile to the institutions of state. Nicholas felt closest to the
heads of his security corps, the guards' officers he knew—the minister
of the court, Count Fredericks; the palace commandants, Vladimir Dediulin and Vladimir Voeikov; and the chief of the palace administration,
Mikhail Putiatin—men who avoided expressing opinions that might
contradict the emperor's.

The one person who enjoyed Nicholas's complete trust was the
empress. Mark Steinberg has made clear that Alexandra's political views
were identical to her husband's on all significant issues—the importance
of the assertion of autocratic power, its divine source, and the devotion
of the people to the throne. Alexandra introduced the Victorian concept of the wife as strong and supportive helpmeet into the Russian
imperial household. Her impassioned advocacy of these views to the tsar
reinforced his beliefs and gave him the reassurance that he sought
among all he trusted.[30]

Nicholas and Alexandra found further support for their views among
the "men of God" who congregated in their chambers at Tsarskoe Selo.
They met Grigorii Rasputin shortly after the publication of the October
Manifesto on November 1, 1905, and considered him a man of the people absolutely devoted to his tsar. In addition to possessing seemingly
miraculous power to stop the tsarevich's hemophilic bleeding, Rasputin
shared their distrust of educated and aristocratic society. He described
both the emperor and empress as defenders of the people and religion
against the enemies of God. Rasputin addressed Alexandra almost as a
saint. She wrote in her notebook a remark that he uttered in 1907: "She
is an ascetic [*podvizhnitsa*], who with experience and intelligence struggles skillfully in a holy manner."[31]

Nicholas was also impressed by Rasputin. The tsar's concern for the
tsarevich was as great as Alexandra's and increased as he began to pres-

ent his son as the hope for Russia's future. He wrote to Stolypin in October 1906, "He [Rasputin] made a remarkably strong impression both on her Majesty and Myself, so that instead of five minutes, our conversation went on for more than an hour." He told General Dediulin that Rasputin was "just a good, religious, simple-minded Russian. When in trouble or assailed by doubts, I like to have a talk with him and invariably feel at peace with myself afterwards." His diaries mention numerous long conversations with Rasputin, without, however, divulging their content. Stolypin warned Nicholas about keeping Rasputin close to him and in 1911 banished him from the capital. This step only confirmed Nicholas's beliefs. That same year he sent Rasputin as a personal emissary to Nizhnii-Novgorod to determine the qualifications of the governor of the province, A. N. Khvostov, to serve as Stolypin's replacement as minister of interior when the prime minister asked to be relieved of that post.[32]

The Revolution of 1905 did not shake the tsar's confidence in his vision of a renewed personal autocracy in Russia. Rather, the defeat of the revolution proved to him that the Russian monarchy could triumph over adversity and that it was his destiny to lead Russia out of a time of troubles, like the first Romanov, Tsar Michael Fedorovich, and to create a restored and powerful absolute monarchy supported by the masses of the Russian people. After 1907, Nicholas showed the resolve to take whatever steps were necessary to realize this vision. The Jews, viewed as menacing this archaic vision of Russia, soon felt its repercussions—the return of the restrictions on Jews' matriculating in the universities and on admission to the bar and the staging of the trial of Mendel Beilis for ritual murder, a step that was clearly meant to please the tsar.[33] The violent confrontations of the early twentieth century must be conceived not as the unsuccessful assault of revolutionary groups against a beleaguered and obsolete autocracy but as a collision of two fiercely opposed insurgent forces, a Russia awakening politically and demanding to be heard and a monarch seeking to create a pure autocracy drawing personal authority from God and the people, unencumbered by institutions of the state or the critical opinion of educated society.

Part II
The Old Regime Confronts Its "Jewish Question"

Chapter 3

A Note on the Jewish Press and Censorship during the First Russian Revolution

DMITRII ELYASHEVICH

During the 1905 Revolution, in contrast to the previous period, few features of the government's censorship policy were specific to Jewish publications. The best way to characterize policy toward the latter is to describe the Russian government's censorship policy in general in 1905–6 and its application to Jewish publications. Nevertheless, there were some features peculiar to the official censorship of printed works in the Jewish languages, Yiddish and Hebrew, at the beginning of the twentieth century.

Until April 1906 the legislative basis for the censorship of Jewish works was the ordinance of 1865 (known as the Temporary Regulations), together with all the supplements and changes that were subsequently adopted over the following three decades. These regulations did not especially single out the Jewish press or Jewish book publishing. Attempts in the 1870s to elaborate special instructions for the Jewish censors were unsuccessful and, at the beginning of the twentieth century, the examination of publications in Hebrew and Yiddish continued along well-established lines. On the one hand, it was based on noninterference in the establishment of Jewish printing presses in the towns of the Pale of Settlement, a practice that had gradually been put in place starting with the early 1860s. On the other hand, it was based on a century-long tradition of relying on precedents. In accordance with this rule of thumb, the fate of a given manuscript depended not so much on statutes or law as on the views and preferences of the censor. Indeed, personal opinions of the Jewish censor had carried considerable weight even during the period when the statutes of 1828 (which had special articles dealing with Jewish publications) were in place. After 1865, however, this subjective opinion became the determining factor for the fate of any given Jewish manuscript or publication, whether original or imported from abroad.[1]

In 1905 a censorship bureau of Jewish publications operated in the Russian Empire in the cities of St. Petersburg, Vilna (Vilnius), Kiev, Odessa, and Warsaw. In these cities, the people occupying the censorship posts were individuals of the old school, who had been inculcated to a greater or lesser degree with such basic notions of the second half of the nineteenth century as enlightenment, the integration of the Jews into the surrounding population, "moral reform" (*ispravlenie*), and so forth. This was certainly true with regard to the censors Rabbi Peisakh Iampol'skii in Kiev, Lev Kliachko in Odessa, and Mikhail Vol'per in Vilna. Even the St. Petersburg censor, Israel Landau, a person with a rather shady biography who formally belonged to an entirely different ideological and educational circle, in practice was also guided by notions from the past. Called upon to influence provincial Jewish censors and, as an official of the Main Directorate on Press Affairs, even to direct them, he did not, in fact, exert any influence on the fate of the Jewish press outside the area of the capital and made no effort to do so. In general, in the period of the 1905 Revolution, there were no truly striking figures such as the earlier censors—Volf Tugendhold, Israel Zeiberling, German Barats, not to mention Iakov Brafman, people who were capable of independently formulating official views on the Jewish press.

This traditional approach, however, was completely unsuited to the rapidly changing character of the Jewish press in Russia. The new situation was related to the breakdown of the traditional Jewish community and the gradual involvement of the Jewish population in the political, cultural, and social life of the country. The Jewish press and book publishing as a mass phenomenon thus no longer fit into the traditional framework familiar to the censors with an old-fashioned, maskilic (enlightened) way of thinking.

During the revolutionary period, the Jewish readership was primarily interested in obtaining information on current events. The composition of the Jewish audience itself changed; now a reader could be either a student (*gimnazist*), factory worker, craftsman, or merchant with various levels of income, in addition to those who were considered (or considered themselves) part of the "Jewish intelligentsia." The Jewish press was compelled to adjust to the spirit of the times: it was no longer as homogeneous as before or as exclusively religious and did not limit itself to a discussion of strictly internal Jewish problems. Indeed, Jewish journals and newspapers now took an interest in the same issues that were found in general Russian publications.

At the beginning of the twentieth century, the circulation of Jewish publications expanded considerably. For example, in 1904 the circulation of the most popular newspaper, *Der fraynd*, reached 50,000 copies.

Moreover, the general number of Jewish periodicals increased notably. In 1907 in the Russian Empire eleven journals and newspapers in Yiddish and six in Hebrew were published.[2]

Traditionally, reference to such issues as the right to full civil equality or the policy of state antisemitism was severely limited in the Jewish press. But after 1903 the primary task of the censors shifted to the struggle against the publication of protests provoked by the wave of pogroms. For years, this issue produced most of the bans and confiscations by the censorship. The brochures *The Case of the Pogrom in Belostok* (Bialystok) and *The Case of the October Pogrom in Simferopol* were confiscated by court order and subsequently destroyed.[3] A similar phenomenon characterized treatment of the notorious Beilis case in the period immediately preceding World War I.

It should be noted, however, that during the events of 1905–6, the general tendency of the censorship (and Jewish publications were no exception) was to avoid outright bans or confiscations in order not to lend oppositional works gratuitous publicity. For example, the censorship did not dare to ban the dissemination of the Russian translation published in Kiev in 1905 of Sholem Aleichem's story "Peace and Harmony: A Story about How Uncle Pinya Lived, Quarreled, and Became Reconciled with Aunt Reiza," a very caustic satire on the Russo-Japanese War and the Russian domestic political situation. In his report on this matter, Nikolai Panteleev, a member of the Council of the Main Directorate on Press Affairs, noted, "At the present time, all our newspapers and journals, even those that are supervised by the censorship, are full of descriptions of the situation in our homeland in the same sense as it is described in the brochure under consideration," and its prohibition in the given case would arouse "interest in the public . . . which, in fact, it does not deserve."[4] There were many similar examples in the work of the censorship in the period 1905–6.

I turn now to the censorship's attitude toward Jewish publications in various languages with differing content and party orientation. Religious publications, which for a long time, up until the 1880s, had been the chief concern of the Jewish censors, found themselves in a better position in the early twentieth century, including the period of the 1905 Revolution, and after. The censorship, to our knowledge, did not make problems for any religious publications in the period from 1901 to 1909. Indeed, the regime and the censorship—and not only in the person of the St. Petersburg censor, Israel Landau, whose sympathies for Hasidism were well known—adopted an almost protective attitude toward the Jewish Orthodox press. They viewed it as a counterweight to the liberal and revolutionary press, as some kind of oasis of stability and immutability. Even Russian translations of individual tractates of the Babylonian Talmud, which until not long before had been considered the cornerstone of Jewish insularity (*zamknutost'*) and perniciousness, were now published without any trouble.[5] Such a development would have been completely unimaginable in the previous period.

The censorship's view on the publication of Zionist literature was complex. It depended to a great extent on the personal views of a given censor; it is known that the majority of them, for example, the above-mentioned Israel Landau, were very unfavorably disposed toward Zionism. At the same time, this dislike, as a rule, led only to petty incidents and misunderstandings that unnerved editors and publishers but did not have a decisive effect on the fate of the publications as a whole. Thus, despite Viacheslav Plehve's circular of 1903,[6] the Zionist press in the first decade of the twentieth century did not suffer significantly from the censorship so long as it engaged in a discussion of the internal issues of Jewish life and the Zionist movement itself. However, as soon as it critically addressed various issues of Russian life in general, it immediately encountered the very same difficulties that were typically experienced by the entire press in Russia at that time.

From a formal point of view, not surprisingly, in the years of the 1905 Revolution and the following period, the Bundist publications suffered the most from the censorship. Even those few publications that appeared legally did not last longer than one or two issues. However, the majority of the Bund publications came out illegally, without the permission of the Main Directorate on Press Affairs, and, accordingly, they were dealt with severely. In 1904–5, the Main Directorate on Press Affairs permitted the publication even of Jewish periodicals with a very bold program but only if the applicants indicated that one of their goals was to oppose Bundist propaganda, illegal examples of which, according to contemporaries, "were disseminated throughout the southwest territory in hundreds of thousands of copies."[7] It should be noted, though, that in reality the regime and the censorship could do little to halt this flood while the revolution was at its height in late 1905 and early 1906.

The situation of the Jewish liberal nonparty press was almost indistinguishable from that of the Russian press in general; in both cases, the censorship zealously employed similar methods to go after material on identical topics. Probably the best-known case in this category was the prosecution of Saul Ginsburg's newspaper, *Der fraynd*. Even the intercession of the censor Israel Landau, who was well disposed toward Ginsburg, did not prevent the temporary closing of the paper at the beginning of 1906. The newspaper *Dos leben*, which was similar in content to *Der fraynd* and replaced it for a few months, also experienced serious difficulties with the censorship.[8]

In contrast to the preceding period, at the beginning of the 1905 Revolution the language of the Jewish press had comparatively little effect on the attitude of the censorship. The censors were interested primarily in how and what the press reported, not in the language in which it was presented. Nonetheless, there were some nuances in this regard. The censors tended to regard practically the entire press in Hebrew as less important, and it was therefore subject to the least scrupulous and captious examination. The censorship paid greater attention to publications in Yiddish because of the Bund's activity, the mass circulation achieved by publications in that language, and a lingering tradition of hostility. For its part, the Russian-language Jewish press was treated more as part of the Russian than of the Jewish press, and, therefore, beginning in 1906—because of its obvious Judeophilic orientation—it was subject to regular harassment by the censorship.

For many decades the Jewish press and book-publishing enterprises had suffered from the burden of censorship, which, no matter what goals it pursued or cultural-ideological purpose motivated it, was invariably harsh. Did the 1905 Revolution ease this burden? On the whole, the answer is definitely positive. After 1905 the Jewish newspapers, in accord with the press in the Russian Empire generally, became much freer and ceased to be totally dependent on the stroke of the censor's pen. The press not only turned into an independent social and political force but also it gained the opportunity to mold the opinion of those who were expected to discipline it. It is known, for example, that Aleksandr Greis, whose job at the Main Directorate for Press Affairs and the St. Petersburg Censorship Committee entailed reviewing works in Jewish languages, attentively heeded the opinion of leading Jewish journalists and frequently corrected his own evaluations in accordance with their express wishes.[9]

In the period from November 1905 through May 1906, the Jewish press was very largely free; during those months neither the Main Directorate nor local censorship committees prosecuted any Jewish publishers or editors. Subsequently, however, as the opposition and tension between the regime and society in general intensified and state antisemitism grew, the Jewish press again began to experience increasing pressure from the supervisory organs. Of course the latter's possibilities for repressive action had been substantially diminished, but from 1906 to 1914 they fully utilized what remained—from the confiscation of press runs up to the institution of court proceedings.

The 1905 Revolution brought about three important changes in the sphere of censorship of Jewish publications. First, it put an end to preliminary censorship, which had been the prime tool of censorship in the nineteenth century. Second, it decisively resolved the language issue: after the Temporary Regulations of 1906 little remained of the state censorship's prejudicial attitude toward the publication of works in a particular language (meaning in the Jewish case, of course, Yiddish). This circumstance, however, was a consequence of a more global and important factor: the events of 1905–6 led to the disappearance of the separate independent censorship of Jewish publications, which had existed for over one hundred years.

After 1906 there were no longer any specific aspects or special rules regarding the censor's examination of works in Jewish languages nor were there any special requirements of candidates for the position of censor of Jewish publications other than knowledge of the respective languages. The supervision of the Jewish press after 1906 became merely an integral part of the general routine work of supervising the publishing activity in the empire without any added ideological coloration or special mission. Less than a decade later, during the years of World War I and the military censorship, the censorship of Jewish publications again acquired specific features, but that is a separate topic.

Chapter 4

The Russian Right Responds to 1905: Visual Depictions of Jews in Postrevolutionary Russia

Robert Weinberg

Notwithstanding the capacity of Tsar Nicholas II to weather the events of 1905, the revolutionary upheaval fundamentally altered the complexion of Russian politics. The capitulation of the autocratic government in the fall of 1905 opened the floodgates of political activity among virtually all segments of society, with activists from the extreme right (popularly known as the Black Hundreds) to the far left mobilizing to influence Russian politics through both legal and extralegal means. Jews and other national minorities found the months following the October Manifesto both conducive and propitious for organizational consolidation, as did various ethnic Russians motivated by a visceral hatred of Jews and categorically opposed to any reform of the autocracy. For individuals of all political stripes, the 1905 Revolution provided an opportune moment to stake out a position in the rough-and-ready arena of Russian politics. Participants in those events took advantage of their new freedoms to express themselves in the public realm with zeal and élan. In particular, parties reflecting the entire political spectrum relied on the print medium, especially newspapers and journals, to disseminate their views, with visual images both reinforcing and complementing the written word.[1]

Not surprisingly, extreme right-wing political parties and activists considered the press an essential ingredient of their tactical arsenal. While the extreme right had been organizing since the turn of the century, it took the events of 1905 to spark the widespread emergence of organizations that sought to mobilize the electorate of various social strata on behalf of the besieged autocracy. The press proved to be of key importance in the effort of the radical right to garner popular support for a program to turn back the gains of the revolution and ensure that Tsar

Nicholas II would be unencumbered by any limitations on his powers. Some very talented historians have written about the ideology and actions of the Black Hundreds during the years from 1906 to the outbreak of World War I in 1914.[2] But these same historians have not examined the illustrations on the pages of various right-wing newspapers and journals. These drawings complement the textual message and add a dimension to our understanding of politics and culture during the final decade of tsarist rule, thereby serving as political commentary on pressing issues confronting late imperial Russia.

To be sure, the messages in right-wing drawings were frequently confused, muddled, and not particularly subtle. Nor were the images unfamiliar in the sense that similar portrayals of Jews were commonplace throughout Europe at the turn of the century. The Russian right did not have a monopoly on antisemitic depictions. But the illustrations, nonetheless, offered readers an education of sorts by exposing them to the main currents of post-1905 politics from the perspective of the extreme right. The crude and straightforward images with explanatory captions enabled readers with little or no knowledge of current events to learn about politics from the perspective of the extreme right. The blunt nature of the cartoons did not guarantee that any uninformed simpleton could grasp their messages. For example, prominent Duma personages, Jewish and non-Jewish, from various political parties were frequently portrayed, and in many instances the artists did not append names to the faces in the illustrations. Furthermore, the accompanying captions did not always identify the persons depicted in the drawings. This suggests that the editors of Black Hundred publications believed their readership possessed more than passing knowledge of current events, particularly developments in Russia's fledgling parliament, the Duma. But it is also reasonable to assume that the editors hoped the interested but not well-informed reader would seek out explanations of the cartoons.

In his book on political cartoons and caricatures, Charles Press describes three kinds of political cartoons: the descriptive satirical, the laughing satirical, and the destructive satirical. The latter is, in Press's words, "meant to be cruel and to hurt . . . the message says unmistakably 'These creatures that I criticize are not human; they should not be allowed to exist.'"[3] Indeed, the depiction of Jews on the pages of various Black Hundred publications falls into the category of "destructive satirical" and reveals an obsession with portraying Jews as the source of all problems besetting Russia. Jews visually represented in the extreme right-wing press are essentially monstrous beings intent on destroying the social, economic, and political fabric of late imperial Russia. As the drawings reprinted in this chapter indicate, the Black Hundred press did not shy away from presenting Jews in the most unflattering light to convey the notion that Russia's Jewish minority threatened to subvert the existing sociopolitical and economic order and to establish Jewish dominion. But just as important were its efforts to contextualize the drawings in current events, with references to specific persons and issues of the time, as a way to edify the people who read Black Hundred publications. In short, the extreme right offered a perspective on the contemporary political scene that was mired in illogic, fantasy, prejudice, and hatred while nonetheless reflecting realities.

As many historians have noted, analyses of visual images require familiarity with the values, attitudes, beliefs, and knowledge of the viewing public for whom these images were created. One function of political art is to "provide a visual script" designed to lead to "new modes of thinking and behavior."[4] But no matter how powerful and persuasive these images may be, no matter how smartly they incorporate popular mythologies, viewers' responses can be unpredictable because visual representations are open to diverse readings. In other words, viewers of these illustrations interpreted what they saw with the aid of the "cultural repertoires" available to them.[5] Not only is it difficult to ascertain how readers may have interpreted the images but it is also challenging to try to pin down what the artists of the drawings intended to convey. On the one hand, political cartoons and propaganda can fail to make an impact if their messages are too opaque and arcane. On the other hand, symbols and other visual images can be politically effective if their meanings are ambiguous, thereby opening them up to multiple interpretations. To be sure, captions and explanatory texts may help viewers decode the images, but even efforts to demystify the drawings do not necessarily lead to a single reading given the polyvalent nature of visual depictions.

The drawings examined here are taken from three Black Hundred publications that appeared in the wake of the 1905 Revolution: *Pliuvium* (St. Petersburg, 1906–8), *Veche* (Moscow, 1905–9), and *Knut* (Moscow, 1906–8). The latter two were published by Vladimir Olovennikov, an activist with close ties to the Russian Monarchist Party and the Union of the Russian People. While the essential messages of these drawings echo what the extreme right asserted in the written word, these illustrations nonetheless offer vivid depictions of the core values and beliefs of the Black Hundreds. All the problems plaguing Russian society were attributed to the machinations of Jews, and all persons and political organizations—Jewish or otherwise—that opposed or challenged the autocracy were considered the dupes of a worldwide Jewish conspiracy. For the sake of brevity and focus, I have chosen to concentrate on a handful of illustrations that address the Black Hundreds' concerns that the Jews were using the newly granted civil liberties of post-October Russia to subvert the autocracy, expand in self-serving fashion the scope of political reform, and dominate the Duma. (These depictions are only the tip of the iceberg; hundreds of similar images can be found on the pages of just these three publications, and I am offering a selective but not arbitrary presentation of the myriad illustrations in these three publications.)

The monthly *Knut* was particularly noteworthy for its wide use of color, clearly an indicator that the publisher did not skimp on expenses. Each issue's cover displayed a colored illustration, and elaborate drawings in color accompanied many of the major articles. For example, the cover of the journal's first issue in 1906 (Figure 1) shows Prime Minister Petr Stolypin holding the reins of a speeding troika whose passenger is Mother Russia. Three horses are pulling the carriage, and the words "indivisible Russia" and the well-known slogan "Autocracy, Orthodoxy, and *Narodnost* [nationality]" are engraved, respectively, on the yoke and the Russian flag flapping in the wind. Several growling bulldogs have surrounded the carriage that a determined Stolypin is trying to drive to safety. The dogs represent three political parties—the Octobrists, Mirnoe obnovlenie (Peaceful renewal), and the Socialist Revolutionaries. Whereas the latter party embraced political violence, the other two were moderate organizations that eschewed radical tactics. Yet they are thrown in with the Socialist Revolutionaries. Generally speaking, most Octobrists did not seek any further diminution of royal authority in post-1905 Russia and certainly did not support the revolutionaries to their political left. Circling above are several anthropomorphized vultures with stereotypical Jewish features. To emphasize that the vultures are Jews, the artist has one vulture sitting on the tree branch wearing a *kipa* (yarmulke) with the word "Bund" emblazoned on its body. The drawing intimates that the Jewish buzzards are waiting for the precise moment to swoop down and feast on the body politic of Russia once it has been destroyed not only by the revolutionaries but also by the reformers. In other words, non-Jews overthrow Mother Russia but Jews will enjoy the fruits of revolution.

Similarly, the cover of issue no. 3 from 1908 (Figure 2) reiterates this message of the Jews' seeking to benefit from the actions of non-Jewish political activists. Above the caption "In Training," a well-to-do Jew with stereotypical looks is teaching tricks to three dogs that bear the names of prominent politicians. The pug is Aleksandr Guchkov, leader of the Octobrists; the small white poodle is Count Vladimir Bobrinskii, a conservative landlord with ties to right-wing Octobrists who opposed efforts to endow the Duma with legislative powers; and the large black poodle standing on its hind legs is Fedor Rodichev, a leading Kadet deputy to the Duma. The other figures in the drawing are evidently Jews because

Figure 1. Cover of *Knut*, no. 1 (1906)

Figure 2. Cover of *Knut*, no. 3 (1908)

they share facial characteristics with the man teaching tricks to the dogs.
Two of the other figures are watching the training session with rapt
attention; another two are talking to each other; and one is walking
away. Again, the artist is asserting the common Black Hundred view that
Jews were orchestrating the efforts of gentile politicians in the Duma to

КОНЦЕРТНОЕ ОТДѢЛЕНІЕ «ПЛЮВІУМА».

САМЫЙ РУССКІЙ ОРКЕСТРЪ ИСПОЛНЯЕТЪ НАЦІОНАЛЬНЫЙ ТАНЕЦЪ «ВИТТОВА ПЛЯСКА» ПОДЪ УПРАВЛЕНІЕМЪ АВТОРА.

Figure 3. Cover of *Pliuvium*, no. 10 (December 9, 1906)

subvert the crown. The extreme right underscored their rejection of parliamentary politics by suggesting that even committed supporters of the reformed autocracy such as Bobrinskii, by no stretch of the imagination a friend of the liberals or socialists, performed tricks at the behest of the Jews and thus had dubious political credentials.[6]

Another variant on this theme of Russian Jewry's orchestrating the destruction of Russia can be found in Figure 3, the cover of the December 9, 1906, issue of *Pliuvium*. The artist shows former prime minister Sergei Witte conducting three leering Jewish musicians who are said to be playing the "national dance, 'The St. Vitus Dance,'" in the "Russian orchestra" and who have evidently supplanted Russian musicians. This cartoon is a jibe at Witte, the official who advised Nicholas II to grant the concessions of October 1905, thereby earning the former the undying disdain and hatred of the political right.

The fact that Witte seems to be looking to his side for direction raises the possibility that he is under the control of someone offstage, someone hidden from public view. Moreover, he himself is tagged as a reli-

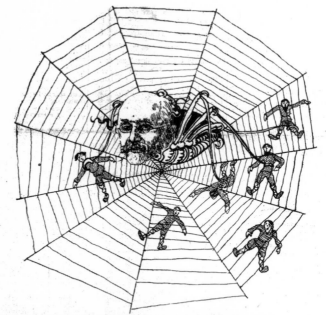

Жидъ Герценштейнъ и православные мужички въ Государственной Думѣ.

Figure 4. From *Veche*, no. 26 (June 11, 1906)

gious Jew by virtue of his wearing the traditional fringed undergarment worn by observant Jews. Depicting Witte as a Jew was, perhaps, the cartoonist's not so subtle allusion to Witte's second wife, who was a converted Jew. Moreover, the Union of the Russian People failed twice in its efforts to assassinate Witte, whom it considered "the most effective agent of . . . the 'Judeo-Masonic' conspiracy" to undermine Russia. Witte also enjoyed the reputation of employing Jews when he was minister of finance in the 1890s.[7] An accompanying caption and poem about Witte suggest that he is attempting a political comeback in order to weaken the government. The poem's final stanza comments:

We Russians have lost heart,
And the Kikes have increased their income.

In a similar vein, the next drawing, Figure 4, illustrates the typical reliance in the Black Hundred press on crass and crude prejudices to convey its political comment. It shows a spider with the head of Mikhail

Gertsenshtein, a Kadet deputy to the First Duma who was assassinated by members of the Union of the Russian People a month or so after this drawing appeared. According to the caption, the "Kike Gertsenshtein" had ensnared several Russian Orthodox peasant Duma deputies in his web. Even though Gertsenshtein had converted to Russian Orthodoxy years earlier, the Black Hundreds nevertheless regarded him as a Jew whose actions in the Duma threatened the interests of the landed gentry. A founder of the Kadet party and a professor at Moscow University, Gertsenshtein was an expert on agrarian affairs and served as the driving force behind the party's advocacy of the compulsory expropriation of private estates for the benefit of land-hungry peasants. Duma deputies representing the gentry opposed this proposal for obvious reasons but so, too, did many deputies representing the peasantry (known as Trudoviki or Laborers). Their opposition, however, was based on the fact that under the Kadet proposal, the local gentry would continue to control the institutions that were to redistribute the land.[8]

There are two ways of interpreting the drawing. First, the artist could be making the case that the Jewish deputies to the Duma had "captured" the peasant vote and were forcing peasants to support policies that would benefit Jews engaged in land speculation. Because the Kadet proposal was designed to assist the peasantry by redistributing land held in private hands, the artist may have been appealing to the interests of the gentry that stood to lose their land if the Kadet proposal were enacted. Given the Kadets' insistence on compulsory land expropriation and the peasant deputies' call for the redistribution of estate holdings into the hands of peasants who worked the land, the second interpretation seems more likely. Moreover, the drawing assumes that the reader has been keeping abreast of developments in the Duma and is aware of the debates over agrarian reform, including the persons involved. The editor of *Veche* evidently believed that readers of the newspaper would grasp the subtleties of the message conveyed in the drawing.

The next drawing (Figure 5) is captioned "The Last 'Shabash' in the Duma, Saturday, July 8." The selection of that date was not random: news of the government's decision to dissolve the First Duma, a result of the standoff with the Kadets over the issue of land redistribution, was promulgated on Sunday, June 9, but announced on the evening of July 8, 1906.[9] The drawing underscores the extreme right's belief that Jews dominated parliamentary politics, even to the point of turning Duma sessions into Jewish religious services. It shows Jewish and gentile deputies to the Duma wearing prayer shawls, although only the Jewish deputies appear to be wearing *kipot* and praying. More Jewish deputies stand on the podium at the front of the room and, in addition to their prayer shawls, they are also wearing phylacteries. Finally, the deputy presiding

Послѣдній „шабашъ" въ Думѣ въ субботу 8-го іюля

Figure 5. From *Veche*, no. 35 (July 13, 1906)

over the meeting, presumably S. A. Muromtsev, a law professor and prominent Kadet, does not possess the facial features of the other deputies in the drawing, although he, too, has donned a prayer shawl and phylacteries.[10] But, like Witte in the previous illustration, the cartoon Muromtsev may be an honorary Jew in the eyes of the artist. Evidently, the fact that only twelve Jews served in the First and four in the Second Duma (both of which had close to five hundred deputies) did not deter the Black Hundreds from imagining that Jews exercised inordinate power and influence in that institution.

Вколачиваніе въ гробъ заживо.

Figure 6. From *Pliuvium*, no. 43 (July 28, 1907): 2

One additional aspect of the drawing merits attention. The substitution of a sibilant "sh" for the final "s" in the spelling of "Shabas" is a play on the imagined, lisping pronunciation of Jews. But "*shabash*" also means witches' Sabbath in Russian, thereby linking Jews to the evil doings of the devil.

Figure 6 highlights the Black Hundreds' insistence that Jews were exploiting the freedoms granted in October to subdue Russia. It shows

Жидова за работой...

Figure 7. From *Veche*, no. 52 (August 23, 1906)

a Jewish man (note the dark hair, thick lips, and large nose and ears) kneeling on the lid of a coffin as he tries to hammer it shut on Mother Russia, struggling to prevent herself from being buried alive. His rough features and workers' clothes distinguish him from the more refined, rich Jews in other drawings. The coffin lid is labeled "constitution," and the wooden mallet has the words "Kike press" written on one side, both phrases indicating that Jews are utilizing freedom of the press and other newly granted civil liberties to bury Russia with a constitution. Of course, post-1905 Russia did not have a full-scale constitution, but the word is used in the Black Hundred press to refer to the political freedoms granted in the October Manifesto and in the Fundamental Laws. The caption "Buried alive" reinforces the message delivered by the drawing.

Another elaboration on this motif is found in Figure 7, titled "Kikes at Work." In a play on the story of Gulliver in the land of the Lilliputians, a man representing Russia—apparently a worker, based on his clothing—has been subdued by a group of miniature Jewish men. Some are hard at work lashing down the gargantuan man while others are resting

ЧУДЕСНЫЙ ЦВѢТОКЪ

Figure 8. From *Veche*, no. 33 (March 22, 1907)

or celebrating the fruits of their labor. One waves a white flag in a sign of victory. Gulliver's upper torso is held down by ropes and three leather straps with the words "equality," "brotherhood," and "freedom" written on them. The artist's message is unmistakable: Jews are exploiting the slogans of political liberty to overwhelm the stronger Russian people.[11]

The last illustration I have selected is titled "The Miraculous Blossom" (Figure 8). It shows the extreme right's confidence that the political tide would soon turn against the forces of revolution. In the first panel, a plant with two leaves emblazoned with the words "The Jewish Question" begins to sprout. The caption reads, "On the fetid soil of the liberation movement, a mysterious plant began to grow." In the next panel, two Jews use watering cans labeled "bribes" and "the press" to tend the plant, which responds positively to the care and attention. As the caption ironically notes, "The benefactors of the human race diligently looked after the flower and gave it various beneficial fertilizers."[12] The fact that the fertilizer used was meant, in all likelihood, to suggest animal waste drove home the point that Jews are feeding shit to society in their effort to promote equal rights for Jews. Panel three shows the plant with a new leaf called "shvaboda" (a play on the supposed Jewish pronunciation of "svoboda," the Russian word for "freedom" or "liberty"). In addition, a stem labeled "equal rights" with a flower ready to bloom has emerged. The caption reads, "The plant grew taller by the hour and soon a shoot with a flowering bud appeared."

In the next panel, various Jews, including a woman who does not look Jewish but evidently represents the movement for equal rights for women, express their glee as they look at the plant and its budding flower. The caption indicates that "the kikes waited from day to day for the flower to bloom. Finally, the bud cracked," only to show the fully blooming flower as three fists giving the *mano in fica* to the Jews, who flee in fright. The *mano in fica*, commonly known as the "fig hand," has been used for centuries in Europe to ward off the evil eye, with many people wearing amulets and good-luck charms with the *mano in fica*.[13] But it is also an insulting, if not obscene, gesture that indicates indignation. It is equivalent to thumbing one's nose at someone or telling someone to "get lost." However, in some contexts it may mean "up yours" or "fuck you," serve as an obscene sexual invitation, or refer to female genitalia. The "fig hand" enjoyed common currency throughout Europe in the early twentieth century, and there is no doubt that it was known among the general populace. Indeed, left-leaning satirical journals also used the *mano in fica* to express their opposition to efforts to reverse the gains of 1905.[14]

These illustrations offer a brief glimpse into the mindset of the extreme right in post-1905 Russia and demonstrate how Black Hundred activists drew freely upon the rich repository of visual imagery in Russian and European culture to convey their views of the dangers Jews posed to society. To paraphrase what other historians have previously noted, the study of antisemitic discourse helps us penetrate the mindset of antisemites, but it contributes little, if anything at all, to our knowledge of Jews. The caricatures that appeared on the pages of Black Hundred publications reveal the consistency of political antisemitism throughout Europe in the early decades of the twentieth century, namely, its tenet that Jews were seeking to enslave host societies by taking advantage of political freedoms and civil liberties. To be sure, there is no way of telling whether the readers of Black Hundred newspapers and journals absorbed the artists' intended message. At the very least, however, the sentiments expressed in the drawings may have reinforced whatever anti-Jewish animus existed among the readership.

Insurmountable problems confronted state and society during the twilight of Romanov rule, and the venom toward Jews displayed on the pages of the extreme right-wing press after 1905 was symptomatic of the deep social and political fissures plaguing late imperial Russia. No fledgling parliamentary system can survive for long in the absence of a broad consensus regarding the fundamental values and norms underlying society. The antisemitic idée fixe of the Black Hundreds underscores the lack of such a consensus in late imperial Russian society, and the inability of the body politic to find a common language contributed in no small measure to the fragile nature of Duma politics. The knee-jerk tendency of extreme, right-wing pro-tsarist forces to assign blame for all the ills besetting Russia to the machinations of a Jewish cabal virtually ensured that such a consensus could not emerge. Given the hatred of liberal constitutionalism reflected in the drawings of the extreme right-wing press, the chances for peaceful coexistence among Russia's fledgling political parties were slim, especially because the radical left, as well as the tsar himself, also rejected a parliamentary solution to Russia's pressing problems. Social and political stability depends on a willingness to negotiate and compromise, a readiness to work through problems in the political arena, traits all too sadly absent in post-1905 Russia.

Chapter 5

The "Jewish Question" in the Tsarist Army in the Early Twentieth Century

SEMION GOLDIN

During the decade before the outbreak of World War I and, especially, after the Revolution of 1905, the high command of the Russian army, with the support of the tsar himself, took a harder line than it had in the preceding decades with regard to Jewish soldiers. This attitude became so harsh that even converted Jews were denied access to officers' ranks. It was also reflected in the drafting of a law that was supposed to halt the conscription of Jews into the Russian army.

In the late nineteenth century and the beginning of the twentieth, Jews who had converted to Russian Orthodoxy were allowed to study in military schools and, subsequently, could be promoted to officer ranks.[1] The situation changed during the rule of Nicholas II, in the context of a switch from a religious to a racial definition of who is a Jew. In 1903, the Military Council (Voennyi sovet) of the Ministry of War decreed, "Young people of the Jewish faith who have adopted Christianity are an extremely undesirable element in our army." The ban on the acceptance of converted Jews into military schools was then supposed to be discussed by the State Council (Gosudarstvennyi sovet). This discussion was postponed by order of the minister of war "until the right time."[2] By the tsar's Decree of May 11, 1910, Jews of lower ranks, "regardless of their declared religion," were no longer permitted to take the examination to become officers.[3] On May 12, 1912, the Supreme Headquarters (Glavnyi shtab) ordered that all Jews, irrespective of their declared religion, be considered "rabbinic" or religious Jews ("evrei–talmudisty"). The restrictions that had previously applied only to those Jews as defined by their religion now applied to all Jews by race.[4]

How was the Jewishness of a candidate for the rank of officer to be defined? In the case of soldiers aspiring to the lowest officer rank (*praporshchik*), commanders were required to "clarify fully the ethnic background of these soldiers" so as to prevent the application of Jews converted to Christianity or of the sons and even grandsons of people "who had been born into the Jewish faith."[5] The gradual replacement in Russia of a religious definition of Jews by a racial one and the corresponding intensified discrimination against Jews during this period have not been sufficiently studied. These issues are, however, critical for understanding the development of the ideology of late tsarism.[6]

As early as 1903, during a discussion of the military budget for 1904, the ministers of war and of finance rejected the idea of replacing military service for Jews with a special tax.[7] When the commanders of military districts were asked, they almost unanimously opposed this proposal, which they considered unfair to other nationalities of the empire (especially the Russians).[8] As a result of the tsar's personal intervention, the proposal was raised again in 1907. Nicholas II added supportive comments in this regard to the 1907 annual reports of the commander of the Vilna military district and that of the governor of Kherson. Both of these reports called for a halt to the drafting of Jews. Citing the experience of the preceding years of revolution, the commander of the Vilna military district reported to the tsar: "A fundamental evil in our army is the Jews, whose harmful characteristics are now fully manifest. . . . The commanders of our troops . . . favor a complete halt to the conscription of Jews into the army." To this the tsar added, "I agree."[9]

The monarch's comment was of major significance because it gave a direction to the bureaucracy in determining the state's practical policy. The issue was sent for review to the State Defense Council (Sovet gosudarstvennoi oborony), the highest government authority for defense policy. Grand Prince Nikolai Nikolaevich headed the council and, subsequently, during World War I was appointed supreme commander-in-chief of the Russian army. The State Defense Council also concluded: " The presence of Jews in the army . . . is a tremendous evil that is extremely harmful to the interests of the army."[10] At the same time, the council ruled out the substitution of a tax for Jewish military conscription because this measure was unfair to the other peoples in the empire and "immoral because it gave the rich the chance to buy their way out of service." It was also claimed that the Jews would pay for this new tax by exploiting Christians, who would have to pay them higher prices for goods.[11] The State Defense Council's decision did not affect the tsar's conviction that Jews should be kept out of the army. The report of the commander of the Omsk military district from 1909 stated: "Closing the ranks of the army to the Jews is as important for the interests of the army as [it is] for the interests of the state." Nicholas added, "I am of the same opinion."[12]

The proposal to halt the conscription of Jews into the army was raised, for the third time, by the State Duma. The Duma's defense committee, "recognizing that people of the Jewish faith are a harmful element in the army," in the spring of 1911 expressed the desire to "introduce draft legislation regarding an end to the military conscription of people of the Jewish religion."[13] In April 1914 a closed session of the Duma itself again proposed a review of draft legislation on ending the conscription of Jews into the army.[14]

After receiving this support from the Duma, and aware of the tsar's fervent approval for such a step, the military bureaucracy considered how to end the conscription of Jews. In 1911–12, the war ministry asked fifty top-ranking military personnel (commanders of military districts and army corps) to express their views about the characteristics of Jewish soldiers and the general desirability of ending the conscription of Jews.[15] With only a couple of exceptions, all of those asked stated that Jews were totally unsuitable for army service; a majority favored the total cessation of their military conscription.

Two practical reasons were given to justify this point of view:

(1) The generals noted that the Jews under their command suffered from physical weakness and a high rate of illness, leading to their inability to withstand the rigors of military service. Due to such weakness it was necessary to exempt Jews from heavy work, participation in maneuvers, and so forth. During the military exercises of 1910 in the Moscow military district, up to 50 percent of the Jews had to be exempted. In the same year, in the Odessa military district, 9 percent of the soldiers excused on grounds of illness were Jews (who constituted approximately 5 percent of the total number of soldiers).[16]

(2) The moral qualities of the Jewish soldiers were, allegedly, low. According to the commander of the Odessa military district, "In general, the Jews are incapable of being honest." Russian military commanders cited Jewish cowardice and lying and Jews' tendency to protect each other, to fake illness, to steal, and to cheat. While it was noted that the Jews' intellectual abilities were higher than those of others, they were said to have used this capacity mainly to avoid the rigors of military service. According to the military commanders, the Jewish soldiers' cautious, crafty nature accounted for the fact that relatively few of them were found guilty of crimes.[17]

In addition, some of the generals gave an ideological justification for their opposition to Jews in the Russian army. General Plehve (commander of the Moscow military district) believed that "the Jews are enemies of Russia and desire its destruction." General Evert (commander of the Thirteenth Army Corps) stated: "Always and everywhere . . . the Jews have been alien and even hostile to the interests of the state in which they lived. . . . A people lacking patriotism and loyalty to the Emperor and Homeland cannot be good soldiers." General Smirnov (commander of the Twentieth Army Corps) believed that "the Jew is a cosmopolitan by conviction, the idea of defending a nation is alien to him." General N. I. Ivanov (commander of the Kiev military district) considered: "It is in the state's interest to have a powerful army, . . . which is possible only if all harmful elements are kept at a distance from it. Such an element is, first of all, Jewry, which introduces a corrupting and demoralizing principle into our forces. . . . Jews do not recognize the army and they reject those elevated ideals that it serves."[18]

Speaking about the desirability of ending the conscription of Jews, several military commanders also called for limiting their civil rights or depriving them of Russian citizenship entirely. In particular, the subsequently famous General Brusilov (at that time commander of the Fourteenth Army Corps) called for the "complete exclusion of Jews from army ranks . . . [and] restriction of their civil rights." The recommendation that Russian Jews be deprived of their citizenship was made by General Martson, the commander of the Vilna military district. Similar calls came from the ataman of the Don Cossack forces, General Mishchenko, who stated: "Then the question of their civil duties and military conscription will be resolved by itself." General Sakharov (commander of the Seventh Army Corps) considered that such a step would be "a real boon for Russia." General Litvinov (commander of the Fifth Army Corps) called for expelling the Jews from Russia or "at least depriving them of all civil status." Litvinov and also General Plehve spoke out about the need to deprive Jews of the right to supply goods to the army.[19]

It should be noted that there were some commanders who opposed ending the conscription of Jews. This was put quite laconically by General Alekseev (commander of the Third Caucasus Army Corps): "All ethnic groups should be subject to conscription itself and should in no case be able to substitute money for it."[20] Grand Prince Nikolai Nikolaevich (at that time commanding the St. Petersburg military district) argued that "Jews are an unavoidable evil in the army." Count Vorontsov-Dashkov (commander of the Caucasus military district), for his part, was concerned that, given the proposed measures, "weak elements" among other peoples might decide to convert to Judaism so that they, too, could buy their way out of the army.

Two generals, Eduard Ekk (commander of the Grenadier Corps) and Nikolai Radkevich (commander of the Third Siberian Corps), were definitely in the minority in their view that Jews might even make decent soldiers. Ekk noted that the harm allegedly caused by Jews in the army "was exaggerated [and that with] strict supervision . . . they were capable of service."[21] Radkevich (who during World War I carried out mass deportations of Jews) believed that Jewish soldiers

would cause harm where strict order was lacking and when there was [insufficient] work with the troops. The revolutionary activity of the Jews between 1904 and 1907, especially that led by the Bund, indicated that the question of the inborn cowardice or lack of military spirit of "the Jews" was no longer of relevance. . . . Since it was not possible to destroy all the Jews and, thus, free the Russian people from the need to coexist with them, one had to be careful in dealing with them.[22]

Radkevich also noted that when it came to maiming themselves to avoid conscription, the Siberians in his corps outdid the Jews. Further, the disruptive influence of Jews in the army was nothing compared to that of the Russian revolutionary parties. In fact, the general believed that serving in the Russian army was a good way to assimilate the Jews. Earlier, in the 1870s, the military geographer and ethnographer A.F. Rittikh expressed a similar view: "For Jews in Russia the military is a great school which in the future can transform these parasites."[23]

The Ministry of War expended a great deal of effort in preparing draft legislation concerning Jewish service in the army. In addition to conducting a survey of military commanders, it compiled historical data. The ministry also collected statistical information about Jews who served in the army. It updated data via continuing contacts with the Ministry of the Interior and sought information from Russian military attachés abroad about Jews serving in foreign armies.[24] As a result, Minister of War Vladimir Sukhomlinov announced to the Council of Ministers in April 1914 that he "definitely favor[ed] halting Jews' being conscripted into the army."[25] In early 1914 the Council of Ministers "in a confidential manner" discussed this issue and prepared legislation to end the conscription of Jews.[26] The outbreak of World War I interrupted this work.

What motivated such strong hostility toward Jews on the part of the military elite of Russia in the early twentieth century? Part of this hostility can definitely be attributed to ideological antisemitism. The remarks of Russian military commanders about Jews often echoed statements of the ideologists of the All-Russian National Union (Vserossiiskii natsional'nyi soiuz), the main Russian nationalist parliamentary party.[27] The leaders of this party believed that "the Jews definitely have all the characteristics of infectious bacteria. Like the latter, the Jews have an amazing ability to reproduce and to poison any organism in which they find a home."[28] A major point of the union's program was absolute opposition to equal rights for Jews. The Jews were "a state within a state. They always were, and will be, separate from the other citizens. Therefore, there cannot be any question of their equality."[29]

A major component of the worldview of the military elite was the certainty that the revolutionary shocks and political reforms in Russia were the result of a global Jewish conspiracy. General G. O. Rauch asserted, concerning the causes of the Revolution of 1905: "Jews the world over are continually pursuing one goal—the attainment of equal rights in Russia in order to then completely subjugate it."[30] Grand Prince Konstantin Konstantinovich (head of Russia's military educational institutions, in addition to being a well-known poet) remarked about the Duma in his journal: "Kikes [zhidy] are increasingly becoming part of it and one should hardly expect any good from this."[31] Thus Russian antisemitism, which was rooted deep in the consciousness of the elite, including the military, created an entire Jewish myth that became a way of perceiving the world and turned into a "catechism."[32]

At the same time, the negative attitude of the Russian high command toward the Jews was also based on what they considered to be "objective" military reasons that provided a new "scientific" explanation for the ingrained antisemitic prejudices. Toward the end of the nineteenth century, war began to be considered as the affair of all the people, of the entire nation, as a cause that would inspire the joy and sacrificial enthusiasm of the individual as part of the collective.[33] The willingness to sacrifice for victory was seen as a crucial resource of the fighting nation at a time when all means were to be mobilized to serve the goals of war.[34]

Insofar as a loyal and patriotic population was now perceived as one of the main military resources of a country, one of the tasks in preparing for war was to determine the magnitude of this resource. Military statistics, which elaborated a scientific approach to the issue, asserted that an ethnically homogenous population speaking one language was the ideal from the point of view of military utility.[35] Moreover, around the beginning of the twentieth century, on the basis of current sociological theories, an understanding developed of the importance and legitimacy of state interference in what constituted the "population."[36] For this purpose the population was divided into separate "elements," each with its own characteristics. The most important feature of each element was ethnic affiliation. Jews were described as an element that was unambiguously disloyal, greedy, and egotistical.[37] In 1911, the famous military figure Dmitrii Miliutin (who was, incidentally, the father of military statistics in Russia) wrote, "In the Jewish population the enemy will find those ready to serve him as spies, scouts, and all kinds of cunning agents."[38]

From the state's point of view, the age-old supposed unwillingness (or inability) of a given group—in this case, the Jews—to be a loyal part of such a mobilization of society represented a serious problem. Any restrictive or repressive measures against such "disloyal" categories of the population became a legitimate means of assuring the loyalty of the fighting force.[39]

Thus, a combination of antisemitic prejudice, allegedly objective military considerations, and the reality of painful changes in the autocracy led the military leadership of Russia to a harsher attitude toward the Jews. This, in turn, was to have a major influence on the fate of Russian Jews during World War I. In the conditions of a war that was difficult and, on the whole, unsuccessful for Russia, the repressive policy of the military authorities was directed at the Jews as a category of the population that even before the war had been defined in a quasi-scientific manner as "unreliable"[40] and "unworthy" of serving in the Russian army.

Part III
1905 as a Crossroads for the Empire's Jews

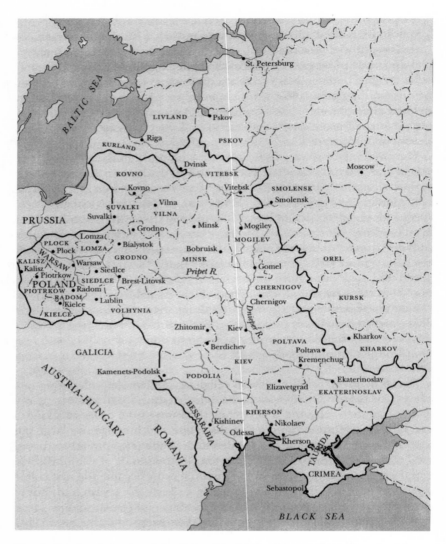

Map 1. Russian Poland and the Pale of Jewish Settlement. Reproduced, with permission, from Benjamin Nathans, *Beyond the Pale* (Berkeley: University of California Press, 2002), p. 2.

Chapter 6

Victory from Defeat: 1905 and the Society for the Promotion of Enlightenment among the Jews of Russia

BRIAN HOROWITZ

The "failed" Russian Revolution of 1905 paradoxically introduced changes in Russia that permitted the Society for the Promotion of Enlightenment among the Jews of Russia to develop in new and positive ways. Processes of egalitarianism and democratization in society powerfully influenced the OPE (the acronym based on its name in Russian according to which the society was known). New leaders who were not members of the Jewish elite emerged and the participation of teachers, students, and workers increased. In addition, a larger number of women, previously a marginal group in the society, were involved in all OPE activities after 1905. Although new leaders in the 1880s and 1890s had tried to make the society more attractive to non-elites, this goal was realized in a meaningful way only after 1905. In fact, one can argue that changes in the composition of the members and efforts to engage the Jewish masses in modern education resulted in a fundamental revitalization of this old society, giving it new tasks to accomplish and a new role to play in late-tsarist Russia.

The OPE was established in 1863, during the reign of Alexander II, by two of Russia's leading Jewish bankers and industrialists, Baron Evzel Ginzburg and Samuel Brodsky.[1] The membership was quickly enlarged to include select maskilim and sympathetic Russian officials.[2] A branch in Odessa came into existence in 1867.

Founded in the wake of the liberation of the serfs in 1861, the OPE initially saw its mission as preparing Jews for legal equality in the Russian Empire. At the time, progressive Jews believed that the government would bestow full equality when Jews were "ready to integrate." Education broadly conceived was seen as the primary means of "transforming" and preparing the Jews for the anticipated moment. In its original charter the society assigned to itself the dissemination of information about the natural sciences and history in Hebrew and Russian as well as the establishment of institutions of secular education for Jews.[3] The Odessa branch of the OPE advanced a specific program of "russification" designed to teach Jews to speak Russian in order to integrate them rapidly into the fabric of the country.

The first attempts to facilitate the creation of private courses for Jews were halted by the government, which suspected so-called Sunday schools of breeding radicals.[4] The Odessa branch closed down anyway, disillusioned by the pogrom that had broken out in the city in 1871. Already feeling the pressure of government scrutiny, the OPE leaders decided to engage in activities that would not arouse suspicion. During the 1870s, St. Petersburg leaders spent the lion's share of their budget on aiding Jewish university students but did little to help the impoverished masses living in the Pale of Settlement. Having lost touch with the realities of Russian Jewish life, the organization became so stagnant that Simon Dubnov announced in 1886 that it was a living corpse, "neither dead nor alive."[5] The number of members was growing only gradually at that time: 551 in 1881, 543 in 1885, and 773 in 1889. Given a population of five million Jews by the end of the nineteenth century, membership numbers were infinitesimally small.

The OPE experienced a change of fortune in the late 1880s, when a new generation of civic activists of unusual energy and vision joined the society. The most important among them were Maksim Vinaver, Leon Bramson, Mikhail Kreinin, Pinkhus Marek, and Boris Brutskus. Not only did these individuals seek to help the mass population in the Pale but they were also ambitious in their plans. In 1894, an OPE historical commission, a school commission, and a commission devoted to strengthening the society's finances were established. Turning away from strictly limited philanthropy, that is, providing financial assistance for individuals, the new leaders hoped to establish permanent institutions, such as schools, libraries, a rabbinical seminary, and a teachers' institute. At that time the OPE in St. Petersburg, and once again in Odessa, made itself into a center for scholarly activity, holding lectures on Jewish history, literature, economics, law, politics, and education.

A central goal of the society by 1900 was to create an extensive system of Jewish schools in which students could receive instruction in secular and Jewish subjects. That seemed an impossible dream, since the OPE budget for schools was limited to a measly 10,000 rubles for nearly one hundred schools in 1898. Despite the plans for change, the OPE still gave individual students over 27,000 rubles in the same year.[6] Fortunately, starting in 1900, the Jewish Colonization Association in Paris began to send grants to the OPE for schools—at first 26,000 rubles, but increasing to 40,000 by 1906.[7] These huge supplements permitted the OPE to offer relatively large subsidies to individual schools; the average amount given was 742 rubles.[8]

OPE leaders understood that their efforts to expand opportunities for modern education were critical because the government's Jewish schools could not satisfy the demand of Jews for secular education and the Orthodox Jewish community in Russia was not interested at that time in establishing schools where secular courses were taken seriously. Given its limited capacities in terms of budget and political power, the OPE concentrated on realistic tasks. The achievements of the OPE before 1905 included the publication of two volumes of archival materials about Jews in the Russian Empire, *Decrees and Inscriptions*; and an exhaustive compendium titled *A Systematic Bibliography of Works on Jews in the Russian Language*, as well as the *Handbook of Questions concerning Jewish Education*.[9] The latter, 681 pages long, was aimed at helping Jewish teachers and civic activists to reform schools and maneuver through the government bureaucracy. Although the school commission showed a preference for funding reformed Talmud Torah schools, in the *Handbook* one could find descriptions of all existing school types, including sample classes, curriculum design, and even building plans for architects. In 1897, the OPE acquired its own school in St. Petersburg, which served as a laboratory to implement theories about the ideal Jewish school.[10]

In 1902, the OPE attempted to gain the trust of provincial leaders by inviting more than thirty representatives to St. Petersburg to discuss how to gain support for the OPE among the masses.[11] The OPE also sent its own school inspectors into the Pale in order to "make contacts and facilitate properly run schools."[12] In addition, the steering committee lowered the cost of membership for provincial members to five rubles. The leaders hoped that outreach would increase membership rolls and funding. Indeed, the number of members solidly increased during these years to 3,010 in 1900 and 3,750 in 1905–6.

The younger generation of leaders had their own concept of enlightenment. Instead of preparing Jews exclusively to integrate into Russian society, they were interested in promoting Jewish cultural autonomy. In the first years of the twentieth century, programs to establish Jewish libraries, a traveling Jewish pedagogical exhibit, and courses in Jewish subjects for future teachers were initiated.[13] In the OPE's own school, Bramson, the director, assigned more hours to Jewish than to secular subjects, paradoxically attempting, in part, to replicate the content of the heder in order to attract children of traditional parents.[14] Influenced by the ideas of Simon Dubnov, such leaders as Leon Bramson, Saul Ginsburg, and Iulii Brutskus wanted to create institutions that focused on the development and preservation of Jewish identity rather than on adaptation to Russia society. The graduate of an OPE school was supposed to become a Jew who identified himself neither as an uncompromising traditionalist nor a renegade. But neither was such a Jew to find himself "between two worlds," as Semyon An-sky (pseudonym of Shloyme Rappoport) had put it.[15] Rather this person was supposed to feel at home in the multicultural capitals of fin de siècle Russia, where individuals of various ethnicities intermingled yet each fostered his own cultural identity.[16]

Although before 1905 the society had undergone important changes that had led to the development of institutions to serve the Jewish masses, it remained, at best, an underutilized resource. This was true despite the fact that, as the only legally recognized society devoted to Jewish education and culture, it housed diverse commissions devoted to historical study, philanthropy, and educational development. The OPE even ran its own elementary school.[17] One of the consequences of the post-1905 reality was that the OPE was able to jettison extraneous activities and concentrate on its educational program.[18] For example, the historical commission became an independent organization—the Historical Ethnographic Society; philanthropic activity was farmed out to newly established independent institutions; and political activity was spun off into the newly formed political parties. In the OPE itself with its growing membership in 1906, leaders were occupied with major initiatives in education and reorganization. They established an institute for higher learning for Judaic studies and a teachers' institute. From 1910 to 1913 they published a monthly journal, *Messenger of the Society for the Promotion of Enlightenment* (Vestnik obshchestva dlia rasprostraneniia prosveshcheniia), devoted primarily to questions of Jewish education. They took ownership of and ran ten schools, eight modernized heders, two nursery schools, two pedagogical museums, and nine libraries.[19] Spending approximately 85,000 rubles exclusively on subsidies for schools in ninety-eight locations in 1910 alone, the OPE was the largest organization devoted to the modernization of Jewish education in tsarist Russia.[20]

In the post-1905 era, the members focused their energies on education. The tsarist government did not permit the OPE to engage in politics. An attempt to govern the OPE through a democratically elected parliament whose representatives would come from the provincial branches was rejected by the authorities. Nevertheless, with the institutions that it established, the OPE was able to do more than just promote education. It successfully managed to foster Jewish national culture and internal Jewish cohesion, acting as a catalyst for cooperation between St. Petersburg and the Pale. By providing opportunities for the participation of non-elites, including women, the OPE took not only a vital role in Jewish education but also a central place in Russian Jewish life. In assessing the accomplishments of the society, as with so much of Jewish history, one has to be sensitive as much to potentialities as to realities, ideas that never attained full realization, as well as realities that were not intended.

During the early months of 1905, the OPE, like many Russian scientific societies and cultural organizations, threw itself into politics, entering into open rebellion against the government.[21] Gathering seventy-seven signatures for the convocation of a special meeting on February 24, 1905, Maksim Vinaver and Maksim Krol' linked the fate of the society with the uprising in the capital. The resolution composed at the meeting expressed deep and longstanding anger at the government:

The general body of the Society for the Promotion of Enlightenment among the Jews of Russia, based on more than forty years of activity, acknowledges that, because of a lack of legal rights for the Jewish people, the condition of Jewish enlightenment in Russia is difficult and abnormal. The whole network of oppressive laws is only a part of the general repression of the Jewish people, which, leading the masses to stark poverty and excluding them from participation in local decision-making, creates conditions that prevent the potentially proper organization of Jewish education.[22]

Another meeting three days later produced an even sharper resolution with concrete political demands. It contained the following points:

The success of the promotion of enlightenment among the Jewish masses is inextricably connected with the legal and economic condition of the Jews and with the general conditions of Jewish life in Russia, and no partial reform in legislation concerning Jews can guarantee the free development of the Jewish people. Strongly convinced that the correct solution to the Jewish question is unthinkable without a radical change in government structure, we consider the introduction of a representative form of government on broad democratic principles to be necessary. Therefore, we demand inviolability of the person and of property, freedom of conscience, the press, assembly, unions and strikes; amnesty for all political religious prisoners; an immediate call for a constitutional assembly of representatives elected by citizens of both sexes regardless of religious belief and nationality and on the basis of general, equal, and direct ballots; the civic equality of the Jews; the creation of institutions that guarantee freedom for the national and cultural development of the Jewish people. In part we want [an institution to deal with] the question of the proper organization of school education and the promotion of enlightenment among the masses. And therefore we consider necessary 1) the right to receive an education in one's native language and 2) free and obligatory general and professional education for all children until age sixteen.[23]

A whole gamut of demands was contained in the resolution. The members demanded a democratic government and institutions to facilitate the national and cultural development of the Jewish people. At the same time, these political demands were linked to a proposal for universal and compulsory education and the use of Yiddish in schools.[24]

Politically the proclamation was too strong for the older generation; Baron Horace Gintsburg, the chairman of the society, did not attend the two meetings and Mikhail Kulisher, a journalist and veteran OPE leader who ran the meetings in his place, voiced opposition and signed on to a minority-approved, less militant document.[25] Interestingly, the St. Petersburg OPE received support in the form of positive telegrams from various urban centers, including Kiev, Riga, Moscow, Gomel, Kovno, Zhitomir, and Vilna. In June the government reacted by threatening to emasculate the OPE, prohibit it from raising money, and, possibly, jail some of the leaders. Apparently, the tsar's October Manifesto, creating a democratically elected consultative Duma and permitting free political expression, saved the OPE from the government's threats.[26]

The revolutionary situation not only stimulated the call for changes from without but also sparked reform from within. Emboldened by their daring attack on the government, the rank and file turned their anger on the old patrician leaders within the OPE itself. An attempt to overthrow the leaders of the Kiev branch occurred at a general meeting on June 23, 1905.[27] The catalyst was the unilateral decision of the chairman, Vladimir Gintsburg, to cut off discussion and deny voting rights to teachers in Jewish schools who had come to the meeting. He claimed that the teachers had not paid their dues and that their membership had not been confirmed in St. Petersburg.[28] A response given by M. L. Tsitron expressed the position of the rank and file:

Jewish teachers were invited as cooperative members and now you set up an inquisition: "Who are you, why have you come?" Isn't it clear that there is an attempt to prevent the most active members from working. [. . .] The life of the Kiev community takes its own course and the Kiev Society for Enlightenment is just a part of this characteristic anti-democratic coalition of power, order, and force. It is obvious that the attitude has become so strongly ingrained that whoever does not have a million does not have the right to speak! But the time is not far off when other people will direct community institutions.[29]

When Gintsburg tried to close the meeting on the grounds that a full quorum was lacking, the rank and file objected, equating the steering committee with the tsarist police. "We don't want the arm of the law, you reactionary," they shouted. Once Gintsburg and other members of the steering committee abandoned the hall, the rank and file held a "private" meeting with Mark Ratner, a young leader and a well-known socialist, who acted as chairman.

Another confrontation took place in St. Petersburg in December

1905, in which members battled one another over the review commission's petition to adopt Yiddish for OPE activities. Opposition to Yiddish on the part of the steering committee was led by the OPE leader and Hebrew writer Lev Katsenel'son, who argued that using Yiddish "contradicted the aims of the society."[30] Conceding that Yiddish could be useful in adult education for those who as boys had never correctly learned Hebrew, Katsenel'son claimed that there was no room for Yiddish in elementary education.[31] Russian and Hebrew were enough.

Defenders of Yiddish charged that the steering committee was ignorant of the real conditions of Jewish life in the Pale. Mikhail Kreinin argued, "The committee follows the dead letter of its charter and is truly afraid to let go of its control over Jewish enlightenment, naively thinking that 'light originates only from Petersburg.'"[32] Israel Zinberg averred that OPE leaders consisted of "old aristocrats who, like the maskilim, shared a preference for russification." In attacking Yiddish, he continued, "The bankrupt element wants to preserve its illusions of reality, but life demands something else."[33]

The conflict worsened as the meeting continued. The members of the review commission asked permission for guests, non-OPE members, to participate in the debate. Although the steering committee was against it, the vote decided in favor of the guests (40 to 6). Soon after, Jacob Gal'pern, the chairman, tried to close the meeting on the grounds that there was not a proper quorum. At this point the meeting descended into anarchy. A certain M. Bolotin shouted out that the behavior of the steering committee was improper and when he was asked to apologize, mocking applause filled the hall in his support.

When the first guest began to speak, two OPE members left, accompanied by loud whistling. Some individuals shouted that those who whistled should apologize. At that point Gal'pern closed the meeting and the members of the steering committee left the hall. The remaining members and guests decided to continue their discussions under the direction of Mikhail Kreinin. Later, those present issued a resolution expressing anger at the closing of the meeting, which they characterized as an "unjustified act of arbitrary rule." It was entirely uncalled for, they claimed, especially since the general meeting was held to discuss the review commission's report, which was critical of the steering committee. The incident alerted members to the flaws in OPE rules that permitted the steering committee to make "arbitrary and undemocratic" decisions. In the future, they demanded, the chairman of the meeting should be elected by a general vote. They called for another meeting as soon as possible.

Discussions about Yiddish continued on January 29, 1906, but this meeting was also wracked by disorder and even violence when Dr.

Tuvim, a partisan of Hebrew, slapped the face of Saul Ginsburg, the editor of the Yiddish daily paper *Der fraynd*. Instead of dealing with substantive issues, the members devoted themselves to a discussion of the proper means to judge and punish Dr. Tuvim. The vote on Yiddish was finally taken at the March 30, 1906, meeting, when the majority agreed, "Yiddish should be considered equal to Hebrew and Russian."[34] One result of 1905 for the OPE was the reversal of the discrimination against Yiddish.[35]

The optimism of the spring turned to mourning in the fall. The pogroms that began in October left their stamp on OPE activity. At the November 21, 1905, general meeting, the first one held after the violence, OPE leaders voiced their horror and anger, vowing to maintain their resolve to struggle for equality and freedom. Blaming both the government and the Russian people, Maksim Vinaver spoke on behalf of the whole society:

> The OPE, on the basis of diverse material in our possession, concludes that the responsibility for the October riots falls on the governing powers. The pogroms occurred everywhere with help from the authorities and in the larger cities under their direct control. Nevertheless, those administrators guilty of supporting and organizing pogroms still occupy their positions and some of those fully involved have not been brought to justice. The OPE cannot help but claim that a large part of the responsibility for the October horrors also falls on Russian society. For twenty-five years Russian society has watched indifferently while the government and reactionary press have persecuted Jews through [establishing] legal liabilities and by inciting the dark masses against the Jewish population. Even today it does not react energetically enough to the horrors of the October pogroms.[36]

Instead of conducting business, the leaders decided to close the meeting as a "sign of mourning" for the pogroms' victims.[37]

While emotions of dismay and disappointment rang loudest in Vinaver's speech, in the coming months a positive spirit began to reassert itself in the society. Under conditions of relaxed police control, the leaders stepped up efforts to create innovative institutions to reinvigorate the OPE.

In 1907–8, the OPE leaders attempted to transform the society by reconfiguring its governance on a truly democratic basis.[38] They wanted to create an OPE parliament that would be responsive to the needs of the members, especially those in the provinces. This body would serve as the legislative arm of the OPE in the country.

In their proposal submitted for the government's approval (1907), the authors suggested that St. Petersburg would have no power on its own but would receive its political legitimacy solely as the meeting place for democratic representatives from OPE branches.[39] Branches were to be established anywhere that twenty-five members submitted a charter for official recognition. The highest organ of the society would be the assembly of "branch representatives" that would convene annually in December of each year and at other times if two-thirds of the members of the steering committee or one-third of the branches requested it. The responsibilities of the general assembly consisted of selecting the steering committee and the members of the review commission; inspecting and approving the budget; as well as creating commissions and appointing their members. The representatives were also empowered to make decisions regarding changes in the charter, to close branches and, if necessary, to disband the entire society. In a word, the representatives held supreme power.

Representatives were to be chosen in elections held at the branches' meetings with suffrage awarded to both men and women. The number would be proportional to the number of members in any given branch; up to fifty members would entitle a branch to one representative whereas branches with a larger membership would have an extra representative for every additional fifty members. Fearing that the steering committee might be dominated by individuals from the capital, Aleksandr Zalkind and Leon Bramson added a clause restricting its influence at the general assembly in order to guarantee the power of the provinces over OPE policy. It stated that only a quarter of the total vote could come from members of the steering committee. This restriction was meant to protect the power of the provincial representatives and block the steering committee from imposing its will in case of absenteeism among delegates.[40]

There is no doubt that the assembly was meant not only to govern the OPE but also to serve as a deliberative body for dealing with the internal needs of Russian Jewry, a kind of national parliament. Since there was no political organization devoted to problems of internal Jewish life, Bramson, Zalkind, and Iulii Brutskus apparently had the idea of allocating that role to the OPE. With representatives in the capital, the Jews of Russia could plan a countrywide comprehensive policy. This project certainly reflected the constitutional democratic approach that Jewish political leaders had hoped to see in the governance of Russia by the new Duma. For example, in 1906, Jews belonging to various political parties ideologically to the right of the Bund formed the Evreiskaia narodnaia gruppa (Jewish national group) to coordinate a political strategy and defend Jewish interests.[41] At the same time, a Jewish representative assembly would provide an opportunity for the OPE to realize the ideas of Jewish cultural autonomy that Simon Dubnov was promulgating.[42]

Some important conditions needed to be met, of course, for this plan to work. One was to obtain the government's approval, which was by no means assured. The branches also needed to be healthy and responsive. Finally, the financing of the OPE had to change. If the OPE was going to give power to the branches as part of a transformation from a financial system based on philanthropy to one based on proportional contributions, increased donations had to come from the provinces. It would not be feasible to give democratic power to the provinces when nearly all the funding for programs still came from St. Petersburg's notables.

The OPE parliament never became a reality because St. Petersburg's chief of police rejected the new charter. Although the vision of a democratic OPE spearheading Jewish autonomous self-rule was considered too risky for the tsar's cautious regime, the inventive blueprint provides a glimpse of what could have been achieved if circumstances had been different.

The version of the charter ratified in 1908 included a financial arrangement beneficial to the provinces. All money derived from the dues of local members was to be spent locally except for a withholding of 50 kopeks from each member, which would be sent to the central office in St. Petersburg.[43] By 1910, there were twenty-five branches in the major cities of Russia, the Pale, and even Siberia. Although not all were active, some, including Odessa, Kiev, Akkerman, Baku, Samara, and Moscow, were successful operations that competently spread modern Jewish education.[44]

For example, in Odessa in 1913, the OPE subsidized twelve schools, serving 1,113 boys and 753 girls. The branch also provided funding for four evening schools for adults, a library, a summer school, and a pedagogical exhibit. There was also support for twenty-three male and twenty-eight female high school students, plus stipends for five university students and two women attending institutions of higher education, including the Odessa Musical Conservatory.[45] In 1909, the Moscow branch, with a budget of 32,650 rubles, subsidized fifteen schools. Led by Zionist supporters, Rabbi Ya'akov Mazeh, Mikhail Kreinin, Pinkhus Marek, and Iulii Brutskus, the branch was so vibrant that it ran its own elementary school and hosted a local historical commission.[46] The Kiev branch was also dynamic. It created the first modern kindergarten in Podol', Kiev's poor district, for sixty children.[47] The branch also devoted efforts to assist students of high school age who were unable to gain entrance into a Russian gymnasium, including the establishment of an "information bureau" where so-called externs could acquire information about opportunities for study, get new textbooks free of charge, and receive other services.[48] With its budget of 14,113 rubles in 1908, the Kiev branch could afford to subsidize sixteen schools.[49] The activities in smaller cities of the Pale were by necessity more modest. Nevertheless, one could see a clear attempt to achieve on the local level and with limited resources the same goals of subsidizing schools, aiding teachers, and helping those groups least able to help themselves, such as the children of poor families, externs, and heders.[50]

Such diverse activities in various cities reflect the rise of a new group of young OPE activists—externs, teachers, young professionals, and worker-activists who had become more involved in the OPE before 1905 but whose advance to positions of authority gained momentum as a result of the increase in opportunities. In particular, young Jewish women were attracted to OPE educational activities and accomplished many of the tasks at the local level because they were already involved with the teaching profession.[51] In addition, the general modernization of Russian society gave these women new understandings of their roles, which included positions of authority. Because the need for education was so great and the resources so slim, the OPE made wide use of whoever was willing to serve, including many women who looked to the OPE as a source of training, experience, and employment.

Aware that the government would not countenance political activity, OPE leaders turned to those undertakings that had a chance of gaining permission and could bring about a gradual improvement in the lives of Russia's Jews. Baron David Gintsburg, for example, strove to establish a Jewish university, a project that leaders had dreamed in vain of achieving in previous decades. (In 1882 and 1894, OPE leaders had sent petitions to the government requesting permission to create an advanced rabbinical seminary. The government rejected the request even though it was aware of the desperate need for educated modern rabbis, in particular, to fill the posts of the so-called state[official, state-appointed] rabbis.)[52]

In May 1906, Baron David Gintsburg saw an opportunity to realize his dream of establishing a postgraduate institution for Jewish studies. Approaching the Free Advanced School in St. Petersburg, the OPE asked whether Jewish courses could be included in the curriculum.[53] The OPE was already funding scholarships there, and the society wanted to give its stipend-holders some instruction in Jewish history, which was especially important given the hope that after graduation these women and men would enter the teaching profession. Because the OPE promised that the courses would not have "a confessional character" and agreed to pay for its own teachers, the administration of the Free Advanced School consented.[54]

The first lecturer invited to teach there was Simon Dubnov, but he taught only one semester.[55] The dream of creating a Jewish university did not die. In December 1906, Baron David Gintsburg organized a meeting with Horace Gintsburg, David Feinberg, I. Markon, and Dubnov to plan such a university for the future. Although the government was not immediately amenable, David Gintsburg spent a year petitioning and cajoling, finally receiving permission with the caveat that the institution bear the "modest" name of Advanced Courses in Oriental Studies (Vysshie Kursy Vostokovedeniia).[56]

The first semester opened in January 1908 with twenty-two students.[57] The expenses for running the school during its first year were 27,800 rubles, part of which was supplied by the educational endowment in the OPE, which had been created in 1903 in honor of Horace Gintsburg in order to promote elementary schools.[58] The budget had to pay faculty salaries—seven rubles per hour—and student stipends; only two students paid full tuition. Of the thirty students in the second year, three were female. According to Dubnov, the majority of the students were "self-taught provincials, university auditors, and former yeshiva bokhers (students) who were educated in Jewish subjects but did not possess a secular education. Only a few satisfied the definition [of educated], the handful of university students who came to our evening lectures. There were also a few girls from the Advanced Women's Courses."[59] Apparently, all these students had their own permits to live in St. Petersburg because the faculty rejected applicants who were unable to get official permission to live in the capital.[60]

During the first semester Baron David Gintsburg offered three courses—the Book of Job, medieval Judaism, and Arabic. Horace Gintsburg taught a course on the Talmudic tractate Sanhedrin, while Dubnov offered an introduction to Jewish history. Lev Katsenel'son gave a course on the Mishnah, Avraam Zarzovskii taught an introduction to the Hebrew Bible, and V. Ashkenazi taught a course on pedagogy. The courses were offered in the evening, from seven to eleven o'clock, first in the building of the St. Petersburg Gymnasium and later in the OPE's own building. During the semester it was decided also to bring on board Daniel Chwolson to teach the Hebrew language and Mark Vishnitser to teach medieval Jewish history. The German and French languages were made obligatory.

The faculty consisted primarily of OPE members, which irritated Dubnov because he felt courses were insufficiently rigorous. He was especially unforgiving toward David Gintsburg, regarding his lectures as epitomizing the school's flaws. "It was closer to something amateurish, intellectual sport, than a scholarly lecture. Two of the Baron's 'Eastern' protégés gave similar chaotic lectures: a bit about the Khazars, the Gaons, the Talmud, etc. It was difficult to view the unsatisfactory realization of such a good idea, but I still hoped that in time the school would improve, in all likelihood by means of natural selection among the professors."[61] Possibly, Dubnov was too harsh. In any case, it is impossible to describe as "amateurish" such individuals as Dubnov himself, Lev

Katsenel'son, and Daniel Chwolson, whose publications indicate a level of remarkable intellectual achievement.[62]

The selection of courses offered in Bible, Talmud, Hebrew, and Aramaic indicates that the OPE was trying to establish a genuine institution of higher Jewish learning and not merely a rabbinical seminary in the narrow sense. The inclusion of courses in modern and medieval Jewish history and the need for knowledge of French and German in order to gain access to contemporary scholarship reveal a serious academic intention. However, the institution was also supposed to prepare modern rabbis. Therefore, by looking at the curriculum, one can see the OPE's conception of an ideal rabbi. He was supposed to be capable of serving the functions both of religious leader and of statistical record keeper, tabulating births, deaths, marriages, and divorces. He was supposed to be completely knowledgeable in Jewish subjects, especially Bible and Talmud, but also capable of interpreting traditional concepts in a modern context and of using Russian to express himself.

From the 1840s, the government had forced Jewish communities to hire rabbis who were educated at one of the two governmental rabbinical seminaries or had acquired a secular education. Since the scholarship and often the personality of these "modernized" individuals did not satisfy traditional criteria, it became customary to have two rabbis coexisting in the same community. One had the job of keeping records and he was often accused, rightly or wrongly, of corruption because he demanded money from individuals for filling out official paperwork or making convenient changes if a "client" wanted them. This individual was known as a "state" rabbi. The other, who in fact led the community's religious life, was referred to as the "spiritual" rabbi. OPE members wanted modern trained rabbis to be able to fulfill both positions, hoping to refute the claim that modern rabbis could not exist in Russia and to show traditional Jews that an alternative to the "state" rabbi was possible.

From the time that the OPE began to devote more resources to education, OPE educators faced the problematic issue of who would teach in modern Jewish schools. Throughout the late 1890s and first years of the twentieth century, the OPE attempted a variety of sensible but unsuccessful projects to prepare teachers. For example, the OPE had only mixed success in convincing *yeshiva bokhers*, self-taught *shreybers* (mendicant Russian-language tutors), and high school graduates to become teachers. Religious Jews tended to avoid the intensive study of secular subjects, while secular Jews often felt antagonistic toward religion. The miserable salary and difficult conditions of a schoolteacher did not attract applicants. Because of the relative openness among Jews toward women's education, the OPE enlisted more women than men to train for teaching. The drawback was that women students tended to be weak in Jewish subjects.[63] In addition, despite having received fellowships, many women did not pursue a career in teaching. Female graduates of a gymnasium or students in university courses tended to resist moving to remote areas, fearing they would find life boring or that it would be difficult to find an educated husband. In addition, the success rate of OPE scholarship recipients in passing the state teacher's examination was not high. Members of the school commission attributed the lackluster results to the absence of an institution devoted to teacher training.

Among those cities where the OPE had awarded scholarships, Grodno boasted the best success rate in passing the state teacher's examination.[64] In 1906, OPE leaders converted the courses being offered informally through the reformed Talmud Torah in Grodno into a full-fledged teaching institute.[65] Appointing A. Kamstam as director and providing a building, the OPE opened the Grodno Pedagogical Academy in the fall of 1907.[66]

In the two-year course, students were instructed in Jewish and secular subjects. They studied Bible, the history of the Jews, the history of Hebrew literature and Hebrew grammar, the Russian language, mathematics, general history, geography, natural sciences, drawing, gymnastics, and singing. There were specialized courses in psychology, pedagogy, and school hygiene. The students received practical training by teaching in Grodno's Talmud Torah.[67]

The OPE received eighty-one applications for its first official class, from which it accepted thirty students. Most of the boys were former *yeshiva bokherim* who had begun studying secular subjects on their own, while the majority of the girls had a secular education. Almost all had previous teaching experience. According to a teacher at the institute, "The students showed themselves well suited because of their great love of learning and strong work habits."[68] The students received monthly stipends of 20 rubles and free medical care. When they graduated they received a loan of between 30 and 50 rubles for pedagogical material, which was to be returned within a year. Among the first group that graduated, all found jobs immediately. The popularity of the program grew quickly so that in 1910 there were 152 applications for the same thirty places.

In 1909, a problem arose over the rights accruing from a diploma from the Grodno Pedagogical Academy. Until that time, a diploma gave students the right to teach in government schools. The government changed its policy and demanded that graduates also pass the official examination for Russian elementary school teachers if they wanted to teach in government Jewish schools.[69]

The institution prepared graduates to teach either in Talmud Torahs or government Jewish schools. From 1908 to 1910, OPE leaders discussed the nature of the ideal modern Jewish school, coming to a fragile consensus that the ideal school should unite aspects of the heder and a Russian gymnasium.[70] The ideal school was supposed to instill national character by teaching Jewish history, Hebrew and Yiddish, and Jewish religion, while providing students with secular knowledge that they needed to earn a living in tsarist Russia.

The pedagogical courses could not, however, solve the chronic problem of a lack of qualified teachers, but the academy was one part of a larger OPE plan to expand modern education among Jews.[71] During this time, OPE members established a job bureau to match suitable candidates with employment opportunities and issued pamphlets in Yiddish and Russian with model curricula and advice on how to improve hygiene in schools.

Although the Revolution of 1905 did not bring about full-fledged freedom and democracy, it did lead to significant changes in consciousness among OPE leaders. For one thing, the days of political silence were over. The attempt to create a Jewish parliament failed, but the idea of organizing the internal life of Russia's Jews was achieved in part through the creation of OPE branches. In 1910 and 1911, branch leaders came to St. Petersburg to decide the society's future direction.[72] The ongoing coordination among the branches can be juxtaposed with the Kovno Conference, held in late 1909 and early 1910, which represented a serious attempt to organize the political life of Russia's Jews.[73] Representatives from the Pale debated the question of who should be considered a Jew and how to define a Jewish community, that is, what philanthropic and religious institutions should be funded by community funds. They also discussed the implementation and uses of taxation, recommending cooperation between religious and secular Jews. Although this meeting officially did not take place under the OPE auspices, its leaders such as Henry Sliozberg, Maksim Vinaver, and Mikhail Sheftel' were intimately involved.

In 1907, when the government curtailed voting rights for Jews and other non-noble groups in elections to the Second and then the Third State Dumas, a situation emerged that in some aspects resembled pre-1905, because Jews did not have adequate political representation.[74] Activists found openly political work stymied by the government and again had to struggle clandestinely and in indirect ways, such as in cultural and philanthropic societies. From 1907 to 1914, many Bundists and Zionists joined the OPE, which led to culture wars among individuals dedicated to the differing goals of liberalism, revolutionary socialism, and Zionism.

Nineteen hundred and five was not a dress rehearsal for 1917, at least for the OPE. Revolution for its own sake was never the society's goal. The leaders needed political reform so that they could expand the society's educational program and foster Jewish national culture. In the Teachers Academy in Grodno, several hundred men and women were trained to teach Jewish and secular subjects in a modern Jewish school. The Advanced Courses in Oriental Studies was an inspiration for the St. Petersburg Jewish University, organized after 1917.

Furthermore, the OPE's educational program proved extremely useful during World War I, when the Russian army evacuated Jews—tens of thousands and more, often without warning and in a brutal fashion—from Poland and the Pale, causing refugees to stream into Russia. Exploiting its network of schools and teachers, the OPE was able quickly to organize schools for refugees. In 1916 the OPE brought instruction to over 18,000 students and in many cases also provided food and clothing. The majority of these classes were taught in Yiddish, the "native language of the children." One may recall that the inclusion of Yiddish as an official language of the OPE was one of the victories of 1905.[75]

Although the OPE never had a large membership (even with a reduced membership fee, the society was unable to attract the masses), it was of central importance in the history of Russian Jewry. Its significance lay not only in the individual projects it undertook but also in its vision of what Russian Jewry should become. OPE members, once clearly aligned with the liberal bourgeoisie, became transformed after 1905, when young women and men from the middle and lower-middle classes entered the organization fully cognizant of the need for individuals to serve at the local level. Although intuitively one would think that this cohort would be more radical than the liberals who came to the leadership at the end of the 1880s, in fact most of the activists shared the hope of facilitating the birth of an educated Jewry, fully equipped to compete professionally and still cognizant of affiliation with and obligations to the Jewish people. OPE members strove to enable Jews to receive an authentic, albeit modern, Jewish education and to accept voluntarily the burdens of membership in the Jewish community. They wanted the communities themselves to adopt the same political ideals of a true democracy and the protection of rights that they hoped would take hold in Russia as a whole. Far from the emancipation of Western Europe, which put its emphasis on individualism, OPE leaders were advocates of collective Jewish institutions.

The OPE, indeed, attracted some of the finest intellectuals in modern Russian Jewry. Individuals who played important roles during the 1905 Revolution, such as Maksim Vinaver, Henry Sliozberg, Iulii Gessen, Mark Ratner, Boris and Iulii Brutskus, Leon Bramson, and Simon Dubnov, were all leaders in the OPE. It is difficult to say whether they were active in the OPE because it was the only legal institution devoted to secular Jewish culture or whether such individuals, having created an atmosphere conducive to democracy and liberalism, sought to be involved in its activities. What is clear is that the determination to create a modern Jewish school system stimulated wide-ranging thought about the future of Russian Jewry that had an impact beyond the educational program. Through the goal of promoting enlightenment, leaders of the OPE, with the help of wealthy patrons, envisioned new relations between the center and the periphery and arrived at new understandings of Jewish national identity and internal self-governance. Of course, those institutions that were actually established were limited by the political and financial constraints characteristic of post-1905 Russia. The central projects nevertheless reflected what one could call a "liberal agenda." The leadership of the OPE placed an emphasis on democratically run institutions, an intensification of educational and professional opportunities for the Jewish masses, and the protection of civil and collective rights.

Chapter 7

The Generation of 1905 and the Politics of Despair: Alienation, Friendship, Community

Scott Ury

Introduction

> Yaakov Bogato went home on Monday and who knows if he'll return at all this summer . . . and I remain here solitary and alone. Oh, how great is my sorrow and how heavy is my heart these days! For even when one is sad, one's load can be lightened when one has someone to whom one can turn and tell one's sorrows and woes. But what could be worse than to suffer so much that your heart is shattered to pieces out of sheer loneliness!!!![1]

With this angst-ridden confession of adolescent confusion, the young David Yosef Green (later to become renowned under his Hebraicized name of David Ben-Gurion as one of the foremost representatives of the Jewish path toward self-empowerment and self-emancipation) relayed his experiences as a young Jewish immigrant in the great turn-of-the-century city of Warsaw. Arriving in Warsaw, home to some 250,000 legal Jewish residents out of a total population of almost three-quarters of a million, in the summer of 1904 to prepare for entry exams as an external student in a technical school, the seventeen-year-old newcomer from the nearby town of Płońsk struggled repeatedly to come to terms with the seemingly irreconcilable conflict between his haskalah-inspired, quintessentially modern dreams of secular education, self-improvement, and social advancement and his bewildering, at times excruciatingly painful, confrontations with daily life in a city of hundreds of thousands of strangers.[2]

While perhaps communicating a somewhat extreme version of his own subjective situation, Green was not expressing the unique experiences of just one young man who suddenly found himself far away from his father's house (*beit avi*) for the first time.[3] In fact, this ongoing conflict between prevailing maskilic-inspired hopes for a new era and the cruel vicissitudes that often accompanied everyday life in the city would haunt an entire generation of young Jewish men (and women) who made similar journeys from familiar environments to large cities and distant lands in search of new lives, new beginnings, and new worlds at the onset of a still fundamentally hopeful century.[4]

Furthermore, while many of these migrants were later able to find temporary solace in friendship circles and other informal support groups that arose in various centers across Eastern Europe, these networks of predominantly male friends ultimately failed to resolve the larger, underlying issues that plagued a generation of Jewish youth at the turn of the century: the pervasive, at times burning, sense of alienation, loneliness, and despair that seemed to grip so many young Jews in European cities, both large and small, from Lodz to Moscow and from Vienna to Vilna. For many of these young Jewish men, the collective series of personal and existential woes brought on by the twin processes of migration and urbanization demanded more radical, all-encompassing solutions. Ultimately, what haskalah-inspired ideology, informal circles of friends, and traditional association could not deliver, modern politics (Jewish and other) was often able to provide. Thus, many of these young men concluded their search for community and belonging in the modern world by joining the growing number of new political movements that began to appear throughout turn-of-the-century Eastern Europe.

This collective journey from urbanization to friendship and from friendship to modern (Jewish) political movements will serve as the framework for this chapter, as I trace the experiences of a generation of young Jewish men. I will argue that the massive influx of Jews into various cities within and outside the Russian Empire contributed directly to a sense of crisis among an entire generation of young Jews and that this sense of crisis served as the background for the participation of thousands of young Jews in the different modes of political organization and action that came to characterize the era. More specifically, I will use the personal experiences of different representatives of this generation to trace this transition from a generation of impoverished Jewish migrants who wandered from city to city in search of little more than a shared room and temporary means of subsistence to a determined group of Jewish revolutionaries destined to come of age through the series of events that would serve as the political baptism of an entire generation of Jews and non-Jews in Eastern Europe—the Revolution of 1905.

Alienation

The late nineteenth and early twentieth centuries witnessed the migration of Jews (and non-Jews) within the Russian Empire and beyond on an extraordinary scale. While most estimates put the number of Jewish immigrants to the New World between one crisis (1881) and another (1914) at approximately two million, we can do little more than guess at how many Jews made parallel moves from small cities and local towns to large urban arenas such as Odessa, Warsaw, and Lodz.[5] Despite this lack of reliable data regarding internal migration, it is clear that both the general and Jewish populations in many of these cities grew dramatically at this time and that a large part of this development was due to the influx of newcomers from other parts of the Russian Empire.[6] Odessa's Jewish population, for example, grew almost fourfold between these two crises, from around 55,000 in 1880 to about 200,000 on the eve of World War I.[7] During the same period, Warsaw's Jewish population grew from roughly 125,000 in 1881 to almost 340,000 in 1914. As a result of this movement to the city, approximately one-half of Warsaw's Jewish residents in 1905 had been born elsewhere.[8] Commenting on the nature of urban society at the time, Daniel Brower notes that cities throughout the Russian Empire were nothing less than "great revolving doors through which passed a significant proportion of the population of large regions of Russia."[9]

This migration of Jews and non-Jews into new industrial centers in turn-of-the-century Eastern Europe is, however, only one part of the story. The ongoing discourse of alienation, loneliness, and depression that pervades so many of the letters, diaries, and other sources from the period is a salient element.[10] Indeed, before it could become the generation that gave birth to such definitive, canonical moments and movements in Jewish history as the Generation of 1905 and the Second Aliyah, the turn-of-the-century generation of Jewish youth that flooded cities across East Central Europe was very much a lost generation.[11] This prevailing sense of helplessness, confusion, and despair was influenced by the wider European discourse regarding the course of modernity that enveloped intellectual circles in locations as varied as London and Odessa.[12] However, while alienation and a larger sense of hopelessness were certainly leitmotifs of turn-of-the-century European society, they were also integral parts of Jewish society and culture. As many of the sources cited herein will demonstrate, many young Jews discussed these very issues among themselves as though they were critical and intrinsic aspects of Jewish society. If anything, this internalization of the European discourse of alienation and despair as though it were part and parcel of a particularly Jewish society and a uniquely Jewish condition only underscores the dynamic of cultural exchange and hybridity that took place as turn-of-the-century European society exerted its influence on turn-of-the-century Jewish society, and vice versa.[13]

One particularly colorful source that helps illustrate this discourse of

alienation and loneliness is, as already noted, a series of published letters written by David Yosef Green during his fateful year in Warsaw from
the summer of 1904 until the summer of 1905.[14] Separated from his family and confused by various aspects of his new life in the city, Green
detailed his mood in personal letters to his childhood friend, role
model, and mentor Shmuel Fuchs—who had already left Plonsk for
London and would soon move on to New York. Writing of his arrival in
Warsaw in the summer of 1904, Green was particularly open about his
somewhat precarious state of mind and his inability to adapt to city life:
"After our train departed, we all went in our own directions, each of us
to his own home. . . . I went home. There I felt so alone as though I had
remained stranded on a deserted island. . . . In an effort to take my mind
off of the loneliness, I began to read and to work. . . . However, none of
this succeeded as my willpower proved unable to overcome my emotions."[15]

Nor was this a lone incident. Green's letters from the period repeatedly refer to debilitating bouts of depression that left him pained and
confused. The following excerpt is typical of the connection that Green
himself often made between his new life in the city and a certain inexpli-
cable, at times uncontrollable, urban malaise. "The next day," he wrote,
"I traveled to Płońsk and returned immediately to Warsaw, and again I
was up all night and couldn't write all day. Since then and until Sukkoth,
I was up almost every night till three and spent the days wandering
around like a ghost because I was depressed on account of many different things."[16]

Such themes of loneliness and depression in the city during this
period of transition appear again and again throughout Green's correspondence with his long-distance friend, Fuchs. Projecting from his own
circumstances, Green attributes Fuchs's apparent state of depression in
London to a set of factors that were strikingly similar to Green's own
situation in Warsaw, where he felt himself "a stranger, lonely and alone,
far away from all those who are close to you."[17]

If misery loves company, then Green and Fuchs were certainly not
alone. In fact, the experiences of the young David Yosef Green are representative of an entire generation of young Jews. The perceived
absence of any and all semblance of community in these new urban arenas constituted a central aspect of the reigning discourse regarding the
fate of the Jewish community in the era of mass society. In his memoirs,
the Zionist political activist Shmarya Levin (1867–1935) recalled his own
arrival in Vilna in terms strikingly similar to those used by the young
David Yosef Green: "I had no relatives in Vilna. I stayed in a hotel and
for two lonely days I tramped the streets, admiring the great houses and
the great shops and approaching no one. I learned for the first time

the curious feeling of loneliness that belongs to the big cities. It seemed incredible to me that among these thousands and thousands of people there should not be one who cared about my fate."[18]

Although Levin's memoirs may have been somewhat tinted by the bias of memory and the influence of broader post-maskilic and early Zionist narratives regarding the Jewish path toward independence and sovereignty, the personal correspondence from this period reflects a similar concern, if not a veritable obsession, with the repeated inability to establish an authentic bond between the newly reconstructed Jewish individual and the increasingly elusive concept of Jewish community. Letters penned by the Hebrew writer Yosef Haim Brenner, his close friend Uri Nissan Gnessin, and others at this time are filled with similar accounts of migration and poverty, loneliness, and depression. Although Brenner also experienced radical mood swings that adversely affected his ability to write,[19] this already influential figure often found himself consoling and mentoring others who were, apparently, more deeply affected than he was by the travails brought on by migration and the accompanying battles with loneliness and depression.[20] Seamlessly passing from his personal experience to that of a generation-wide sense of crisis and a specifically Jewish sense of impending disaster, Brenner implored Gnessin not to surrender to the forces of cultural despair that he himself had already clearly internalized by the year 1900. Here, in particular, Brenner's comments reflect the steady flow of ideas between the Jewish and non-Jewish spheres as a wider pan-European sense of despair was almost automatically translated, reinterpreted, and integrated as part of a particularly Jewish condition: "Can we really take our minds off of the present for one moment? Do you know the state of our youth? Do you realize that we are the last of the Mohicans? Do you know that our people are going to die? Do you know that the world is sick? Do you know that desperation kills souls? Do you have eyes?! Uri Nissan!!!"[21]

Gnessin himself was already deeply immersed in the same discourse of loneliness and despair. In an 1898 letter to Shimon Bichovski, Gnessin touches upon many of the central themes that occupied an entire generation: "Look inside, my brother, look and don't delay . . . What will you find there? . . . Emptiness! . . . Empty vessels! . . . Is there no room for love? Faith? Look, is there no hope either . . . ? Where? Look: Horrible despair! That is the only thing that remains; only it can fill the vast emptiness of the heart. Did you hear me? The vast emptiness of the heart will be filled with horrible despair and nothing more! . . . How terrible, how heavy, how painful is such a situation! . . . The heart is dry, and shriveled up . . . Shriveled up! . . ."[22]

Nor was this a mere passing expression of desperation. In a letter to Anokhi (Zalman Yitzhak Aronson) several years later, Gnessin speaks painfully of some of the more debilitating aspects of the pervasive sense of crisis that gripped him and so many others: "Aronson! My brother! You speak of insanity; and I, I fear—You should know that my headache gets worse from day to day, and at night, covered in sweat, my head burns and my body is on fire; I think a lot, and I also think about this." Gnessin continues the letter by turning directly to themes of solitude, loneliness, and the need for community. "And, Anokhi, it has been already close to three weeks since I have spoken to a soul, seen anyone, in the normal sense."[23] The new century that had seemingly offered the generation of young Jews on the move so much promise and hope was, at least at its onset, a bitter, painful period in which "the vast emptiness of the heart" was "filled with horrible despair and nothing more!"

Friendship

This sense of confusion and crisis was often assuaged by the support and comfort of close male friends. Alone and far away from their families, young Jewish men gravitated toward one another in search of friendship and community that could, theoretically, alleviate some of the more crippling effects of modernity. Ideally, these friends, friendship circles, and other less formal gatherings offered young Jews alternative frameworks that could somehow replace traditional family and communal structures in changing times. As George Mosse notes in connection with friendship circles in England and Germany: "The importance of such male friendships as a social and political force cannot be overrated. They provided a home and a shelter for modern man."[24]

One such expression of this search for friendship and belonging in the city is Haim Nahman Bialik's poem "On a Summer's Day." Written in 1896 and originally dedicated to Bialik's cousin and close friend Yisrael Bialik, the poem speaks passionately and painfully of the search for community and meaning in the urban arena. For the better part of this poem, friendship between men is the sole solution to the individual's bitter encounters with the cruel conditions of urban life. In the summer,

> When high noon on a summer's day
> makes the sky a fiery furnace
> and the heart seeks a quiet corner for dreams,
> then come to me, my weary friend.
>
> · · · · · · · · · · · · ·
>
> Later, in the winter:
> When the black cold of a winter's night
> bruises you with its icy pinch
> and frost sticks knives in your shivering flesh
> then come to me, blessed of God.[25]

Several years later in 1900, after the poem had been published under the title "Friendship and Solitude," life imitated art as Yosef Haim Brenner and Uri Nissan Gnessin spent an evening together in Gnessin's Warsaw apartment on 21 Dzielna Street, memorizing and reciting Bialik's poem about urban society, loneliness, and friendship between men.[26] A decade or so later, in a volume dedicated to Gnessin, who tragically died at the age of thirty-four, Brenner recalled this particular private performance of friendship as follows:[27]

> And one night, he [Gnessin] brought from the streets a new copy of *Luah ahiasaf* that came out that very day from the publisher; on a night that we actually had bread, and tea, and oil in the lamp, and a hot stove. The two of us sat over dinner and began. . . . And after an hour or so, at the end of the meal, we were already standing in front of one another and had memorized the poem. . . . "A shady carob grows in my garden," he said, word by word with an obvious, real sense of pleasure. "When the black cold of a winter's night," I roared back towards him. . . . "My dwelling is modest, lacking splendor," he shouted with joy in a playful manner.[28]

According to Brenner, the two friends continued until, at the end of their reenactment, tears welled in Gnessin's eyes and the two suddenly found themselves in a brotherly embrace with: "A fire in the grate, on the desk a candle."

Nor was this the only time that Brenner turned to Bialik's poem "On a Summer's Day" to express his own need for friendship and comfort. In a letter to Anokhi from the summer of 1903, while Brenner was serving in the Russian army, he again found in Bialik's poem from *Luah ahiasaf* inspiration, hope, and meaning. This particular letter leaves little doubt about the extent to which he, too, was dependent upon such friendships, particularly in trying times. Brenner's letter opens: "My brother, my beloved brother, my dear friend, my brother unto the grave! I wept tears of joy when I received your brief letter as I was very, very worried since your expulsion from Kiev." Returning to his more familiar position of the older, wiser friend and mentor, Brenner reassures Anokhi that even in the worst of times, hope, meaning, and redemption are just around the corner in the form of friendship between men.

Moreover, for Brenner, hope in 1903 is similar, if not identical, to the same type of hope described in Bialik's poem of 1896, subsequently reenacted by Brenner and Gnessin in Warsaw in 1900 and later recalled by Brenner (and vicariously relived by his readers) in 1913. For Brenner, Bialik, Gnessin, and Anokhi, male friends were, at times, the sole rays of light in exceptionally dark times: "Life is cursed, but death is also cursed. And who knows; perhaps we should not wait for the good life, but for a life of purpose, a life of love and friendship in one city and, perhaps, in one room—perhaps we should hope [for this]. Only two and a half years remain for me to lie alive in this grave [the army], and then—we will be together, we will live together, and, perhaps, travel together. Find comfort in your own greatness, in your deep and great understanding of the world and of life, and, when you desire, also in my great and deep love for you."[29]

While these and other expressions of friendship and intimacy in Brenner's fiction and life are well documented,[30] I want to use these particular examples to illustrate the extent to which many young Jewish migrants across Eastern Europe often sought and found solace in particularly intense friendships with other young men. Indeed, throughout the correspondence and other sources, one finds very few references to women either as comrades or potential partners. As Dan Miron observed in regard to this generation of Hebrew writers, they "resisted continuous, real relationships with women, postponed the creation of their own families and the like."[31] In this sense, this was not only a generation in which "loners come together," but also one in which lonely men came together.[32]

In this context, the letters of David Yosef Green are again relevant as they reveal a male-only world in which *landsleyt* and friends were dependent upon one another as they left old worlds and entered new ones. Green himself was dependent upon different male friends including his mentor and role model Shmuel Fuchs. With Fuchs on his way to London, the impressionable Green waited anxiously for news of his fate:

> Several days passed. My situation became even worse; and this was exacerbated by worries about you. No letter arrived. At night, I dreamt that you were caught and brought back to Płońsk in chains. And not only at night. Also during the day, horrible thoughts regarding you entered my head. Every day I did nothing but wait for your letter. And here, on Monday, the sixteenth of Sivan, in the early evening . . . two letters. . . . And so I opened your letter and there, instead of the detailed letter that I had hoped for, there was some sort of tiny note in indecipherable handwriting. I was very angry, but after reading it (which was rather difficult as the handwriting was so unclear) other feelings replaced my anger.[33]

Green's obsessive sense of dependence was not limited to his attachment to his "older brother" Fuchs,[34] and it was soon replaced by a somewhat similar dependence upon other *landsleyt*, including his close friend and occasional roommate Yaakov Bogato ("Yes, I will be lonely this summer, because, beyond a shadow of a doubt, Yaakov Bogato will not return before the winter, and afterwards, who knows. . . .").[35] Far away from his family and unsure of his place in rapidly changing times, the young David Yosef Green apparently had a pattern of becoming dependent upon male role models.

The personal, intimate language used in many of these letters further

reflects the passion that characterized and cemented many of these relationships.[36] Green, for example, repeatedly uses greetings such as "my
brother,"[37] "my dear brother,"[38] "my older brother,"[39] while he referred
to himself as "your poor suffering brother."[40] Brenner was particularly
effusive in his correspondence, as confidants were greeted as "my
beloved brother!"[41] or as "my brother, my beloved brother, my dear
friend, my brother unto death!"[42] Other missives were closed with
phrases such as "with much love,"[43] "dedicated to you in heart and
soul,"[44] and "goodbye and a kiss, a real kiss."[45] Gnessin reciprocated to
Brenner with the same level of intimacy, referring to himself as "Your
brother who loves you dearly" and "your brother forever." To Anokhi,
Gnessin was simply "Your brother, UriNissan, UriNissan, UriNissan."[46]
Whether or not this sense of intense closeness between Jewish men had
its origins in wider European concepts of friendship, it was clearly of
central importance to an entire generation of young Jewish men. As
David Biale commented with regard to earlier adherents of the haskalah: "The maskilim also replicated in the Jewish setting a general tendency in Europe since the Enlightenment to create a community of
male friendship (*Männerbund*)."[47] Male friendship mattered to these
young Jewish men because they needed some way of coping with the
avalanche of problems that they encountered in the urban environment, and joining close circles of male friends was one of the easiest,
most acceptable ways of creating a sense of support and belonging.

   Although the subject of male friendships and its relationship to homosexual bonds and identities in turn-of-the-century Jewish society deserves
a study of its own, I would like to make several preliminary comments.[48]
First of all, the near total absence of any mention of women as peers,
comrades, or partners in most of these sources underscores Miron's
point that this was a distinct subculture created by and for young men
on the move. On the economic and social planes, the forms of urban
leisure that would eventually create opportunities for heterosociability
had, apparently, not yet taken root in Jewish centers in Warsaw, Lwów,
Odessa, or even London. As Judith Walkowitz has shown in her pathbreaking study of women in Victorian London, the movement of women
into many parts of the public sphere as full, if not equal, members of
urban society was a slow, erratic, and, at times, dangerous transition, and
this apparently was also true for many Jewish women.[49] Thus, it could be
argued that there were relatively few public spaces and institutions in
which young Jewish men and women could meet, interact, and bond as
equals. As a result, many Jewish men—in particular, those who were too
old to be in educational institutions and not yet ready, for whatever reason, to marry—remained in the company of other men.

   On the educational and ideological plane, women were still not viewed by many as equal members in the nascent world of Hebrew belles-lettres and national regeneration.[50] Traditional educational systems in Jewish society continued to promote the education of young boys, and, as a result, many young women were denied access to those educational institutions and practices that would have enabled them to achieve reading and, no less important for a budding republic of letters, writing skills in Hebrew. Hence, from the very outset, far more men were able to acquire the basic literary tools that would enable them to enter these tight circles of post-maskilic Hebrew writers and cultural activists. Moreover, the propagation and cultivation of these male-dominated, if not male-only, circles of friends and comrades served an additional, equally critical purpose, the potential salvation of a Jewish masculinity that many felt was in a growing state of crisis.[51] Sedgwick notes that members of similar male-only circles often "perceived the exclusion of women from their intimate lives as virilizing."[52]

Finally, by excluding women these circles also helped create spaces that enabled and encouraged homosocial interaction, behavior and, in many cases, desire. On this note, Sedgwick's differentiation between homosocial behavior and male homosocial desire is particularly relevant.[53] Indeed, many of the citations discussed herein reveal an intimacy or passion "between men" that went far beyond networking, socializing, and other forms of male bonding and into what Sedgwick so brilliantly coined as "homosocial desire."

The question remains, however, whether or not Sedgwick's comments regarding "the potential unbrokenness of a continuum between homosocial and homosexual" also apply to this generation of young Jewish men. Despite the wealth of materials available, I was not able to find any which illustrated a link between intense bonds of male friendship and passionate expressions of love between men and open homosexual relationships or discernible homosexual identities.[54] While that does not mean that physical encounters, closeted liaisons, and secret relationships did not take place, it does make it difficult for me to claim that they did. What I can say, at this stage, is that turn-of-the-century Jewish society lacked the cultural institutions and social structures necessary for the construction and maintenance of a homosexual subculture (as opposed to a dominant heterosexual or heteronormative culture) that would have allowed for, enabled, or given social legitimacy to open homosexual relationships and discernible homosexual identities.[55] As a result, even if some of these young men had wanted to pursue open homosexual relationships and identities, they had relatively few options available to them other than "to settle down." And settle they did. David Yosef Green soon overcame his adolescent insecurities and immigrated to Palestine where, together with Paula Munweis, he worked to create a

Jewish state; Bialik, the great Hebrew poet, married Mania Averbuch when he was barely twenty and eventually found his way to the Hebrew city of Tel Aviv; and even the restless Brenner resettled in Ottoman Palestine and managed to have one child—whom he named (how not) Uri Nissan Brenner—before his own death in 1921.

That said, the impact of these friendships and networks did not end with this widespread turn to and apparent embrace of bourgeois concepts of family and society. In fact, in many cases these circles helped set the stage for what was soon to become the next phase in the larger process of confrontation with migration, modernity, and the city—the transition from male friendship circles and informal societies to modern Jewish politics in general and to Jewish nationalism in particular. As Mosse has noted with regard to male friendship and nationalism: "Nationalism in absorbing the ideal of friendship was able to strengthen itself, to collaborate still more effectively with bourgeois society in order to support ideas of respectability, to control a 'nervous' age, and to contain sexual passions. The nation must transcend sexuality even as friendship must be stripped of eroticism. The love between male friends should not be projected upon each other but upon the nation; in this way, homoerotic temptation would be overcome."[56]

To paraphrase Mosse, nations and nationalism offered these young Jewish men the opportunity to bond together as brothers (and comrades) "forever," "unto death," and "with much love" in a manner that would not disrupt the existing bonds of friendship and the (heternormative) nature of turn-of-the-century Jewish society.[57]

Politics

The transition from male friendship to modern Jewish politics represents the final phase in the search for community and belonging. It was the need for more sweeping solutions to a wider sense of crisis that eventually led many of these young men to turn to action and to the fate of the collective as a means of overcoming their combined individual and generational crisis.[58]

Before turning to modern political movements and ideologies, many of these young men first attempted to overcome this sense of hopelessness and helplessness by pursuing various individual projects of self-improvement. Often their choices derived from the same maskilic ideals of self-productivization and secular re-education that had originally led them to the city. Green, for example, first came to Warsaw in order to prepare for the entrance exams to various technical schools in that city and, once there, immediately applied himself to studying math, physics, and Russian. "Here in Warsaw another technical gymnasium will open this year. And maybe I will be accepted even this summer. And, if not, in May of 1905 I will be one of the students at the Wawelberg technical school. Of that I am sure."[59] Brenner, too, was equally concerned about his future professional prospects and what he felt was his substandard preparation for his entry into a new world. Thus, he complained bitterly to Anokhi of his own chances of being able to rescue himself from the dismal fate that he had inherited: "pity that I didn't study anything and that I don't know any languages or sciences."[60]

Speaking of similarly poor prospects with regard to his upcoming resettlement in Ottoman Palestine, Berl Katzenelson also placed his faith in secular education and professional retraining. "I would even be satisfied right now if I were to have at least a knowledge of bookkeeping and if I knew one European language."[61] For these and other young Jews, a fundamental lack of professional skills and education compounded the reigning sense of hopelessness.[62] Despite their faith in the potentially redemptive power of secular education and professional retraining, these young men discovered that their plans to construct their modern Jewish selves often failed to materialize.

Influenced by Brenner and others, Gnessin declared his own blueprint for salvation.[63] Here, in particular, the fate of the individual was bound to the concept of work and to the potentially redemptive act of dedicating oneself to an infinitely higher goal, the fate of the collective:

> Yes, work and suffering: work even though you suffer; work even though you sometimes doubt your actions; overcome all of the obstacles, internal and external, that you encounter along your way—Work! Because we need work! . . . We must consecrate ourselves, purify ourselves. . . . Because all of these doubts and questions are nothing more than the result of our own profanity. Once our souls are purified, these [matters] will also disappear. . . . For the time being, dedicate your energies to the needs of the local community so that you can later be of use to the entire people of Israel. . . . Work, Work, Work![64]

Gnessin's comments, which were a clear reflection of Brenner's own thoughts on this and related issues, were not an isolated instance. Writing to the respected Zionist figure Menahem Ussishkin on behalf of "a group of young (single) students," David Yosef Green similarly details how his own search for individual salvation was transformed into a need to work towards collective redemption: "We are prepared to dedicate all of our fresh forces, our skills, and our human desires to the service of the goal that we have set ourselves. We are prepared to work and to suffer, to toil, and to abide silently with patience and without delay in order to attain the ideal that is the law of our life, there in the land, only there can we find the total solution to all of our bitter questions."[65]

Green's declaration to Ussishkin was not a momentary expression of youthful exuberance. Several months later, in May 1905, while reiterating that his "entire existence is pointless, superfluous, desolate and sorrowful," he again turned to the redemptive value of work and to the need to dedicate one's own life to the collective. Once lost and confused, Green was now on fire with the commitment and faith of the newly converted:

> With regard to the question of "why" and "what for," there is only one solution, unique and special . . . and that is to work. Indeed, I am thirsty for work, work in which I can invest my entire soul, work that will extinguish all of my senses, all of my thoughts, that will alleviate all of my wild emotions, make me forget all of my cursed, troubling questions—but, where can I find such work, where? I ask! . . . I can tell you with an honest heart that all of my soul's desires, life's worth, life's breath is—Zionism—in other words the rebirth of our people on its land. . . . My brother! I don't ask for a single thing from life, I yearn for neither pleasure nor education, neither respect nor love; I'd give up everything, everything, only one thing I ask for—hope!!![66]

Such sentiments were clearly taking hold among significant sections of the youth, hitherto so marginalized. The potentially redemptive aspects of work were repeatedly linked to the fate of the collective and to the individual's willingness to subordinate his own individual needs to those of the collective body.[67] And thus a generation of runaway Jewish rebels was able to find salvation by dedicating itself to the newly reconstructed concepts of the Jewish nation and community.

Epilogue

For a generation of young Jews that suddenly found itself in radically new environments, cities across turn-of-the-century Eastern Europe were foreboding, frustrating, and befuddling arenas. The personal and collective problems created by modern society demanded modern solutions. Although this crisis was not political, the solution that many young Jews embraced was certainly a political one.

Ultimately, the modern political institutions, parties, and ideologies that developed in and around the Revolution of 1905 offered many of these young Jewish men much of what they had lost by tearing themselves away from familiar environments and traditional surroundings. They gave them coherent communities of activists and supporters, modern ideologies that lent order to an increasingly chaotic world, and collective bodies that confirmed and validated their sense of place and purpose. And thus the lost generation of turn-of-the-century Eastern Europe was able to find, transform, and reinvent itself into the much-celebrated Generation of 1905: a dedicated, committed body of political activists and leaders determined to revolutionize, heal, and redeem the sick Jewish world.

In his definitive studies *Prophecy and Politics* and *The Damascus Affair* and in other influential pieces, Jonathan Frankel has repeatedly pointed to the critical role that larger political crises play as both catalysts and turning points in the course of modern Jewish history.[68] While these particular crises are, more often than not, watershed political events that force entire generations of Jews to reconsider their social status, political strategies, and future options, the end result, one of radical political and communal reconceptualization and reorganization, is, almost always, a fundamentally positive one. Hence, scurrilous blood libels ultimately lead to international Jewish solidarity and organization, and violent pogroms bring about the birth of Zionism.

While I have certainly applied the Frankel model of crisis and change in Jewish history to a generation of Jews and their particular crisis, I am somewhat less optimistic about the inherently positive aspects of the path of modernity in general and its influence on Jews in Eastern Europe in particular. In fact, throughout this essay, I have argued that the birth of modern Jewish politics should be seen not only as a direct by-product of the very crisis brought on by the impact of two quintessentially modern experiences—mass migration and rapid urbanization—but also as a direct response to, if not against, two key aspects of modernity: the individual and the city. Time and again, the repeated inability to resolve fully the constant struggle between the individual search for self-actualization and self-fulfillment, on the one hand, and the need for belonging, community, and purpose, on the other, led David Yosef Green, Yosef Haim Brenner, Uri Nissan Gnessin, and many others to modern Jewish politics.

In this sense, such transitions to modern Jewish politics were not radically divergent from the tumultuous path of many other young Europeans at this time, the fin de siècle. Thus, what Arendt, Mosse, and others identified and defined as "selflessness," "self-abandonment," and transcendence also applies to those young Jews who embraced various political movements as a means of escaping their own existential dilemmas, protracted generational crises, and collective sense of impending disaster.[69] Like many of their non-Jewish contemporaries, they, too, suddenly found themselves in radically new worlds for which traditional societies and ostensibly modern educations were unable to prepare them, and they, too, rebelled against both these new worlds and the existing solutions available to them.[70]

Finally, while this process often helped alleviate the prevailing sense of helplessness and despair that plagued many, it also demanded the surrender of many of the same maskilic ideals that originally brought these young Jewish men to the city. There in the urban arena, where maskilic (or, at the very least, maskilic-inspired) visions crashed violently and painfully on the cruel pavement of East European cities, the path of Jewish modernity passed through an equally violent and, perhaps, equally irreversible transition from haskalah-inspired, individually centered searches for meaning and self-fulfillment to collective fantasies of community, purpose, and nation.[71] Ultimately, the reformulation of prevailing concepts of community would demand parallel reconceptualizations of the delicate relationship between the individual and the collective. Or, as the late master and victim of the horrendous twentieth century Czesław Miłosz reminds us so brilliantly: "To belong to the masses is the great longing of the 'alienated' intellectual."[72]

Chapter 8

The Jewish Socialist Parties in Russia in the Period of Reaction

Vladimir Levin

It became dark and misty in tsarist Russia in the second half of 1907. It was like being on a boat, cutting through a thick fog on a murky night. And you stand and look, to see whether you will recognize a sign, a ray of light. But all efforts are in vain. The darkness oppresses you and fills you with a heavy sadness, and it seems that the boat itself is borne by a gloomy force. Thus the darkness descended over all of Russia and aroused a horror that gripped the heart.[1]

This is one of many passages that describe the period after the 1905 Russian Revolution in ominous terms, endlessly repeating the words "darkness" and "gloom."

After the coup d'état of June 3, 1907, everyone understood that the revolution was over and that the hopes for the downfall of the tsarist regime and for the establishment of a new and better order had disappeared. However, a new, unprecedented period in Russian history began that year. On the one hand, antigovernmental activities were almost totally suppressed. On the other hand, there were greater opportunities to establish voluntary nonpolitical associations and censorship became less restrictive. As a result, public social activities developed and open discussions appeared in the newspapers. The elected parliament—the State Duma—became the center of public political life and the main political forum of Russia.

In this new atmosphere, the role of revolutionary parties, including Jewish socialist parties that had been so prominent in the prerevolutionary years and especially during 1905–7, became marginal. According to Jonathan Frankel, at the end of the revolution, "the Jewish Left crashed down" and was reduced "to the barest shadow of its former self."[2]

The breakdown of all four Jewish socialist parties—the Bund, the Zionists-Socialists (the Zionist Socialist Labor Party or SSRP according to the Russian initials), the Seimists (SERP), and the Poale Zion—began already following the elections to the Second Duma in February 1907. Despite the very stormy campaign and a bitter struggle among the Jewish parties, the results were deeply disappointing. Only three Jewish deputies, all liberals, were elected to the Duma, whereas no candidates supported by the Jewish socialists won.[3] The Jewish revolutionaries, who had thought in 1905 that they ruled the Jewish street and that they had powerful allies among non-Jewish comrades, were disappointed. From that point on, they began looking for new ways of winning influence among the Jewish masses.[4] However, the sudden coup d'état on June 3, 1907, presented them with another challenge—not that of gaining new followers but of retaining the old ones. This chapter will examine the measures that the Jewish socialist parties undertook in order to maintain their influence and standing in Jewish society, the implementation of these measures, and their results.

The Decline

The main symptom of the decline in the standing of the socialist parties was the crisis in the local party organizations. The attraction of being directly involved in the struggle against the old regime significantly diminished after two years of revolution. The resurgence of governmental power, the successful and brutal suppression of all kinds of mass unrest, and the general exhaustion of the population, combined with the loss of hope and interest, rendered socialist activities almost impossible. The parties' local organizations, which basically consisted of groups of like-minded young people united by "revolutionary" idealism and romanticism, devotion to a certain ideology, and the desire to participate in practical revolutionary activities, lost their main raison d'être. As a prominent Seimist, Yisroel Efroikin, wrote, "The period when a worker would not answer the question, 'what time is it?' without first asking the party committee is now over."[5]

It is very hard to calculate the number of members in an underground party. Among Jewish socialists parties, the available information relates only to the Bund and it shows a decline of about 20 percent in membership at the end of the revolutionary period: in August 1906, 33,890 members in 254 local organizations participated in the elections to the Sixth Congress of the Bund, whereas in April 1907, only 25,468 Bundists sent representatives to the London Congress of the Russian Social Democratic Labor Party (RSDRP).[6] After June 3, 1907, the decline in all the parties was even more drastic, but the exact numbers are unavailable. However, the circulation of party publications served as an indication of the rapid fall in membership. For instance, in the beginning of 1907, 5,000 copies of the Seimist weekly *Folks-shtime* were printed, in June 3,000 copies, and in August only 1,500 copies. The sharp decrease forced the party to cancel the publication.[7] The Zionist-Socialists experienced similar problems, and in October 1907 Nahman Syrkin's wife wrote to him that the party organ ought to be closed because its circulation was very small.[8] The Bund continued publishing a daily newspaper as long as the authorities permitted it, but its circulation also shrank from 20,000 copies in early 1907 to 16,000 in the spring and to 9,000 copies in the autumn of the same year.[9] The lack of interest in the socialist periodicals combined with the police repressions brought about the closing of all Jewish socialist periodicals before the end of 1907.

Party leaders blamed the members themselves for the declining membership and emphasized the workers' utilitarian attitude to party organizations. A leading ideologist of the Bund, Vladimir Medem, wrote: "[Workers] have not developed fully the feeling that the organization is not a place where 'they' are obliged to give something to 'me,' but a place where 'we' gathered for struggle. [. . .] There is no feeling that if I am dissatisfied with the organization, it means that, first of all, I am not satisfied with myself, because it is 'my' organization and not the organization of somebody else, of 'them.'"[10] The leader of the Poale Zion, Ber Borochov, expressed similar thoughts: "No party has fostered the ability of the masses to organize themselves. To organize from the outside is, in reality, to disorganize."[11]

Thus, in 1907, many of the members of the Jewish socialist parties had already lost interest and begun to leave, and by the end of that year, the majority of local party organizations ceased to exist. However, it was mainly the rank and file that disassociated themselves from the parties in the second half of 1907. The leadership, on the contrary, stayed in place and was ready to continue its work and to guide the parties in the new political situation. Only a minority of the leaders, most of them theorists, left Russia in 1907;[12] the majority looked for ways to adjust to the new reality. Thus, at the end of December 1907, the Poale Zion convened a party council in Belostok[13] and the Zionist-Socialists held their Third Conference in Vilna;[14] in March 1908 a conference of Seimists met in Vitebsk,[15] and a broadened consultation of the central committee of the Bund took place in Grodno.[16] Notwithstanding these forums, the members continued to drop out. A prominent Bundist, A. Litvak, wrote subsequently: "During the summer of 1907, in all of our organizations, people used to speak about the crisis, argue, and look for reasons. In 1908 there was almost no one left to speak about the crisis."[17] The rare available statistics confirm this impression: during the inspection trip of the Bund's central committee members in the winter of 1907–8, only twelve organizations were found in seventeen localities;[18] and in October 1910, only 404 members in ten organizations participated in the elections to the Eighth Conference of the Bund.[19] Not only organizational connections but also personal contacts among the former revolutionaries suffered as a result of these developments, as could be seen from the following example: a prominent Poale Zion leader, Zerubavel, was arrested in April 1908 in Vilna. Soon after that, the remnants of the Poale Zion fighting unit tried unsuccessfully to organize his escape from prison. A year later, however, the Poale Zion had nobody in Vilna who could lobby on his behalf; thus Yitzhak Ben-Tzvi from Palestine had to ask the General Zionists to do so.[20]

Indeed, the year 1908 was a catastrophic one for the socialist parties. By then, the majority of the socialist leadership had joined the rank and file in leaving the movement and looking for other occupations in Russia or abroad. At the same time, many leaders were arrested. The only existing study of the Bund's leadership in the period of reaction, that written by Henry Tobias and Charles Woodhouse, states that the leaders with a better education and with higher positions in the party were more eager to find a new occupation than those local leaders with a poorer education, who preferred to remain involved in underground activities.[21] I would argue, however, that, on the contrary, many of the party leaders who did not emigrate moved on to other public activities—they worked as journalists for Jewish and Russian newspapers or filled various positions in Jewish societies, schools, and other such institutions. In this way they continued to participate in Jewish public life and could influence it to some extent. Even many of those who earned a living in the private sphere often retained an involvement in public affairs: "In Kiev I met also with Novakovskii [a leading theorist of the Seimists]. He was then the manager of an office in a sugar factory. In the evenings he wrote about social [*gezelshaftlikhe*] questions."[22] The members of the central committee of the Bund, who in 1908 found "legal" occupations, did not abandon their party work, but, understandably, it became less intensive.[23] Many émigrés, especially top-ranking leaders, also continued to write and to publish their articles in both general and party periodicals issued in Russia. The extensive development of the public sphere, and especially of Yiddish journalism, enabled the socialist leaders to express their opinions publicly and even to earn their livelihood in that way.

In other words, the Jewish socialist parties (like their non-Jewish counterparts) did not disappear completely from the political and public arena. Their organizational structures that had carried out the practical work and had been so prominent before 1907 collapsed, but their voices were heard, and their ideologies and ideas retained some influence. The years just before World War I saw a certain revival of the local organizations of the party and press, although its scale could not be compared with that of the period before or during the first Russian revolution (for example, the Bund claimed twenty-three organizations in 1912 and forty in 1914; its legal weekly *Di tsayt* was printed in 9,000 copies in late 1913[24]). But it was only with the fall of the tsarist regime in February 1917 that all four Jewish socialist parties could resume an important role in Jewish politics.

With the onset of the crisis, beginning in late 1906, all Jewish socialist parties sought ways to preserve their organizations and deter members from dropping out. They therefore felt obliged to seek some alternative areas of activity other than the strictly political. The first two such fields to which all the parties turned were trade unions, on the one hand, and cultural and educational associations on the other, spheres with which the socialists had previous familiarity. The third such arena, the Jewish communities, began to attract their attention only in 1907 and was completely new to them. During the years of reaction, party leaders intensified their activities in several additional spheres, for example, the struggle for the rights of Yiddish (the so-called language war) or the attempts to defend Jewish interests through the State Duma and the bills discussed there. However, activities of this latter kind were not directly related to strengthening or preserving the parties' organizations and membership; therefore, they fall outside the scope of this essay.

Trade unions, cultural societies, and Jewish communities were included within the framework of "legal opportunities," meaning associations and institutions approved by the authorities. By 1907 it was understood that there could be no return to the focus on underground activity that had existed before the revolution. Through participation in the legal institutions, the Jewish socialists hoped to preserve their contacts with the workers because the conspiratorial revolutionary organizations had lost their attraction. It was for this reason that no conflict existed in the Jewish parties between the legalists and antilegalists—*likvidatory* and *otzovisty* in Lenin's terminology—as there was among the Russian Social Democrats. The only exception concerned the Bund, which was part of the Russian Social Democratic Labor Party but, in reality, both the Bund's legalists and antilegalists adhered to centrist positions and easily came to practical agreements. Notwithstanding the theoretical differences about the developments in Russia—a peaceful, gradual transition to democratic society or a new revolution—the Jewish socialists saw, or believed that they saw, immediate needs and problems through which they could retain their influence.

Trade Unions

Jewish revolutionary parties first turned toward the trade union movement. Although the socialist movement had long been engaged in the struggle for improving the workers' economic situation, before the revolution it could not operate openly. During 1905 and 1906, semilegal and legal trade unions were established, but it was much easier to resolve problems between employers and employees through powerful party committees and their *boevye otriady* (armed units of party members that served simultaneously as self-defense units against the pogroms and as a fighting force in the struggle against the authorities). In 1907, and especially after the coup d'état, the picture changed and all parties intensified their union work, hoping to attract workers who no longer wanted to be involved in political activities. In the summer of 1907, the parties set up special commissions under their central committees to deal with the trade union movement;[25] began publishing special periodicals in Yiddish devoted to trade union theory and practice;[26] and established central trade union bureaus in several cities.[27] The congress of Poale Zion in Cracow even decided that all party members were obliged to participate in a trade union. This decision derived from the assessment of current conditions: "Now in Russia, economic struggle, if properly directed, can serve as a starting point for a new and broad popular uprising."[28] The Poale Zion was the most radical Jewish party, but its counterparts also believed that trade unions could, to a certain degree, replace the collapsing party organizations.

Although the Bund advocated party-affiliated unions, and the three other parties supported the idea of nonparty unions, there was almost no difference between the two types of organizations. The majority of Jewish trade unions could not exist on their own and were dependent on a single party. While criticizing the Bund for its position, the Zionist-Socialists, the Seimists, and the Poale Zion were no less proud of their exclusive control of the unions. Such close connections to the parties proved to be harmful, and most of the unions collapsed in late 1907 following the collapse of the party machinery or were closed by the authorities.

The few unions that stayed afloat after 1907 were almost entirely ineffective and often closed on their own without the intervention of the authorities. The Bund's press complained that "after the closing of unions, their leaders do nothing in order to preserve the connections with the workers in their profession; as a result [. . .] the relations among the workers do not meet the demands of workers' solidarity."[29] In December 1908, the editors of the *Shtime fun Bund*—the new illegal Bund periodical—opened their survey of the trade unions with these words: "The trade union movement [. . .] struggles with the persecution of the reaction on the one hand and with the depressed mood of the masses on the other; [it] struggles and suffers losses. Only ruins remain from the [once] mighty movement."[30]

A typical example of the existence of a legal trade union is given in the memoirs of Leib Blekhman—the famous Abram der Tate, the organizer of the Garber-Bund, the Union of Jewish Tanners established illegally under the Bund's auspices in 1898 and revived in February 1907. When the conference of the Garber-Bund in December 1908 decided to halt its activities until better times,[31] Blekhman became a secretary of the legal trade union of shop assistants in Berdichev, which was connected to the Bund and whose membership had dropped from five hundred in 1907 to ninety people by the end of 1908.[32] At that time many shop assistants violated the existing work agreements, acceding under pressure from the employers to a longer working day. Other union members demanded that the union undertake measures against this subversion. The union board faced a dilemma. The right response in such circumstances should have been the declaration of a strike. But nobody was sure that the workers would follow the union's declaration, in which case it would go down to total defeat. Moreover, if the strike indeed were to begin, nobody doubted that the authorities would immediately close the union. Instead of calling a strike, the board organized cheap medical help for the members, in order to "show the members that the union can still do something." However, the initial revival of interest in the union rapidly declined, the money ran out, and these circumstances forced Blekhman to leave his position and emigrate from Russia to the United States,[33] while the union collapsed.[34]

The reasons for the trade unions' impotence were very obvious. Despite the socialists' belief in the intrinsic value of every proletarian organization, the workers expected an immediate benefit from their unions. By late 1907, however, this was very hard to achieve because, after two years of revolution, contractual agreements were relatively satisfactory in the main areas where the Jewish socialist movement operated. The employers could not withstand the workers' pressure, which was frequently supported by the party's fighting units. On the other hand, the economic crisis, growing unemployment, and the strengthening of the authorities made further such successes almost impossible. In the years after the revolution, the majority of strikes failed, and working conditions deteriorated in all branches of "Jewish" industry. As the Bund's report to the Second International states, by late 1910 "almost all of the workers' economic achievements from the revolution had already been lost. The proletariat suffered as a result of the unbearable working conditions and its trade union organizations generally disappeared."[35] Only occasional workers' strikes in the northwest region proved to be successful, and that was the case because the Bund leaders were able to raise money in St. Petersburg and abroad for the striking workers.

In the following years all the socialist parties continued to speak about the trade union movement and to argue about its affiliation with political parties, but until the revival of the workers' unrest in 1912–14, there were no significant developments in this field. The hopes of retaining the parties' influence among the workers through the trade unions proved illusory.

Cultural Work

Lacking an opportunity for successful activities in the economic area, the parties hoped that cultural and educational activities would provide a worthy substitute. Education and culture was indeed the second arena in which the parties intensified their work in 1907.

According to the socialist outlook, an education should instill class consciousness in the workers, enabling them to struggle for their rights as trade union or proletarian party members. Educational activities occupied the most important place in the work of the first Jewish socialist organizations in the late 1880s and early 1890s, but they were pushed aside by growing political activity.[36] In 1907 the Jewish socialists again turned to educating their workers. They proclaimed that the desire for knowledge among the workers was great, and they hoped that the educational and cultural enterprises within the trade unions would serve to shore up the waning popularity of their parties. However, the unions, for the most part, proved to be too weak to fulfill that role, and even the existing joint bureaus of all the unions in a city in the second half of 1907 were unable to bear the burden successfully.

The party leaders therefore began to establish societies and associations specifically to deal with education and culture. The idea of thus withdrawing to the sphere of voluntary associations characterized not only the Jewish socialist parties but also the Russian opposition as a whole. Even the central committee of the Constitutional Democratic party discussed transferring the center of its activity from the political arena to "cultural societies, public unions and associations."[37] The idea was borrowed from the experience of the German Social Democratic party, which, although prohibited by Bismarck from 1878 to 1890, succeeded in retaining its influence through a variety of voluntary associations. The Bundist activists hoped that in Russia, too, such associations would be able to serve as an organizational basis for the party and hence wanted them to be party affiliated.[38] The Bundists as well as the Zionist-Socialists also demanded that power inside the educational societies be given to the workers and not to the intelligentsia.[39] The Bundist Society for the Education of Illiterate Adults in Warsaw was even organized according to such a formula: the so-called active members paid a ruble a year and could vote in the general assembly whereas the "passive" members had to pay four rubles and had no voting rights.[40]

As our sources show, the Bund was the most active in establishing the cultural societies; the three other Jewish socialist parties were significantly weaker in this field.[41] The Bund's cultural activities were particularly influenced by the example of Polish democratic and progressive circles, which by 1905–6 had already organized broad cultural and educational enterprises. The Bund's most successful associations that interacted with hundreds and even thousands of Jewish workers existed in Warsaw, Lodz, and Vilna, where Polish cultural activities were especially developed; in many cases the Bund's cultural enterprises started as Yiddish sections of the Polish associations. In the summer of 1907, when the Bund's newspapers started to agitate for a shift of emphasis to work in the field of culture and education, they pointed directly to the Polish examples.[42]

In Lodz, two cultural institutions were guided and influenced by the Bund. The first was the Yiddish section of the Polish Towarzystwo Krzewienia Oświaty (TKO, Association for the Dissemination of Enlightenment), which organized lectures and maintained a library. The second institution was the Society for Music, Singing and Drama—Harp. Established in the spring of 1908, it concentrated on public lectures, amateur theater, and a choir. The TKO was a joint enterprise of Polish democrats and Jewish "assimilationists," while the Bund's influence was restricted only to its Yiddish section; the Harp was established by the Bund but also included many workers affiliated with the SSRP. An SSRP activist from Lodz wrote later:

The main activity of the Jewish workers' parties [. . .] in Lodz was centered around the Singing and Culture Society—Harp. The leaders there were the Bundists. The nonsocialist, Yiddish-democratic elements were concentrated around the second society, Dramatic Art [. . .]. Both societies contributed to the development of the Yiddish language, literature, and culture. In fact, their connection with the revolution and socialism was slight. However, the Harp building did serve as a broad, legal, inter-party *birzhe* [meeting place].[43]

The Harp's activity reached its peak in 1908; later it declined significantly and in 1910 the society was closed by the authorities. The activities of the TKO shrank to the support of two Yiddish libraries, and in 1911 the Bundists were forced to leave the TKO because of a conflict with the nonsocialists and anti-Yiddishists.[44]

In Warsaw the Bund sponsored the Yiddish department of the Polish University for All. Established in February 1907, it operated autonomously, free from the direct control of the university board, offering courses and lectures in Yiddish. At the same time, a school for adults was established (after splitting from a Polish society headed by Jewish "assimilationists"), providing an elementary education, also, of course, in Yiddish. Both institutions attracted hundreds of Jewish workers but were closed by the authorities in 1908.[45] Their place as a cultural, but not an educational, establishment was taken by the Warsaw branch of the Jewish Literary Society. The latter was founded in December 1908 in St. Petersburg by "bourgeois" Jewish activists and closed by the authorities in 1911.[46]

The Bundists' cultural work in Riga met a similar fate—the Yiddish section of the general association Vestnik Znaniia (Herald of Knowledge) worked actively for several months in 1909 until the association was shut down by the authorities. A new Jewish society, Carmel, was established in 1910, but the Bundists could not control it, as can be seen from the society's name (which had Zionist connotations) and from its activities.[47] According to the memoir of a Seimist, "around Carmel there grouped Seimists, Bundists and [other] radicals who fought for [the rights of] Yiddish."[48]

The Bund's operations in Vilna were similar to those in Warsaw: the elementary school for adults provided basic literacy, while the Society for Music, Singing and Drama organized public lectures and concerts. The content of their activity was purely Bundist, and one Zionist even complained in January 1908: "Many people abstained from attending the musical-vocal evenings because the stormy political atmosphere [in these meetings] permitted neither the soul nor the head to enjoy the sounds and the poetry."[49] Both Bundist institutions in Vilna continued to exist for many years and succeeded in retaining a "Bundist" atmosphere.[50] This was the exception rather than the rule.

After the first year of cultural activities in the legal organizations, the editors of *Shtime fun Bund* wrote: "Unfortunately, the fate [of the cultural associations] has proved to be no better than that of the trade unions: the broad working masses ultimately lose interest in them. In Belostok all the democratic elements [i.e., socialists] left the 'Jewish Art' circle and it turned into an 'amateur troupe'; the 'Harp' in Lodz also has trouble functioning; in other cities the cultural associations do not show any signs of life and suffer severe harassments [from the authorities] (regarding the choice of topics, lectors, and a ban on speaking Yiddish)."[51]

A. Litvak, who actively lectured in many Bundist cultural societies, wrote later: "At one time it even seemed that the socialist movement could hide itself there during the bad times. But the hopes that were placed on the cultural societies were realized only on a small scale." He attributed this to the persecution by the authorities and the scarcity of intelligentsia in the movement: "Sometimes the activities of the cultural societies were so worthless [*nishtik*] that the better workers treated them with contempt. In Dvinsk the workers called their literary and art society '*kunts-kaykl-dreydl*' [an untranslatable play on words mocking the society]."[52] In addition, Rafael Abramovich complained, "In fact, many legal associations consisted of the same people over and over again, and the members also included non-Bundists."[53]

In other words, the cultural and educational institutions did not succeed in replacing the political organizations and serving as a basis for party activities during the period of reaction. At the beginning they did function as meeting places for the former and still active party members, but very quickly their "cultural" role as amateur theaters, orchestras, choirs, or literary discussion groups became dominant and their political-organizational tasks were pushed to the background or completely disappeared.

The police repressions played a significant part in this process. In many cases, even the socialist directors of such legal institutions faced a choice: a strictly socialistic content and closure by the authorities or less socialism and more education and culture. Ultimately, the need for education pushed aside the socialism. The cultural associations offered some party activists legal jobs and a place to give public lectures; sometimes, as noted below, they even provided the socialists with a basis for participation in the reorganization of the Jewish community.

The weakest point in the parties' effort to control the cultural and educational associations was their inability to provide them with sufficient operating funds. The fact that the fees of the "proletarians" could not cover the expenses, even when they were willing to pay, rendered the participation of the "bourgeois" public essential. Moreover, the party organizers could not prevent their ideological rivals from joining the institutions even if they succeeded in promoting a narrow ideological line that differed from broadly defined Yiddishism. In most of the cases described above, the socialists worked within frameworks established and supported by "nonsocialist" segments of Jewish or even non-Jewish society. The socialists took advantage of the existing structures, dominating certain branches of the Jewish Literary Society[54] or of the OPE (Society for the Promotion of Enlightenment), but only in rare cases were they able to run these organizations alone. The massive participation of the nonparty intelligentsia and huge differences in the educational level between that social stratum and the simple workers transformed the cultural associations into intelligentsia clubs whose role in the development of Jewish culture, especially of Yiddish literature and theater, was very important whereas their significance as *Kulturträger* had little impact on the Jewish population as a whole. Their importance for the socialist parties per se likewise proved to be minimal.

The Jewish Communities

The completely new field to which the Jewish socialist parties turned in 1907 was that of the Jewish community. In the prerevolutionary years as well as during the revolution, the socialists paid no attention to the existing communal institutions. The hopes for a bright socialist future, on the one hand, and the need to organize the "proletariat" so that it would not be subject to the influences of the existing bourgeois order and of traditional Jewish society, on the other hand, led the socialists to ignore communal structures or, at most, to criticize them severely. Anticipating the socialist parties' turn to communal affairs was their proven desire during the revolution to influence not only the "proletariat" but also the poor Jewish masses—the "bourgeois democracy" in the Marxist vocabulary of the time. It seemed to them in 1905 that they were, indeed, heading the revolution and that broad strata of the Jewish population were following them. However, the failure of the socialist call for a boycott of the elections to the First Duma in February–March 1906 demonstrated how limited their influence actually was.

A year later, the electoral campaign for the Second Duma, in which the socialists participated in opposition to the Jewish "bourgeoisie," reaffirmed their weakness.[55] It proved that in the minds of most Jews, at least those of adult age, the traditional communal leadership still had authority. When the choice had to be made, the majority of Jewish voters preferred to cast their ballot not for the socialists with their revolutionary slogans but for the old, familiar leaders who had the support of the traditional elite of the local communities. Vladimir Medem even complained: "The Jewish masses, which consist mainly of [. . .] the bourgeois democracy, gave their votes willingly to the lists of the Jewish Electoral Committees. [. . .] The Jewish bourgeois democracy has demonstrated political confidence in people whose political outlook it knows nothing about, or even in people who, as it knows, have no political outlook at all."[56]

Reflecting on the experience of the elections to the Second Duma, Medem called upon the Bundists to become involved in the existing communal institutions in order to win the confidence of the "bourgeois democracy": "Only by implementing the proposed tactics [. . .] can the Jewish proletariat come to occupy the place in Jewish society that it rightfully is entitled to [. . .]—the leader of bourgeois democracy in the bourgeois revolution of the twentieth century."[57] At the same time, the conference of the Seimist party discussed the proposal of its central committee to begin work in the Jewish communities in order to "organize the broad Jewish working masses."[58]

The Seimists easily accepted this proposal as their program demanded autonomy for Jews based on the national Seim (parliament) and on the local community whereas Medem's appeal initially did not find many followers in the Bund. Only in the summer and autumn of 1907 did all parties seriously start to speak about taking part in the existing communal institutions and working there for the benefit of the masses. Thus, in late 1907 the Bundists took part in resolving the problem of high kosher meat prices and the question whether or not to invite a new rabbi, and the Seimists participated in community discussions about the return of Jewish representatives to the municipalities.[59]

In the early twentieth century the status of the Jewish community did not satisfy even its own leaders, not to speak of democrats and, especially, socialists. First of all, Russian laws (and their implementation in practice) were extremely inconsistent concerning the Jewish community. On the one hand, ever since 1844 the community as an institution uniting all Jews in a given locality was not recognized officially, but, on the other hand, the Jews of every town and shtetl had certain rights concerning the levying of state taxes on Jews (the tax on kosher meat and that on candles). In order to deal with these matters, the law recognized that the "well-to-do and settled" Jews would serve as representatives of the "Jewish *obshchestva*" (an amorphous term meaning all the Jews of a given locality). Thus, the community did not exist officially, but in practice the Jews were legally united on a local basis, even having their own representative institution, however ill-defined.

Second, the kosher meat tax was the main source of funding to maintain Jewish communal institutions (the Talmud Torah schools, Jewish hospitals, synagogues, philanthropic associations), but, in the opinion of the majority of contemporary observers, it placed a particularly heavy burden on the poor strata of Jews by making kosher meat very expensive. Third, the community, in fact, consisted of numerous unconnected institutions—synagogues, traditional *hevrot*, modernized philanthropic societies—which usually were ruled by an oligarchy over which the broad strata of the Jewish population had no influence.

Jewish socialists who were willing to work in the community first had to justify such work, define the structure and functions of the community, and develop a socialist program of activities. Every socialist who wrote about communal work felt obliged to prove that the existing community was not a philanthropic voluntary "bourgeois" institution but a compulsory structure with semigovernmental functions and obligations that included, in reality, all the Jews living in a given locality. This definition provided a rationale for the socialists' participation in communal affairs (as in the affairs of other state institutions—the parliament and municipalities) in order to defend the interests of the "proletariat" even before the victory of the revolution and the achievement of the socialist program-minimum (meaning the democratization of Russia and the establishment of Jewish national autonomy). Via participation in communal affairs, the socialists sought to protect the interests of the workers and the poor masses, thereby organizing and influencing them. All the parties proposed similar tasks: the introduction of direct taxes instead of the tax on kosher meat, the transformation of Talmud Torah schools into secular public schools; the transfer of all welfare matters from philanthropic associations to the community, which was obliged by the existing law to support the poor; and the introduction of public control over community expenditures.[60]

Thus, by advocating the immediate reorganization of the community on a democratic basis, the socialists found themselves in the mainstream together with the "bourgeois" political movements. In 1907 all Jewish bourgeois parties—the Liberals, the Zionists, and the Autonomists— started to develop models of community reform, and in the following years the question of community reorganization became the major topic in Jewish politics.

The high point in the political reorientation toward community reorganization was the Kovno conference of Jewish public activists in November 1909 and the conference of rabbis in the spring of 1910. The rabbinic conference was out of the socialists' sphere, but the Bund sent four representatives to the Kovno conference, and the Seimists were represented by Nokhem Shtif; all of them came as delegates of the cultural associations.[61] The socialists' appearance at the conference of Jewish public activists devoted to communal reorganization so surprised the organizers that it took a long time to approve their mandates.[62] "[The delegates were] afraid of the [socialists], distrusted them, and commented several times in the corridors that they had come to destroy the conference. [The delegates] were astonished: how had they [the socialists] become interested in community affairs? How is it their business [*vos iz dos zeyer zakh*]?" However, in the end, the relations between the socialists and the majority were normalized: "By the final day, the conference became somewhat accustomed to the new elements; it saw them, naturally, as opponents, but not as those who wanted to destroy, or disturb. People listened to them more closely."[63]

The Bund's report, written by A. Litvak, stressed the importance of the Bundists' participation in the conference, but, in reality, their vision of the future community structure did not differ from that of the democratically inclined "bourgeois" participants: a secular community with the legal rights to impose its discipline and its obligatory taxes on all the Jews in a town or shtetl, universal suffrage, and progressive taxes. The only demand especially stressed by the Bundists (and other socialists) was that all religious matters should be completely excluded from the community's competence. They raised this demand in Kovno but, not surprisingly, even the nonsocialist leftists at the conference (who in principle advocated the same decision) chose not to support this demand in order to keep open the possibility of reaching some degree of consensus.[64]

Participation in community reorganization raised anew the question of the competence to be assigned in the future to the national-cultural autonomy that was finally included in the Bund's program in 1905. The majority of the Bundists considered that the sphere of activity of the existing or reorganized Jewish community should be much broader than the strictly cultural-educational definition of autonomy to be found in that program. Some leaders (Medem, Kossovsky) proposed distinguishing between the community and the future autonomy,[65] while others, with A. Litvak at their head, proposed expanding the framework of the autonomy to include those spheres that they believed should be dealt with by communities in the present: public health, welfare, and the "regulation of emigration."[66] After an acrimonious discussion in October 1910, the Eighth Bund Conference could not reach an agreement and it decided only on the "first steps that our party has to take now in the new realm and on the general character of its activity": the Bundists should "gain access into the ruling institutions [of the community] and struggle there for our demands against the oligarchy and rabbinic clericalism."[67]

At the same time, three other Jewish socialist parties also declared their readiness to participate in the reorganization of the community: the Vienna Conference of the Russian Poale Zion in September 1909 included "the struggle for the democratization of the Jewish community" in the list of possible spheres for cooperation with other socialist parties;[68] the Third Conference of the Seimists in late 1910 described the desirable type of community and criticized the decisions of the Kovno and rabbinic conferences;[69] and the Fourth Conference of the SSRP in the spring of 1911 decided on "active participation in communal institutions."[70] However, the Jewish socialist parties' differing approaches to the community question reflected their different ideologies: the Bund and the Seimists, which both assigned priority in their programs to national autonomy for the Jews in Russia, paid considerably more attention to the reorganization of the communities than did the SSRP and the Poale Zion, which placed greater emphasis on emigration from Russia as the answer to the "Jewish Question." Nonetheless, all the parties were willing to work in the communities even though this entailed a significant degree of cooperation with the bourgeoisie. This was true both of the SSRP, which since 1907 had worked with the bourgeoisie in the Galveston project (involving Jewish emigration to

America) and in general territorialist matters, and of Poale Zion, although in 1909 it walked out of the World Zionist Organization in order not to participate in a "bourgeois" institution.

Nonetheless, the estimation in various party circles that the socialists' involvement in communal affairs was unlikely to be successful proved correct. The Bundists, for instance, tried to participate in several unofficial attempts to establish a surrogate community but without any success.[71] In addition, the hopes that the Russian government would support some reorganization of the community and that a law regulating the Jewish community could be passed in the State Duma faded in 1911. When the Jewish liberals dismissed the community issue as unrealistic, the socialists' interest in this question also sharply diminished, because, among other things, they simply could not continue alone. After 1911, the communal question disappeared from the socialist periodicals and party forums. The discussions of 1907–11, however, paved the way for the socialists' participation in Jewish communal politics in the 1920s and 1930s in Russia (until 1919), Poland, and the Baltic states.

Conclusion

The year 1907 transformed the tactics of the Jewish socialist parties along the same lines adopted by many other political organizations in the Russian Empire. While their strategic aims did not change—the establishment of a democratic regime in Russia that would allow a struggle for a socialist society—the practical emphasis shifted from revolutionary activism to the preservation of the parties' infrastructure and of their ties with the population. Some of the socialists (such as the Bolsheviks) regarded such activity, which they termed "small deeds," as only a temporary means until a new revolutionary upheaval, whereas other factions (such as the Mensheviks) believed in the vitality and importance of such work for the development of civil society and the democratization of Russia.

The tactics adopted by the four Jewish socialist parties in 1907 and applied in the subsequent years to cope with the crisis did not satisfy their expectations. Neither trade unions nor cultural associations could replace the parties as political organizations, and the existing Jewish communities failed to become an arena for the pursuit of class politics. However, the activity in these spheres led to a significant modification in the socialists' rejection of joint participation with the bourgeoisie in general Jewish projects. The theoretical principles of separate proletarian politics gave way to what was seen as the necessity to preserve contacts with the Jewish masses through participation in everyday Jewish life. The new possibilities for public activities were too attractive and the fear

of finding themselves completely marginalized was too real. Cooperation with the bourgeoisie, although not total, of course, characterized
the activity of Jewish socialist parties in Russia until World War I and the
Revolution of 1917.

Although most of the Jewish socialists were not involved in any party
work during the years of reaction, their basic ideological positions did
not change. Many of them continued to participate in public activities,
no longer under "party labels" but simply as free-floating socialists, Yiddishists, or territorialists. In 1917 many of them returned to politics and
played prominent roles in the revived Jewish socialist parties.

The tactics of the parties in the postrevolutionary period did not
achieve the immediate goals and did not attract the masses back into
their ranks. But, combined with the political activities of the skeletal
party organizations and with the journalistic activities of their members,
past or present, they did contribute to the survival of the socialist movements. The preservation and development of the ideologies together
with the nucleus of organizations made possible the remarkable revival
of all the parties in 1917.

Chapter 9
1905 as a Watershed in Polish-Jewish Relations

THEODORE R. WEEKS

The Revolution of 1905 marked a clear watershed in relations between Poles and Jews in the Russian Empire. By the early twentieth century, the liberal Polish conception of assimilation as the solution to the "Jewish Question" had already become questionable; the revolution and its aftermath, however, considerably exacerbated relations . Both the "successes" of the revolution (a lessening of censorship and the formation of a modest but weak legislature) and its overall failure (in particular, to bring autonomy and broad cultural-linguistic rights to non-Russians) set Poles against their Jewish neighbors. In short, 1905 may be seen as a significant step toward the major break of late 1912, when the failure of a Polish nationalist to win election to the Fourth Duma led to an anti-Jewish boycott.

Following the failure of the January 1863 Polish insurrection against Russian rule, liberal Polish society generally saw the solution to the "Jewish Question" in education and the acculturation of Polish Jewry, culminating in the formation of "Żydzi-Polacy"—individuals who spoke Polish, felt Polish, and differed from other Poles only in their religious beliefs.[1] Obviously, the Russian government opposed these efforts to strengthen the Polish cause by linking the Jews to it, but the weakness of this ideal of assimilation went beyond St. Petersburg's disapproval. In essence, this liberal solution assumed the inferiority of Jewish ritual and Jewish culture, taking for granted that Jews would happily shed their language (Yiddish), ritual practices (such as *kashrut*), and, indeed, their entire way of life in order to accept Polish culture. One can already see the discrediting of assimilation as the main solution—from the Polish side—to the "Jewish Question" before 1905, but the events of that year and the disappointments that followed it dealt this ideology a decisive blow.[2]

Initially in 1905, Poles and Jews struggled side by side against the Russian authorities. Or, more precisely, as spontaneous demonstrations, terrorist attacks, and strikes took place in major Polish cities and spread into the countryside, ethnic concerns were eclipsed by the social revolution. The "Jewish Question" played almost no role in these disturbances, and the fact that Jews (usually extremely Polonized individuals) figured prominently in certain revolutionary parties (in particular Rosa Luxemburg's SDKPiL [Social Democratic Party of the Kingdom of Poland and Lithuania], which opposed Polish independence) seemed initially of little import. During the year 1905 (at least until the autumn) the social questions far outweighed national issues, and one can find articles in both the liberal-conservative, middle-class *Kraj* and assimilationist *Izraelita* warning about revolutionary excesses.[3] At the same time, the antisemitic National Democrats were already expressing grave reservations and even condemnation of the revolutionary movement—even when led by ethnic Poles—seeing it as "chaos" that would in the end bring only grief and further government repression.

For most Polish Jews, the revolutionary years signified not liberation but the threat and reality of violence. Indeed, after the Kishinev pogrom of 1903, Jews in the Kingdom of Poland had been worried about the possibility of violence against them.[4] In 1905 and especially as government repression gained momentum in 1906, a rash of anti-Jewish attacks took place. To be sure, most of these pogroms occurred in the Pale of Settlement, but a veritable pogrom-panic swept the Polish Kingdom: a Polish weekly reported in the summer of 1906 (in the aftermath of the Belostok pogrom) that trains leaving Warsaw were full of fearful Jews.[5] Indeed, a pogrom did break out in Siedlce, one of the Kingdom's eastern towns, in September.[6] The Polish press was unanimous in denouncing these acts of violence, seeing in them the work of reactionaries and "people of a moral level lower than that of beasts."[7] Compared with the pogrom wave of 1881, these attacks were far more vicious—over two hundred Jews were killed in Belostok, and around one hundred in Siedlce. The threatening atmosphere that Polish Jewry (especially its Orthodox majority) endured during these months certainly affected the tenor and rhetoric of exchanges between Poles and Jews in 1905 and afterward.[8]

As predominantly urban dwellers, Jews were probably affected even more directly than Poles by the revolutionary events of 1905. Yet the proposals for Polish autonomy, schools, courts, and the like rarely, if ever, acknowledged the fact that a good portion (around one-fifth) of the population in the former Kingdom of Poland was not ethnically Polish but mainly Lithuanian and Jewish.[9] Despite the fact that Jews constituted around one-third of the residents of Warsaw and Lodz, to mention only the two largest cities, and even larger percentages in smaller towns, Jews per se were almost never mentioned in discussions of local autonomy and the reformed school system. When the Polish Koło (a parliamentary group in the Duma) presented a project for autonomy, it failed to mention the Jews—a fact noted even by the very pro-Polish *Nowa Gazeta*.[10] Allowing equal rights for the native tongue of Poland's Jews—Yiddish—was never considered (and the Lithuanians of Suwałki province were similarly ignored). Whereas no group in Polish society in the revolutionary years advocated eliminating or curtailing equal rights for Jews, very few Poles seemed even to recognize that the non-Polish population was entitled to some kind of cultural and linguistic concessions, at the very least. At the same time, young Jews were very visible in the revolutionary movement (particularly in the Bund), and many Poles considered that their demands for specific Jewish rights ran directly counter to Polish national interests.[11] Could Jewish identity—even of a mitigated, acculturated type—be included as part of the Polish nation? This was the fundamental but unspoken question of those years.

The organ of the Polish-Jewish assimilationists, *Izraelita*, answered the question with a resounding "yes!" As always, the weekly denied the existence of "Jewish solidarity" and argued for the incorporation of Jews into Polish society. An editorial early in the year, just as street violence and strikes were spreading, restated a common theme: "In relation to our countrymen [*rodaków*] of different religions, above all we have upheld the principle of social harmony in the broadest possible sense." Social harmony—*zgoda społeczna*—was precisely what was lacking in the Russian Empire and, in particular, in Warsaw at that moment. *Izraelita* could offer no new arguments but merely repeated its standard line that "the basis of the Mosaic religion is pure love toward one's neighbor" and that Jewish religious customs did not in any way imperil close relations with non-Jews. As a nod to the revolutionary events of the day, perhaps, the editor went on to state that *Izraelita* also wanted to "go forward with the flow of life."[12]

By autumn, the convocation of some kind of legislative body in St. Petersburg seemed a certainty. In late September *Izraelita* argued that Jews should participate in elections to this body on an equal footing with all residents of the empire and the Kingdom of Poland, and it also expressed the hope that the new Duma would be a first step toward equal rights for all the Jewish subjects of the tsar.[13] But what sort of representative should be elected? *Izraelita* polemicized with the Hebrew-language newspaper *Hatzefirah,* which had stated its preference for a "humanitarian Christian" rather than a Jew "divorced [*oddalony*] from his nation [*naród*], a Jew for whom all of Judaism weighed no more than a fly's wing." Predictably, *Izraelita* insisted that an "assimilated" Jew could both understand and defend the specific religious interests of Jews, and it explicitly rejected the designation of Jews as a "nation."[14] Clearly, the inauguration of politics in the form of elections and legislative representation would not put an end to internal disputes in the Jewish community.

At the end of the year, *Izraelita* announced the formation of the Union of Poles of the Mosaic Confession. This was a major departure for so-called *assimilated* Polish Jews who had hitherto argued against the need for specifically Jewish political movements. An article by the prominent jurist Józef Kirszrot explained that because many political programs had surfaced in Polish society after the publication of the October Manifesto, assimilated Jews should therefore similarly formulate their own. "On this platform should be found those Jews who consider themselves Polish citizens [*poczywający się do obywatelstwa krajowego*], who together with the entire Polish nation wish to march forward [*kroczyć*] along its preordained historical path." At the same time, as Poles of the Mosaic confession, they could not regard the fate of the Russian Jews as a matter of indifference. Furthermore, this religious connection with Russia would, so the announcement declared, enable the members of this party to help bridge the painful gap that history had created between Poles and Russians. In other words, while "assimilated" Jews—"Poles of the Mosaic confession"—continued to exhibit characteristics different from those of Christian Poles, these differences would benefit the Polish nation.[15]

The National Democrats ("Endeks" or "Endecja"), to be sure, would not have agreed. But for most of 1905, the leadership of this nationalist and judeophobic party was in a state of semi-shock and panic due to the unexpected violence of the revolution. Neither of their major organs, *Gazeta Warszawska* and *Przegląd Wszechpolski,* devoted much space to the "Jewish Question" during that year. Politically speaking, the National Democrats found themselves in a highly uncomfortable and embarrassing situation.[16] As *the* avowedly Polish-nationalist party, one might have expected the Endecja to be at the forefront of the struggle against Russian domination. In fact, however, the fear of disorder and chaos displayed by the Russian authorities was shared by the National Democrats' leader, Roman Dmowski, and his lieutenants. Writing some years later, Dmowski described the revolution as artificial and anachronistic (that is, romantic—harking back to pre-1863 traditions), organized and led by three parties antipathetic to Endek aims (the Bund, the SDKPiL, and the Polish Socialist Party [PPS]) and doomed to failure. Even worse, the revolution further demoralized Polish society: "The feeling of civilized people, whether educated or not, was despair and doubt regarding our own value as a society capable of survival [*społeczeństwo zdolne do życia*]. And there was a general consciousness that this resulted directly from the weakening of Polish cultural independence [*samoistność cywiliza-cyjna*] as a consequence of Jewish and Russian influences."[17] While these words were written nearly two decades after 1905, an article in *Gazeta Warszawska* in late 1905 similarly blamed the revolution on the machinations of the socialist parties, especially the Bund, SDKPiL, and PPS.[18]

Dmowski was entirely correct in his sober evaluation of the very dim chances for the revolution's success, but the result was that in 1905 the National Democrats appeared to be supporting the status quo (read: the Russians) over the revolution (read: the Poles). One finds, for example, Dmowski's signature, along with those of archconservatives such as Count M. F. Zamoyski and Prince Z. Lubomirski, on a petition to the Russian government of November 1905.[19] Indeed, when Dmowski met with the Russian prime minister, Sergei Witte, in late 1905, rumors abounded (spread by the socialists) that Dmowski had promised to help crush the Polish insurgents in exchange for a leading role in the administration of the Polish provinces.[20] Dmowski's adamant opposition to the revolution made it easy to attack the Endecja as retrograde, antidemocratic, and collaborationist.[21] Certainly the gap between doctrinal national radicalism and strategic "collaboration" with the Russian authorities may explain the increasingly ferocious anti-Jewish rhetoric of the National Democrats. But this rhetoric developed mainly in the aftermath of the revolution itself, during elections to the State Dumas.

The National Democrats were not alone in their opposition to Jewish national rights and their accusations of "Jewish separatism." In late summer 1905, an article in the progressive but hardly judeophilic *Głos* on the disturbances in the Kingdom of Poland identified many Jews as revolutionaries, casting them in a very negative light. The article furthermore specified that the Bund not only was carrying out revolutionary agitation and actions but also—and even worse—"lately [the Bund] has begun to form armed units [*drużyzy bojowe*] and increasingly betrays [*zdradzać*] more and more aggressiveness toward the Christian population of the Western provinces."[22] Of course, *Głos* had been publishing anti-Jewish articles for a long time, but as an avowedly progressive journal, it had seldom attacked Jewish socialists per se. By the autumn of 1905, when the revolution was reaching its apogee, accusations that "foreign elements" (*obce żywioły*) were foisting revolution on innocent Polish workers were clearly in the air. In the Polish situation, these "foreigners" were most often identified with Jews, in particular the so-called litwacy or Jews from the Pale of Settlement, who were accused of acting as agents of russification. An article in *Kraj* late that year specifically argued against these charges that had been made in an anonymously published brochure by the conservative and patriotic novelist Henryk Sienkiewicz, who was to receive the Nobel Prize for Literature in 1905.[23]

In the article, Professor Jan Baudouin de Courtenay (writing under a pseudonym) argued against Sienkiewicz, saying that Poles needed to accept responsibility for the events in their native land rather than look for scapegoats.[24]

As violence and anarchy grew in late 1905, and perhaps even more in 1906 when government repressions lashed out rather indiscriminately at revolutionaries and bystanders, the desire to find scapegoats grew even more intense. Predictably, the "father of Polish antisemitism," Jan Jeleń-ski, and his notorious weekly, *Rola,* vociferously opposed the revolutionary events of 1905, blaming them on Jewish intrigues. From late 1905 into 1906 the tone of Jeleński's anti-Jewish, antisocialist, and antiliberal campaign became increasingly hysterical. An article titled "God, Faith, Fatherland" set down the three pillars around which Jeleński aimed to rally "true" Poles. Jeleński argued for "national self-defense" (*samo-obrona narodowa*), the "nationalization" (*unarodowienie*) of the country's riches (that is, putting them in Polish hands), and an end to strikes and other disturbances.[25] Although Jeleński did not mention the Jews by name, it is clear whom he meant when he referred to "foreign elements that have always been hostile to us" and that dominated the country's economy.

Jeleński continued his crusade in brochures published for a broad audience in 1905 and 1906. His brochure addressed to the "Polish worker!" warned that workers should not listen to voices calling them "comrades," even in pure Polish. Jeleński claimed that he, a Christian journalist, had the best interests of the Polish workers at heart, whereas behind the agitators stood "the German and the Prussian Jew" (*żydowin pruski*). At their hands, "Jewish-German industry will take over Polish industry"; moreover, their calls for strikes and socialism were simply a means of destroying Poles and Poland. Strikes would not bring the desired results but would only lead to higher prices and to the elimination of industry and jobs. The tone of the brochure became ever more feverish, as if Jeleński feared the battle already lost. "Say what they will, I will never believe that you, my brother, a Polish worker, want to break with the faith of your forefathers and cease being a Pole."[26]

Unfortunately for the socialists, vocal criticism of the revolutionary left was by no means the monopoly of extremists such as Jeleński. Already in late 1904, Polish liberals led by Aleksander Świętochowski had formed the Progressive-Democratic Union (Związek Postępowo-Demok-ratyczny, ZP-D). Building on an alliance with Russian liberals (in particular through the person of Aleksander Lednicki, a close associate of the Russian Kadet leader, Pavel Miliukov) and the previously existing Polish liberal group, Kuźnica, the ZP-D aimed to provide a middle-of-the-road alternative for Poles who rejected both the radical program of the socialists and the nationalist chauvinism of the Endeks.[27] From the start, many acculturated Jews like Henryk Konic, Józef Natanson, and Stanisław Kempner were active participants in the progressive party. The reason was obvious. As middle-class or even wealthy men of liberal but hardly radical outlook, they would have felt out of place in the PPS, SDKPiL, or other socialist groupings. Jews were also prominent in professionally as lawyers, physicians, and journalists—precisely the groups that tended to support the liberals. The National Democrats rejected the possibility of Polish identity for the Jews (even fully acculturated, Polish-speaking Jews). Hence the progressive, liberal parties attracted a disproportionate amount of support among middle-class, assimilated Jews.[28]

The Polish progressive parties, both the ZP-D and the Polska Partia Postępowa (PPP), were middle-class, center-left groupings. Their members and constituency were drawn almost exclusively from urban professionals or, to use the not exactly equivalent Polish term, *inteligencja*. They advocated human rights, Polish autonomy within the Russian Empire, and, of course, the use of Polish in schools, offices, and courts within the Kingdom of Poland. Economically the liberals did not espouse a doctrinaire laissez-faire program but certainly rejected socialism as a solution to the economic problems facing Poland.[29] It was the progressives' tragedy that their program could hardly attract a broad following in the revolutionary situation of 1905–6. As is well known, in periods of political upheaval, proposals of moderation and liberal reform tend to be sidelined by more radical solutions. The National Democrats were more successful in wooing the urban petty bourgeoisie, and workers were far more likely to support socialist parties (or even the National Democrats) than progressives.

On the "Jewish Question" the progressive party programs were quite unambiguous. The "Jewish Question" in Poland would be solved by education, assimilation, and toleration. Essentially, the progressives continued the line of the positivists. For both parties, *polskość* ("Polishness") was broad enough to include Jews defined as a religious group. As we would expect, the progressives firmly rejected any suggestion that the Jews constituted a nation, and they opposed Zionists and the Bund every bit as much as they condemned the Endeks' chauvinism. Yiddish was seen as a negative survival of Jewish backwardness that would disappear as Polish education spread among the Jewish masses. Whereas a few progressives were prepared to countenance the idea of using Yiddish as a pedagogical tool to further colonization, for the overwhelming majority (including Świętochowski and Iza Moszczeńska), the idea of allowing Yiddish in "Polish" schools was an absolute taboo. On the whole, however, the progressives preferred to avoid the Jewish issue rather than to confront it head-on—quite unlike the Endeks.[30] Like their ideological forefathers the positivists, the Polish progressives of the early twentieth century acted as if the "Jewish Question" did not exist—or, if it did, they hoped it would soon disappear.[31]

Elections to the First Duma revealed the lack of talent of the progressives—and, one may say, of the Polish liberals generally—when it came to electoral politics. Many liberals felt that to participate in elections under the prevailing circumstances would amount to endorsing Russian repression in the Polish provinces. Even Świętochowski was somewhat swayed by such arguments but in the end he felt that the benefits of elections outweighed such scruples.[32] When the Progressive-Democratic Union did decide to participate in the elections, a group split off from it, calling itself the Democratic Union (Związek Demokratyczny). By the time this decision had been taken, the National Democratic party had already positioned itself as the front-runner, a position it would never lose. Attempting to make up for their organizational weaknesses and their very late decision to participate in the elections, the progressives took the logical but ill-fated step of allying with the Jewish Electoral Committee (Żydowski Komitet Wyborczy) and putting up joint candidates in seven of Warsaw's twelve electoral districts.[33] The voting for electors took place on March 28, and the Endecja carried the day. In Warsaw, for example, sixty of eighty electors were identified with that party (and, as Kiepurska points out, one of these was of Jewish background) and the other twenty were Jewish.[34] Political disagreements had been translated into ethnic differences.[35]

The electoral agreement between the progressives and the Jewish Commitee gave the Endeks a golden opportunity to accuse the liberals of "selling Poland out to the Jews and Russians." From this point onward, the Endeks portrayed themselves as the only true champions of Polish rights, and the Jews (and their liberal Polish allies) as the primary enemy. While anti-Jewish rhetoric and action had always been a part of the Endek political platform, antisemitism now took on a central role.[36] More significantly, the Endek assertion that the Jews constituted the greatest threat to Poland (even more so than the Russians) became increasingly accepted in Polish society in the next few years. In 1906, however, while anti-Jewish rhetoric did play a significant role in the Endek campaign, it still lacked the obsessive quality that it was to acquire in the following few years.[37] The rhetoric of the National Democrats during the campaign preceding the elections to the First Duma concentrated more on "unmasking" the impractical and dangerous ideologies of the socialists and progressives than on the Jews per se.[38] Indeed, *Gazeta Polska* even agreed, though grudgingly, with Władysław Studnicki's argument that, constituting 13 percent of the population in the

Kingdom of Poland, the Jews deserved their own Duma representative.[39] On the whole, however, the anti-Jewish slant of Endek rhetoric was clear.

A postelection article in *Biblioteka Warszawska* insisted that the "slogan of racial struggle" and hatred of the Jews did not play a significant role in the campaign, nor did antisemitism dominate Polish society. This was, the article argued, "not a battle with the Jews but rather a battle with Jewish separatism, which should not exist in Poland" and which would be "quickly buried" once a proper constitutional order was inaugurated.[40] In essence, however, this kind of argumentation simply meant that Jews could be tolerated in Polish society but only if they shed their separate identity. The denial of racial and antisemitic motives in the electoral campaign rings hollow, and certainly *Izraelita*—which also in its own way battled "Jewish separatism"—perceived the elections and the Endek victory as a triumph for antisemitism.[41] The battle lines were already being drawn in the elections to the First Duma, with Poles on one side and Jews on the other.

After all the excitement, the First Duma convened in St. Petersburg on May 10, 1906 (new style). The Polish representatives organized themselves into a separate parliamentary group, the so-called Koło, directed primarily at pressing for specifically Polish rights.[42] As matters turned out, however, the Koło was unable to promote any specific projects during the Duma's short life. In July, Tsar Nicholas II dissolved the Duma, and new elections were called.[43] The Russian authorities were discovering that managing a parliamentary system was far more complex than they had imagined. At the same time, the government felt itself strong enough to replace possibly fruitless dialogue with repression. And heading the government from July 1906 was the energetic, intelligent, and anti-Polish Petr Stolypin. The tide had turned in the Russian Empire against progressive reform and toward a restoration of imperial power, which could have only a negative effect on the rights of national minorities.

News of the dissolution of the First Duma was received with more resignation than indignation. In Lodz the governor of Petrokov province wrote that the population reacted "indifferently" (*bezuchastno*) and reactions were similar elsewhere.[44] The failure of the government to find a *modus vivendi* with the fledgling parliament discredited liberals and encouraged radicals of both the right and left. The socialist parties that had boycotted elections to the First Duma decided to participate in the new elections, and the government also actively attempted to support monarchist, Orthodox, and conservative elements, in particular, the Union of the Russian People.[45] The Pedecja (Progressive Democrats) once again attempted to take on the National Democrats (a splinter group called the "Polish Progressive Party," however, joined the Endeks and the "Realist Party" in an electoral block called the "National Concentration").[46] The Pedecja continued to push the idea of autonomy, toleration, and minority rights and to agitate against the Endeks.[47]

Świętochowski denounced Endek threats that if Jews did not support its "national concentration" (*koncentracja narodowa*), then "pogroms could be expected," and he called on Jews to support the progressives.[48] *Nowa Gazeta* published a long series in 1907 titled "Material on the Jewish Question," and it made the excellent point that while Jews were very sympathetic to Polish autonomy, their specific interests (such as the use of Yiddish) had been completely ignored in autonomy projects hitherto.[49] While *Nowa Gazeta* admitted that "at the present moment," Jews certainly made up a "separate nation" (*odrębny naród*) in Poland, it saw this as a passing stage only, and it argued that Jews in the Polish milieu increasingly melded into the larger Polish society.[50] Along similar lines, *Izraelita* called on Polish Jews to support "progressive candidates" who upheld the principle of equal rights for Jews.[51]

On the other side, the National Democrats and their allies painted an apocalyptic picture of the results of a hypothetical progressive victory. In his pamphlet *Away with the Enemies of the Fatherland!* Jan Jeleński fulminated against socialists and progressives, many of whom were "enlightened Jews" (*oświeceni żydzi*, that is, acculturated Jews), utterly alien to Polish and Christian desires, interests, and hearts.[52] In *Rola*, Jeleński's denunciations became, if anything, even more exaggerated, claiming that the progressives were out to establish "national-Jewish representation" in the Duma.[53] Along similar lines, the National Democrats campaigned on a platform of order, stability, and autonomy for Russian Poland, blaming the anarchy and bloodshed of the previous years on progressives and Jews.[54] The elections took place under tense circumstances, following mass arrests and continued terrorist attacks against Russian officials.[55]

As in the elections to the First Duma, the National Democrats swept the field in the Second Duma. *Rola* bore the headline "The Sacred Victory of Poland's Capital!" to celebrate the election of two Endek representatives, Roman Dmowski and Franciszek Nowodworski.[56] The Polish Duma representatives went rather soberly to St. Petersburg in February 1907, hoping, perhaps, to achieve some measure of legal amelioration for Poles in the Russian Empire but, just as likely, not quite believing in that possibility. As it turned out, the conservative Polish *Koło* was quite out of place in the polarized Second Duma, divided sharply between Russian nationalists and monarchists on the right and socialists and radicals on the left.[57] In such an atmosphere, the possibility of passing a bill for Polish autonomy was extremely unlikely. The complete impossibility of compromise between the government and the highly polarized Duma made its dissolution only a matter of time. In June 1907 the inevitable occurred and the Second Duma was dispersed, marking the end of the revolutionary period.[58]

The Second Duma had lasted just over three months. Upon its dissolution a new electoral ordinance was published, quite contrary to the spirit and letter of the October Manifesto. The imperial manifesto that accompanied the new electoral law specifically mentioned the issue of non-Russian representation in the Duma: "The other [non-Russian] nationalities making up a part of our state should have representatives in the State Duma for their own needs, but not in such numbers as would allow them to interfere in purely Russian matters."[59] Practically, this meant that representation from the Kingdom of Poland dropped from three dozen delegates to one-third that number. Furthermore, two of these were specifically designated as Russian (or Orthodox) representatives. Warsaw, for example, would thus have in the Third Duma only one representative from its over half-million non-Russian population.[60]

The news of the Second Duma's demise was met with dull apathy and resignation. Earlier in the year the labor movement had been dealt a decisive blow by a massive lockout in Lodz, and while banditry, terrorist acts, and strikes continued, it was clear by mid-1907 that the government was gaining the upper hand.[61] The educational society Polska Macierz Szkolna was shut down in December of 1907 and the governor of Warsaw province wrote that all was quiet and that revolutionary and antigovernment forces had been crushed or at least driven underground.[62] The revolution was over, order had been restored, and the high hopes for increased cultural and political rights for both Poles and Jews had been dashed. The disappointment of these failed hopes combined with the oppressive political atmosphere of the following years would push Polish-Jewish relations to their breaking point.[63]

The years 1904–7 form a crucial watershed in Polish-Jewish relations. The Russo-Japanese War and the ensuing revolution reawakened hopes for increased Polish rights, hopes that had been set aside or downplayed since 1863. In 1905 it appeared that autonomy would be restored in the former Kingdom of Poland, that Polish would be restored to schools and offices, and that a Polish legislature would convene in Warsaw. Most Jews did not oppose, indeed welcomed, Polish autonomy and struggled against tsarist authority in that revolutionary year. Unfortunately, once the Russo-Japanese war was over and St. Petersburg began to restore order on its own terms, Polish rights and those of the other minority nationalities were quickly forgotten. Furthermore, the undemocratic nature of the Duma elections, favoring the urban population and landowners over peasants and workers, sharpened perceptions that Polish and Jewish interests did not coincide and were even directly opposed.

More important, however, Poles failed to recognize that by this point, Jewish national and cultural considerations could no longer be ignored. With Jewish rights seen as antagonistic to Polish needs, progressive Poles opened themselves up to accusations of "selling out to the Jews" in their electoral alliances with Jewish voters. In any case, the National Democratic party, which swept the field in both the first and second Dumas, learned the effectiveness of antisemitic slogans and charges in the electoral campaigns. It was a lesson they would build upon in later Duma elections with fatal results for Polish-Jewish relations.

Part IV
Cultural Reflections of Revolution

Chapter 10

Polish Literature's Portrayal of Jewish Involvement in 1905

Agnieszka Friedrich

The Revolution of 1905 had a strong impact not only on Polish society and politics but also on Polish literature. Numerous authors, including the most prominent, faced the challenge of coping with this momentous event. Literary works created during the years following 1905 that were related to the revolutionary "heat," as it was commonly called, numbered in the dozens; yet, their significance lies not only in their quantity. According to the picturesque formulation of a researcher, this was the moment when Młoda Polska (Young Poland) turned gray.[1]

No monumental masterpiece stands out among the numerous works. As Krzysztof Stępnik, who studied the literary record of the events of the revolution, has pointed out, the literature of this period is neither novel nor revolutionary in character. On the contrary, the reader encounters the mechanical copying of familiar literary conventions and patterns. Stępnik explains this phenomenon by the authors' assumption that literature should serve the revolution. The familiar literary devices that were already rooted in the reader's consciousness were considered the most effective way of transmitting an ideological message in favor of the revolution. As a consequence, the majority of literary portrayals of the revolution are trite and formulaic.[2]

Such an approach detracts from the artistic value of this literature. However, this ideological and schematic treatment allows for a relatively faithful reconstruction of contemporary attitudes toward the revolution in general, as well as toward secondary issues such as the role of the Jews in 1905. According to a commonly held belief at that time in Poland, Jewish participation in the revolution was significant, if not indispensable. The publicist Iza Moszczeńska,[3] who was deeply involved in the revolution, confirmed the prevalence of this belief in a statement published in 1906 in *Izraelita*, a Jewish journal that supported Jewish integration.

Moszczeńska stated that, on the one hand, the participation of Jews in the revolution was really essential and on a large scale; on the other hand, she noted that the opponents of the revolution were exploiting this fact in order to discredit it in the eyes of the nationalist-oriented Polish masses.[4] The latter tendency was particularly noticeable in statements concerning the Marxist SDKPiL (Social Democratic Party of the Kingdom of Poland and Lithuania), in which several people of Jewish origin, such as Rosa Luxemburg, occupied important positions.

The most striking evidence of the nationalist-oriented public's dislike of both the Marxist left and the Jewish participants in the revolution was found in an article written by Julian Unszlicht.[5] He wrote: "Such organizations as the so-called 'Left,' 'Workers Solidarity,' and especially the SDKPiL are exceedingly dangerous and led by 'litwacy' [Russian Jews who moved from the Pale of Settlement to the former Kingdom of Poland] and Jewish nationalists as well as a few Polish renegades who aim at denationalizing and russifying the Polish people, at breaking down and splitting Polish society from within into its parts in order to strike at the divided parts [. . .] and in this way to 'thoroughly kill' execrable Poland."[6] Unszlicht, who had Jewish roots himself, presented in an extreme form a conviction that was quite common.

Not all writers held this view of Jewish participation in the revolution. In fact, the broad range of authors' views found expression in diverse literary portrayals. A fundamental aim of this chapter is to describe this diversity. First, I ascertain the extent to which a Jewish theme appears in works dealing with the Revolution of 1905 in general. The key studies of Polish literature of that time[7] point to about sixty works of fiction, written between 1905 and 1914, referring directly or indirectly to the revolution. An extensively elaborated Jewish theme appears in many of them (approximately one in every four) but Jews are the main characters in only two: a short story by Maria Konopnicka, "Żydóweczka" (A little Jewish girl), and a longer story by Andrzej Niemojewski titled "Boruch."[8]

It is thus clear that issues concerning Jews occupy a relatively minor place in the literary record of the 1905 Revolution. The large number of works with Jewish characters, however, makes it possible to differentiate among the various portrayals of Jews involved in the revolution and the hidden attitudes of the authors. I will do so by examining the above-mentioned group of literary texts.

Obviously, the most common type is a revolutionary character, an active party member, a fighter; and the most radical revolutionary character is one who attempts a terrorist act. Such is the title character of "Boruch" (1907) by Niemojewski,[9] modeled on Boruch Szulman, a member the PPS (Polish Socialist Party), who in May 1906 carried out a successful attack on a Russian police commissar known for his sadism.[10] Niemojewski quite faithfully reconstructs these events, adding a convincing depiction of a young fighter's parting from his parents. The father, giving his blessing to his son destined for death, is compared to the patriarch Jacob. This scene places the title character in a traditional Jewish environment, the one he comes from, and emphasizes his Jewish roots.

The highlighting of these roots is important because for Niemojewski, Boruch becomes a personification of the alliance between Jews and Poles, Jews and Christians, an alliance made possible only because of the social revolution. Niemojewski's narrator, commenting on Boruch's burial place, declares, "You could say that his dead body in this grave filled in some great gulf between two religions,"[11] and further, "Here, in this sacred grove, at Boruch's graveside in a concordant and fraternal choir of workers, Aryan and Semite alike, arose the song of faith, hope, and love—those evangelic virtues brought to naught by predators and pastors but now brought to life by people of the hammer and the spade."[12] This effusive description confirms Stępnik's observation that supporters of the revolution employed metaphors linking the current revolutionaries to the early radical stage of Christian history.[13]

A similarly heroic, more complex portrayal of a Jewish revolutionary is found in Andrzej Strug's[14] 1910 novel *Dzieje jednego pocisku* (The history of one bullet). In the part of the novel in which the author describes the breakdown of the revolution, he portrays Izrael Miński, an ideological and brave anarchist who shortly before his death formed a revolutionary group in a provincial town. The gang quickly turned into a band of common thugs that included an equal number of Jews and Christian Poles. Strug writes that although Miński stemmed from "the tiger line," his followers were like rats.[15] In this description as well as in the rest of Strug's novel—an exceptionally ambiguous and complicated one in comparison to the other works under discussion—a disquieting aspect of revolutionary dynamics was revealed, with politically motivated violence unexpectedly degenerating into common banditry.

The ideological message of a novel published in 1907 and fully devoted to the revolution, *Dzieci* (Children), by Bolesław Prus,[16] is less complex. Here, the character of David Regen, a Jewish revolutionary, partially echoes that of Boruch Szulman. Regen, like Boruch, throws a bomb at a Russian police superintendent, but the motivation Prus ascribes to this perpetrator is quite different. The writer singles out the desire for vengeance as a result of police harassment, suggesting that Regen is mentally ill. Prus's introduction of the character demonstrates the ironic distance he placed between himself and Regen, who had become a revolutionary "by chance"—"a young Jew, haggard, with a straggly beard. He wore a revolutionary cloak and a very revolutionary hat." The protagonist of the novel, a noble ideologist named Kazik Świrski, is repelled by the bomb attack.[17] Prus's attitude toward the act of terror differs from that of Niemojewski. Both writers situate the perpetrator squarely within his Jewish environment. Niemojewski uses this fact to deliver a clear ideological message, but Prus does not reach any general conclusions on the basis of Regen's Jewish roots. Nonetheless, Regen can perhaps be seen as in some way representative (let us add—not in a very favorable way) of the Jewish involvement in the revolution. Above all, his personality confirms Prus's primary thesis that the revolution represented immaturity or even pathology.

The element of personal revenge that characterizes Regen reappears in Teodor Jeske-Choiński's[18] 1909 novel *Po czerwonym zwycięstwie* (After the Red victory). This work, which Tomasz Weiss labeled "a lampoon on socialism,"[19] presents a vision of Poland after the victory of the revolution. One of the revolutionaries depicted in the novel is (as described by the writer) the "żydek" (Jew boy) Fajgenbaum, who, together with his colleagues, ensconces himself comfortably in a luxury restaurant, thus compensating for his previous indigence. In this case the character's Jewish origin is of no significance as the rest of the participants taking part in this feast are Christians. Fajgenbaum's Jewish roots are more significant in another scene, a public meeting at which he adopts an antibourgeois and anticlerical position, urging the destruction of the monuments erected in honor of Polish kings, writers, and scholars, suggesting that they be replaced by monuments memorializing Marx and Bebel. Another participant retorts: "Don't touch what isn't yours." Undoubtedly, in this way, a determined antisemite such as Jeske-Choiński wanted to point to the national alienation of the Jews that could not be overcome even within the internationalist socialist movement.

In his novel *Hetmani* (Hetmans) (1911), Józef Weyssenhoff[20] similarly depicts Jewish revolutionaries in an antisemitic light. This work portrays Rubin Held and his companion Szmul Krótki among other Jews involved in the revolution. Held is, as depicted by Weyssenhoff, a repulsive character not only because he serves the cause of Jewish nationalism instead of the socialist ideal and gives preference to Jews in using the party's money but also because he uses violence even against workers when they do not meet his expectations.[21]

Another novel by Weyssenhoff, *W ogniu* (In the fire) (1908), includes a schematic portrayal of a revolutionary agitator, undoubtedly a Russian Jew, who advocates progressive slogans that are received by "a welcoming Polish mob."[22] When Demel, a Polish ideological socialist, dies, it is left to dubious Jewish revolutionaries—implicated inter alia in the death of Demel—to defend socialism. (They are scornfully called "a black million"[23] by the writer, an ironic reference to the ultra-nationalist and anti-semitic Russian "Black Hundreds.")

Marian Gawalewicz[24] presents an extremely grotesque portrait of a Jewish revolutionary in his novel *Bez celu* (Aimless) (1907). The character Zettelman—a strict internationalist and a member of the SDKPiL—favors the use of terror and rejects Polish independence. Such formulations were contrary to the personal views of a conservative writer opposed to the revolution. As Gawalewicz did not promote antisemitic attitudes in his works,[25] his selection of a Jewish character to advocate internationalist, anti-independence opinions should therefore be treated as indicative of a literary strategy in which a writer uses a commonly accepted stereotype for the sake of simple communication with the reader.

Niemojewski portrays a different kind of Jewish internationalist in a short story titled "Jur" (1906). An old Jew delivering a speech during a public meeting recalls with emotion the time of fraternization between Poles and Jews in the years 1861–63. Later on, he says affectionately: "Now I have lived to see the day when there is again a common cause and again holy blood is sprinkled on these paving stones. That is why a Christian or Jew should go to his own place of worship and say his 'Holy Mother' prayer."[26] These words exhorting brotherhood are motivated by humanistic rather than revolutionary values.

Evidently, the old Jew from Niemojewski's story is not a revolutionary; however, even nonideological motivation may play a significant role in revolutionary activities. Maria Konopnicka[27] conveyed a moving portrayal of a Jewish revolutionary in a brief story (only three pages long) titled "Żydóweczka" (A little Jewish girl) (1908). In this short text Konopnicka succeeded in presenting the dynamics and drama of the process of leaving the traditional Jewish community for the new reality of the socialist world. The heroine of the story, who is deeply devoted to the revolution, describes to the narrator her break with her Orthodox Jewish parents, who do not accept their daughter's revolutionary vocation. She is fully aware that "they [her parents] had to repudiate me." However, the cause that took her from her family home is so great that she felt that she had no choice, despite the pain involved. The human suffering to which she was responding was "greater than her father and greater than her mother."

Konopnicka's portrayal of the heroine, although concise, even formulaic, is the clearest and most purely humanistic statement in the Polish literature of the period, and it goes beyond a mere ideologically motivated sketch of revolutionary engagement. Konopnicka deliberately does not inform the reader as to which political organization the main character belongs; the latter says simply: "I'm from the party" (she probably means the PPS, or the Bund or, more likely, the SDKPiL). A matter of a crucial importance concerns gender: both Konopnicka and her character represent a "feminine" point of view expressive of a direct sensitivity to human unhappiness and misery. The heroine is motivated by total devotion to the cause; and although she surely sees in its victory the only chance to improve the universal situation, nothing is said about party politics in this story, which reinforce's the work's humanistic, non-ideological message.

Jewish revolutionary women also appear briefly in Niemojewski's short story "Jur," mentioned earlier, in which the title character discovers the admirable intelligence and bravery of Russian Jewish women who are carrying out propaganda work in the army. The narrator writes about them with amazement: "These women, despite their awful accent, glaring mistakes in their very first words [. . .] did not provoke any sign of antisemitism in this primitive military setting."[28] The narrator attributes this amazing lack of antisemitism to the influence of the revolution; however, he leaves some room for the possibility that the soldiers' response was due to the influence of a gentle feminine factor.

Weyssenhoff presents a more complex portrayal of a Jewish woman involved in the revolution in the character of Hela Latzka in *Hetmani* (Hetmans). On the one hand, she participates in her father's deceitful and repugnant activities; but, on the other hand, she is deeply and sincerely committed to the revolution. She does not arouse animosity because she seems to be exploited as ruthlessly as others by her father.

The character of Hela's father, Wawrzyniec Latzki, is unequivocally negative but at the same time difficult to classify from a typological point of view. His involvement in the revolution hints at certain positive traits (although this is not the author's ultimate intention), while his high position in society as well as the unseemly political game that he plays create the image of a wheeler-dealer who exploits the revolutionary situation to advance his personal affairs. Or, as Weyssenhoff puts it, the fundamental issue appears to be that national Jewish ambitions are being advanced at the expense of the Poles, including the Polish proletariat. This fact discredits Latzki as a true revolutionary.[29] Moreover, Latzki is too modern in a negative sense: he tries to manipulate public opinion through the press, insinuating vague connections between the authorities and financial capital. The main character and narrator of the novel, Sworski, is impressed with Latzki's dash, power, and determination.[30] However, the ultimate action that discredits Latzki is his plotting of the murder of Wojciech Piast, an ideological embodiment of Polish traits and of all positive features of the novel. The repellent depiction of Latzki is not surprising given the unmitigated antisemitic thrust of the entire novel, which most unequivocally (in comparison to other contemporary literary texts) presents a vision attributing the responsibility for the revolution and its misfortunes to the Jews (in this case, which is worse, in cooperation with Prussians).

A figure somewhat similar to Latzki is Herman Lancet, one of the main characters in the novel *Wir* (Whirl) (1908) by Gawalewicz. He is also characterized by quick wits and shrewdness as well as an uncompromising tenacity in pursuit of his personal goals. A fundamental difference between these two characters is that whereas Latzki supports the revolution with all the means at his disposal, Lancet, as a capitalist and factory owner, tries firmly to reverse the revolutionary outlook of his workers. The portrayal of Lancet is an exceptional attempt to present a Jewish capitalist in the Polish literature of the period. In this respect, it goes beyond the stereotypical depiction of the Jews as on the side of the revolution. Gawalewicz's novel presents a diversified portrait of Jewish characters that are confronted with revolutionary events: an old Jew, the capitalist Fienwurzel, who—contrary to his partner Lancet—tries to come to an agreement with his workers; Lancet's wife, who, on the one hand, takes the time and effort to read Polish Decadent writers and, on the other hand, in the face of danger behaves in an extremely practical way; Berek Gutweib, an owner of a tenement house, who, anticipating the approaching revolution, tries to hide his wealth "in order not to be out of line";[31] and, Gutweib's manager, Izydor Sanfkind, who, in order to feel safe in the street in times of revolutionary turmoil, puts on a red tie, hoping to be taken for a socialist.

The gallery of Jewish characters in *Wir* is exceptionally rich and diversified; moreover, it is the only novel about the Revolution of 1905 with a Jewish setting. Other works in which Jewish themes are more marginal offer a few additional types but they do not contribute much to the entire spectrum of characters.

The portrayal of a Jew confronting the 1905 Revolution in Polish literature from the years 1905 to 1914 thus tends to be highly standardized, with the most important place reserved for the Jewish revolutionary. Other types, as we have seen, do appear sporadically, although in two cases they occupy a central position—Latzki in Weyssenhoff's *Hetmani* and Lancet in Gawalewicz's *Wir*. This classification according to type to a large extent derives from the paramount importance of ideological formulations as opposed to literary values. Paradoxically, the most complex figures are Jewish characters such as Latzki and, especially, his daughter Hela who appear in the most ideological works. This complexity, however, is superficial and is the result of the enormous narrative inconsistency in Weyssenhoff's novel caused by its ideological bias.

In conclusion, let us consider to what extent these ideologically influenced portrayals reflect the opinions of the writers in question. The elevated portrayals of the revolution and its Jewish participants that are presented by Niemojewski result from his PPS orientation at the time—a preference that was not tinged with antisemitism. Konopnicka displays a similar friendly attitude, one that was devoid of a party affiliation, toward the revolution and Jews. Choosing a Jew as the heroine in her short story, she continued the trend—insignificant numerically but vivid ideologically—of presenting Jews as co-citizens deserving respect.

Prus presents a more complicated case. His negative attitude toward the revolution as seen in *Dzieci* was a direct consequence of his antirevolutionary views that were clear in his journalism. He was a declared opponent of revolutionary terror. It is striking that he selects a Jew as a feverishly excited perpetrator overwhelmed with rage. Presumably, this was some kind of automatic reflex connected with the above-mentioned stereotype of the Jewish revolutionary as well as a typical tendency in Prus to merge factual events (in this case the bombing carried out by Boruch Szulman) into his fiction. One certainly cannot ascribe to Prus any antisemitic intentions, although the portrayal of Jews in *Dzieci* (there are some other Jewish characters in addition to Regen in the novel) is not unambiguous, which is typical of his later works. The attitude of Gawalewicz is likewise complex. He was an opponent of the revolution, which is reflected in his texts; yet his portrayal of Jewish characters is diversified and multidimensional, which could be explained by the fact that he was not a dyed-in-the-wool antisemite. In contrast, in the period under discussion, Weyssenhoff and Jeske-Choiński displayed in their works a clear antisemitic bias that was connected to the obvious aversion to the revolution typical of such conservatives. Weyssenhoff was, in addition, a declared supporter of the National Democratic Party. Now and again one can find direct parallels between antirevolutionary, antisemitic journalism of that time and literary depictions. For example, Weyssenhoff almost directly lifted the scene in which Jewish revolutionaries made Poles take off their caps in front of a red banner from the antisemitic journalism of Jeleński.[32]

It is worth noting that, despite the ideological motivation, in terms of propaganda, the portrayals in literature are less radical than those in journalistic essays. This difference is vividly seen in the case of Jeske-Choiński. His journalism, imbued with radical antisemitism, would lead one to assume that similar elements would appear in abundance in his antirevolutionary novel. Yet Jewish characters and themes are relatively few, and even those Jews he depicts in a negative way (e.g., Fajgenbaum) are not different, in principle, from their Polish, non-Jewish companions. It is striking that Jeske-Choiński himself, in his study *Żyd w powieści polskiej* (The Jew in Polish literature) envied Weyssenhoff's antisemitic zeal, writing that it was his novel that overcame the "narrow [. . .], (local) framework of our [Polish] Jewish novel."[33] According to Jeske-

Choiński, the type of Jews created by Weyssenhoff derived precisely from the revolution.[34]

In principle, literary portrayals reflect, although not always exactly, an author's political views or ideological motivation. In some cases, however, these views undergo revisions in the process of literary composition. This is probably the case with Andrzej Strug, a member of the Polish Socialist Party whose literary vision of the revolution was free of a propagandist bias. At this point, it is useful to focus on an insignificant Jewish subplot in the portrayal of the revolution by another outstanding writer, Władysław Stanisław Reymont.[35] His short story "Z konstytucyjnych dni" (From the constitutional days) (1905) contains a very heroic scene of the accidental death of an old Jew during a demonstration for freedom. Considering the strong antisemitic component in his earlier work, *Ziemia obiecana* (The promised land), one could conclude that the events of 1905, to a certain extent, influenced the reformulation of his point of view (however, one should keep in mind the dissimilarity of the described worlds—in one instance Jewish capitalistic exploiters, in the other, a demonstration).

It is also worth considering which authors do not deal at all with the role of the Jews in the revolution. Among the highly rated authors are Sienkiewicz[36] and Orzeszkowa.[37] Sienkiewicz, who devoted his novel *Wiry* (Whirls) as well as his short novel *We mgle* (In the fog) to the problems of the revolution, presenting issues from the conservative viewpoint, totally omitted Jewish themes—a tendency that was, in any case, characteristic of this author's writing as a whole. Yet the silence of Orzeszkowa is more surprising. This writer, who often discussed social problems in her works, did not produce any literary work about the revolution nor, as a consequence, any portrayal of a Jewish revolutionary. Orzeszkowa, called *żydolubka* (Jew-lover) by contemporaries unfavorably disposed toward her, did present, in her writing, portrayals of Jews attempting to change the world (the clearest example is Meir Ezofowicz). In the light of this evidence, the gap left by the neglect of 1905 is surprising.[38]

In sum, the portrayals of the Jews confronting the revolution conveyed to us by Polish literature are as diversified and ambiguous as were the attitudes of the Poles toward the actual revolution and toward the "Jewish Question," which was so intertwined with 1905.

Chapter 11

Rebellion in Writing: Yosef Haim Brenner and the 1905 Revolution

HANNAN HEVER

Brenner and the October Pogroms

The 1905 Revolution left a substantial impact on Hebrew and Yiddish literature, mainly in response to the wave of pogroms that followed in its wake. The pogroms of 1903 had provided authors with a yardstick for relating to the new atrocities; particularly fresh in their minds was Bialik's long poem *Be'ir haharegah* (In the city of slaughter), written after the Kishinev pogrom of 1903.

By that time, Yosef Haim Brenner had already earned a reputation as a Hebrew author of major importance. In 1903 he had published his great novel *Bahoref* (In the winter), an account of the experiences of a Jewish youth torn between the life of a modern maskil, his family, and the world of the shtetl. Brenner, helped by the Bund, had escaped Russia to avoid military service, settling in England. Arriving in London on April 2, 1904, Brenner was quickly caught up in a welter of political activity, becoming one of the two leaders of Poale Zion in London (together with Kalman Marmor).[1] He then worked for the anti-Zionist Social Democratic weekly *Di naye tsayt* but was at the same time active in the Socialist Revolutionary movement in London[2] and in a Yiddish-language edition of the party's journal.[3] Later, Brenner also worked on the anarchist journal *Di fraye arbayter velt*.[4]

All this variegated political and editorial activity was merely a backdrop for Brenner's Hebrew literary work. At this time, his literary output focused in particular on the life of Jewish immigrants in London's East End, against the background of the anti-Jewish pogroms during the period of the 1905 Revolution in Russia.

The 1905 Revolution was provoked by public unrest following a series of defeats suffered by Russia in the Russo-Japanese War and it gained momentum with the growing confidence of the revolutionary parties.

Tsar Nicholas II was consequently forced to issue the October Manifesto, which promised basic civil liberties. The very next day, on October 18, 1905, a wave of pogroms, incited in large measure by radical right-wing organizations loosely known as the Black Hundreds, inundated hundreds of Jewish communities.[5] "In the course of only twelve days, from October 18 to 29, pogroms took place in no less than 660 towns and villages. As some communities suffered repeated attacks, the number of pogroms at this time totaled 690, sowing considerable death and destruction. About one thousand Jews were killed and many thousands wounded. Damage was done to the property of more than 200,000 Jews, to the tune of some 63 million rubles."[6] In Belostok, from June 1 to 3, 1906, eighty Jews were murdered and many hundreds wounded; the Jewish delegates to the Duma placed responsibility for the pogrom on the police and the army.[7] Eight hundred Jews lost their lives in Odessa on October 18, 1905. Even before the October events, twenty-nine Jews were murdered in Zhitomir in late April 1905, one hundred in Kiev on July 29, and sixty in Belostok on August 1, 1905.

The Zionist movement, despite initial reluctance, eventually supported the revolution and in May 1905 joined the demand for constitutional change in Russia.[8] Simon Dubnov, however, in a series of articles titled "The Lessons of the Terrible Days" published in December 1905, rejected the view of the pogroms as merely counterrevolutionary, arguing that they were primarily a manifestation of the old brand of antisemitism. Criticizing Jews who had joined the revolutionary ranks under other national flags or to support the cause of internationalist class warfare, he dubbed their actions "slavery in the midst of revolution."[9] In response, Dubnov's opponents (such as S. An-sky) insisted that the pogroms had been organized by the authorities in order to "douse the revolutionary fire with Jewish blood"[10] and that the spotlight should be focused exclusively on the bloodstained guilt of the tsarist regime. Indeed,

to the great majority of the politically active youth, to the socialists of all kinds this [Dubnov's] basic thesis was utterly unacceptable. In late 1905 and the early months of 1906, the revolution absorbed their entire lives. For some it was social revolution, for others political; for some the internationalist theme was all-important; still others saw the revolution as primarily a national war, providing the Jews with a chance to defend their collective honor and to take revenge against the regime responsible for the pogroms and the endless humiliation.[11]

When news of the events of 1905 in Russia reached London, Brenner was shocked. He was particularly affected by the murder of Chaya Wolfson,[12] Brenner's model for the character of Yeva (Havah) Isakovna Blumin in his novel *Misaviv lanekudah* (Around the point). As told by

Shoshana Cohen (Narodnitzky), when Brenner "received news from Russia that his fiancée had been killed in the pogrom, he shut himself in his room, allowed no one near him, and when [Shoshana Cohen's] mother brought him food, he sent her away with it."[13]

Brenner gave direct expression to his mourning in a story, "Hu siper le'atzmo" (He told himself), published together with another story, "Beino leveino" (Between him and himself), in a special pamphlet titled *Lo-khlum* (Nothing).[14] In addition, Brenner wrote an article titled "Mikhtav arokh katav lah" (A long letter he wrote her), which Rabi Binyamin (Yehoshua Radler-Feldman) described as an immediate reaction to Chaya Wolfson's death:

> The profound sadness, the October pogroms touched Brenner directly. One of his relatives, I believe, was murdered then, "in those black days." And alas, that same Chava was also murdered then.[15] . . . He mourned her for weeks, months. . . . The personal pain burned and raged, raged and burned. But the public pain burned and raged no less. He drew up a large pamphlet, intended almost entirely for a few friends ("A Long Letter He Wrote Her").[16]

Brenner's Politics

In that article, "A Long Letter He Wrote Her," Brenner gave vent to his disillusionment with Zionism, socialism, and the very prospect of Jewish survival.[17] In general, Brenner's political biography is replete with upheavals and reversals. While still in Russia he had joined the Bund, whose members helped him to escape military service, but he later expressed greater sympathy for the Socialist Revolutionaries (SRs).[18] This change of viewpoint was probably motivated by Brenner's increasing alienation from the Bund's dogmatic Marxism and cosmopolitanism, as against the moderate internationalism of the SRs and their more humane socialism.[19] In later years, Brenner would write admiringly of Grigorii Gershuni, a key figure in the terrorist organization of the SR party and a Jew who saw the policy of selective political assassination as justified, among other things, by the pogrom policies of the tsarist regime.[20]

Brenner's politics during his London period were fraught with contradictions. On the one hand, he worked for the anti-Zionist *Di naye tsayt* and translated articles for that journal; on the other, he was then writing his novel *Misaviv lanekudah* and was unswervingly loyal to Hebrew and to Hebrew literature.[21] In fact, at the time, Brenner seemed to be systematically opposed to any political platform. For example, he attacked the territorialists, who had seceded from the Zionist movement at the Seventh Congress in Basel (July 1905). During June and July 1905, Brenner published an antiterritorialist pamphlet in Yiddish, which was essentially a reworked version of Jabotinsky's articles: *Far vos vilen mir dafke Eretz-Yisroel un nisht a teritoriye in der velt arayn.* In addition, he was opposed to the Helsingfors Congress, mainly, it would seem, because of the resolution endorsing "the participation of the Zionists in the liberation movement of the territorial nations in the Russian state."[22]

In his article "Klayne felyeton," while attacking territorialism, Brenner deplored the interpretation of the pogroms as a counterrevolutionary reaction by the authorities, rather than antisemitism pure and simple. Reviewing the journal *Das naye leben* published by Poale Zion, he bitterly rejected the view of the pogroms as instigated solely by reactionary, counterrevolutionary circles. This view, he wrote, was based on the misconception "that everything that happens to the proletariat will also happen to our proletariat; that the cause of our emigration is the cause of the emigration of all the proletarian masses: the development of capital; that the slaughter of our babes and the rape of our sisters are nothing but transient counterrevolution."[23]

Brenner essentially persisted in his opposition to the Jewish intelligentsia, which supported the revolution as a protest against the government's adoption of antisemitism as an official policy. The intelligentsia's position was reinforced by the authorities' protection of the pogromists, on the one hand, and by the role of the socialists—including non-Jews—in the organization of self-defense, on the other. As Jonathan Frankel has written, the pogroms that broke out immediately after the publication of the October Manifesto undermined the Jews' confidence in the revolution. Nevertheless, the anti-Jewish violence also strengthened the revolutionary resolve of many in the opposition.[24]

Hame'orer

In the first eight issues of *Hame'orer* (volume 1, 1906), Brenner published a long story, "From A. to M." An account of its hero's imprisonment for revolutionary activity (he was arrested while reading a journal called *Revolutionary Russia*),[25] the story is actually a long, convoluted journey into the innermost workings of Russian society at the turn of the century. As such, it signaled the emergence of what Yitzhak Bakon has rightly termed "a new Brenner." In the view of Rabi Binyamin, the transformation was the result of "the October disturbances," which, he writes, "laid bare the basics of human existence."[26] Brenner describes Russian society in all its ugliness and brutality, including, in particular, its hatred of Jews. He thus highlights his view of the pogroms and his utter rejection of the argument that they were initiated exclusively by the government.

The hero also expresses his detachment from politics:

Vanity, vanity of vanities, shameful and disgusting things, evil and grotesque things, filthy nonsense, any contact or dealing with which is an ineradicable disgrace—such seemed to me then all those "political movements" to which I had formerly devoted my life. What use are they? what good? What are they good for with their falsehoods, deception, and inner contradictions? What good are they with their weakness, their triviality, their futile sacrifices?[27]

He concludes that "only one alternative is left for the multitude of people who are not animals, who were born with all their faults, and do not wish to gorge on moldy sausages: to assemble in the desert, to embrace one another and slaughter one another, with the sharpest of knives [literally: with knives used by ritual slaughterers]."[28] Whatever is political is meaningless, and murder is the only possible existential conclusion.

The narrator is speaking as a person despairing of life and poised to commit suicide.[29] The pogroms, as they impact upon the story, are indeed a fait accompli, beyond politics. His fellow prisoners, mainly common criminals, found great pleasure in recounting "stories about 'plundering the Jews'. . . . They almost never uttered the word 'pogrom.' Simply—looting, murdering, with nobody to resist you."[30]

The ground is thus well prepared for a mocking representation of Jewish revolutionaries in the story. For example, Kaber the "theoretician" interrupts

his "practical" comrade and, in a loud, hurried-hurried voice, tongue clucking and clicking at breakneck speed, preaches the avant-garde position that the Jewish workers should—and do—occupy in the movement; about the new, revolutionary element, the new and revolutionary chapter in Jewish history, from the time a proletarian party was established among them; and about their nationalism, that of the Jews, who must be very, very careful about that, lest it be considered—God forbid!—a self-sufficient entity, a faulty, reactionary opinion; that is to say, when they no longer consider it *national* and it becomes *nationalistic*.[31]

Elsewhere, Brenner scoffs at Poale Zion, whose Zionist consciousness was "weak even for them," and "all their efforts were wasted merely on showing and proving to their opponents that they, too, Poale Zion, despite their, indeed, being workers of Zion, were nevertheless not regressing, they were not bourgeois!" Or: "The spiritual ancestors of today's Zionist Socialists, most of whom were imprisoned here for the crime of defending themselves, were members of their nation, a nation of weak nerves, whose remnant is gradually dying off and has practically nothing left but discussion."[32]

That same Kaber believed—a belief that Brenner deplored—in the cooperation of Jewish and Russian revolutionaries: "For now, 'all the pogroms in the world' will not revive Zionism; to confront the pogroms, the Jewish proletariat will stand and fight, shoulder to shoulder with its Christian brothers, at the head of the camp, leading the way for everyone!"[33]

How did Brenner react to this situation, having lost hope in any clear-cut political program and statement? After the 1905 pogroms, the Jewish press of Eastern Europe seemed to have been struck dumb.[34] This was why Brenner founded *Hame'orer* in London, as a voice in the wilderness, uncommitted to any single political position; he himself explained that the paper had been founded as a direct reaction to the pogroms of the 1905 Revolution:[35]

It is in these unparalleled days of anguish, anguish without and within, anguish occasioned by death and bewilderment, that *Hame'orer* is being published. It was founded immediately after the October days of last year and has continued to appear through the days of Belostok and Siedlce, of wicked stupidity, indifference, self-deprecation, and putrefaction at home. And it will defend its existence and its continued existence. While everyone is busy promising complete salvation to the world, the masses, the proletarians, it guarantees nothing, does not address its message to thousands, does not predict comfort in the future, offering no hope for redemption.[36]

Describing the Brenner of the post-October days, Yitzhak Bakon discerns a sharp turn toward what he terms "a sublime pessimism" and a "romantic-mystical attachment to the language of the Prophets."[37] *Hame'orer* saw the light of day at a time when Hebrew literature was in sharp decline. Joseph Klausner wrote that he was publishing in Russian because he had nowhere to publish and because Hebrew was being supplanted by Yiddish.[38] Or, as Brenner put it in 1906: "Who understands Hebrew? For what purpose and for whom is Hebrew being written? Can one possibly write properly in a dead language? The people read a jargon [= Yiddish]. . . . In any case, the Hebrew reader can also read Yiddish. . . . And the year passes. Two more years pass. In any event, there is nowhere to print something new in Hebrew. All the publishing houses have died off."[39]

The lonely voice of *Hame'orer* had its source in the desire not only to preserve the dying flame of Hebrew literature but also to challenge any other settled ideology. Brenner rejects any official political solution to the Jewish problem—a fixed location for a Jewish homeland; a state; the ingathering of the exiles; Bundism; the British East Africa (Uganda) proposal or territorialism ("Zangwill's territorialism is not the opposite of the Zionist consciousness of Herzl, the breath of our life").[40] Even when he speaks approvingly of finding a territory for the Jews, he does so from a position opposed to any institutional brand of territorialism.[41]

Bakon attributes this negative attitude to Brenner's association at the time with the anarchists, whose journal *Di fraye arbeter velt* he was helping to edit.[42] More likely, however, his stance stemmed from a far broader position of rejecting any solution, of refusing "to make false promises."[43]

"To Cast Off the Falsehood of Programs of All Kinds"

Brenner's objections to the way in which the political establishment interpreted the pogroms of 1905 were rooted in his general refusal to adopt any specific position in the Jewish political arena. Rebelling against Jewish political discourse, he sought to distance himself from it. Thus, in a letter to A. Tziyoni, he rejects an article submitted by the latter to *Hame'orer*, telling him, "I cannot possibly print it! The attack on our revolutionaries, which you have articulated time and time again, in this very style, and when?—while the dead are still falling from the wall. . . . And now the view of the Helsingfors Conference that lacks any overall vantage point that might grasp the whole [comical] catastrophe."[44]

In a letter sent at the time to Joseph Klausner (March 25, 1907), he writes: "I wrote a terrible article for issue 3 [of *Hame'orer*] and omitted it. I must not speak of current affairs—I, a person who sees not even a hint of hope. Within a year I shall go to Palestine, but not as a believing, hoping Zionist, rather as a person pining for the sun. I want to work there as a farm laborer."[45] A few months later he writes Rabi Binyamin (in Yiddish): "Once again, I am not going to Eretz Israel; I hate the chosen people and I hate the dead land, the so-called 'Land of Israel.' Ough! [. . .] I hope to flee, at long last, from the Hebrew world and the literary world in general. I hope to bury myself in some hidden corner of London, to work in a school and hold my tongue."[46]

In his article "Pinkas katan" (A little notebook), he writes: "The life of wounded dogs, yes. . . . But if so, why speak any more of the Jewish people in our time? No to pogroms; yes, yes to emancipation. . . . But why speak any more of national rights and cultural autonomies? Why should we continue to deceive ourselves?"[47] And he goes on, in reply to a letter that he had recently received: "You ask me, 'Why do I hate Marxism, why do I hate socialism?' Here is my answer to you: 'I do not hate Marxism, I do not hate socialism. I am quite cold toward them; what I do hate—as one hates snakes—is the Marx of the Jewish ghetto, the socialism on "the Jewish street." It is a socialism that has no battleground; no workers to fight; no hold whatsoever on reality; it is the socialism of self-satisfied people who lack sensitivity, of bourgeois scholastics.'"[48]

And again:

But, alas, has the time not come to realize that this present trouble is an eternal trouble, that this present trouble has not ceased and will never cease; that it can never cease; that pogroms, albeit not necessarily of such a mass and organized character, are not a passing phenomenon at all; that antisemitism is not something that one can dismiss by merely protesting and calling out "Shame!"; that the hatred for us and the punishment inflicted upon us are normal, unchanging sights? In certain circles jeers are commonly heard against what they call the *"Pogrom-Zionisten!"*; but those who mock do not understand that the entire history of our nation is nothing but one long pogrom, that all the nations who despise us—and rightly so!—repeatedly try to destroy us. . . . And we take flight and go into exile from one place to another.[49]

Brenner expressed similar ideas in his article "A klayner felyeton," published in the anarchist organ *Di fraye arbayter velt* (December 8, 1905) and in an unpublished essay titled "The Jewish Press in London," published by Bakon in Hebrew translation:

Here something must be said that is relevant to each one (of the newspapers) separately, but the wound is still fresh and sensitive to the touch. I am writing for an anarchist paper. Most of my readers will not agree with me; but, nevertheless, I would like to convey the impression that the recent events made upon me. Knowing perfectly well what a government is in general, and the Russian government in particular, nevertheless, I can't listen to all those platitudinous phrases that it isn't a pogrom at all, just the government's counterrevolution; that it's an attack by the police and hired "hooligans" on Jews, students, etc. This formula, "Jews, students, etc." is so idiotic, so vulgar! Are the students a separate population, a different race? Students have been beaten and arrested in the street for their revolutionary views; but the Jews with their dancing and prancing had nails hammered into their heads in their homes, for saying Psalms. [. . .] Such actions are part of the chaotic situation in Russia, but they are, nonetheless, uniquely Jewish calamities, that is to say, suffering inflicted only upon us, the Jews. I believe that as free people we should have cast off the falsehood of programs of all kinds. The truth of life must take precedence over everything else. All the Jews are being killed. All the Jews are threatened with death, whether they are students or devout *kloiznikes* [students in a beit midrash].[50]

Given these sentiments, what, then, was Brenner's positive message? What we hear in these passages is an extreme, radical version of the affirmation of humanity, of human existence per se, coupled with the negation of any "established" social or political program. The only thing Brenner holds sacred is the human individual, untrammeled by any ideology, as he writes in "Pinkas katan":

We, the surviving Hebrew authors, should not be impressed by them in any way, not even by their medals and titles: "Progressive authors" and "Revolutionary literature." We rebel with all our might against all the governments marked by ugliness and malignity, against all domination of life by the satiated and the base, but not in the name of rebellion for its own sake. We have one principle, namely, the sanctification of man in all its manifestations, the fullness of his existence, the wealth of his soul. Here lies the root, moreover, of our Zionist awareness, Zionism pure and simple, without any treatises on—or worship of—the march of Progress; here lies the root of our negative attitude to the Ussishkins and the other leaders of present-day Zionism; it is this distinction that also governs our approach to all the new, high-sounding conceptions.[51]

Brenner had already formulated his negative view of the Zionist response to the 1903 Kishinev pogrom in his novel *Misaviv lanekudah* (1904). He was probably responding here to a manifesto that had been published over the signatures of Aḥad Ha'am, Abramovitch (Mendele Moykher Seforim), Ben-Ami, and Bialik, deploring Jewish cowardice and calling on the Jews to take up their own self-defense. Brenner was apparently pained, in particular, by Bialik's long poem *Be'ir haharegah*, in which the poet deplored the victims' helplessness and failure to retaliate. Brenner's was one of the few voices that criticized Bialik's position; he questioned anyone's right to judge the victims. In one scene— perhaps the climax of the novel *Misaviv lanekudah*—he describes an argument between Ya'akov Abramson and several onlookers in reaction to the arrival of Eva Isakovna with news of the pogrom in Kishinev:

"Pogroms?"—Abramson stared at her and his voice was like an echo.
"You have also heard the news?"
"I? No. I know vaguely. After all, I am living here all the time. I haven't heard, I know vaguely."
All heads turned toward him. The room fell absolutely silent. Everyone felt they had to ask for details. To express sympathy . . .
"God, how terrible it is!" cried Rosalia Maksimovna at last.
"And the Jews went like lambs to the slaughter?" asked Samuel. "They didn't defend themselves?"
"Now the Zionists will make use of what's happened," added Haverstein. "They'll call meetings, produce colorful descriptions, bewail the blood, and claim it as proof of how the non-Jews hate us . . ."
"And they'll start a hue and cry: 'To the Holy Land!'" concluded Frankel.
"It's embarrassing to speak of such things in the presence of Grigorii Nikolaevich," whispered Zinaida Maksimovna, first to Rosalia Maksimovna and then also to Eva Isakovna.
Grigorii Nikolaevich said nothing for a while, and then broke out, "Agitation, propaganda, the party, popular education, the *Lumpenproleteriat* . . ."
"Shut up!" shouted Abramson suddenly, hitting his head with his fist, "Stop for a moment, you vile chatterers! That Mr. Haverstein, . . . he . . . dares . . . at such a terrible time . . . his calculations . . . his work . . . his loss of work . . .
All eyes were filled with fear and surprise.
"But Abramson, you be the judge . . ."
"Judge?"—with a furious glance at *her* too, "Judge?! Who am I to judge? I don't want to judge! I don't want to speak! A curse upon me! . . . A curse upon you! . . ."[52]

Brenner rejects any attempt at judgment. While he does object to the vilification of Zionism, his position is based on an opposition to any condemnation of the victims as expressed by Bialik in his poem.

Writing Instead of Speech

Brenner's was a radical, almost unconstrained, position that strongly influenced the patterns of his literary writing in reaction to the pogroms. Underlying his writing is a mood of consistent negation, challenging the very use of literary speech as a suitable medium for relating to the mass violence. Brenner is effectively rejecting any possibility of Jewish political activity and is thereby challenging the very possibility of Jewish national discourse. In so doing, he is rebelling against the wealth of political options then available in the Russian Jewish world. He rejects them all as worthless alternatives, thus casting grave doubt on the possibility of establishing a modern political Jewish subjectivity.

Nevertheless, Brenner had no intention of rejecting literary creation per se. He continued to write literature, in fact, at a great pace. Throughout, however, he was radically confining his literary output to its most essential basis, namely, the act of writing as such. But while doing so, he emphatically rejected the idea of literature as an imitation of human speech. In the passage quoted above from *Misaviv lanekudah,* Abramson exclaims, "I don't want to speak!" After the pogroms of 1905, this position became more comprehensive and consistent in all Brenner's works.

Brenner's main concern in this group of works, of which the most important was his play *Me'ever lagevulin* (Beyond the limits), is the issue of the Jewish response to the pogroms and other anti-Jewish actions during the revolution. This question takes on a variety of guises, but the main problem is whether it is even possible to respond, to say something and write something when confronted with such horror. Concrete political questions—how to relate to the revolution—give way to questions involving the very representation of the horror. In this respect Brenner evolved a very complex position. He argues, in effect, that nothing can be said about the pogroms. On the one hand, no spoken words can encompass the terror and the pain. The death of his friend Chaya Wolfson in the pogroms only intensified the feeling of impotence that imbues his writing.

On the other hand, Brenner proposes an alternative. Instead of speaking, he says, let us write. Writing itself is a suitable response to the horror. Such horror cannot be described without developing expressive means to portray the terrible "otherness" of the pogrom. Speech falls short of this task because it is self-contained. Speech falls short because it presents the option of expressing itself in the name of and for the sake of the group, formulating collectively held positions, in this case—nationalism. Gayatry Spivak has distinguished between "to speak for" and "to speak of."[53] One might say, accordingly, that Brenner was caught on the horns of a dilemma in the attempt to speak for the victims of the pogroms. "Is this description of the spoken word," asks Edith Wyschogrod, "not also a condemnation of the monological character of speech? Does the living voice not place the world at the self's disposal rather than the self at the disposal of the other?"[54] Speech is opaque, full of itself. Writing, in contrast, crumbles, takes things apart, and does not revolve around a center.

Writing, or speaking to oneself, covers a broad spectrum of interpretative and implicative possibilities, possibilities not available in the second-person mode of face-to-face speech, which conveys a living, immediate and therefore clear-cut, unambiguous meaning. This was precisely the perspective from which Brenner examined the revolution, and the difference became even sharper when he tried to cope with the question of how to refer to the pogroms, the slaughter of Jews during the revolution. The title of the text that he wrote upon receiving the news that Chaya Wolfson had been murdered—"Hu siper le'atzmo" (He told himself)—thus betrays in its solipsism the limits of human communication in reaction to the atrocities that had taken place during the revolution. Here, too, speech acquires an obvious moral significance:

However, in one of those many, many hours, many and fleeting, fleeting, in an hour of that curious-normal headlong rush, in which, when you think of it, you lose your bearings, which became utterly confused and rushed along with it [that hour]—it was then that the healthy man stood, in the center of his room, and told himself things.

And it was not silent in the room, for surely it was filled with the clash of wheels, the noise of the city, clamor and talk, business talk . . .

But there was nobody in the room but he. And his eyes did not change color because of a stranger's look. And no human eye desecrated the expression on his face at that hour.[55]

The ability to speak of the disaster is confined to a situation of loneliness. Then, says Brenner, when no stranger is looking, the expression on the face of the person speaking to himself will not be defiled.

But what is the substitute for interhuman communication in speech? Brenner insists that the solution lies in writing. As Jacques Derrida has argued, Western, logocentric culture prefers speech to writing. However, contends Derrida, writing is prior to speech and encompasses a broader range of possibilities. Writing is capable of providing a great variety and breadth of implicative possibilities that undermine the seemingly stable meaning of speech. It enables the lost voices and the excluded possibilities to be heard, or, better, to be written.[56]

As far as Hebrew was concerned, Brenner rejected Hebrew speech and preferred writing: "It was not only that during his London period, Brenner was never enthusiastic about the ideas of the 'Hebrew speakers'; he, in fact, treated them with scorn and belittled their efforts. Marmor describes Brenner's clear distinction between Hebrew writing, of which he was a sworn advocate, and Hebrew speech, to which he never committed himself."[57] Brenner, as Marmor related, was utterly opposed to speaking in Hebrew to Jews whose mother tongue was Yiddish.[58] Moreover, the absolute writtenness of Hebrew is clearly implied by the fact that "Hebrew writing does not come easily to him, although its sources, notably the Bible, the Mishnah, the Midrashim and, in particular, Mendele were more than familiar to him. Nevertheless, he has first to think everything out in Yiddish and only then does he work hard to decide how to transplant one concept or another into a Hebrew word that will express his intentions."[59]

Writing, for Brenner, makes it possible to express what is inexpressible in speech, or what speech, committing a moral offense, silences. Describing the face of a person speaking to himself, he writes: "However, no one said anything to it, no one examined it or looked at it. It implied a desire to grasp something that could not be grasped. It implied everything together, everything and then something that had never been there."[60] Therefore, since the face "implied a desire to grasp something that could not be grasped," he glances aside and immediately realizes the proper means of expression—written letters: "Only those letters, in Russian, were lying on the table, a large bundle; and he stood in the middle of the room—it was astonishing!—and began talking to himself."[61]

This writtenness is the key to holiness. The written text ultimately becomes a fetish, to be worshiped; hence writing, as a response to the horrific disaster, is, in a way, an act of sanctification and purification. As Brenner wrote in a previously cited passage, "We have one principle, namely, the sanctification of man in all its manifestations, the fullness of his existence, the wealth of his soul."[62] This is also the gist of his philosophy as reflected in Rabi Binyamin's eulogy (Brenner was murdered in 1921 in Jaffa), which described Brenner's reaction to the events of October, his inability to utter a spoken word:

Do you recall, my dear Brenner, the October pogroms in our London days? When the news came of the murder of your dear friend? Silently you struggled, day and night, day and night, unable to utter a word. "Thus saith the Lord: Set thy house in order, for thou shalt die and not live." Always, my dear Brenner, you always heard this absolute imperative, you ever struggled with it and always, constantly, prepared for it; and now, here it is, awful and tremendous, just as it had to come! What a harmonious end! What a beautiful death! What martyrdom! What a sacrifice of being! What purity![63]

Brenner's despair in the face of various political nationalist formulae ultimately channels itself into theology. Indeed, when Brenner describes the woman in "He Told Himself," and, mourning her death, reveals so cruelly that he had not been in love with her, he calls her "a high-school student who chronicles her soul, her innermost thoughts, who commits all her warmth, all her sanctity, to white paper, ending with a plea to be forgiven for her chatter."[64] Writing enables her to express her most intimate, ephemeral notions, her struggle to find expression for her thoughts, and becomes a kind of holiness. He thus quotes what she wrote to him:

Oh, how many important things I have to tell you, Benjamin! But first, I beseech you to let me hear your voice, at least once, properly. So write soon, quickly, not a few words but much more! I'm waiting for . . .—well, how shall I say it—for a revelation of the soul! I would like to know the reasons: Why this lack of faith? Why such apathy? Surely it is painful, terribly painful, that people like you should be living like that! After all, one can find something proper and sublime in life! Oh, the sorrow of it all! Why is there no word for this in my language? I haven't the slightest idea how to state what I want explicitly. . . . You mustn't, mustn't live like that! That's what I believe, but perhaps I'm wrong! Possibly. No![65]

In fact, much of what Brenner "tells himself" is a reconstruction of his correspondence with Chaya Wolfson. At any rate, that is the case until he sees the name of her town in a list, probably the location of the pogrom, and "then you sat down and wrote her . . . But she no longer answers."[66] Correspondence is the correct, true channel of communication, through which he can reconstruct her ties to him and mourn her loss. When she died, Brenner asserts, relying on the written communication, she had his image in her mind: "And when the ax was raised over her head, over her will, over her ambitions, over her hopes, over everything, and her future became clear; and when her terrified eyes opened, never again to be opened—your name was in them!"[67]

His name was in her eyes—not in her memory, her consciousness, but, literally, in her eyes, a kind of material inscription, like an act of writing. Writing, writing the story, was the only mechanism through which Brenner could experience and reconstruct the horror of the 1905 Revolution. Instead of speaking, he says, one should write. Writing itself is the appropriate response to the horror. As opposed to constructing a homogeneous story, the act of writing deconstructs the narrative into different, contradictory possibilities and so does not impose itself on the story of the other, whose fate the narrator is mourning. This is particularly true because Brenner considered the act of writing in Hebrew in a heroic light; it was the determined stand of "those who remain last on the wall," of those who at this turn-of-the-century juncture were preserving the embers of Hebrew culture and literature—just when Hebrew creativity was in broad retreat and the hope to create a national home for the Jews in their land was fading.

"Hu amar lah" (He told her)

"He Told Her" was first published as a pamphlet in London in 1905. "In one of his papers, B. notes, 'Written on the day after the pogrom that took place at Zhitomir.'"[68] Brenner repeated this information in a letter to Kalman Marmor (March 22, 1906), in which he discussed the publication of a Yiddish translation of the story in the *Yidisher kemfer.*[69] Publication of the story "was a kind of symbolic expression of a certain crisis in Brenner's life that took the form of abstention from any party activity, humanist-Jewish introspection, and—the main point in the crisis, as mentioned previously—disappointment in the labor movements (both Russian and Jewish) because of their attitude to the pogroms."[70]

The story essentially represents a son's appeal to his mother before embarking on a campaign of revenge for his fellow Jews slain in the pogroms. He pleads with her not to hold him back for several reasons—in particular, he invokes the image of his cowardly father, who had been murdered by peasants. He recounts the never-ending chain of pogroms, including the massacres of 1648–49 Underlying everything he tells her, however, at both the beginning and the end of the story, are written texts. He begins with Solomon ibn Verga's *Shevet Yehudah,* from which she used to read to him, and which he designates as one of the reasons for his present behavior. Above all, he refers to the book of Psalms that his father had left at home before leaving, never again to return.

This adherence to the written text is attributed to the influence of a local rabbi, who ruled that Jews fearful of murderers should recite the ten chapters of Psalms "from 'Happy is the man that walked not . . .' to '. . . so that he shall no longer be terrified of an earthly mortal.'"[71] Only later does it become clear that the narrator is referring in particular to the end of Psalm 10, the last words of the Psalms recited on the first day of the month (chapters 1–10), including a whole verse of which Brenner cites only the end. The entire verse is, "To champion the orphan and the downtrodden, so that he shall no longer be terrified of an earthly mortal" (Psalm 10:18), which implies that the speaker's being an orphan is his motive for revenge.

Brenner presents a basis for the son's vengeful reaction in both the Jewish tradition and in the family's fate. But even more important is his designation of the printed word as something stronger than speech. For his father, oral recitation derived its authority from the printed text: "He knew all of Psalms by heart; but nevertheless, when he was reciting those

Psalms, he used to hold the book of Psalms in his hands and recite them directly from there." This was the bond between him and his father, but it was also what separated them: "Mother! Some twenty-five years have passed since those days,[72] the time when—a few years before he fell in the village—my still living father hid in this corner, his terror-widened eyes turned upwards, the bundles ready around him, the familiar verses hovering in the watching and waiting air, and in his trembling hands— that *Tehilim* [book of Psalms] with those *Ma'amadot*, as a good-luck charm."[73]

It was the familiar verses hovering in the air (without a written text)— precisely *because* they were known by heart—that made his father such an easy prey for the murderers. He himself, the son, no longer recited Psalms. He had abandoned his ancestral faith. But his ambiguous attitude to that faith—his rejection of cowardice and his affirmation of a commitment to heritage and nation—finally obliged him to rely on that same book of Psalms: "Let me be, I'm going. Accursed be he who says, 'Hide!' All I shall hide is this book of Psalms. Let it arouse wrath and let it recall the evil to Ivan's sons, to future generations."[74]

"Beino leveino" (Between him and himself)

The hero of Brenner's story "Between Him and Himself"[75] is Kitin, a Russian emigrant, who speaks only Russian and is struggling to make ends meet in London. As an emigrant, he is a member of a political association that reacts to the 1905 Revolution. "At any rate, Kitin opened books, did his job, was even a member of 'The Association for Aid to Political Emigrants,' and would sometimes go himself to see Amalia Ivanovna, an old maid with a veil over her face, and talk to her about the public lesson on their previous day of rest [Sunday] and about the new radical paper and the new reforms."[76] All this political activity relating to the 1905 Revolution and the period of the reforms—probably of October—is contrasted with his suicidal inclinations. At that point, though, Brenner writes immediately, "and that thing was postponed."[77]

The contrast, however, is then developed and practically reversed. Kitin constantly returns to his plans for suicide, torn between the choice of whether to drown or gas himself. Then he thinks of the name of a journal that Maxim Gorky had edited, *Znanie* (Knowledge), and of the name of a novel by Gorky, *Man*, but feels them to be "so far away."[78] Letting his thoughts wander, he recalls: "It was autumn outside. Today, standing on the steps leading to the reading-room on the third floor, there was a lot of mud. And there that person saw him. That person had a sharp, acrid tongue. He spoke in special accents, exaggerated, despicable. Gorky would surely have approved of them. He describes his poverty in bright, full, garish colors."[79]

In mid-November 1906 Brenner wrote Rabi Binyamin about *Man*: "I am puzzled by your decision to send me Gorky's *Man*; it is so trivial and ugly. Perhaps it makes a better impression in German. No, stop that! Leave Gorky to me!"[80] Brenner thought the book to be pathetic and superficial,[81] and it is therefore significant that he portrayed Gorky as the antithesis of Kitin's death wish.

But a new element now came into play—speech, verbal expression. Kitin sees in fluent speech something despicable and exaggerated. These verbal expressions that "Gorky would surely have approved of" were to be kept at a distance. Kitin, in his intense desire to die, prefers to remain silent or to speak in nonfluent tones. The revolution is seen as a factor that works against suicide, but its hopes are to be loathed. The revolution belongs to a false world, far removed from the individual's personal distress. He views society around him through the eyes of a silent observer, eager to appear in public only as a dead person, incapable of speaking. Hence, for example, he believes that if he had drowned himself, as he had planned, he would have had to leave a letter, that is, to write, "But now, surely, everyone will see, everyone will see him face to face."[82] Finally, he decides to address the letter to himself, so that "if he is no longer there, it will lie there until someone opens it and everything is known."[83] He cuts himself off from the world, regarding the world of the revolution as something beyond the pale, in fact, as a moral offense:

Only if Amalia Ivanovna decides to go to see him, Kitin, in his room, and to talk to him about what's happening in Russia—No! That's already forbidden, that may no longer be, that is no longer permissible, it's already immoral. . . .
    Animals! A barrier between him and them. A painful barrier. And the river, . . . the river will not remove the barrier; but the river will remove the pain, the pain.[84]

The revolution is speech. And speech is a moral offense because it violates the solitude of a person who is tired of living. Kitin is apparently a Russian, not a Jew; Brenner opposes the revolution (which had not completely subsided at the time described in the story) on a universal basis that, through the prism of the individual, cuts through to the foundations of the collective representation. Speech, verbal representation, is an act involving responsibility and moral sin.

Mikhtav arokh katav lah (A long letter he wrote her)

A Long Letter He Wrote Her was the title of a special pamphlet, subtitled "And in the letter, the following was written." At the top of the title page was the byline "Prepared for the press by Y. H. Brenner." The pamphlet was printed at the Narodnitzky Press, London, 1906. A list in Brenner's literary estate contains the note "Written after the granting of the constitution in Russia" (October 1905), but it was clearly completed at a time when news of the pogroms had reached London.[85] The article begins as follows:

And in the letter, the following was written:
    It is not a letter of greeting but a writ of confession that I would like to send you, brother.
    For you see, dear brother, even if I have nothing to say, if, indeed, every word that I put on paper at this moment slashes my heart; if, indeed, every syllable that I produce at this time tears me apart—at this time, brother, at this very time, the lives of my brethren, my people, are being taken, with indescribable pain—if indeed I really feel now, every single instant, the burden of sin in every deed, in every move that is not intended to save—despite all this, I say, my brother and partner, let me tell you what is in my heart, let me pour out my speech before you, let me talk. . . . So that I may rot in my sorrow, so that I shall never, never know relief.[86]

The speaker of the text includes reflexive references to the text itself, as a written text: "In brief, my brother, I see from the increasingly confused course of my discourse (because of which, perhaps, I seem to you to be merely copying a newspaper article!) that I cannot describe all these things as they are, as they are in reality."[87] The writtenness of the text derives directly from its political stand. In his ultimate grief, from which "I shall never, never find relief," Brenner creates an inconsolable text, expressing the lack of any institutional solution immersed in the political reality of his time. In contrast to the presenting of speech as expressive of something that exists, of a subject replete with meanings, Brenner imposes upon his text a dynamics of writtenness, which precedes speech and makes it possible.

In the article he describes a meeting he had with a territorialist "who, while I was talking to him, uttered a few confident sentences about history driving the Jewish proletariat of Russia to the realization of territorialism. And I, naturally, was furious: 'Why Russia, of all places?!' And I yelled my heart out: 'What kind of drive?! The realization of Zionism is conditional: If there are no pioneers among us, we are lost.' "[88] National redemption is thus reduced to a few elite pioneers, untrammeled by any ideology, whose very actions demonstrate the bankruptcy of any such ideology. Brenner's analysis reduces Zionism to its starting point, to a situation in which "No, Zionism has not died—it simply never existed in the way that we imagined it."[89]

Writing is a kind of death wish whereas speech, on the contrary, breathes life. Writing is a yearning for a holy death, theology becoming a substitute for the national politics of which Rabi Binyamin spoke in his eulogy for Brenner.[90] Nevertheless, the objective is not to die finally and absolutely but to yearn for death, to come as near to it as possible. This is precisely the significance of the written text as prior to speech—*it precedes the realization of communication, but the latter is nevertheless conditioned by it.* To speak from death is to speak without hope, to undermine the prospect of speaking about reality from a perspective of promise. From this vantage point, history is what Walter Benjamin, referring to allegory, called a process of decline and perpetual disintegration, not a hopeful progression toward salvation.[91] Brenner speaks from a place of death, which precludes the possibility of speaking representatively about the pogroms from any collective national stance. The view from this position of destruction and loss does not allow one to speak in a positive national voice. Loss, after all, stands in opposition to national speech; for national speech tells a teleological story, a story with a message of purpose.

Jacques Derrida, in his eulogy for Roland Barthes, insisted that his speech could never reach Barthes;[92] but in his eulogy for Sara Kaufmann, he wrote, echoing her comments on Rembrandt's *The Anatomy Lesson* and the substitution of a written corpus for the corpse: "The book [*lui*—masculine pronoun—*Trans.*] stands up to, and stands in for, the body: a *corpse* replaced by a corpus, a *corpse* yielding its place to the bookish thing, the doctors having eyes only for the book paper, as if by reading, by observing the signs on the drawn sheet of paper, they were trying to forget, repress, deny, or conjure away death—and the anxiety before death."[93]

Hence this absolute reduction of the possibilities of hope yields the impossibility of second-person, communicative speech as a privileged moment of interpersonal communication. It is the lowest possible point of despair in national speech: "What have we to do with the ancestral land, with the beautiful land, to which no path leads? What good is our past if the past is nonexistent, if we have neither past nor future, only present upon present—the middle ages?! It is a cave that we seek, a cave for the fugitive. . . . Let us have a cave and we shall hide in it."[94]

Brenner then goes on to address his correspondent, who is puzzled why he "is sitting and writing such letters, and in the holy tongue." His answer, as we might expect, expresses deep despair: "If only there were in my heart the slightest shadow, the smallest fraction, of hope." His formulation of the answer pits the metaphor of writing in the holy tongue against the metaphor of speech: "Were it not *inscribed in fire on the tablet of my heart*: 'They shall perish among the nations and die there,' I would indeed not waste any effort, not one single thing of all I possess. For I would devote the clothes on my body to construction; naked and barefoot, I would roam the streets and *shout out loud*: 'You, the surviving remnant, give yourselves no rest! To the wilderness!'" The text concludes with his reasons for writing: "For I know not, know not how to do anything else."[95]

Clearly, therefore, Brenner rejects all the routine interpretations of the pogroms. They were not, he writes, engineered by the Russian government—this would acquit the Russian people of responsibility. The pogroms were due, on the contrary, to a profound hatred for the Jews; they were not a result of any particular social configuration. Essentially, he rejects the very attempt to explain them:

Like the people, like its rulers. Cruel, brutal, throughout its history, ignorant, it trampled corpses all through its past and has always been the most abject slave. Harsh slavery, harsh ignorance, harsh servility.

And now those stunted, cunning impudent people [the Jews], who crawl, who are hated and despised, are emerging to rebel, to cut through the living, dry, congealed flesh, to heat up the wound and tear the skin—shall they not be slaughtered for this?

But even without this they shall be slaughtered. Whether old or young—they shall be slaughtered! Why should they not be slaughtered if no one demands vengeance for their blood, if no one *ever* demands vengeance for their blood, the blood of these stunted, foreign, exiles?

They seek reasons, those chatterers, reasons for the slaughter of those who, having no place in the world, have remained on the summit of a mountain about to erupt. Many of them, having no choice, have made it their business to try to tame the volcano, and many, many of them have stoked the burning embers within it.

Woe to them![96]

In an article titled "Mikhtavim lerusiyah" (Letters to Russia), published in the first issue of *Hame'orer* (January 1906), Brenner explicitly refers to the speaker's silence, saying that whatever he writes, he speaks, "as long as my lips have not fallen silent." Silence gives way to writing: "And you shall say to your soul then, 'Be silent! For whatever you utter—nothing shall be said! For whatever you say will leave out that one thing which alone, that alone, is worth telling; for however it is written, the writing will be the fruit of disaster, the fruit of disaster. . . . Therefore, my soul, you had best shut yourself up in rock, in earth, completely, absolutely. . . . The last hour of the burial of souls has arrived!'"[97]

Here, too, Brenner denies any possibility of a concrete political solution. He ridicules the Bund and the Bundists. On the other hand, when he argues, "How wretched are the S.S. [or SSRP, members of the Zionist Socialist Labor Party], who are jealous of this branch of 'the only organization' [the Bund]," he immediately adds that "it is also folly for others to fight it,"[98] for:

Forget all the various routine argumentations! Forget all the trivialities, all the second-class arguments! Abandon your hollow idols, your useless beliefs! Set your eyes on one goal, one goal alone: Salvation and refuge. Seek a way of salvation and refuge. Seek the means to achieve what our hearts yearn: to gain a country!

It is not for our faith that we are being slaughtered, O, Children of Israel, not for our iniquity that we are being slain, not for our righteous deeds that we are being stabbed, not as martyrs that we are being burned. Everyone's hand is against us only because we are hated. And we are hated because all those human wolves hate and are hated, but they live in their own forests, while we are exiles, strangers. Enough of being strangers among them. Let our sons leave them. Let us prepare for our grandchildren a land where no other person may set foot. *Let us abandon theories!* In the flashing brilliance of the knife—their light is dimmed; let us try to save, if salvation there be.[99]

Me'ever lagevulin (Beyond the limits)

Brenner probably completed his play *Beyond the Limits* in mid-December 1906, as he then wrote Shimon Bichovsky, asking him to include an announcement about the imminent publication of the play among the advertisements in *Hame'orer* (December 26, 1906).[100] In his letter, Brenner asked Bichovsky to inform Hillel Zeitlin of the play's existence: "Tell him that something very deep has been born, but that he should take care not to criticize it until he reads the fourth act through."[101] In a letter to Rabi Binyamin, however (January 4, 1907), he seems full of hope: "(My song has indeed been sung before, or, to be precise, I have never had song in my life; but my writing has not yet ceased, and in the last few days I have written something amounting to five printed sheets or more, superior in quality to everything I have written till now). If we must despair, let it be only for material distress, but why is the present any worse than last year? Brenner is still alive and in good health!"[102]

In the play, there is a dialogue between Yohanan, a writer, and his former lover, Dobeh, a revolutionary who is about to return to Russia. She asks him about his work, and he explains his advocacy of a poetic stance that he calls "symbolic realism," which includes "the symbol of life, the pole of life, characters and portrayals that will encompass the secret, the very essence, of all life."[103] While he insists on talking about his general attitude to literature and life, she begs him to tell her the content of the long poem. Brenner avails himself of the *spoken* genre of the play to present a character who stubbornly speaks of the conditions of *writing*, while she, Dobeh, wants him to speak of his poem. Essentially, Yohanan refuses to recount in speech something that is inherently written. He tells her of his doubts about his work and about his ability to go on creating. These doubts evaporated, he tells her, when he held his first printed volume in his hands; it was then that the materialistic nature of writing confirmed that he was not engaging in the naturalistic business of "bread to eat and clothing to wear," but "the new gods of poetry were stirring within me. So then I went to work."[104]

Yohanan expresses his despair of any political solution, also doubting the viability of the territorialists' idea, for "the view that the Jews are a single nation in all lands is false. [. . .] In fact, the Jews are no longer fit for anything!"[105] He then goes on to describe the grotesque figure and position of Naftali Edels, a member of Poale Zion.[106]

Hebrew creativity is nothing but the result of rejecting all established political ideologies. Writing itself is the reverse of any positive, monological expression. When Dobeh asks Yohanan about his work for the Social Democrats' newspaper *The Friend of the Times*, edited by her brother, Birfeld, he replies, "I am a slave there, but I do not write for him."[107]

Dobeh judges Yohanan's answers solely in relation to the available political options. (How can he write a poem when he does not believe in socialism? If Zionism has been replaced by territorialism, what is the point of Hebrew literature?).[108] She is portrayed as a person whose political outlook blinds her to everything else. Yohanan, for his part, replies that the need for Hebrew literature is ultimately something quite private and personal, not associated with any political system: "'Hebrew literature,' you say. What is the practical difference, what market need is literature supposed to satisfy? Is it a kind of commerce, dependent on 'demand'? It is I, I, a Hebrew from the land of the Hebrews, who needs it, or, more precisely, I did need it."[109]

In the last act, which Brenner considered the most important in the play, Yohanan reads from a written text. His concentration on this text highlights the act of writing, as a contrast to speaking, of the war:

Yohanan (reading): "Here they are, complaining and grumbling about the horrors of war and its outcome, speaking in the name of physical and financial losses, bringing all sorts of proof from the press and from the writers, talking in their language about the cruelty and bestiality of all these shootings, skirmishes, attacks" . . . (*rubs his hands together, looks at the darkness out the window, reads on*) "For indeed, accursed is the land by its inhabitants—except for those few who have not even seen this, who do not want to see, who cannot see, and some even speak approvingly of the sword, of the war" (*throws the page on the table; very agitated*). Of course! War! Bloodshed! How red the blood is! How beautiful the blood is! How beautiful the red blood! . . . (*screaming "Ay," short-breathed*) And I say: "Let me lay aside the red blood and write down—write down a few sketches—about the red courtyards, the courtyards before the blood. What Eliahu [Hizkuni] has told me, I shall leave for a time of emergency, for a time of war. Let me remember that time of peace that preceded it—and what Eliahu has revealed to me—the time of everlasting peace."[110]

Writing is the situation that makes it possible to reveal the general illusion, including the illusion in the very act of writing: "[*Yohanan to Eliahu Hizkuni:*] And whoever is privy to the secret of the constraining power of the alphabet—shall he create properly any more? There is no more pleasure, and I am wallowing like a birthing mother in the pieces of paper all around me. I still cherish my writing: Once it has been written, I feel a little relief. For a moment, I delude myself; for what I really need is the great thing, the great thing and something else."[111]

In the final analysis, then, writing itself is also an illusion, and it, too, cannot satisfy the death wish. Yohanan tells Eliahu that, sitting in jail, he had planned to write about a person who was struggling to write a great work and thought that he had created something great. One day, however, realizing that he had failed completely, he resolved to drown himself_but reconsidered. Only a year later, when he went to bathe in the river, there was a flood and he was drowned.[112] Writing itself could not be the source of a heroic act of death, given the worthlessness of creation.

Chapter 12

The Revolutionary Origins of Yiddish Scholarship, 1903–1917

BARRY TRACHTENBERG

They were extremely young in 1905, utterly committed both to the cause of revolution and to that of armed Jewish self-defense against the pogroms. Almost to a man they had become fervent Marxists by 1906, and even those who had not . . . now advocated (philosophically) a monistic determinism and (politically) proletarian class war. By 1906, the revolution had absorbed their every waking moment, every ounce of strength and every hope. However, to them the revolution meant a struggle not only for social equality and political freedom, but also for national, for Jewish, liberation.[1]

Since the appearance of Jonathan Frankel's magnum opus, *Prophecy and Politics*, more than twenty-five ago, we have perceived the revolutionary currents running through late nineteenth- and early twentieth-century Jewish Russia primarily through the representational lens that he constructed. In terms of the impact of the 1905 Revolution on the course of Jewish development, his oeuvre has shaped our understanding of this period as one defined in part by the intersection of a Jewish generational shift and the emergence of mass radical politics. Although his work continues to provide the terms for our understanding of this period, with few exceptions the challenges posed by his historiographical legacy have not made their way into studies of the development of Yiddish and Yiddishism. An examination of the impact of the generation of 1905 and its embrace of radical politics shows, however, that these forces had a profound and fundamental influence on the shape of the Yiddish language and its culture.

Studies of modern Yiddish and the Yiddish language movement have been primarily limited to the generations on either side of those who came of age in 1905. Much attention has been paid to its "classical" era in the final decades of the nineteenth century, when figures such as Sholem Yankev Abramovitch (who adopted the persona of Mendele

Moykher Seforim, or Mendele the Bookseller), Isaac Leib Peretz, and Sholem Aleichem first crafted Yiddish into a language of serious modern literature. In no small measure as a result of the success of these early literary artisans, some Jewish thinkers looked to Yiddish as the basis for a reinvigorated Jewish national identity. Appropriately then, attention has been paid to the first "architects" of the linguistic nationalistic movement of Yiddishism such as Chaim Zhitlowsky, Nathan Birnbaum, and Peretz himself.[2]

Similarly, much scholarly focus has been dedicated to the period that is often thought of as the "Golden Age" of Yiddish culture in the decades between the two world wars. During that time, in the Soviet Union, the United States, and the newly reconstituted Poland, Yiddish achieved some of its greatest forms of creativity and artistic expression. This was the moment when Yiddish fully came into its own as a cultural idiom and became the basis of a secular Jewish renaissance, complete with vibrant Yiddish school systems, publishing houses, theaters, and other cultural institutions. This, too, was the age of important Yiddish poetic circles such as the expressionist groups Di khalyastre (The gang) and Yunge vilne (Young Vilna) and of renowned writers such as Kadya Molodovsky, Peretz Markish, Uri Tsvi Greenberg, Itsik Fefer, Itsik Manger, Avrom Sutzkever, and dozens of others. Among the crowning achievements of this era was the ascendance of three major centers for the study of Yiddish in Poland (Vilna [then called Wilno in Polish]) and the Soviet Union (Kiev and Minsk).

The generation of writers, activists, and ideologues that links these two great epochs, however, is only recently becoming a topic of study. This lack of attention has been to the detriment of students of Yiddish; for it was during the first two decades of the twentieth century that Yiddish shifted from being thought of as a mere jargon spoken by an unsophisticated people to being the foundation of an ideology of Jewish liberation and the basis of a new scholarly discipline. The years 1903–17 witnessed an explosion of Yiddish cultural activity in Russia, first motivated by the revolutionary optimism that ignited the emancipatory expectations of a generation of youth and then, with the suppression of the revolution in 1907, by the new Jewish national pride that had captivated them.

This essay examines the origins of a scholarly idiom in Yiddish at the turn of the twentieth century. In particular, it is concerned with what can be considered the "prehistory" of the once famous Yiddish research centers that emerged in the mid-1920s and provided a much-needed institutional foundation for the field of Yiddish studies. Like many of the cultural and political movements that dominated the European Jewish world in the first half of the twentieth century, the roots of this new branch of Jewish scholarship are best located amid the tumult of the 1905 Russian Revolution—a time when Yiddish rapidly developed ever more sophisticated forms of expression.

According to most studies on the subject, *Yidishe visnshaft* (Yiddish studies/scholarship[3])—by which I mean in this case scholarship that was written both *in* the Yiddish language and *on* Yiddish, its literature, and the culture of its speakers—began with the 1913 publication in Vilna of a volume titled *Der pinkes* (The record), which is widely thought to have led, after World War I, to the rise of the three centers.[4] *Der pinkes* was a monumental achievement in the history of Yiddish scholarship, as it was the first compendium dedicated to the scientific investigation of the Yiddish language to be written in Yiddish. Previous studies on Yiddish had been written in, for example, Latin, German, English, and French, dating as far back as the sixteenth century, but even by the turn of the twentieth century there had been no such efforts to employ Yiddish as the medium for scholarly discourse.[5]

Der pinkes was a bold and daring undertaking in that only a decade prior to its publication there were very few Yiddish speakers (including some who ultimately contributed to the volume) who imagined that their spoken language was sophisticated and mature enough for such a daunting task. If Yiddish in Russia was so stunted—both developmentally and legally in the notorious year of 1903—how were scholars able by 1913 to publish one of the most substantial works ever of *Yidishe visnshaft?* What occurred was a near total revolution in Russian Jewish life that led to a fundamental reassessment by Russian Jews of their status in the empire, their life in the Diaspora, their relationship to a religiously orthodox way of life, and the many assumptions about the limits of their language.

A study of Yiddish writing in this period demonstrates that *Der pinkes* not only provided the impetus for what is thought of as modern Yiddish studies but also represented a culmination of a decade's worth of rapidly changing attitudes toward the language. This shift took place during the pivotal decade that began with the 1903 pogrom in Kishinev and concluded with the publication of *Der pinkes* ten years later. During this short period, Yiddish went through three important bursts of expansion: (a) its widespread use in revolutionary propaganda; (b) its use for literary and cultural criticism in the aftermath of the revolution; and (c) its use as a medium for critical scholarship.

At the outset of the twentieth century, Yiddish culture in Russia was meager. As a result of severe restrictions on Yiddish publishing and a long legacy of perceptions about the language's limitations, in the year 1900 there were no Yiddish newspapers, literary journals, or textbooks, no legal Yiddish cultural clubs, theater companies, nor secular Yiddish schools in the empire.[6] This situation existed despite the fact that there were more than five million Jews in the Russian Empire, 97 percent of whom claimed Yiddish as their primary language. Yiddish culture was transmitted either through materials imported from abroad or through the publication of occasional novels and miscellanies. Yiddish was largely restricted to the same functions that it had served for much of the Middle Ages: as a language of day-to-day communication, in the shops, in the homes, in the marketplace, and in religious school instruction. Yiddish book dealers tended to sell either religious material intended for those who were incapable of reading the more esoteric and legalistic materials published in Hebrew or cheap, disposable *bikhlekh*— short stories intended for a marginally literate audience. The Bund, the increasingly radical Jewish worker's movement, was still publishing most of its material in Russian, and the Zionist movement was not yet the powerful cultural force it would later become.

Just as the 1905 Revolution accelerated many of the modernizing changes already underway in Russian Jewry's economic, demographic, and religious realms, so too did it prompt changes in the perception and use of Yiddish. Jewish participation in the revolutionary movement affected the creation of a Yiddish scholarly idiom in significant ways. First, a new generation of young, militant Jewish activists emerged who quickly assumed the leadership of Jewish political and cultural life. Second, the newly established revolutionary political parties turned to Yiddish as the medium for their propaganda and, in doing so, began to lay the foundations for the development of a scholarly, critical stance toward modern Yiddish culture.

The importance of the 1905 Revolution for Russia's Jews can be seen clearly in the new leaders who rose to power. This cohort grew up in a world dramatically different from that of their parents and grandparents, one that was experiencing rapid waves of industrialization, urbanization, and proletarianization. By the time that they reached young adulthood, they were fully part of the revolutionary and nationalistic currents that were sweeping across Russia. Frankel has described the generation as "very young, numerous, possessed of precocious political and organizational experience, confident in itself and its methods, trained by the Marxist method to think in terms of world-historical categories and change, ready to lead whenever the opportunity came."[7]

What separated the 1905 generation from the preceding one was, most of all, a desire for action. As youths, they were less concerned with nurturing their ties to the past than they were with fleeing the *kheyder*— the famously oppressive religious elementary schools where children were taught the basics of the Torah—for the utopian worlds promised by socialism and nationalism. When they went off to study, it was not to *yeshivot* to master Talmud and Torah but rather to universities abroad to train (if only for a short while) in philosophy, linguistics, sociology, demography, ethnography, and history. They formed self-defense units to counter anti-Jewish attacks. They were the ideological core of the Second Aliyah (wave of emigration) to Palestine and dedicated themselves to creating a new world through Hebrew labor. They participated in the ranks of the Marxist parties that hoped to overthrow the tsar and usher in a workers' paradise. They advocated regime change—at times through violence and terror if necessary. Most importantly for the development of Yiddish culture, this generation also included those who did not accept the theretofore perceived limits of Yiddish and ultimately expanded its uses to all realms of thought and expression.

The generation of 1905 was not one of great Jewish thinkers like the one that came before it. Rather, it was made up of activists who drew their ideas from those who preceded them and infused their theories with a revolutionary ethos. In their late teens and twenties, often intensely engaged in the upheavals of 1905, these new figures included labor and Zionist leaders such as Vladimir Medem, Esther Frumkin, Vladimir Jabotinsky, Ber Borochov, Yitzhak Ben-Zvi, and David Ben-Gurion. Rosa Luxemburg, Leon Trotsky, and Adolph Joffe were among the "non-Jewish Jews" who became major figures in revolutionary politics. Others such as Avrom Reyzen, A. Vayter (Ayzik-Meir Devenishski), Sholem Asch, Shmuel Niger, Dovid Bergelson, and Joseph Opatoshu were responsible for much of the burgeoning modern Yiddish literary culture, while Haim Nahman Bialik, Shaul Tchernichowsky, Yosef Haim Brenner, Shmuel Yosef Agnon, and Zalmen Shneour modernized Hebrew literature. Finally, and most significant in terms of this study, this generation also includes those who brought Yiddish and Hebrew to new forms of mature scholarship such as Jacob Lestschinsky, Nokhem Shtif, Noyekh Prilutski, Ben-Zion Dinaburg, and Joseph Klausner.

The new leadership helped form several new Jewish political parties, each of which merged Zionist and socialist ideals into a unified platform and did so in the Yiddish language. These groups included the Zionist Socialist Workers' Party, known by its Russian initials S.S., and the Jewish Socialist Workers' Party, known as the SERP (or the Seimist party).[8] Prior to the appearance of these groups, the Yiddish political newspapers, journals, and tracts that circulated in the Pale of Settlement employed Yiddish more out of practical reasons than out of conviction. Most Russian Jewish revolutionaries initially could not conceive of Yiddish as a suitable vessel for political propaganda but came to realize that if they wanted to attract a mass audience to their platforms, they would have to communicate in the language of the workers. However, what began out of necessity rapidly turned into a matter of ideology as many

Jewish revolutionaries began to view Yiddish as an integral part of their national identity.

Two weekly journals in particular—the S.S.'s *Der nayer veg* (The new way) and the SERP's *Folks-shtime* (People's voice)—incorporated some of the first attempts to apply critical scholarly methods in Yiddish and they provided important antecedents to the scholarly forums that would appear later.[9] They thus marked the beginning of a new, important phase in the expansion of Yiddish and helped lay the groundwork for *Yidishe visnshaft* to develop in the post-1905 period. While neither party organ lasted past the end of the 1905 Revolution, they served as a proving ground for many of those who would later found the Yiddish journals that expanded the language further.

Reflecting the editorial conviction that Yiddish should be regarded as a language equal to any other, these papers contained some of the earliest efforts to use Yiddish in the study of politics, economics, literature, and the social conditions of Russian Jewry. They thus served as the first forum for some of the initial avant-garde Yiddish literary productions and critical studies of Jewish economic and cultural life. For example, in the debut issue of *Der nayer veg*, Sholem Asch's short story "In a frilinge-nakht" (In a spring night) appeared alongside essays on May Day celebrations in Germany and elections to the Duma, a statement of party principles, and a lengthy examination of the conditions of Jewish workers. Elsewhere, the future literary critic Shmuel Niger first examined the relationship between the Yiddish language and the Jewish intelligentsia; the future demographer Jacob Lestschinsky documented the economic transformation of the Jewish workers in Russia; and the future linguist Nokhem Shtif began to set out a populist agenda for the Yiddish language.

With the decline of the revolution in 1907 and the waves of repression that followed, the use of Yiddish for political propaganda was sharply curtailed. Membership in the Bund and Poale Zion declined dramatically and the S.S. and SERP newspapers were forced to close, reflecting the virtual disappearance of the parties. Many activists fled the empire and sought to continue their struggle in the United States, Palestine, or Britain. At the same time, however, new avenues for Yiddish were opened as many activists began to pursue their commitment to Jewish nationalism through the advancement of Jewish cultural institutions such as the new Yiddish and Hebrew press, theater, school systems, and various self-help organizations. As a result of these efforts, the decade between the two Russian revolutions—from 1907 to 1917—saw an explosion of the Yiddish press as a variety of newspapers, journals, and publishing houses sprang up throughout the Pale. Unlike the Yiddish press during the 1905 Revolution, the new postrevolutionary periodicals were mostly independent undertakings and not the organs of any particular political party. Lacking an institutional base (as well as a reliable readership that could afford a subscription), these new initiatives emerged and disappeared with great frequency. Many lasted but a few issues while some continued for years. With their independent status and greater dependence on the vagaries of the marketplace, they presented a broader ideological and aesthetic range to their readers than did the revolutionary press.

In light of this change of fortunes, while drawing on their early success at propaganda, Yiddish writers quickly expanded the language into a medium for increasingly sophisticated forms of fiction, poetry, journalism, and scholarly essays that sought to emulate the best European forms; in the process, these works gave shape and form to this "awakening" cultural nation. The emphasis on culture and the new significance given to the status of Yiddish through the ideology of "Yiddishism" were hailed in some quarters as marking a new age in the development of the Jewish nation and decried in others as a betrayal of the revolutionary passions that had so recently been ignited.

One of the most recognized milestones of the Yiddish language movement in the immediate postrevolutionary period was the issuance in 1908 of the literary monthly *Di literarishe monatsshriften,* which sought to launch a literary renaissance in Yiddish. A second marker in that year was the conference in Czernowitz, where activists proclaimed that Yiddish was a national language of the Jewish people.[10] Even more important to the development of a Yiddish scholarly genre was the appearance of a new crop of journals that combined Yiddish literature with articles covering a broad range of cultural and societal topics. Modeled in large measure after Russian periodicals as well as highly successful Yiddish ones in the United States, literary/*gezelshaftlekh* journals such as *Lebn un visnshaft* (Life and science, 1909–12) and *Di yidishe velt* (The Jewish world, 1912–16) not only featured some of the best new Yiddish fiction, plays, and poetry but also contained articles on general and Jewish history and political essays on the state of Russian Jews, Jewish workers, and global politics.[11] Similar to the Hebrew periodicals of the early haskalah such as *Hameasef* (The gatherer) and *Bikure ha'itim* (First fruits), which, as Meyer Waxman argues, served as "the seminary in which the early writers, poets, and scholars . . . of the second Haskalah period were nourished, trained, and prepared for their future activity," these journals served as a type of surrogate university for early Yiddish intellectuals.[12] The folklorist, linguist, and newspaper editor Noyekh Prilutski credited the rapidly maturing Yiddish press as the most important factor in the transformation and maturation of the language: "Thanks to the Yiddish press our *mame-loshen* has quickly developed over the past few years. From the language of the marketplace, home, folk creations, and *belles lettres* there has been created a language with which to speak of politics and diplomacy, the military and armored ships, social and communal questions, science and criticism, and sculpture and painting."[13]

Under the editorship of A. Litvin (pseudonym for Shmuel Hurvits, 1862–1943), *Lebn un visnshaft* was founded in Vilna with the express purpose of bringing popular works of science, culture, and politics to the broad masses of Russian Jewish youth who had no access to formal university training. Like *Di literarishe monatsshriften, Lebn un visnshaft* was decidedly unaligned politically and promoted the centrality of culture as key to the Jewish national awakening: "cultural work in general and Jewish cultural work in particular must stand above all parties."[14] However, unlike the purely literary journal that was aimed at a sophisticated readership, Litvin's monthly was a forum for a wide variety of political views and sought a popular audience. The editor envisioned a journal that would serve as a bridge between the Jewish and the non-Jewish worlds: "We must have a Jewishly-educated and educated Jewish *intelligentsia*. And sadly, we barely even have this! Our educated intellectuals are almost entirely not Jewish and our Jewish intellectuals are too poorly educated."[15] *Lebn un visnshaft* was to remedy this unnatural condition.

Litvin's opening statement for the journal displays an almost maskilic conviction of the power of knowledge to emancipate the Jewish people. A full generation older than those who came of age in 1905, Litvin combined the Enlightenment embrace of science with the revolutionary *geist* of more recent years: "We proceed with this difficult work, because we know very well how our nation's youth—the young generation of the old "people of the book"—thirsts for a word of science, yearns for education, because we believe deeply in the strength of the sciences and education, because we are convinced that science—in the broadest sense of the term—is the unwavering fiery pillar that illuminates the dark path of life's desert and will one day bring general happiness to humanity."[16]

Over the next several years, *Lebn un visnshaft* published the writings of some of the best-known novelists, poets, and scholars. Literary works by David Einhorn and Avrom Reyzen appeared alongside translations of Guy de Maupassant, Bialik, and Henry Wadsworth Longfellow. It included popular essays on nature, family dynamics and child rearing, and astronomy. In addition, *Lebn un visnshaft* was the forum for works by scholars such as "Dr. X" (pseudonym for Ludovic L. Zamenhof, the founder of Esperanto), Prilutski, and the linguist Mordekhey Vayniger, who advanced proposals for Yiddish language reform (such as changing its alphabet from Hebrew to Latin, the use of proverbs, and the issue of *daytshmerizms*).[17] Others contributed essays on Yiddish literature and theater.

Critical works in Yiddish appeared not only in journals such as *Lebn un visnshaft*. The years after the revolution also saw the publication of several monographs and miscellanies dedicated to *visnshaftlekh* methods of promoting and enriching the Yiddish language and culture. In 1908 Zalmen Reisen published one of the first basic Yiddish grammars with the goal of proving to skeptics that such a task could be accomplished: "Often discussed is whether it is possible [to create such a work]. I am inclined to think . . . that there has been imposed a veil of fear around that which is called 'Yiddish grammar.' . . . My grammar . . . which is, understand, only a first attempt, will demonstrate . . . that the fear is unnecessary—that a Yiddish grammar is *clearly* possible, and even relatively easy to write. . . . Mistakes, should they be found, will lead to the perfection of Yiddish grammar. This is the path to the scientific basis of the Yiddish language."[18]

Along with the new emphases on Yiddish grammar, literature, and literary criticism came a renewed interest in folklore. Noyekh Prilutski, for example, motivated by a thirst for Yiddish folklore, published *Yidishe folkslider* (Jewish folksongs) and *Noyekh prilutski's zamelbikher far yidishen folklor, filologye, un kulturgeshikhte* (Collections of Yiddish folklore, philology, and cultural history).[19] He hoped his new collections would preserve and make available for examination the rapidly disappearing traditional Jewish ways of life. His attachment to folklore was, to a large degree, an effort to document and preserve the traditional Jewish world that was by that time in its last throes:

> I believe that the need for a special Yiddish organ for our folklore, philology, and cultural history has long been apparent. There already exist several such periodicals in German. The time has come, however, to produce a Yiddish ethnological periodical in the same language as the researched material.
> . . . We request that you send to us 1) folksongs, folk stories, Purim plays, phrases, witticisms, colloquialisms, expressions, riddles, and the like; 2) folk stories about historical events and personalities; 3) odd documents, letters and family archives, pages from old storerooms [*genizes*]; and 4) descriptions and photos of old cemeteries, rituals baths, homes, housewares, kitchenware, and the like.[20]

Also during this time, Zalmen Reisen published the first edition of his monumental *Leksikon fun der yidisher literatur, prese un filologye*, a comprehensive guide (edited by Niger) that was the first such effort to establish systematically the canon of Yiddish writers and scholars.[21]

With the publication in 1913 in Vilna of *Der pinkes*, Yiddish scholarship reached one its most sophisticated expressions in the post-1905 period. Under the editorial stewardship of Shmuel Niger, *Der pinkes* was a tour de force of the new Yiddish scholarship. Reflecting on its impact upon later research, many scholars have credited *Der pinkes* for launching the field of modern Yiddish scholarship.[22] While its role in laying a foundation for subsequent scholarly investigations into Yiddish is undeniable, the volume also was a result of nearly a decade of scholarly investigations into the Yiddish language and its history and culture, as well as the socio-logical, economic, and demographic status of its speakers. Published by the press of B[oris]. Kletskin, this compendium is rich with the sort of linguistic, literary, folkloric, and bibliographic essays that were scattered throughout the Yiddish press after the 1905 Revolution. Not only was it the first volume to showcase the new Yiddish scholarship but it also sought to establish the agenda for future research by featuring a state-ment on the future of Yiddish language scholarship by the leader of the Poale Zion, Ber Borochov. In his essay "Di oyfgabn fun der yidisher filo-logye" (The tasks of Yiddish philology), Borochov represented Yiddish language reform as a primary step toward the national revitalization of Russian Jewry.[23]

Der pinkes marked a transition in Yiddish scholarship. Prior to the vol-ume's appearance, most studies of Yiddish were conducted by those researching the development of other Germanic languages, without any particular concern for Yiddish. The appearance of *Der pinkes* was an effort to wrest control of Yiddish language research away from these scholars and to tether it instead to the agenda of Jewish national libera-tion by placing it squarely in the hands of its strongest advocates. Much like Borochov's influential manifesto, the volume is itself a type of pro-grammatic document that hoped to set the tenor and tone of future lan-guage research by infusing it with the revolutionary pride developed during the 1905 Revolution. Beyond Borochov's "Oyfgabn," *Der pinkes* contained a broad range of articles on Yiddish literature and culture: essays on Yiddish phonetics and Hebrew sounds; memoirs and remem-brances of literary figures such as Abramovitch, Avrom Goldfaden, and Avrom Reyzen; studies of the Yiddish theater, the early Yiddish press, and Russian Jewish folklore; and reviews of recent Yiddish scholarly work. The volume concluded with a bibliography of Yiddish philological works written by Borochov.

Although Niger's introduction to *Der pinkes* was brief, he articulated a bold agenda. He envisioned it as the first in an annual series that would serve as a permanent archive of the accomplishments of Yiddish publish-ing and as an aid to scholars in comparative studies charting the growth and development of the language, literature, and literary studies. In effect, he was proposing that *Der pinkes* should be the first Yiddish schol-arly institution, one that would not only preserve and store the wealth of Yiddish literary and scholarly activity but would also preside over its development by establishing standards for the budding discipline. Just as five years earlier, with *Di literarishe monatsshriften*, he had displayed faith in the Yiddish language's ability to elevate Russian Jewry, Niger subsequently hoped that *Der pinkes* would further the legitimization of Yiddish and its acceptance in the world at large. He saw it as a vehicle that would set new standards for Yiddish orthography, establish a regular grammar for the language, and lay the agenda for future scholarly endeavors. This agenda-setting impulse is most evident in the emphasis that Niger gave to the question of orthography. At the time, there was no agreed-upon basis for spelling and each press tended to follow its own standard, or in some cases, no identifiable standard at all. Niger named orthography reform as one of the first issues that needed to be addressed: "[*Der pinkes*] will be able to assist in answering the practical-scientific questions of Yiddish literary life. Among the most vital of these questions is, without a doubt, the question of its orthography."[24]

Niger hoped *Der pinkes* would serve Yiddish scholarship and the Jewish community in two additional ways: "by gathering and cultivating various material that has a relationship to scientific investigations of Yiddish literature and language in general," and "by collecting and systematizing the relevant materials of each year."[25] His hope of providing an annual record of Yiddish was not realized as the 1913 edition was the only volume to appear, but his goal that *Der pinkes* begin a process of creating a broad variety of forums for scholarly research into the Yiddish language and Russian Jewry was attained.[26]

Niger's vision for *Der pinkes* was partially realized. While it could not be sustained beyond the first volume, several of its contributions continue to inform Yiddish scholarship until the present day.[27] More important, however, was the tone taken by the volume. In several ways—via its opening declarations, the broad range of its ambitions and contributions, even its handsome binding and formal printing style—*Der pinkes* boldly proclaimed that the Yiddish language and its culture were capable of embodying the most sophisticated realms of intellectual expression, and its speakers were worthy of inclusion among the nations of Russia.

As much as it launched the field of *Yidishe visnshaft* as a serious field of modern Jewish scholarship, *Der pinkes* also marked the climax of a process of transformation of the Yiddish language that had been occurring over the previous half century and was accelerated and transformed by the 1905 Revolution. The language that its native speakers once had to abandon in order to take up serious scholarly pursuits had become, by the eve of World War I, the language for some of the most critical scientific studies into all aspects of Russian Jewish life. Once marginalized as an immature jargon unfit for sophisticated works, it now stood at the very center of a new national project.

1905 as a Jewish Cultural Revolution? Revolutionary and Evolutionary Dynamics in the East European Jewish Cultural Sphere, 1900–1914

KENNETH B. MOSS

The years before the First World War saw dramatic changes in the East European secular Jewish cultural sphere. In the arts, the burgeoning of a mature multigeneric and experimental Jewish literature in Hebrew and Yiddish[1] paralleled the emergence of fledgling Jewish art, music, and theater;[2] aesthetically, stylized folk culture vied with Symbolist and Decadent literary conceits; and new, vigorously modernist currents made themselves felt in ever-quickening succession.[3] Institutionally, numerous newly hatched cultural organizations and journals provided a far larger and more differentiated framework for these developments while forging a complicated relationship with nationalist and radical tribunes and the burgeoning popular press.[4]

These developments took shape, moreover, around new axes of cultural-ideological commitment. Yiddishism emerged as a full-fledged cultural ideology and provoked a confrontation between increasingly separate Hebraist and Yiddishist camps. Within Yiddish culture, a redoubled valorization of East European Jewish "folk culture" sat uncomfortably with a newly assertive demand among some Yiddishists for a modern Yiddish "high culture" suited to the aesthetic sensibilities of the intelligentsia.[5]

Finally, the relations between this culture-in-the-making and the nationalist and leftist politics that had midwifed it grew much more complicated. First, to take the Yiddish case, this period might be seen as *cementing* the close ties between Yiddish culture and the Jewish left; yet it was also a moment of party collapse and retreat. In some ways, this ensured closer ties, as party activists turned their efforts to legal cultural activity. But on the other hand, this also meant unprecedented open confrontation between party-affiliated cultural activists and a new kind of expressly apolitical or even antiparty cultural activism and discourse. Many of the leading writers and cultural journals of the day hewed to a nonparty line, and party and nonparty activists fought each other for control of cultural institutions; at stake was the question of whether and how the new culture was to align itself with nationalist and revolutionary visions.[6]

This chapter addresses the relationship of these critical developments to the revolutionary conjuncture of 1905–7. It does so against the back-drop of a powerful narrative bequeathed us by contemporaries who took part in 1905 about how these developments—and indeed virtually every important aspect of the new secular Jewish and, especially, Yiddish culture that took shape in twentieth-century Eastern Europe—grew out of the revolutionary experience.[7] During 1905, this narrative runs, a new generation of *inteligentn* mobilized around a nationalist and leftist politics that inclined them, in principle, toward a deepened commitment to Yiddish, to the "folk" or workers, and, consequently, to the more intense cultivation of a secular, radically inflected Yiddish culture. Full-fledged Yiddishism, born of 1905's Jewish revolutionary populism, found expression in both the urge to a Yiddish culture rooted in folk culture *and* the urge to a self-contained European-style Yiddish high culture. When the revolution was suppressed in 1907, many of these activists threw themselves into "cultural work" as a substitute for *or* as a renunciation of politics. Concomitantly, the very idea of a freestanding Yiddish high culture could be seen to mark either an embrace or a betrayal of the revolution's Yiddishist logic: either an organic outgrowth of 1905[8] or a sickly response to its defeat in 1907–8.[9]

Meanwhile, the narrative maintains, literati—a distinct subgroup—reacted to the revolutionary events by shifting from Hebrew to Yiddish, developing new genres to capture their own experience, and "searching" for a new poetic voice to express their postrevolutionary despair. Thus, the generic and aesthetic developments that characterized pre-1914 Yiddish culture were the product of postrevolutionary searching *or* of decadent ideological betrayal. Above all, this view attributes the persistent concern of Jewish writers and artists to assert the independence of their art from the mobilizational demands of nationalist and radical politics to the atmosphere of despair prevailing in the half-dozen years prior to World War I. The very idea of aesthetic autonomy, which became a critical enduring source of controversy in the cultural sphere, was, in this view, a product of 1905 politics frustrated or betrayed.

None of these claims is, on its face, ludicrous; certainly, it would be merely perverse to dismiss the formative impact of the revolution's matrix of ideology and experience on its participants. Moreover, no one would gainsay that there are real empirical phenomena at the root of this narrative. The turn to Jewish cultural activity by substantial numbers of young Jewish revolutionary activists played a central role in the 1908–14 burst of cultural institution building, innovation, and debate. Contemporaries on all sides of postrevolutionary debates over aesthetics and cultural politics clearly felt that the "great yearning for spiritual-cultural creation,"[10] the rising status of Yiddish vis-à-vis Hebrew as a culture-language, and the new aesthetic trends that characterized Yiddish cultural life were all deeply connected to the failure of the revolution. At least one scholar of our own day, Mikhail Krutikov, has recently given flesh and bone to such contentions with his persuasive argument for the importance of the revolutionary experience and associated discourses in the development of a specific genre, the Jewish novel.[11]

Yet much of what we know about Jewish culture and about how cultural spheres develop more generally points to the gap between any concatenation of events, no matter how important, and a process as complex as cultural development. In this chapter, I assay two somewhat contradictory endeavors. First, I raise some questions concerning commonplace assumptions about the importance of 1905 in the development specifically of the Yiddish cultural sphere. Here, I take my inspiration from two landmark works. The first is Jonathan Frankel's classic revision of the insider narrative tradition about the origins of the Bund's nationalities policy in which he dug beneath a near unanimous memoiristic explanation of the Bund's national turn to find its more tangled roots.[12] The other source is Dan Miron's revisionist history of the crisis of Hebrew culture circa 1905, which locates a revolutionary-era print crisis in longer-term processes of readership decline and literary shift.[13]

Epistemologically, I have set myself two distinct critical goals. First, without disputing the causal importance of the 1905 Revolution for the post-1907 Jewish cultural sphere, I will nevertheless raise some objections to assigning it priority in certain matters, both by suggesting the impact of prerevolutionary cultural developments and by highlighting some postrevolutionary cultural developments that are better explained by factors other than the revolution itself. Second, implicit in my brief to assess whether 1905 was a "turning point" in the history of the Jewish cultural sphere is a *counterfactual* question: how differently would that sphere (and especially the Yiddish subsphere) have developed without the events and legacy of 1905–7? I will attempt to show some developmental trajectories in prerevolutionary Yiddish culture that suggest that, even without the 1905 watershed, there would nevertheless have emerged in Eastern Europe a distinct Yiddish high culture undergirded by an increasingly assertive Yiddishist ideology and allowing an ever-broadening array of modes of literary and cultural expression and interiority.

Against this backdrop of critique, the second part of the chapter sketches some concrete cultural impacts of 1905–7 largely ignored in the standard collective narrative. Finally, I return to the traditional account and suggest that the core of the revolution's impact lay, ironically, in the fact that its suppression propelled the Jewish left *not* into an empty cultural field waiting to be plowed but rather into an already burgeoning Yiddish cultural sphere, with profound and disruptive results.

First, regarding the impact of 1905–7 on the post-1905 Jewish cultural sphere, there is much evidence to suggest that one central feature of modern Yiddish culture, the neo-Romantic recentering of Yiddish literature around folk culture, which some on the left denounced as a kind of consolatory or anesthetizing postrevolutionary turn,[14] was far more a product of the 1890s through 1904 than of 1907 and beyond. Y. L. Peretz's *folkshtimlekhe geshikhtes*, which set the pattern for efforts to transform a moldering Jewish folk culture into a purified well of symbols and narratives that could be put to artistically productive or nationally redemptive uses, were written mainly between 1901 and 1904. The larger resonance of these ideas and strategies was already becoming evident before 1905 in such works as Sholem Asch's *Dos shtetl*. So, too, Haim Nahman Bialik's turn to "folk" culture (albeit in a Hebraized mode linked to a posited rabbinic-era folk culture) may have resulted in the *Sefer haagadah* only in 1908, but as Mark Kiel's research reveals, it took shape in this prerevolutionary period through Bialik's intensive contacts with Peretz and the Warsaw scene.[15]

Second, several pre-1905 developments in the literary sphere should be understood as decisive causal influences on ostensibly 1905-centered developments. In his *Nashi zadachi* of 1907, the socialist-nationalist Mark Ratner attributed party commitment to full-fledged Yiddishism not to the abstract dictates of ideology but rather to the fact that "recently, the 'zhargon' literature has attracted to it Jewry's finest literary powers— whether in literature or in publicistics [. . .]"—a situation that he regarded as an inevitable development in a language nourished by "living roots and deep wells of folk-life."[16] Likewise, when Shmuel Niger sought to define the new Yiddish canon in his 1908 *Literarishe monatssh-riften*, the canonical figures he chose were precisely the leading figures of *pre*-1905 literary life: Peretz, Asch, Nomberg, Bialik.[17] These cases suggest that if Yiddish culture as idea and reality had not been well consolidated by 1905, no amount of abstract conviction could have convinced so many that it was a viable option; and the specific evolution of that culture since the 1890s gave form to the revolutionary Yiddishism of 1905's socialist-nationalist youth.

Turning from the impact of the revolution to the impact of its *failure*, we should also question the assertion, advanced particularly by Bundist memoirist-historians, that the emphasis on aesthetic culture as an *end*, the defense of aesthetic autonomy, and the sharp distinction between art and politics were inventions of disillusioned *inteligentn* rejecting revolutionary politics. These notions had already sunk roots in the East European Jewish cultural milieu by the turn of the century and were espoused by figures as far apart in their political and aesthetic sensibilities as the Zionist-Hebraist literary critic Joseph Klausner and the experimentally inclined, politically alienated Hebrew writer Uri Nissan Gnessin.[18] Perhaps more strikingly, we can also find them clearly embraced by Jewish revolutionaries themselves in the full fire of the revolution. At the Seimists' First District Conference in Vilna in March 1907, vigorous debate over the question of art-literature and its place in party work led to the conclusion that it had to command more attention from the party and its journal.[19]

Significantly, the conference wrote into party dogma a surprisingly sharp distinction between art and politics: "We must strive [to ensure] that everything printed in our organ will have literary value and not merely narrow party content [. . . .] Art-literature and art must take their proper place, and the time has come to supply literature to the conscious worker in its pure and true form." Though dating the dynamics of revolutionary triumphalism and revolutionary despair is notoriously difficult, significantly, these decisions were taken well before the formal counterrevolutionary rollbacks of 1907 (including the suppression of the legal socialist press[20]) and were adopted not by people who had abandoned party and revolution but by those committed (at least at that juncture) to realizing aesthetic and political goals in concert with them.

On the other side of the chronological divide, as we turn to the rapidly changing Jewish cultural sphere of 1908–14, we must also be careful not to attribute undue weight to the supposed cultural aftereffects of 1905–7. Thus, younger figures who adopted the various ideological and aesthetic stances described above *after* 1907 were not necessarily reacting primarily to the revolution. In memoirs dealing with the blossoming of the Yiddish cultural milieu in late imperial Kiev, Nahman Mayzl notes that "the Russian Revolution of 1905–1906 did little to plow the Jewish earth in Ukraine for a strong growth of the Yiddish word." Rather, his memoir suggests, both the Yiddishism and the new literary departures that characterized his Kiev circles of 1908–14 were born of the *continuing* influence of prerevolutionary *Hebrew* literature in its "rebellious" forms

(Gnessin, Brenner); the influence of Russian literature; and a local, individual process of unwittingly retracing the road from Zionism to socialist-nationalism walked by so many in the revolutionary generation. This process entailed the strange experience of finding one's own efforts to articulate a "synthesis between nationalism and socialism" unexpectedly anticipated in Seimist or SSRP pamphlets discovered well after the revolutionary movement had fallen into eclipse.[21]

By the same token, one of the most distinctive aesthetic developments in postrevolutionary Yiddish culture was the emergence, beginning in the years just before World War I, of a new lyric poetry profoundly different from both the poetry of national lament and the radically inclined "civic" voice that had hitherto dominated the fledgling Yiddish poetic tradition. Produced especially by a circle of writers from the Kiev region such as Dovid Hofshteyn or Osher Shvartsman, who were no older than sixteen when the revolution broke out, this belated invention of a Yiddish lyric voice can be attributed to the revolution or its failure only by going to great lengths. I would suggest that these new departures were shaped less by a revolution that these authors (to say nothing of the still younger cohort that gathered around them) could barely have experienced than by the prerevolutionary Hebrew lyrical revolution (especially that of Bialik, who personally influenced both Hofshteyn and Shvartsman), contemporary Russian and Ukrainian poetry (and in Shvartsman's case, Polish poetry that he encountered during his 1911 army service[22]), and the very fact of a burgeoning postrevolutionary Yiddish literary sphere *against* which this cohort was reacting.[23]

Thus, we may identify several key aspects of post–1905–7 Jewish culture for which the revolution and its suppression clearly acted as powerful catalysts but should be seen as stimulating cultural norms and practices already developing before 1905, born of deeper factors, and exerting independent effects on new cohorts long after the revolution's suppression. Turning from causal to counterfactual argumentation, let us examine the relationship between the revolution and the rise of a robust Yiddishist ideology. Clearly, on the revolutionary left, the rapid ideological delineations of the revolutionary period and the drive to realize ideology in practice did push many toward a Yiddishist cultural ideology and thus deeply shaped post-1905 Yiddishism. Yet cultural Yiddishism was a development well under way before 1905 and one that had the same deeper causes as all East European minority cultural nationalisms. The intellectual outlines of the Yiddishist ideology voiced most famously at the 1908 Czernowitz Conference to the effect that Yiddish (rather than Hebrew or any non-Jewish language) could serve as the language for a full-fledged modern Jewish secular-national culture and civil society were already taking shape before the revolution. Jonathan Frankel's pioneering treatment of the maverick Russian Jewish radical Haim Zhitlovsky suggests that his turn-of-the-century Yiddishism enjoyed real resonance among Jewish students in the Central European Russian student colonies—many of them later leaders in 1905—seeking a cultural ideology compatible with their nationalist and radical impulses.[24] In Russia itself, the Socialist Zionist Vozrozhdenie student circle also evolved toward a similar (theoretical) Yiddishism: thus, in 1904 the socialist Zionist Ben-Adir (Avrom Rozin) attacked Bundist cultural theorists for failing to embrace the idea of a generically encompassing Jewish national culture in Yiddish.[25] In other words, Yiddishism was well on its way to consolidation (as *theory*) in some Jewish socialist circles because of intrinsic ideological dynamics *before* the alembic of the revolution.

Nor was this a development peculiar to the hothouse theoretical circles of Russian Jewish student radicalism. The young, traditionally educated provincials who made up the literary circle around the Warsaw Yiddish-Hebrew writer Y. L. Peretz also evolved toward a similar Yiddishism in the 1903–5 period. Thus, Avrom Reyzen introduced his 1904 journal *Dos yudishe vort* (co-edited with Peretz's intimates Sholem Asch and Baal-Makhshoves [Isidor Eliashev]) by asserting all of the most radical formulations later made at Czernowitz: *"Dos yudishe vort* is the first periodical that unambiguously declares its firm conviction that the language that has been and continues to be called Jargon by many publishers *is the national language* and that it considers the literature of this language not as a means *but as an end in and for itself."*[26]

Similar complexity can be seen in the notable shift of Hebrew writers and Zionist publishers to Yiddish circa 1905. Yitzhak Dov Berkowitz recalls that in Vilna the circle of young writers linked to *Hazman*—Z. Anokhi (Zalman Yitzhak Aronson), Perets Hirshbayn, Zalman Shneur, and Yeshiyahu Bershadski—held several "intimate meetings" in the summer of 1905 about the literary-language question and resolved that they must write in Yiddish as well as Hebrew and try to disseminate their work "among the folk."[27] The founding of two *Yiddish* papers in 1906 by the "Hebrew-oriented" editors Ben-Tsion Katz and Yosef Luria also undoubtedly reflected the effort by Zionist circles to find a new voice that might appeal to the real or imagined radicalized "folk."[28] The revolution's social reality and ideological currents clearly played a critical role in both cases. Yet here, too, the revolution should be understood at least in part more as a *catalyst* reinforcing ideological and cultural shifts already underway. Hirshbayn had come of age as a writer under the influence of the solidly bilingual Peretz; Berkowitz began a Yiddish story while still in Ekaterinoslav in 1904.[29] Luria had played the role of a Hebraist-Zionist editor of Yiddish journals that took Yiddish literature seriously since 1902 in *Der yid* and *Der fraynd*.[30] More generally, the shift to active literary bilingualism was clearly the norm in the literary sphere by 1901–2, thanks in good measure to Yehoshua Khone Ravnitsky's journal *Der yid* and to Peretz's example and direct influence.[31] However much the language choices of Jewish writers were, in fact, affected by the revolution, the shift from Hebrew to at least bilingual literary creativity was under way before 1905.

One of the most significant assertions of the 1905-centered narrative is that the implosion of revolutionary hopes provoked some of the central developments of modern Yiddish literature. Krutikov argues that the revolution generated its own aesthetic dynamic: driven to seek formal correlates for this unprecedented political event, Jewish writers converged on the novel as the appropriate multivocal but also realistic narrative form; on narrative strategies that replaced cyclical "shtetl" time with irruptive political-historical event time; and on devices such as using female characters modeled on the revolutionary "new woman" to represent and enact the principle of change.[32] The contemporaries of 1905 emphasized a far broader shift: they attributed to the revolution a decisive wholesale transformation of Yiddish literature from having been guided by a social mission dictating "progressive" realist and naturalist tendencies or a redemptive national-folk romanticism to a modern literature open (for better or worse) to a full range of postrealist literary sensibilities. In this account, the revolution's failure drove a generation of writers disillusioned with collective and redemptive visions toward the willfully idiosyncratic referential structures and penchant for mysticism characteristic of Russian Symbolism and, even more so, toward the themes and images of unbridled individual self-exploration, eros, decay, madness, wandering, and masculinity gone awry that contemporaries tended to cluster under the term "Decadence."

Certainly, there is warrant for this account. The writer Peretz Hirshbayn, typical of his half-forgotten generation, records that he responded to the revolution's failure by "consciously [striving] to create symbolic characters that could in part present a model of beings of the future."[33] Conversely, the writing of his entire generational cohort (many clustered around the journal *Literarishe monatsshriften*) and the works of more innovative younger writers like the novelist Dovid Bergelson and the symbolist short story writer Der Nister (Pinkhas Kahanovich) are replete with themes of decay, exile, the unconsummated, and equivocation that resonate with the failure of the revolution and its epochal promises.

Yet without denying the actual impact of 1905 here, I would suggest that these tendencies would have made their presence felt in Yiddish letters regardless of the 1905 experience. Hamutal Bar-Yosef has demonstrated the ubiquity of Decadent modes in turn-of-the-century Hebrew literature under the impact of the 1890s Silver Age Russian culture,[34] and both these literatures were powerful influences on younger Yiddish writers independent of 1905. But more directly, these trends were already becoming visible in prerevolutionary Yiddish writing despite its freight of assumptions about its expressive capacities and "civic"/public tasks.[35]

To return to the pivotal figure of Peretz: much of his work even in the ostensibly "realist-radical" 1890s is replete with the Decadent motifs of despairing wanderers, madmen, and grotesque and symbolically freighted imagery ostensibly peculiar to the literature of post-1907 despair. Though he often embedded such elements in "defusing" narrative and thematic frameworks that yoked them to the more acceptable social-critical tone expected of Yiddish literature, stories like "Der farsholtener brunem" (The accursed well) with its devouring well and "Meshiekhs tsaytn" (Messianic times) with its uncanny vision of the onset of divine redemption present concatenations of fantastic elements so strong as to nearly overwhelm such constraining narrative devices (an unreliable narrator and the device of a dream, respectively). Just as significantly, "decadence" was already becoming visible not only in Yiddish texts but also as a recognized phenomenon in extratextual literary discourse about Yiddish literature: thus, between 1898 and 1900, Peretz warned the now-forgotten Yiddish writer Yitshok-Yankev Propus against a "*dekadentizm* [. . .] quite often as appetizing as wormy Swiss cheese."[36]

Finally, blurring my distinction between causal and counterfactual concerns, I would like to pinpoint the revealing difficulty of assessing the impact of 1905 in individual works. Peretz's 1908 symbolist masterwork *Ba nakht afn altn mark* (At night in the old marketplace) seems to offer a textbook case of a literary expression of postrevolutionary despair. Beyond the clear 1905 references within it—the "*dergreykhers*" in the "*hoykhe fenster*"[37] confronted by the workers on the street and the mock-hero with the martyred pogrom victims in tow—the play offers a full-fledged and bitter satire of Jewish political and cultural hopes in all their forms. Among its cast of symbolic characters, such moderns as poets ("artistic" and "folk" poets), assimilated Jews, Zionists, and even the workers prove unable to offer anything but phraseology. Moreover, in a rebuke to his own localist and national romanticism, Peretz represented his beloved religious and "folk" past, epitomized by the dead Jews of previous generations, as a realm of worthless decay, while the vicious "medieval" stance of the symbolically charged Polish nationalist characters, knights and churchmen, suggests despair about the Polish Jewish future. *Ba nakht* also subjected Peretz's own hopes for literature as a saving cultural power to a devastating and resigned critique: the jester, a liminal figure who bridges tradition and modern art through the grotesque, renounces the very hopes for a transcendent "word" that had powered Peretz's culturally and socially reconstructive agenda since 1891.[38]

Thus, the Zionist activist Yitzhak Grünbaum seems to be on solid ground when he pronounced *Ba nakht* a product of Peretz's own jaundiced revolutionary experience at the mass meetings of revolutionary Warsaw.[39] Yet Chone Shmeruk's archaeology of the play suggests deep problems with this view. Many of the play's central symbols and motifs— the wanderer, the devouring well at the center of the town—can be traced back to a long evolution in Peretz's poetry and prose of the 1890s. More broadly, the impulses of political and cultural despair that undergird the play were powerful, if partially submerged, forces in Peretz's thought and work well before 1905. As Shmeruk and Dan Miron argue, Peretz's dark vision of Jewish cultural collapse as represented through a phantasmogoric shtetl was the core structuring principle of several of his foundational works (most notably the 1891 "Rayze-bilder" [Travel scenes]) and reemerged at various junctures through the 1890s in such works as "The Dead Town" and "The Accursed Well" in jarring dissonance to the optimistic social-progressive postulates underpinning much of his writing in that decade.[40]

Peretz's related doubts about the very undertaking of Jewish literature and national salvation through cultural creation were, in turn, already thematized in two works, "Stories" and "The Pond," written at the height of his "folk-romantic" phase (1903–4). Both called into question the power, purpose, and even moral legitimacy of precisely the kinds of folk stories Peretz himself was then writing by situating such "redemptive" storytelling side by side with deflating representations of all-consuming poverty, ethnic hatred, and cultural collapse.[41] In short, Peretz's conviction that the solutions preferred by the Jewish leftist and national movements were empty may have been redoubled by 1905's failure, but his larger sense of a proverbial crisis of values and cultural possibility in Jewish life would have continued to permeate his work regardless.

Similar caution ought to be exercised in examining even literature infused with "self-evident" postrevolutionary angst. Although Der Nister did experience the revolution as a *vozrozhdenets* and felt that experience deeply, his letters suggest that his profound internalization of the urge to be a writer, his particular concepts of literary value, even his themes (dualism of the sacred and profane, for instance[42]) derived from the larger fin de siècle Russian scene.[43] More generally, it is significant that figures like Bergelson and Der Nister came of age not just circa 1905 but also at a moment when Yiddish literature and culture were increasingly well defined and when Russian culture had become second nature to educated Jewish youth. Their literary work was at least as much a response to the Warsaw-centered Yiddish literary establishment (which they held in contempt) and to prerevolutionary Russian and Hebrew literature in its Chekhovian or symbolist modes (as many critics have noted, Bergelson's work shows clear traces of Gnessin's influence) as it was to the revolution or its failure. In generic terms, too, all of these writers, from the postrealist Bergelson to the symbolist Der Nister to the lyric poet Hofshteyn, shared a commitment to genres that presupposed complex forms of reading and engagement in multiple literary traditions. The revolution and its Yiddishist tendencies may have helped channel these writers into Yiddish rather than Hebrew or the Slavic languages in which many of them experimented. But their genre commitments were not "produced" by the revolution but rather imported from the Russian and Hebrew literary spheres that were their natural point of reference and would have been so regardless of 1905.

Having questioned some assumptions about the revolution's expressly ideological and aesthetic role in the formation of the new Yiddish culture, I now tentatively suggest some hitherto uninvestigated ways in which 1905–7 *did* impact the cultural sphere. First, we might ask how distinctly revolutionary experiences and structures of mass mobilization left their mark on ways of organizing cultural life. One of the most striking features of the immediate post-1907 period was the proliferation of organized "art clubs" (*kunst-faraynen*). One observer described these as "a movement like any other: with activists, slogans."[44] Further research on these organizations may reveal a peculiar transposition into the cultural sphere of the whole political ambience associated with public meetings, organized party life, and democratic sentiment forged in 1905.

Second, we might ask whether the distinctive *psychological* sensibilities forged in the revolution had implications for how the Russian Jewish intelligentsia related to culture. One of the hallmarks of post-1905 Yiddishism evident in the trajectories of young *inteligentn* such as Shmuel Niger, Nokhem Shtif, and a good many others is the intense concern to Yiddishize not only their cultural production but also their private lives (a trend mirrored, as we know, in Second Aliyah circles). Thus, in a 1908 letter to Niger, the Hebrew-turned-Yiddish writer and revolutionary Anokhi implored Niger's wife to write him "in Yiddish, only in Yiddish."[45] In the Bundist press in 1911, Moyshe Olgin called on Bundists to bring Yiddish into their private and personal cultural lives by force of ideological commitment, despite what he acknowledged to be its perceived inferiority to the Russian culture so many of them valued as private individuals.[46] The contrast with the norms of pre-1905 Yiddish culture is striking: figures like Sholem Aleichem or Peretz felt no compulsion to Yiddishize their private lives. It bears asking whether this type of personal Yiddishism reflects the revolutionary's distinctive will to self-transformation in accordance with ideology.

Less speculatively, we may pinpoint one clear and unanticipated impact of 1905 on the Jewish cultural sphere. An undeniable concrete legal gain of 1905 for Jewish culture was the sharp reduction of restrictions on journalism and theater in Jewish languages.[47] This, in turn, allowed an explosion of market-driven Yiddish popular culture on stage and in the Yiddish press, as well as the invigoration of a middlebrow Yiddish culture that mixed the intelligentsia's exalted notions of "art" with a desire for entertainment and accessibility.[48] David Fishman and other scholars have observed that this fact in itself marked a major impact of 1905 on the Yiddish cultural sphere.[49] This argument can be taken a step further. A largely unremarked issue in the standard account is the Jewish cultural intelligentsia's tremendous resistance to both developments; many of them were compelled to work and write for the mass press and thus loathed it all the more.

This very reaction against market-driven culture deeply shaped postrevolutionary Yiddish high-culture initiatives. Nahman Mayzl and the Kiev compatriots who shared his contempt for Warsaw's market-oriented literary collections and their aesthetic "mishmash"[50] founded a literary publishing house in Kiev to bring out "purer" art. The famous 1908–10 efforts of Peretz and A. (Aleph) Vayter (Ayzik-Meir Devenishski) to organize a Yiddish art theater were in good part a reaction to the explosive development of Yiddish sensational theater in the wake of the 1905 legalization.[51] When Vayter and Niger presented the 1908 journal *Literarishe Monatsshriften* as a way to rescue Yiddish literature from the low level of its readership, they were in part confronting the unexpected offspring of the revolution's legal implications and pent-up Yiddish popular demand.[52] Significantly, none of this had to do with the specifically *ideological* dynamics of the revolution: rather, the confrontation between "high" and "low" so central to postrevolutionary Yiddish culture was a product of the precipitous interplay of a purely *legal* outcome of the revolution with a preexisting audience for post-traditional but accessible culture.

Returning, finally, to historiographers' enduring focus on the importance of the revolution as an *ideological* phenomenon for modern Jewish culture, I should like to suggest a more complicated analysis of the revolution's role in shaping the central question of the East European Jewish cultural sphere, namely: what should be the proper relationship between what contemporaries considered "culture" and what they called "politics"? Almost all the insider histories of the era trace this tension, as I have said, to the revolution and its suppression. I have argued, contrarily, that it is *not* the case that 1905 and its failure created the all-important distinction and tension between "culture" and "politics"; these were already intrinsic to the Jewish national intelligentsia's three-fold undertaking of creating a modern culture, a social revolution, and a nation.

Yet it is no accident that so many memoirists trace this axial opposition to the fateful year 1907–8, when the revolution expired and, not coincidentally, there was an upswing in Jewish cultural activity. That juncture saw a host of discursive and institutional struggles around the problem of "politics and culture" in the context of the already *clearly emergent* revival and expansion of active cultural engagement in many circles. First, there was a sharp discursive confrontation between those—Niger, Zerubovel, Shtif—who declared that the upswing in cultural engagement was a national victory in the midst of sociopolitical failure and those—above all the Bundists A. Litvak and Mark Liber—who saw it as a symptom of that failure and a betrayal.[53] Second, there was an equally sharp exchange (with overlapping players and additional partners such as An-sky) over the question of whether the intelligentsia should now cultivate a distinct Yiddish aesthetic high culture *insulated* from the influence of the masses or redouble its efforts to bring culture to the masses in accessible and acceptable form.[54] Third, there was a confrontation between those who demanded that culture should be "emancipated" from direct political determinations and those who insisted that it remain linked to party-political goals. This last confrontation expressed itself not only in discourse but also in the life of the cultural *fareynen*. Thus, while the Warsaw Literary Society saw a friendly symbiosis between *literatn* such as Peretz and the Warsaw Bundists who used it as a front, in the Lodz Harp, some sixty members led an organized campaign to resist efforts to politicize the organization; and at a Vilna literary evening, Litvak was publicly heckled for a Marxist analysis of Sholem Aleichem.[55]

Perhaps the question about the revolution's impact on the cultural sphere must be framed thus: what was it about the revolution's outcome that caused the intrinsic tensions between cultural and political activity to move to center stage in Jewish cultural life? All the memoiristic accounts insist that the actuating development was the willful *disassociation* of part of the intelligentsia from the revolution and the left in the name of independent culture—a treason, as it were, to the supposedly intrinsic alliance between the left and Yiddish culture. Yet I would argue that quite the opposite happened: the new factor that the revolution introduced into the Yiddish cultural sphere was *precisely* the left itself. Here, we should take note of an ongoing revision of the assumption that the left, and especially the Bund, played a key role in the prerevolutionary development of Yiddish culture. As Fishman, Ruth Wisse, and others have demonstrated, this is a retroactive account that greatly exaggerates the organized left's actual role in prerevolutionary Yiddish literary culture, while underestimating populist-Zionist institutions on the one hand (like *Der yid*) and individual groups of writers on the other, such as Peretz and his circle.[56]

It was, in fact, *after* the revolution that the Bund and other radical parties involved themselves centrally in the now burgeoning Yiddish cultural sphere, creating their own literary journals and organizations while seeking to influence others.[57] They did so, as we know, in order to redirect their radical energies in the face of political suppression. They—figures such as A. (Aleph) Litvak, Borekh Charney-Vladek, Liber, Ansky—also brought with them robust demands that cultural practice serve their ideological ends. But they did not recreate the Yiddish cultural sphere from scratch nor in accordance with their desires. On the contrary, the organized left, and those of the left who abandoned revolutionary politics, becoming its bête noir, happened to have entered cultural life in earnest at a moment when a host of unrelated *longer-term* developments—the formation of a potential mass readership and mass press; a new generation of educated writers schooled in Russian literature; aesthetic and generic differentiation in Yiddish literature itself—were coming to maturity, in part released or amplified by the revolution; and none of these developments easily fitted the leftist visions of an engaged culture.

In other words, the chief (and ironic) significance of 1905's failure was that it generated a *stronger* relationship between the suppressed but still powerfully committed left and the evolving Yiddish cultural sphere, and it was precisely this relationship that turned the distinction between art and party-political ideology from a *given* into an *issue*. It is here that we see most clearly the truth of the significance accorded 1905 as a turning point in Jewish cultural history; for it was this issue—the irresolvable conflict between the will to create a full-fledged modern Yiddish culture and the will to harness that culture to a revolutionary politics—that remained the central organizing conflict of the Yiddish cultural sphere for the rest of its pre-Holocaust history.[58]

Chapter 14

Jewish Cultural Associations in the Aftermath of 1905

Jeffrey Veidlinger

The political upheavals of the 1905 Revolution and its aftermath also brought about a transformation of sociocultural activity in the Russian Empire. As a result of the reforms associated with 1905, the decade before 1917 saw the proliferation of public spaces in Russia devoted to the dissemination of national cultures. Recent studies have shown how the commercialization of leisure through theaters, nightclubs, restaurants, tourist groups, and movie houses transformed the ways that middle-class Russians spent their time.[1] Cultural activity was institutionalized and nationalized in parallel with the commercialization of leisure. The spontaneity of the fairground and the casualness of the *kruzhok* (circle) were curtailed with the establishment of formal voluntary associations, premised on the bourgeois values of stability, transparency, and accountability. Such associations also served as guides for the navigation of new environments. Unsure of how to act in modern society, their constituents benefited from the opportunity to explore the world in the comfort of a group. Voluntary associations helped direct and channel newfound desires for leisure, intellectual enrichment, and social activism.

Adapting Jürgen Habermas's theories on the structural transformation of the bourgeois public sphere in early modern Western Europe,[2] scholars have often credited the post-1905 proliferation of voluntary associations in Russia with the genesis of a civil society. Most, though, have recognized the problems of grafting Habermas's theories onto tsarist Russia, where governmental restrictions prevented the formation of any truly autonomous public organizations.[3] David Wartenweiler, for instance, proposes that "far from grafting a potentially anachronistic notion onto late Imperial Russia, the ideas and representations at the heart of a civil society were, on the contrary, very much present in contemporary liberal thought."[4] Edith Clowes, Samuel Kassow, and James West, in applying the concept of civil society to imperial Russia, note that "the presence of civil society implies agreement on two things: the state should not and cannot do everything, and people are public as well as private creatures."[5] Although the nature of the relationship between public spaces and civil society in Russia remains controversial, the discourse of the public sphere urges us to look anew at the proliferation of voluntary associations that occurred in the interrevolutionary period.

The Jews, who had so few legal rights and so much to gain from a civil society, were among the most vocal proponents of the movement to establish formal voluntary associations within the public sphere. The Society for the Promotion of Enlightenment among the Jews of Russia (in Russia it was referred to by the initials OPE) was, of course, the oldest and most prestigious Jewish voluntary association in Russia. But there were also hundreds of others that pursued more culture-oriented paths toward the attainment of Jewish civil rights. The degree of public debate that existed among Russian Jewish intellectuals about the future of Russian Jewry is truly remarkable, as is the sheer number of cultural forums in which these issues were discussed and elaborated. In the words of Simon Dubnov, writing about the second half of the first decade of the twentieth century:

At that time, after the political disillusionment and that which was called rotten decadence in several circles of youth, a strong need for broad national-cultural work was felt in the healthy part of Jewish society. . . . In order to raise the level of social energy it was necessary to utilize the only achievement that was intact from the recent revolution: the relative freedom of the press and the right to conduct public lectures. The new law facilitated the establishment of societies and unions for cultural purposes . . . everywhere one noticed societal animation, everywhere discussion groups could be observed not only on cultural, but also on political themes, as long as the authorities did not suddenly wake up.[6]

Some scholars have recently turned their attention to the ways that Jews in Russia utilized voluntary associations in order to create new community structures. Christoph Gassenschmidt, for instance, has noted the role that the Jewish Saving and Loan Co-operative and other such organizations played in the economic development of the Jewish community, while Heinz-Dietrich Löwe has written on how mutual aid societies informed Jewish social policy in the decade after 1905.[7] These works have shown how modern Jewish voluntary associations gradually usurped the communal leadership roles previously played by traditional religious and secular authorities such as the kahal and hevres (brotherhood). With the waning of public trust in the traditional centers of power after the pogroms of 1881, voluntary associations helped reassert patterns of leadership. A crucial innovation in the character of such associations was that they were based upon the premise of inclusiveness. In stark contrast to the policies of selectivity that characterized many late nineteenth-century Jewish political and intellectual movements, voluntary associations aimed at disseminating knowledge or spreading cultural tastes to as broad a segment of the population as possible. Although few achieved the mass popularity that they sought, membership recruitment and expansion were always of paramount importance. In addition to giving political voice and financial stability to the bourgeoning Jewish public, though, Jewish activists also sought to mold the cultural tastes of that public.

This chapter will focus on two very different types of "societal animation" in order to point toward the variety of organized cultural activity that was underway in the interrevolutionary period. Both cases to be examined involve voluntary associations formed in accordance with legal principles as a forum in which individuals from different social networks could interact with each other on the basis of common interests. Both were also cultural in the sense that their primary goal was the dissemination of cultural ideas rather than tangible products. In contrast to mutual loan societies or societies for the aid of the poor, in which the distribution of economic goods was the primary goal, cultural societies, such as literary, historical, or music societies, sought to disseminate their own ideas and notions of culture. First, I discuss the Jewish Historical and Ethnographic Society (JHES), which drew its membership primarily from the upper-middle-class acculturated Jews of the imperial capital. Despite its efforts, the society failed to garner the type of mass membership it sought. I then turn to the provinces, where the decade after 1905 witnessed a trend toward the foundation of public libraries, established as official voluntary associations. Although they were never as widespread as their supporters desired, memoirs attest to the lasting impact that public libraries had on the small towns of the Pale.

Both types of institutions shared the goal of spreading education (a primary aim, too, of many other voluntary associations). In the first decade of the twentieth century, Russian liberal educators, acting with government acquiescence, set out to establish academic institutions designed both to cultivate citizenship in those excluded from the universities and to pursue research projects not supported by the government-run universities.[8] They believed that full civil emancipation and the formation of a civil society were possible only through the dissemination of education and that the formation of civic and national identities could best be cultivated through research into the past and present of the nation. Jewish activists soon followed with attempts to establish their own institutions to further education among the nascent Jewish middle class.

Many of these associations sought to promote public enlightenment through specialized research and the development of independent scholarly disciplines. The Jewish Historical and Ethnographic Society, among the most productive of such organizations in the empire, was modeled on similar historical societies in Western Europe with both research and public educational agendas. Before becoming an officially recognized society, the group that constituted its leadership had already been meeting since 1891 as a commission of the OPE. The commission, in turn, was an outgrowth of a circle of lawyers that compiled compendia of Russian law in order to ascertain the legal situation of Russian Jewry. In 1908 this circle evolved into the JHES. Among the members of the JHES were liberal activists of all stripes as well as both amateur and professional historians and ethnographers. They included the preeminent historian of Russian and Polish Jewry Simon Dubnov; the lawyer, political activist, and future Duma member Maksim Vinaver; the lawyer, publicist, and amateur historian Mikhail Kulisher; and the writer and ethnographer Solomon An-sky (Rappoport), whose famous ethnographic expedition to Volhynia and Podolia in the years preceding World War I was conducted under the auspices of the JHES.

Many of the activists involved in the formation of the JHES and other similar organizations were a close-knit group of people, mainly lawyers, who interpreted the failure of the Duma to abolish Jewish restrictions as a general failure of parliamentary politics. They turned their attention instead to the cultural realm in an effort to reconstruct Jewish society through "organic work." Members of this JHES founding group also helped establish the Jewish Advanced Courses in Oriental Studies in January 1908 and the Jewish Literary Society in October of that year.

The formulation of statutes in March 1908 marked the first step toward structuring the historical-ethnographical group as an official society, couching the society's goals in the language of scholarship and academic research:

1) The goals of the JHES are: a) studying and researching all realms of Jewish history and ethnography; and b) elaborating theoretical questions of historical and ethnographic scholarship.
2) To reach these goals the Society will: a) arrange meetings of its members, with proper permission from the authorities, for the purpose of academic reports and discussions; b) arrange public lectures about Jewish history and ethnography; c) publish, in fulfillment of these tasks, works in the form of single books, collected volumes, and periodical publications; d) propose problems to be solved by awarding monetary prizes and rewards.[9]

In addition, the society had the sociopolitical goal of rejuvenating Jewish identity and national awareness based on the idea that the Jews should be recognized and should recognize themselves as a nation as well as a confession. In the words of Maksim Vinaver, "We didn't even discuss the 'national idea,' we felt its invigorating effect."[10] Despite the legalized and detached language of their official statute—written in accordance with strict governmental guidelines—the members of the society clearly believed that they were writing not merely the Jewish past but also its future. "Through an understanding of the past, lies the path to the future," as Vinaver put it.[11]

Dubnov was even more blunt in his memoirs:

I have lost faith in personal immortality, but history teaches me that there is a collective immortality and that the Jewish nation can be considered relatively eternal, for its history coincides with the entire course of world history; therefore the study of the past of the Jewish people connects me to this type of eternity. This historicism united me with the national collective, guided me from the realm of individual problems to the social expanse, less deep but more authentic. National sorrow was closer than universal. There the path to a national synthesis was found in which the best elements of the old thesis are combined with the new antithesis, Jewish and universal ideals, the national and the humanist.[12]

The first meeting of the constituent assembly of the JHES took place on November 16, 1908, in the Aleksandrovskii Hall of the Choral Synagogue of St. Petersburg. Kulisher, with Vinaver and Dubnov sitting by his side, chaired this first meeting, which was attended by sixty-five participants.[13] Dubnov spoke, again emphasizing the role that the society was expected to play in the national rejuvenation of the Russian Jewish people:

I am speaking here about history not only as a scientific discipline but also as a vigorous factor of national culture. If we are truly to be called an "eternal people," we must clearly understand the eternal thread that connects our past, present and future into a single unity. . . . In the great struggle for our national existence—what does the energy of one generation mean when it is cut off from the great accumulation of national energy that builds up thanks to the heroic strength of a hundred generations? . . . My warmest hope is that our new society will become authentically historical, that it will serve to play a historic role in the history of our people.[14]

Over the course of the year, the society came to include 362 paying members. Within two years of its foundation, the society's membership included 427 individuals, 254 of whom lived in St. Petersburg.[15] This number rose steadily throughout the society's existence, reaching 823 in 1918, the last year for which statistics are available.[16]

The chief activity of the society was the publication of *Evreiskaia starina* (Jewish antiquity), a quarterly journal that met the highest standards of academic scholarship for its time. Each article contained a full academic apparatus, with all sources properly cited in footnotes. The full text of important documents was given in the original language either in the text of the article or in a footnote; the provenance of sources was discussed either in footnotes or in the text; and articles were written as part of an ongoing dialogue with the preexisting historiography.

Another major project of the JHES was the establishment of an archive of Jewish historical documents.[17] It included unpublished rabbinical and secular manuscripts; collections of hasidic legends; records of taxes and of property exchanges; photographs of synagogues, records of Jewish courts, rabbinical correspondence; and etchings taken from Jewish gravestones. The most numerous collection, though, was of minute books (*pinkasim*) from Jewish communal organizations, such as burial societies, synagogue committees, and, most important, from individual kahals (Jewish communal administrations). The society also allocated considerable funds to publishing as a supplement to *Evreiskaia starina* the minute book of the Council of the Lithuanian Land, which had likewise been acquired by its archives. Only in 1914 was publication of the minute book forestalled due to wartime censorship regulations forbidding the publication of Hebrew texts.[18] The society also published a third volume of Sergei Bershadskii's collections of early regulations and inscriptions relating to the Jews of Russia, Poland, and Lithuania.[19] The publication of such documents consumed 13.5 percent of the society's budget its first year. In addition, the St. Petersburg society provided grants to other cities toward the publication of their own historical documents.[20]

The society also emphasized its role in the area of youth education. It proposed the creation of a monthly journal for children that was never published—at least partially because of financial constraints. But it did oversee the publication of a Jewish history reader for schoolchildren. The first volume of the reader, covering the biblical period, was published in 1911 under the editorship of Leopold Sev and Kulisher.[21] Although plans were made for additional volumes, financial considerations and the poor sales of the first volume seem to have prevented their realization.[22]

The society also sponsored regular public lectures, delivered both by members of the society and visiting historians, on historical themes of general interest. In his lectures to the society, Dubnov presented some of his most salient observations and explications with regard to his sociological conception of Jewish history. One of the issues of most interest to the audience, probably in part due to the large number of lawyers who composed the society's membership, was the question of legal rights and juridical philosophies as elaborated throughout Jewish history. A brief examination of the topics raised in these talks reveals much about the issues and attitudes that predominated within the society. Some speakers followed the enlightenment tradition in positing a universal law that differed between cultures only in form but not in essential content, whereas others adopted romantic notions of the law, arguing that legal precepts expressed the national spirit of the people.

At least three speakers lectured on ancient Judaic law, all of whom tried in some way to situate Judaic law in the context of the legal norms and customs of the times. For instance, in his talk on the recently discovered law code of Hammurabi, Kulisher drew upon the newest scholarship to demonstrate that many biblical laws were borrowed from the Law of Hammurabi.[23] Similarly, when Rabbi Chaim Chernovits, the progressive rabbi of Odessa, came to speak to the group on the topic of Jewish law, he approached the subject from a comparative perspective, explaining the differences between Jewish and Roman law, while noting the changes that had occurred in Jewish law over time. The essence of Jewish law, he argued, was founded on the principles of universal morality, and it was worthy of study both because of the centrality of the Talmud, in particular, and also because of its relevance to the principles of law in general.[24]

When S. I. Aizenshtadt addressed the group on the topic "Ancient Jewish Law and its Principles" in October 1911, he, too, adopted a humanistic approach, drawing comparisons between Judaic and Roman law and arguing that, ultimately, the most important principles of Jewish law are the equality of all before the law and the freedom of the individual. The principle "love thy neighbor as thyself" stood for the sum of Jewish law. But Aizenshtadt also argued that Mosaic Law was derived from the customs of the folk—it was therefore national law in the modern sense rather than a "revealed legislation" as Moses Mendelssohn had argued. In fact, whereas Mendelssohn attempted to show the universality of law to argue that Judaic law did not differentiate Jews from the rest of society, Aizenshtadt's point was precisely the opposite: that Judaic law demonstrates the distinctness of the Jewish nation.

The notion of Judaic law as national or customary law was the subject of another report given in January 1913 by Ia. I. Treplitskii titled "Jewish Daily Law as an Element of National Culture." He maintained that the principles of Jewish family, contract, property, civil, and inheritance law all reflected the internal conditions of Jewish existence and therefore had and retain a great cultural significance for the Jewish nation.[25] Inspired by these talks, the members of the JHES decided in January 1913 to establish a separate division of the society dedicated exclusively to the study of Jewish law.

Finally, the society sponsored numerous ethnographic expeditions to Jewish population centers. By far the most important of these was Ansky's 1911–14 ethnographic expedition to the Pale of Jewish Settlement, in which he and his team visited over 70 sites, collected over 1,800 folk tales, took over 2,000 photographs, collected over 300 objects of religious and cultural significance, and made over 500 wax cylinder recordings. The JHES also sponsored expeditions to the non-Ashkenazic Jews of the Crimea, the Caucasus, and Turkestan led by Shmuel Vaysenberg and followed his work among these groups closely. Visitors from these regions were also welcomed at the JHES meetings. The Sevastopol archaeologist A. Ia. Gidalevich, for instance, presented a report on sketches he had made of old Jewish synagogues in the Crimea. [26] He later donated a series of engravings he had made of Jewish gravestones from the town of Mangup-Kale, which included fifty inscriptions from the sixteenth and seventeenth centuries.[27] But ultimately, the JHES was more successful in collecting relics from the provinces than in spreading its vision of enlightenment there.

Provincial Jews, however, were not only the passive subjects of ethnographic expeditions sponsored by societies based in the capitals but also active participants in the movement to establish voluntary associations in their own regions. "After 1905, the time of confusion in Russia," wrote a native of Lipkany in Bessarabia, "when a little freer air began to blow, one could find in Lipkany a group of young nationalist and worldly, educated students who, having studied in larger cities, became infected with progressive ideas and the spirit of those times."[28] University students returning home for the summer brought with them the organizational skills and social aspirations that they had acquired in the big cities. Dovid Roykhl, for instance, recalls the summer of 1909 when he returned to Kremenets from his studies in Odessa, where he had belonged to a *krayzl* (small circle). Upon his return he coordinated with several fellow students from neighboring towns for the purpose of acquainting the youth of the region with the activities of enlightened circles in the cities. He established a group of activists to disseminate journals through subscriptions that could be paid for in installments; as a result, thirty-four new subscribers were recruited in Kremenets. The group then negotiated agreements with booksellers in Vilna and later Warsaw that entitled it to receive a 40 percent discount by paying in cash for books, a reduction that was then passed on to the consumer. In this manner, the group was able to disseminate the works of Mendele, Peretz, Sholem Aleichem, Sholem Asch, and others, and an informal circle was transformed into a more formal literary society.[29]

Most common folk who were able to obtain secular books did so either from traveling booksellers or from private libraries in the shtetl. Avraham Slutski, for instance, tells of how he read secular books as a youth in his Belorussian town in the early 1900s:

In the shtetl, one could find intelligentsia and men of means who owned private libraries, in some of which one could from time to time read a book, but it was not convenient for us young people of poor parents to call upon the well-to-do aristocrats very often. One read what came to hand. From time to time a traveling bookseller would arrive in the shtetl. People would buy from him stories and jokes about Hershele Ostropoler or novels by Shomer or Elyakum Tsunzer. This type of literary work would from time to time be read by one of us at a gathering [*farzamlung*] of boys and girls.[30]

The turn toward a more binding kind of organization came, in Slutski's case, when he and a group of friends secretly subscribed to a Bundist journal: "Around us quickly formed a circle [*krayz*] of listeners, who with great thirst would listen to what one of us read." The conspiracy of subscribing in secret required a level of trust and commitment greater than that involved in simply sharing the cost of a book. Slutski makes the distinction between the informal gatherings and the circle of subscribers clear by referring to the former as a *farzamlung* and the latter as a *krayz*.

Typically, many of the memoirs tell of the formation of formal and informal societies for the purpose of sharing books; and the most widespread voluntary associations founded in the years after 1905 were libraries. The first secular Jewish libraries in the empire had been established in the late nineteenth century. The Lithuanian town of Mir, for instance, famous for its yeshiva, was also well known for its library, which was founded in the late 1890s by a group of young enlightened thinkers who had left the yeshiva. Because they were unable to obtain official permission for the creation of a Jewish public library, the founders of the library camouflaged their institution as a bookstore, even putting false stamps in the first books. Funding came from private cash donations, and the books were acquired mostly through donation.[31]

The major impediments to the formation of public libraries in Russia prior to 1905 were legal. Censorship regulations restricted acquisitions by public libraries to a list distributed by the Ministry of Education. Private libraries for which admission was charged were permitted to carry any books in any languages that were not specifically banned, whereas free libraries were permitted to carry only books that were specifically approved to that end by the censors, a figure that amounted to only approximately 8 percent of all books that went past the censors. Organizations seeking to form a library were also required to submit their charters to the provincial governor for approval. Many local authorities, with little interest in educating the general public, routinely turned down petitions requesting permission to establish a library.[32]

The Jewish population faced additional impediments to the establishment of Jewish libraries. For instance, not a single book in Yiddish was on the list of books approved for free public libraries, and only a few in Russian on Jewish subjects were listed. Moreover, Jewish readers, who were on the average poorer than their Russian counterparts, were more likely to need a free library. The bureaucratic hurdles that stood in the way of obtaining permission to establish a formal library also discouraged many would-be patrons from attempting to do so.

In a series of laws passed in late 1905 and early 1906, however, the procedure for obtaining permission to establish a library was streamlined, and it was then that the OPE began a massive campaign to establish public libraries throughout the Pale. Although there were many more informal reading circles and illicit libraries throughout the region, the society believed that only public libraries with open reading rooms accessible to the entire community were fully capable of serving as sources of enlightenment. The campaign began with a survey of the existing situation that concluded that the spread of Jewish public libraries was haphazard, with many large cities still lacking such institutions in 1905. Furthermore, nearly three-quarters of the existing libraries were not fully communal in that their charters had been issued to private individuals rather than to communal organizations or to the community as a whole. The OPE encouraged the formation of libraries with charters issued either to the community as a whole or to a communal organization, such as a local mutual aid society, synagogue, or trade organization.

The OPE also sought to disseminate information on the methods of cataloging and collecting books; to make specific recommendations with regard to acquisitions and to reading programs; and to subsidize the establishment of local libraries. As one activist wrote, "Whereas our fathers and grandfathers saw in books the key to an understanding of God and his commandments, the young generation of Russian Jews, having become part of general European civilization, together with the already adult and soon-to-mature thinking proletariat, search in books for solutions to all their troubling problems—general, cultural, national, and political."[33]

Typical of the development of libraries in small towns was the aforementioned Bessarabian town of Lipkany. At the turn of the century, the only secular reading materials widely available were mayse-bikher (popular stories) and romances that could be rented from traveling booksellers. But in 1907 the Eliezer Steinberg Memorial Library, named after the Jewish fable collector and Yiddish writer who had been a native of Lipkany, was established. It did not have a permanent home but rather moved from private house to house. It was open daily from two in the afternoon until late at night and served not only as a library but also as a gathering place for the community. This formalized structure contrasted with the informal individualism of the bookseller.[34] Not long afterward, the local branch of the Society for the Lovers of the Hebrew Language established another library in the town.

Following the 1905 Revolution, the number of Jewish public libraries in the Russian Empire increased nearly threefold from about 100 in 1905 to nearly 300 in 1910. Library development, though, was uneven. Some regions, such as Chernigov, still had no Jewish public libraries in 1910, whereas others, like Mogilev, Kherson, and Bessarabia, each had over twenty. On average the distribution of Jewish libraries was about one for every 17,500 people, far below the one for every 8,000 that was considered ideal. Within the Pale of Settlement (not including Poland), though, the ratio was somewhat better at about one for every 15,000. The most dramatic increases in this period were achieved in Mogilev and Vitebsk, two regions in which the Moscow OPE concentrated its efforts at encouraging and subsidizing library development.[35]

Perhaps even more important than the sheer numbers was the percentage of libraries that were run by public organizations. Whereas individuals of enlightened inclinations could, and often did, establish libraries that were open to the public, they lacked the institutionalized grounding, governance transparency, and perceived stability of libraries established by formal voluntary associations. It is therefore of great significance that the percentage of libraries run by such associations increased in the five years after 1905 from 36 to 55 percent of all Jewish libraries open to the reading public. It is also significant that associations with specific cultural agendas increased their share of libraries in this period. In 1905, some half of the libraries were run by such organizations as mutual aid societies and societies for aid to the poor, whereas only 21 percent had been established by organizations interested primarily in enlightenment. By 1910, in contrast, 69 percent of the libraries were in the hands of organizations whose primary goal was the spread of enlightenment, typically literary societies, branches of the OPE, or even associations formed explicitly for the purpose of developing a library.[36]

Libraries were not just storehouses of books. Rather, they were, for the most part, bustling centers of intellectual and social exchange, where users—mainly young men and women—could meet in a realm beyond the restraints of traditional society. An evening at the library was a communal activity. Not only was reading itself often communal but also the library functioned as a surrogate community center. In Baranovits, for example, the Jewish Literary-Artistic Society, which was founded in 1907–8, established a reading room and a library, as well as a small theater hall occupying the second floor of the building that housed it. "It was located in the very center of the city," according to one former resident, "and everybody could feel at ease and at home there. . . . In the years before World War I, [it] was a lively nerve center of social life in Baranovits and the only place in which cultural activity was concentrated. Here theater performances, concerts, anniversary celebrations, Hanukah festivities, and traditional Purim balls would take place as well as literary evenings and other activities."[37] When celebrities such as Sholem Aleichem and Mikhail Gnessin visited the city, they would give public lectures or presentations at the library. One resident of Kamin-Koshirskii in Northern Volhynia recalls, probably of the interwar period, that the library was "the cultural center of our shtetl. There the youth would get together, regardless of political affiliation" and would meet for literary discussions and meetings.[38]

Jews began to establish formal voluntary associations on a mass scale in the Russian Empire around the time of the 1905 Revolution. That is not to say that individuals had not formed voluntary groupings prior to this period. But what occurred around 1905 was qualitatively and quantitatively different from what preceded it. These differences were recognized even by contemporaries, who used a variety of terms for these new associations. The Hebrew term *hevre*, which was used for traditional and religious organizations, and the Yiddish terms *zamlung* (gathering) and *krayz or krayzl* (circle), both of which referred to informal gatherings parallel to the Russian *kruzhok* (circle), were replaced by the Yiddish term *gezelshaft* (society). *Gezelshaft* was used as a translation of the Russian *obshchestvo* (society), a formal voluntary association with a charter and bylaws approved by the state. A *hevrat koneh sfarim* (brotherhood for the purchase of books), for instance, would be expected to purchase only religious books, whereas its Yiddish equivalent, a *bibliotek gezelshaft*, would be expected to purchase secular books.

Voluntary associations institutionalized culture, creating a public space where individuals with common interests could socialize and enjoy their leisure time together. They functioned as social equalizers, providing opportunities for new social mixings considered taboo by traditional Jewish society. For instance, women were included in many of these societies, turning them, along with the burgeoning political organizations, into one of the first social groupings in which young Jewish men and women could freely interact. It was not just gender but also class differences that the voluntary associations helped overcome. The daughter of a *melamed* whose home housed a public library in Luninets recalls, "Every Friday afternoon in our house, visitors came from among the dressmakers, servant girls, clerks, and workers—cobblers and tailors—who would remember, coming from the baths, to stop by Avraham Hershl the melamed's [house] to take a book for Shabes . . . the library had a great influence on the readers."[39]

Men and women alike recall how these societies helped open their eyes to a larger world. "It did not take long for several of us small-town more developed youth (you understand, with a talmudic education and religious upbringing) to begin to see for ourselves a new world with entirely different horizons," wrote one.[40] "The small-town folk became familiar with the larger world," wrote another; "it opened their eyes and they realized that there is a big world with problems outside of Luninets and even beyond Pinsk."[41] By taking leisure out of the home and into the public arena, the voluntary associations transformed the structure of Jewish social and cultural life. Libraries in the provinces provided a common public space for learning, socializing, and entertainment. Likewise, the JHES and similar organizations in the capitals provided such space for the intellectual exchange of ideas and for the institutionalization of networking cells.

Chapter 15
Writing between the Lines: 1905 in the Soviet Yiddish Novel of the Stalinist Period

MIKHAIL KRUTIKOV

In his introduction to *Di klyatshe* (The mare, 1873), one of his most ambitious and complex novels, Mendele Moykher Seforim offered the reader a key to the text:

> *Di klyatshe* is written in a lofty manner, the style of the ancients. Each reader will comprehend it in accordance with his intelligence and on his own level. For people on a superficial level, it will simply be a lovely tale, and they will enjoy the plot. But those on a deeper level will also find an allusion, an application to us sinful human creatures. I, for example, on my level, found in it nearly all Jewish souls, all our beings, and the secret of what we are doing in this world.[1]

Mendele's formula—which is obviously rooted in the medieval tradition of scriptural exegesis—can be applied not only to the works of the founding fathers of modern Yiddish literature but also to those of their followers. This chapter attempts to look through Mendele's prism at the multilayered narrative of Soviet Yiddish prose produced during the 1930s under the severe ideological pressure of the Stalinist period.

Soviet critics perceived the 1905 Revolution as an important although somewhat underrepresented theme in Soviet Yiddish literature. In his survey of Soviet Yiddish prose in 1939, the critic M. Dubilet described Dovid Bergelson's *Baym Dniepr* (At the Dnieper) and Lipman-Levin's *Dem shturem antkegn* (Toward the storm):

> Our writers pay great attention to the representation of the past, and especially to the theme of the 1905 Revolution. . . . These works are of great principal importance. As is known, the 1905 Revolution has hardly been reflected in Yiddish revolutionary prose. Now our writers are filling the gap. Only now does the "dress rehearsal" receive a correct reflection, one that is both broad and deep. The working class, which in the prerevolutionary works of Yiddish prose was left standing somewhere in the background, is now being moved up to the front stage.[2]

Whereas *Baym Dnieper*, Bergelson's two-volume autobiographical epic and his last novel, has received some attention from contemporary scholars,[3] the other book mentioned by Dubilet, Lipman-Levin's[4] *Dem shturem antkegn*, appears to be completely forgotten. The other example, the unfinished novel draft *Fun finftn yor* (From the year 1905), by the great Yiddish modernist author Der Nister, was not published until years after his death.

The Revolution of 1905 was one of the most glorious episodes of the Soviet Jewish usable past as it was constructed during the 1920s and 1930s. It created an opportunity to celebrate a heroic Jewish character in the setting of the all-Russian revolution, provided, of course, that the narrative conformed to the normative historical scheme that was current at the moment of publication. The very dynamics of the revolutionary events offered a plot scheme that had been aptly captured already in Sholem Aleichem's 1909 story "Baranovich Station." Summarizing a typical conversation among Jews traveling in an archetypical third-class railroad carriage, the fictional narrator followed a pattern that could fit in almost every Jewish narrative of 1905. Regardless of the starting point, the subject of those train conversations in the post-1905 Pale of Settlement invariably shifted "to the war with Japan, while after barely five minutes of fighting the Japanese, we moved on to the Revolution of 1905. From the Revolution we passed to the Constitution, and from the Constitution it was but a short step to the pogroms, the massacres of Jews, the new anti-Semitic legislation, the expulsion from the villages, the mass flight to America."[5] Indeed, the three-part "War-Revolution-Pogroms" scheme was first utilized by Sholem Aleichem himself in his novel *Der mabl* (The flood, 1907) and then reproduced, with some variations, by Sholem Asch in his 1911 novel *Meri* (Mary). A similar scheme can be found, fully or partially, in virtually every Yiddish work of fiction about 1905 written since then.[6]

The revolutionary theme presented writers both with an opportunity and a challenge, a chance to combine a romantic story of adventure with an ideological message, and Yiddish literature was no exception. Thus, to convey his Zionist message, Sholem Aleichem used the symbolism of Exodus, whereas the diaspora-nationalist ideology of Sholem Asch was evident in his opposition to the urban civilization, which he perceived as a threat to Jewish authenticity. Unlike their predecessors, the Soviet Yiddish authors did not enjoy freedom of choice when it came to matters of ideology, and they had to cleave to the line that was imposed by the party leadership at that particular moment. As a result, any Soviet work of fiction had to contain explicit ideological statements. Any other meanings—if they existed at all—were accessible only to the attentive reader capable of reading "between the lines."

These additional narrative layers could potentially carry subversive messages that clashed with the rigid master narrative of socialist realism. A general principle regarding this kind of writing was formulated by Leo Strauss:

If an able writer who has a clear mind and a perfect knowledge of the orthodox view and all its ramifications contradicts surreptitiously, and as it were in passing, one of its necessary presuppositions or consequences that he explicitly recognizes and maintains everywhere else, we can reasonably suspect that he was opposed to the orthodox system as such and—we must study his whole book all over again, with much greater care and much less naïveté than ever before.[7]

Guided by this rule, as well as by common sense, we can try to imitate the process of textual "deconstruction" that must have been familiar to those among Soviet Yiddish readers who had received training in traditional scriptural exegesis and were at the same time familiar with the conventions of modern Yiddish literature established by Mendele, Sholem Aleichem, and Peretz. Without being able to determine precisely the intended audience for such hints, we can reasonably assume that any author who placed such coded messages must have intended them to be noticed by at least some of his readers.

Lipman-Levin, the author of *Dem shturem antkegn* (Moscow, 1938), was, in his own way, a unique phenomenon in Soviet Yiddish letters. Born in Mogilev in 1877, he began his literary career writing for the Cracow Yiddish newspaper *Der yid* in 1900 and soon earned a reputation as a prolific and popular Hebrew and Yiddish author. His short stories, novellas, and articles appeared regularly in the Yiddish papers *Der yid, Der fraynd, Di yidishe tsaytung*, as well as in the Hebrew periodicals *Hashiloah, Hazman*, and *Luah ahiasaf*; two collections of his Yiddish stories came out in Vilna (1909, 1914), and a collection of his Hebrew stories appeared in Warsaw (1908). Demobilized from the Russian army in 1917, he briefly served as the secretary of the Moscow Jewish community. During that period he was engaged in writing an epic trilogy in Hebrew titled *Beaviv haolamot* (In the spring of the worlds) that was to cover the period between the 1905 Revolution and World War I.

The trilogy remained unpublished, but Lipman-Levin presumably used it as a draft for his two Yiddish novels: *Doyres dervakhte* (The awakened generations [Moscow, 1934]) and *Dem shturem antkegn*. Unlike some other Soviet Yiddish writers, Lipman-Levin did not go into exile after 1917, but he remained silent during the 1920s. When he resumed his writing activity in the early 1930s, his texts appeared to be meticulously attuned to the requirements of socialist realism. Titles such as *Merke di pionerke* (Merke the pioneer) and *Di konstitutsye oysnveynik* (The constitution memorized) give an idea of the direction Lipman-Levin's writing took in that period. He survived the war and died peacefully in Moscow soon after his seventieth birthday, which was widely celebrated in Yiddish literary circles.[8]

The novel *Dem shturem antkegn* opens in the early spring of 1905 with the release from prison of Slavke Ginzburg, the only daughter of a wealthy merchant in a provincial capital. Arrested for the possession of revolutionary literature, she is freed in a few weeks, apparently after her father makes an effective intervention on her behalf to the authorities. For the young and beautiful woman, the ideal of the revolution is embodied in the person of a handsome young man named Dovid Blyum. Unfortunately for Slavke, Dovid had to leave town a day before her release from prison. In accordance with the rules of the romantic adventure story, the reunion of the hero and the heroine is delayed by various circumstances until the final chapter. The intervening space is packed with various revolutionary activities. The action shifts back and forth between the provincial capital, a remote shtetl, and its surrounding villages. Within two to three months, Slavke undergoes a transformation from spoiled and wealthy girl to professional revolutionary.

In contrast to most other authors of novels in Yiddish focused on 1905, including Sholem Aleichem and Sholem Asch, Lipman-Levin did not carry his tale up to the October pogroms. Instead, he chose to replace the pogrom by a theatrical travesty. When the authorities try to incite pogromist feelings in the provincial capital by sponsoring a performance of the antisemitic play *The Smugglers* by a touring Russian theater company, the joint forces of Jewish and non-Jewish Bolsheviks ingeniously thwart this provocation by spreading sneezing powder and revolutionary leaflets around the theater.[9]

This episode is based on a real incident that took place on November 23, 1900, when an organized group of students staged what became "the worst riot in the history of Russian theater" by raising "a prearranged cacophony of yelling, stomping, rattling, and whistling," "supplemented by a variety of projectiles, including potatoes, cucumbers, rotten apples, binoculars, gloves, and boots," at the first performance of *The Smugglers* (the creation of an apostate author named Litvin-Efron) at the St. Petersburg Malyi theater, which belonged to the notorious antisemitic editor and journalist Aleksei Suvorin.[10] The play was then taken on tour, and, as Simon Dubnov relates, "in a considerable number of cities where the play was presented, such as Smolensk, Orel, Kishinev, Tiflis, and others, violent demonstrations took place in the theaters" that led to clashes with the police.[11]

The impact of those theater riots was such that: "[L]ooking back in 1908, a high-ranking police official, determined to see a Jewish conspiracy as the driving force behind Russia's recent revolutionary upheaval, reported to Prime Minister Stolypin that 'the beginning of the Russian Revolution must be reckoned not as January 9, 1905 ["Bloody Sunday," the massacre of peacefully marching workers in front of the Winter Palace], as the revolutionary parties are accustomed to doing, but November 23, 1900.' "[12]

Moving this episode nearly five years ahead in time enabled Lipman-Levin not only to place the 1900 theater riots in the immediate context of the 1905 Revolution but also to portray it as a Bolshevik action. The coded language of those Bolsheviks betrays their familiarity with Jewish tradition: one of them refers to the revolutionary leaflets as "shirhamayles."[13] (If the tsarist police official had had a chance to read the novel, he probably would have found the image of a Jewish Bolshevik in full conformity with his stereotype.)

In the novel, the theater riot takes place in the spring rather than in the autumn, which enabled Lipman-Levin to incorporate it into the buildup to the First of May rally. Ideologically, May First was celebrated in opposition to the traditional Passover as the festival of liberation. From a compositional point of view, however, the First of May and Passover both play the same role: they are events that serve to unite all the major characters in a show of hope. Led by Dovid Blyum, the Bolshevik Moses, the revolutionary forces walk into their first open confrontation with the modern-day pharaoh.

In contrast to Slavke, Dovid Blyum undergoes no change during the novel's action, which is indicative of the socialist realist representation of gender roles. A committed Bolshevik of impeccable working-class origins, Blyum has apparently received a solid Jewish education, which has enabled him to expose his Zionist opponent not only as an ideological reactionary but also as an ignoramus in Hebrew. A competent entrepreneur, Blyum is put in charge of the entire cycle of propaganda production, from drafting the texts through printing and distributing thousands of leaflets; an inspired speaker and teacher, he is equally good at mass rallies and in underground classes on political economy and revolutionary theory. His handsome looks make him irresistible to every woman he meets, sending a strong erotic current running through the entire narrative. In short, David Blyum embodies an ideal combination of youth, Bolshevism, and Jewishness that could not fail to appeal to a certain segment of the Yiddish-reading audience in the Soviet Union.

Whereas some parts of the novel were obviously reworked in order to suit the requirements of the socialist realist master narrative, others appear to have been adopted from the pre-Soviet, perhaps Hebrew, version with little alteration. In the latter sections the everyday life of the Jewish middle class is portrayed in a way that brings to mind Dovid Bergelson's prerevolutionary writing. Less innovative and original than Bergelson, Lipman-Levin was also more sympathetic to the concerns of the older generation that had to deal with the new revolutionary passion that took possession of their children's minds and souls. Worried about their daughter's future, Slavke's parents turn for help to the *gvirisher shadkhen* (the matchmaker for wealthy families), Nakhmen Zhuravitsher, a character who closely resembles the Talmud teacher Yankef-Nosn Viderpolyer, a hero of David Bergelson's unfinished novel *Yoysef Shor*, who tried his hand at arranging a match between two modern young people.

A shrewd businessman, Nakhmen quickly realizes that the revolutionary movement opened up new market opportunities. He sets off to Moscow with a plan to arrange a match between Slavke and the son of a merchant family who also had the misfortune to have spent a few months in prison for *hayntike mayses* ("today's affairs," meaning involvement in politics):

"So, both of them have warts: if this is a defect, both of them have the same defect; if this is a nice thing, let them be happy and enjoy it." (Oyb azoy, zaynen dokh beyde mit brodavkes: iz dos a khesorn, hot ir beyde eyn khesorn, iz dos a kheyn, az zol es aykh lib un nikhe zayn.)[14]

Needless to say, within the rigid ideological framework of the socialist realist novel, Nakhmen's efforts are doomed to failure. Slavke has no time for the wealthy young Muscovite who turns out to be a Jewish nationalist. Without hesitation, she leaves the comfort of her parents' bourgeois home when the party needs to send her on a secret mission to a remote shtetl.

The adherence to the rules of socialist realism did not prevent Lipman-Levin from borrowing motifs and situations from his prerevolutionary predecessors. Dovid's methods of educating the shtetl youth in the foundations of Marxism-Leninism have their parallel in the maskilic stories "The Sins of Youth" and "Behind a Mask" by S. An-sky; the depiction of the worker's "birzhe" in a provincial town closely resembles the passages in An-sky's novella *In a New Stream*, while the episode in which teenage revolutionaries mislead a policeman by using heavily Hebraized Yiddish—*shabes loshn*—obviously comes from Sholem Aleichem's novel *Motl, the Cantor's Son.*

In order to fulfill one of the key requirements of the socialist realist style, Lipman-Levin took great care to maintain the exact balance between Jewish and non-Jewish participation in the revolution. He probably drew the correct conclusions from the critical discussions of the late 1920s, when most of the leading Soviet Yiddish authors were accused of singling out Jewish participation in the revolutionary movement. Similarly, Lipman-Levin excludes the Bundists and Zionists not only from all revolutionary activity but also from Jewish self-defense, reducing their image to caricature and limiting their role to parlor talk. The active characters, such as Dovid and Slavke, never fail to adhere to the decisions of the Second Congress of the RSDRP (Russian Social Democratic Labor Party) and the latest directives emanating from the newspaper *Iskra* before taking action. They never have moments of doubt and always obey directions from the invisible party leadership.

In short, *Shturem antkegn* could be presented as a perfect example of the socialist realist Yiddish novel created by an experienced and skillful author. Keeping silent for nearly fifteen years, Lipman-Levin must have learned a lot from the fierce debates that were going on in Soviet Yiddish literature. He made sure "to cover all his bases" and to preempt the possible accusations of bourgeois nationalism, modernism, or anti-historicism. With all that, his novel remains firmly grounded in the Yiddish literary tradition familiar to a significant segment of his readers that also offers keys to an alternative reading of the narrative, placing the emphasis on the hidden meanings rather than on the overtly socialist realist declarations.

Der Nister (Pinkhas Kahanovich, 1884–1950) is remembered today mostly for his early symbolist tales and the historical novel *The Family Mashber* (1939–48). This novel, which presents a broad panorama of Jewish life in the aftermath of the Polish uprising of 1863, was apparently intended to serve as the first part in a series of novels that would lead to the 1905 Revolution. The author's arrest in 1949 and his subsequent death in a prison hospital in 1950 prevented him from completing his planned series. However, a short draft manuscript of the last part, titled *Fun finftn yor* (From the year 1905), survived and was published in 1964 in the Moscow Yiddish journal *Sovetish heymland.*[15] Unlike other works by Der Nister, this fragment was not received favorably by Yiddish critics outside the Soviet Union, including Chone Shmeruk, who dismissed it as "unambiguously realistic and [. . .] marked by an almost hackneyed ideological and artistic conception."[16] The only notable exception was Eliezer Podryatshik, who deciphered the manuscript and prepared it for publication while he still was in the Soviet Union but did not change his positive opinion after his immigration to Israel. In his insightful analysis of the fragment, which took into consideration also the unpublished second part, Podryatshik made a convincing attempt to recover the autobiographical and historical elements in Der Nister's fiction. Contrary to Shmeruk, Podryatshik placed *Fun finftn yor* in the category of the *genize-shafungen* (secret writings) of Soviet Yiddish authors.[17]

Like *The Family Mashber, From the Year 1905* is set in an anonymous city that can be easily identified as the author's native Berdichev. The two characters, Leybl and Milye, come from the upper and lower rungs respectively of Berdichev Jewish society, which enables the author to depict the range of social differentiation. Their encounter and mutual attachment is presented as a direct outcome of their involvement in the revolutionary struggle. Leybl's selfless idealism, which is described as typical of the revolutionary youth, stands in contrast to his mother's obsession with money and status. A domineering businesswoman, she works hard to find a right match for her only son, but when she discovers that he has fallen in love with Milye, who is socially unacceptable to her, she loses her mind. Blinded by her rage, she denounces the entire revolutionary organization to the authorities, sending her own son to prison. Eventually she commits suicide, unable to cope with the disaster that she has brought upon herself.

Milye's mother, on the contrary, chooses to join the revolutionary movement and dies under the bullets of the tsarist police, when, red banner in hand, she leads the first protest demonstration in town. Certain structural and thematic parallels between *Shturem antkegn* and *Fun finftn yor* may suggest that Der Nister was not only familiar with Lipman-Levin's novel but also tried to imitate his narrative strategy. Indeed, the popularity of Lipman-Levin's novel provides grounds to assume that other Soviet Yiddish writers were acquainted with it. Thus, both novels end in a similar fashion, putting the revolutionary demonstration in the place of the "traditionalist" pogrom. Similarly to Lipman-Levin, Der Nister emphasizes the intellectual dexterity and the entrepreneurial competence of Jewish revolutionaries. In both novels, the revolutionary Jews are engaged mostly in producing propagandistic literature and smuggling weapons from abroad, the kinds of activities that are closer to traditional Jewish occupations than direct revolutionary violence.

To clarify the ideological message of the novel, Der Nister employs the didactic narrative voice of an "implied author," in which he explains the meaning of the events from a monistic perspective closely resembling orthodox Marxist historical materialism but nevertheless differing from it in certain substantial points. The spring of 1905, this voice tells us, marked one of those special moments in history when the poor masses, nature, and a young couple happened to be affected by the miracle of awakening. The tragedy of Leybl's mother, as well as that of all other wealthy Jews, was rooted in their inability to sense the changing spirit of the times because their natural sensitivity had been blunted in this situation by their pursuit of wealth and status. Anyone familiar with Der Nister's earlier symbolist works can identify hidden references to the secularized pantheistic messianism that informed his artistic philosophy during the 1920s.

It is difficult to agree with Shmeruk's assertion that "this conception fits well the principles of the ruling Soviet 'proletarian' criticism of the period 1928–1932" because proletarian criticism rigidly required a representation of the internationalist working class as the active agent of historical change. Neither workers nor non-Jews play a significant role in Der Nister's fragment, which is overpopulated by young Jewish intellectuals. Indeed, Shmeruk's opinion that "the novel is free of any ideological deviations that might have forced the author to keep it in his 'drawer,'" and that therefore "it could have been freely published at any time after Der Nister's return to the Soviet Union, and every Soviet publishing house would have been delighted to accept it,"[18] seems to underestimate the erudition and critical intelligence of Stalinist censors. *Fun finftn yor* could appear in print only when it actually did—during the short-lived period of Khrushchev's "Thaw."

The most intriguing episode in the fragment is the depiction of a secret gathering attended by the representatives of different Jewish socialist groups. Their fierce debate is conducted in a form similar to that of a talmudic dispute and, like the famous discussion of the sages in the Passover Haggadah, goes on until the morning. Podryatshik identified this event as the Berdichev conference of December 1905, at which the leadership of the Poale Zion tried to work out a new strategy in the light of the evolving revolutionary situation. According to the two leading Poale Zion activists, Zerubovel and Rachel Yanait, the young Pinye Kahanovich (Der Nister) was also present at that conference.[19] For understandable reasons, Der Nister chose not to describe in detail the ideological debates between different groups, all of which were, of course, branded as nationalist and reactionary by the official Soviet historiography. Instead, he concentrated on portraying the character of the participants, all but one of whom remains anonymous in his novel.

Among the participants of the revolutionary "Sanhedrin," as the meeting is referred to in the novel, is

a certain comrade Borekh-Ber, as he was called, still a young man, but overgrown—not so much with the hair on his head and his beard, as with an excess of knowledge and information. He had been made nearly blind by his penchant, developed from childhood, for every kind of book, from which he scooped treasures with full hands, a sharp but an undisciplined and casuistical intellect . . . (eyner a khaver Borekh-Ber, vi me hot im gerufn, nokh a yunger mentsh, ober a shtark bavaksener, nit azoy mit hor fun kopf un fun der bord, vi mit fil kentenish un yedies, velkhe hobn im gemakht blindlekh-kurtszikhtik fun hobn tsu ton fun yungerheyt on mit farsheydene bikher, fun velkhe er hot geshept fule oytsres mit fule zhmenyes, a sharfer bal-moyekh, ober nit genug organizirter, a tsedreyter. . . .).[20]

As a high school student, the young prodigy Borekh-Ber mastered Kantian philosophy and then moved on to the social sciences; he had also made a remarkable contribution to the study of a language that he himself tried to learn. He arrives at the conference as the leader of "one of the Jewish territorialist parties."

Der Nister's portrait of Ber Borochov, the founding father of the Poale Zion movement, is interesting in respect to both what it says and what it omits. Der Nister even avoids defining the object of Borochov's linguistic interest as Yiddish, thus leaving the nature of his philological pursuits vague. Neither does he mention the word "Zionism," preferring the more neutral term "territorialism." While the latter omission is perfectly understandable in the context of the 1930s, the former is difficult to explain. Despite the somewhat convoluted language, the real Borochov emerges vividly in Der Nister's description, but only for those readers whose knowledge of the political context of 1905 goes beyond the official version of events. The Berdichev episode was one among the many occasions on which Borochov himself engaged in fierce ideological debates with other groups. As Jonathan Frankel relates in his account of Borochov's political career:

From Poltava, Borochov traveled with Ben Zvi straight to Berdichev for a conference of Poale Zion in the southwest. He arrived, after a train journey much delayed by strikes, with a heavy cold but, nonetheless, he single-handed conducted the battle against the Vozrozhdentsy led by Moyshe Zilberfarb. The contest raged, Zilberfarb later recalled, for an exhausting eight days, but always at a "high intellectual level," and although most of the delegates remained loyal to the Vozrozhdenie, it was generally agreed that Borochov had more then held his own.[21]

From a historical point of view, it is, of course, important that the Berdichev conference took place in December, when the revolution was in severe crisis, and the Jewish revolutionaries had to decide what to do next. As a writer, Der Nister was less concerned with historical accuracy than with artistic "truth." He therefore decided to change the chronology and move the Berdichev conference back in time. In the novel the conference occurs in the late spring, in the very midst of the revolutionary buildup. Borekh-Ber and his opponents embody the new wave of springtime energy that revives both nature and people. From this point of view, the ideological differences among them are much less significant than the sense of revolutionary optimism that they share.

Der Nister's Jewish radicals, most of whom come to the revolution straight from the yeshiva bench, excel in revolutionary theory, education, and organization. They are less successful, however, when they try to take up arms and fight: an entire unit of Jewish self-defense is rounded up in a certain "particularly backward village" and brutally murdered by peasants who had been subjected to antisemitic indoctrination by the authorities. The narrator is fascinated by the intellectual brilliance of Jewish revolutionaries and their commitment to the study of ideology, but he becomes vague concerning the details of the disagreements between the Bolsheviks—whom he calls "the main party"—and their opponents, the "splinter groups."

The published draft of Der Nister's unfinished novel offers a unique opportunity to explore the difficult process of creating a dual narrative according to the principle formulated by Leo Strauss: "a popular teaching of an edifying character, which is in the foreground; and a philosophical teaching concerning the most important subject, which is indicated between the lines."[22] Der Nister's narrative style is deliberately slow and sometimes repetitive, his syntax heavy and convoluted, and his vocabulary overloaded with archaisms and Hebraisms—all these qualities clearly indicated to an attentive reader that the text had to be read slowly and beyond the framework of socialist realism. The numerous statements in which the narrator asserts his loyalty to the official Communist party history stand in marked contrast to the style of his narrative. Judging by the draft, it is difficult to imagine what final form the novel could possibly have taken, but one can assume that Der Nister would have made every attempt to hide the "between-the-lines" meaning of his text as deeply as possible under the cover of the "popular teaching of an edifying character."

One of the chief requirements of socialist realism had to do with the representation of the leading role of the proletariat in general and of its avant-garde, the Communist Party, in particular. Both Lipman-Levin and Der Nister tried to satisfy this requirement by employing basic images and motifs drawn from the Soviet stock repertoire, such as red banners, strikes, and demonstrations. At the same time, they heavily idealized the character of the Jewish Bolshevik, endowing him with qualities that were traditionally held in high esteem in the Jewish community, such as intellectual agility, social commitment, and entrepreneurial skills, while downplaying the violent side of the revolution.

Even though the two writers manifestly endorsed the socialist realist master narrative, they also, to use Leo Strauss's language, "surreptitiously contradicted" that narrative by inserting into their texts details and references that did not fit in with it. Such events as the 1900 theater riots or the Berdichev conference of 1905 were obviously not part of the officially approved history of the 1905 Revolution. By incorporating those and other events into their works, Lipman-Levin and Der Nister not only acted to preserve them in the Soviet Jewish collective memory but also created their own version of the revolution in which Jews played a more active role. What makes these novels interesting is the detailed and quite sympathetic depiction of traditional Jewish life, which had all but disappeared by the time they were written. By turning to the 1905

Revolution, Soviet Yiddish writers of the oldest cohort—as Lipman-Levin and Der Nister already were in the 1930s—recreated the most glorious episode of the usable past available to Soviet Jews.[23] The events of 1905 offered an opportunity to incorporate Jews into the official socialist realist discourse and to celebrate, in a somewhat "surreptitious" way, a young Jewish hero as an active participant in Russian history. Reading these texts along the lines suggested by Leo Strauss could perhaps offer a momentary relief to the readers of the Stalinist era.

Part V
Overseas Ripples: 1905 and American Jewry

Chapter 16

The 1905 Revolution Abroad: Mass Migration, Russian Jewish Liberalism, and American Jewry, 1903–1914

REBECCA KOBRIN

Samuel Dinerstein recalled fondly in his autobiography the festive mood that filled his hometown of Ekaterinoslav in Ukraine on October 17, 1905 (old style), the day the October Manifesto was issued.[1] Promising a semiparliamentary system of government, a relaxation of censorship, and concessions to non-Russian ethnic groups, the manifesto thrilled Russian Jews seeking fuller participation in Russian civic life. It seemed to mark the beginning of the fulfillment of the dream of Russian Jewish liberalism—a movement that in its most simple terms strove for civic emancipation, economic integration, education, and social inclusion. The elation of Ekaterinoslav's Jews diminished rapidly, however, as new protests against economic conditions and tsarist oppression set in motion a three-day anti-Jewish riot.[2] The violence and anarchy that filled Ekaterinoslav's streets convinced Dinerstein's father that the 1905 Revolution was a failure. A successful merchant in Ekaterinoslav, he saw his three dry goods stores and home looted in the riots. Despite receiving a grant of one thousand rubles to rebuild his businesses, he "did not have the faith to rebuild in Russia."[3] Realizing that his educational, economic, and civic aspirations for his family could be achieved only elsewhere, Dinerstein's father took advantage of the new system of acquiring steamship tickets and with his wife and three sons embarked on a journey to America on January 31, 1906.[4]

Dinerstein's father was not alone in his reaction to the revolution. Dozens of other post-1905 Russian Jewish immigrant writers relate the ways in which the revolution's failure, deteriorating economic conditions, and the concurrent rise in anti-Jewish violence prompted them to rethink their commitment to the Russian Empire, setting in motion a truly monumental revolution: mass Jewish emigration. Indeed, over the course of the next decade, Jewish emigration from the Russian Empire would profoundly affect the demographic and cultural map of world Jewry: from 1903 until the outbreak of World War I (when war, not a lack of desire, halted Russian Jewish emigration), approximately 2.5 million Jews, nearly 78 percent of all emigrants leaving Russia, set out to seek their fortunes in Europe, North America, South America, and Palestine.[5] While many scholars have discussed this mass Jewish population shift—the largest voluntary demographic transfer in modern Jewish history—most mistakenly begin the metanarrative of Russian Jewish mass migration in 1881.[6] Yet, as John Klier notes, 1881 was, in fact, "not a great turning point" because "the pogroms of 1881–2 and the May Laws of 1882 did not produce an immediate or sustained mass emigration of Jews from the Russian Empire."[7] U.S. immigration statistics record an average of only twenty-seven thousand Jews entering the country during the five years following the upheaval of 1881.[8] In contrast, the 1905 Revolution did produce precisely such a mass outpouring, leaving an indelible mark on world Jewry. The upheaval surrounding the 1905 Revolution impelled 784,274 Jews to immigrate to the United States and approximately fifty thousand to move to Argentina.[9] The flood of Russian Jews did not abate. By 1920, post-1905 Russian Jewish migrants constituted over 35 percent of the Jewish community in the United States and approximately 70 percent of Argentine Jewry. From the perspective of Russia, the events of 1905 may have failed to achieve any long-lasting reforms, but from the vantage point of the Americas—where post-1905 Russian Jews formed the backbone of the immigrant community, emboldened the nascent labor movement in each of these countries, nurtured a world of *yidishe kultur*, and molded the overarching character of Jewish life—1905 did indeed mark a revolution.[10]

Why did the revolution and its failure trigger such an upheaval in Russian Jewish emigration in contrast to earlier crisis moments such as 1881? What precise constellation of variables came together in 1905 to prod so many Russian Jews to vote with their feet and to abandon Russia to pursue their dreams in other parts of the world? American Jewish historians often discuss Russian Jewish mass migration, but few systematically assess it diachronically, exploring how Russian Jews or the process of migration changed over the course of the late nineteenth and early twentieth centuries. As the following pages illustrate, a concatenation of technological, commercial, social, and ideological factors intersected around 1905 to impel so many Jews to leave Russia. First, advances in technology, shipping, and print transformed the practice of overseas migration, enabling thousand to contemplate leaving Russia. But most important, Russian Jews' distinctively new attitudes, economic aspirations, and political expectations that derived from their exposure to intellectuals and new modes of thought in fin de siècle Russian Jewish society ultimately drove many Jews to give up on the dream of transforming Russia after 1905.

My analysis of the autobiographies and organizations of post-1905 Russian Jewish immigrants highlights an intriguing lacuna in American Jewish history: despite American Jewry's close identification with the ideals of liberalism and integration, American Jewish historians essentially ignore the background of liberal Jewish politics in tsarist Russia. Russian Jewish immigrants' embrace of liberalism is depicted as taking place exclusively on American shores.[11] As Frankel's *Prophecy and Politics* unequivocally demonstrated over two decades ago, it is most fruitful to view Russian Jewish politics through a transnational lens.[12] My focus on liberalism here does not imply a denial of the importance of other ideologies, such as socialism, in molding Russian Jewish society and the Russian Jewish diaspora. Indeed, many Russian Jews were involved in illegal revolutionary political movements—ranging from socialist to anarchist—and migrated out of fear of arrest, incarceration, or exile.[13] The ways in which socialism and other Jewish radical political beliefs mobilized a new Jewish politics in the aftermath of the 1905 have, however, already been well documented. Far less understood are the ways in which the ideals espoused by the fin de siècle Russian Jewish liberal intelligentsia, such as personal autonomy, individual economic betterment, education, professional status, rule of law, and political integration, also influenced immigrant Jews in this period.[14] As Dinerstein's recollections hint, elements of Russian Jewish liberalism were very much alive in those who voted with their feet. Still stirred by their ideological commitments after their arrival in their new homes, post-1905 immigrant Jews displayed a seemingly "paradoxical mix," to use the words of Daniel Soyer, of liberal commitments and "working-class politics."[15]

Endeavoring to explore the legacy of Russian Jewish liberalism in America is complicated by the virtual erasure (until recently) of Jewish liberalism from the annals of Russian Jewish life.[16] Russian Jewish liberalism followed the path of liberalism in general in Russia, which at first struggled to gain devotees as an ideological force. But by the end of the nineteenth century, it emerged as a strong and influential intellectual movement that drew its inspiration from Western Europe.[17] As Russian liberals, conservatives, and radicals all sought some form of change in Russia, they forged "a dialectical relationship" with one another, creating a situation in which "one cannot comprehend any of these three strains that dominated Russian thought except in relation to one another: for all their hostility, they were intimately related."[18] As Russian liberals struggled to create a vibrant civil society within the framework of Russia's rigidly authoritarian state, the major socialist parties in tsarist

Russia—the Social Democratic and the Socialist Revolutionary—were committed to the attainment of parliamentary ("bourgeois") democracy as their immediate goal (their "minimal" program). A full-fledged socialist revolution was usually seen as far off in the future, an abstract ideal, only marginally relevant to everyday aspirations.

Russian Jewish liberalism also developed in a dialectical relationship with Russian Jewish revolutionary movements, drawing on similar ideological currents.[19] In the sources I have studied it is difficult to distinguish definitively between the liberal and socialist influences shaping immigrants' motivations, desires, and decisions, but the ambiguity in itself is telling. Accordingly, it is not surprising that many immigrants expressed individualistically oriented liberal tendencies—such as the pursuit of economic autonomy, education, professional status, and civic integration—that they did not see as excluding radical impulses invested in the collective good. Thus many immigrant Jews dedicated themselves to opening their own sweatshops so that they could attain higher status and move out of the wage-earning class, while simultaneously ferociously fighting for higher wages and better working conditions for all.[20]

Scholars have traced the roots of these seemingly contradictory political ideals and economic practices back to Russian Jews' encounter with America, but I argue that differing intellectual streams in Russian Jewish society planted the seeds of this ambiguity long before Russian Jews arrived in America.[21] The voices captured in immigrant autobiographies and organizational records help us hear these often overlapping intellectual streams that percolated down to shape the inner worlds of Russian Jewish immigrants. As they discuss their rationales for migration, those immigrants highlight the complex constellation of political attitudes they harbored, yielding a fuller picture of the rich complexity of political life in Russia during this era of epochal change.

The Promise and Pitfalls of Autobiography: Some Notes on Sources and Methodology

Autobiographical materials, the main source for my discussion, have been called by Virginia Woolf "a treasure trove" as a result of the information they contain on the lives and dilemmas of individuals who might otherwise remain unknown.[22] Since Woolf penned this observation in 1925, however, scholars have cast a shadow on her view of autobiographical sources, raising questions about their utility for the study of the past because they present only a self-selected, meticulously constructed version of an individual's life experiences.[23] From a literary standpoint, they are difficult sources to interpret, as Alan Mintz points out, because the author conveys a tale in which he or she is both the narrator and the subject, or, in other words, the author acts as both "retrospective analyst" and "experiencing character."[24] For the historian, these sources, rich with candor and detail, pose even greater challenges. As Michael Stanislawski oberves, a historian must continually question "how to use such inherently problematic texts as historical sources [so that all can see with accuracy] the lives they open up, the time or place they depict, [or] the societies they so eloquently describe."[25]

Bearing these methodological issues in mind, it is critical to note from the outset that the YIVO (Yidisher visnshaftlekher institut) autobiographies of American Jewish immigrants that I circumspectly utilize in this study differ from most standard (and at times problematic) autobiographies. First and foremost, all the writers were nonprofessional and had no literary aspirations. Moreover, the YIVO rules stipulated that autobiographers write in a "detailed," "precise," and "sincere" manner, encouraging them to be as candid as possible in their assertions.[26] To be sure, immigrants penned their recollections close to thirty years after migrating. During those three decades of adjustment to life in America, they may have acquired a new vocabulary infused with elements of New Deal liberalism (which bore a resemblance to social democracy) to describe their former passions and beliefs. Nonetheless, I firmly believe that these autobiographical texts provide an unparalleled prism through which to view the inner world and belief systems of ordinary immigrants whose voices would otherwise go unheard.[27]

One must appreciate that when YIVO immigrant autobiographers sat down to make sense of their lives for themselves and their readers, they wrote in response to specific questions and were influenced, both knowingly and unknowingly, by traditions of life-story writing rooted in the haskalah, or Jewish enlightenment, as well as American culture.[28] Whereas several Jews wrote autobiographical works prior to the nineteenth century, the second half of the nineteenth century witnessed an explosion in Jewish autobiographical writing, which emerged as the genre of choice for young Jewish authors seeking literary fame.[29] Often young acculturating Jewish authors would use their autobiographies to express their new beliefs as well as their frustrations with Russian society, East European Jewish culture, and the constraints of Judaism.[30] America provided a sharply different model for writing one's life story: the autobiography of Benjamin Franklin, who "worked his way up" and crossed class barriers, was recast in the fictional yet widely popular story of Horatio Alger. Inspirational American tales of success prodded individuals from various national groups to write celebratory accounts of their humble origins and their ultimate economic success.[31]

Despite the blossoming inclination in both Jewish and American cultures to chronicle one's own life, hundreds of Russian Jewish immigrants would not have written their autobiographies were it not for the YIVO Institute for Jewish Research, an institution founded in Vilna in 1925 and dedicated to the study of East European Jewish life.[32] During the 1930s, YIVO had run several markedly successful autobiography competitions focusing on the challenges facing Jewish youth in Eastern Europe.[33] Arguing in 1942 that the mass migration of the previous six decades had set in motion a historical transformation in Jewish life that had yet to be fully documented, the leaders of YIVO who found refuge in New York proposed an autobiography contest on the theme "Why I left Europe and What I Have Accomplished in America."[34] The contest's main advocate, Max Weinreich, contended that while "scholars and intellectuals had outlined the general contours of this profound population shift, the great masses of immigrants who [had] struggled and with their own hands rebuilt personal lives and communal institutions in the New World, had not yet had their say."[35] Weinreich and other organizers of the contest hoped it would provide information on the socioeconomic context of Jewish migration, typical challenges facing East European Jewish immigrants, and the "social-psychological" dilemmas they were forced to tackle.[36]

The organizers of the contest sought the participation of the fullest range of Jewish immigrants in America, announcing the contest in Yiddish, English, and German newspapers that spanned the ideological spectrum. Promising the honor of publication and cash prizes to the winners, the organizers emphasized that age, education, class, occupation, and political affiliation were of no consequence; the contestants had only to compose a minimum of twenty-five notebook-sized pages and to sign their works with pseudonyms, enclosing their real names in separate envelopes. Embracing this effort to capture the voice of the people, the socialist *Arbeter ring* (Workmen's circle) encouraged many of its members to submit essays.

The response to the YIVO contest was overwhelming: within less than a year, Jewish immigrants in the United States, Canada, Mexico, Argentina, and Cuba representing a broad ideological and age spectrum submitted 223 autobiographies supported by photographs, diaries, and other personal documents. The vast majority of the entries—over 190 autobiographies—were composed in Yiddish by East European Jews who entered the United States between 1887 and 1924.[37] Among those 190 autobiographies, over 104 were written by Russian Jews who arrived in America in response to the events of 1905.[38] To be sure, the submissions do not embody a representative cross section of East European Jewry or of the Jewish immigrant community.[39] Yet they nonetheless yield extremely valuable insights because the contest, with its assurances of anonymity, encouraged many to reveal the most personal aspects of their lives. Thus they captured the yearnings and aspirations of an immigrant generation that rarely had an opportunity to share their vision of the world in written form.

Technological and Commercial Innovations Facilitating Migration

Surfacing vividly in the autobiographers' accounts is the fact that the revolution in Jewish migration of 1905 would not and could not have taken place if not for developments in overseas shipping and print communication. Between 1895 and 1905, American industrial productivity rose dramatically, enabling the transatlantic steamship industry to blossom.[40] Eager to fill their boats for the return voyage to the United States, steamship companies began pursuing a new approach to the business of migration in the late 1890s: instead of waiting for travelers to make their way to port cities in Western Europe, shipping companies used newspapers along with a system of agents to entice potential emigrants in their hometowns scattered throughout Southern and Eastern Europe.[41] Working on commission, these agents, usually members of the local community, did their best to drum up business, boasting of the successes achieved by earlier emigrants and offering classes on how to answer the questions of immigration officials or how to conceal a disease from an American inspector.[42] These agents were critical, as Solomon Horowitz points out in his autobiography, to the "mass migration of Jews" that took place throughout Eastern Europe at the same time that his family left in 1906. Jewish families like his own were open to agents' persuasion because they finally had the financial resources to purchase tickets. Moreover, as a result of changes in the method of international money transfer, many Russian Jews found they also had the help of "at least one relative living abroad who eagerly sent them money" to pay for their passage after hearing of the news of the revolution and ensuing violence.[43]

Agents' efforts were aided by an explosion in the publication of Yiddish newspapers focused on emigration issues. Although many scholars note that in the Russian Empire—where Jews had a literacy rate almost twice as high as that of non-Jews—the breakdown of traditional authority and the growing strength of revolutionary political movements were instrumentally aided by the development of a popular Jewish press, fewer address the role of the press in fueling mass migration.[44] Beginning in the 1860s and 1870s, a handful of Jewish newspapers printed in Russia reshaped how Jews debated the contours of their identities and,

more significantly, thought about their futures in the tsarist empire.[45]
From its very inception, the Jewish press openly wrote about and partially fueled a Russian Jewish "emigration mania," with contributors to
Rassvet (published between 1879 and 1883) and *Nedel'naia khronika vosh-
koda* (published 1882–97) constantly sparring over the centrality of emigration to the Jewish communal agenda.[46] By the turn of the century,
the Jewish reading public could enjoy not only monthly and weekly
newspapers but also a Yiddish daily, *Der fraynd,* that boasted a readership
of over 100,000 subscribers.[47] In these publications, Jewish journalists
inculcated in their readers the idea that if they were disaffected with the
Russian Empire, migration offered a viable solution to their predica-
ment.

The monthly Yiddish newspaper, *Vuhin* (Whither), published in Kiev
in the aftermath of the 1905 Revolution, illustrates the new and innovative ways in which the press was deployed to facilitate this mass exodus.
Vuhin's editors in Kiev sought to create and nurture a reading public
that regularly exchanged information about the complex process of
moving from one country to another. The world conveyed in the pages
of *Vuhin* was defined by feature stories such as "The Emigration Congress," or "The Immigration Question in America."[48] Supported by
Jacob Schiff as part of his Galveston plan to entice East European Jews
to settle outside New York, *Vuhin*'s regular comparative reports on the
cost of renting apartments in Milwaukee, St. Louis, Memphis, and New
Orleans or the earning potential of typical Jewish workers in New York,
Boston, Providence, Philadelphia, and Louisville armed prospective
immigrants with essential information that helped them negotiate for
lower rents and higher wages wherever they settled.[49]

With contributors who would later be recognized as literary giants,
such as Dovid Bergelson and Moyshe Litvakov, and correspondents
reporting from London, the United States, and Argentina, *Vuhin* was a
well-regarded literary publication that included poetic reflections on the
process of emigration along with charts conveying critical practical
information. With its front page and back cover devoted to steamship
advertisements, its focus upon emigration as the locus of world news,
and regular comparative features on immigrant life throughout the New
World, *Vuhin* helped its readership address the two central questions
shaping their lives: not only whether they should leave Russia but also,
as *Vuhin*'s title painfully queried, where was the best place for them to
go?

The practical economic guide to the mechanics of migration offered
in *Vuhin* was reinforced by a multitude of emigration organizations that
sprang up throughout Russia at the turn of the century focused on facilitating Jewish immigrant settlement. The Jewish Emigration Organiza-

tion in Kiev (Yidishe emigratsye gezelshaft in Kiev), for example, regularly published lists filled with names of Jews from areas throughout the Russian Empire who had settled in America. These lists highlighted the career shifts individuals might have to make upon migration in order to earn a living: David Margoles, a lawyer from Lutsk, earned nine dollars a week as a merchant in Oklahoma City, for example, while Binyomin Liberman, a merchant from Mogilev province, earned twelve dollars a week as a factory worker in Kansas City, Missouri. Others such as Reuven Cohen, a metal worker from Vilna, were able to find work in the metal industry in San Antonio. Accenting the benefits of settling in places such as Omaha, Houston, and St. Paul, these lists, similar to *Vuhin*, had the effect of encouraging Russian Jews, who were greatly concerned with economic success and integration, to contemplate pursuing a wide range of occupations and settling in barely known locales throughout the world.[50]

Although it is difficult to assess precisely the broader impact these new types of newspapers and organizations had on the ultimate trajectory of Russian Jewish migration, one fact is indisputable: whereas over 20 percent of Russian Jews who emigrated in the 1880s and 1890s returned to Eastern Europe, less than 7 percent of those who arrived on American shores in the wake of the events of 1905 made their way back to the Russian Empire.[51] Such a low rate of return must be viewed in the context of the new developments that facilitated post-1905 Jewish migration. These initiatives, no matter who sponsored them, enabled prospective Jewish migrants to arrive in the United States better informed and better prepared for the trials and tribulations of finding a new job, renting a new apartment, learning a new language, and immersing oneself in a new community. As Shloyme H. summed up in his YIVO autobiography, with the information he had garnered from publications, organizations, and other *landslayt* (townsmen), he was able to "succeed very quickly," securing for himself a job that paid twice as much as other newcomers earned, thereby easing his initial adjustment to life in America.[52]

Ideology and the 1905 Russian Jewish Emigrant

Advances in travel and information dissemination, as significant as they were, cannot alone explain why such considerable numbers of Jews chose to leave the Russian Empire in response to the 1905 Revolution and its failure. Anti-Jewish violence clearly alarmed many; yet few autobiographers draw a direct correlation between their migration and these violent outbursts.[53] Some even note that prior to migrating overseas they had moved to larger cities within Russia that had been the sites of vicious anti-Jewish riots during the years 1903–6, such as Kishinev or Bialystok, clearly believing, as the historian Shaul Stampfer observes, that "the economic opportunities outweighed the risk of violence."[54]

Frustration with tsarist Russia's autocracy, particularly as it related to the Jews' acquisition of political rights and economic integration, was the main factor compelling YIVO autobiographers to leave their homes. As Jacob Sholtz rhetorically queried and answered on the opening page of his autobiography, "Why did I leave my old home [*alte heym*] in Lithuanian Russia [*rusland-lita*]? Well, that is not a difficult question to answer: Russia's unfavorable political situation."[55] While he earned a very good living as a traveling salesman in Russia and possessed a fierce loyalty to his birthplace, the incessant discrimination and the lack of hope that the political situation would improve for Jews, or for anyone else, convinced Sholtz that if he wanted his children to have more political and educational opportunities, he would have to leave Russia.[56] He concludes his memoir with the triumphant election of his cousin David Sholtz as Florida's governor, implicitly underscoring that America provided the most fertile ground for Jews to pursue their commitment to political integration.[57] Anon. (Ish Ikor) was even more direct in his response to why he left Russia: "the political and cultural injustices [Jews] suffered" made it a burden to live there. Even though, he added, all "his youthful dreams" were nurtured and rooted in Russian culture and the Russian Empire's landscape, he could not bring himself to remain under the despotic tsarist regime.[58]

Exposure to Russian liberal thought pushed S(amuel) Rubin to leave Russia after the revolution's failure. Settling in Pittsburgh in 1906, Rubin believed the "freedom of America" provided the best environment to achieve the goals instilled in him by Russian intellectuals such as Alexander Herzen and Vissarion Belinskii. Rubin describes in detail his obsessions with political integration and equality that grew out of his extensive reading of the works of Russian writers such as Nikolai Gogol, Fedor Dostoevsky, Ivan Turgenev, Alexander Pushkin, and Dmitrii Pisarev.[59] After 1906, however, he realized that the promising future these writers and liberal thinkers had inspired him to fight for could not be achieved in Russia but only elsewhere.

Other autobiographers affirmed that the desire to live in a society governed by the rule of law and characterized by participatory politics— values rooted in Russian Jewish liberalism—was the motivation fueling their migration. B. Rosen, who immigrated to New York from Bialystok in 1907, proclaimed that "America offered Russian Jews" who wanted to gain rights "their only hope." Thus, even though "the pious consider America impure" and revolutionaries consider "fleeing to America cowardly," he considered overseas migration a "natural" decision for anyone sharing his opposition to governmental arbitrariness and his belief in the possibility of Jewish integration.[60]

Anon. (Ish Ikor) describes how he endeavored for years to learn English so that he could become a citizen of the United States as quickly as possible. Driven by a deep faith in the rule of law, Anon. described his acquisition of citizenship as "giving [him] the greatest spiritual pleasure, especially when [he] compares the benefits of his citizenship to the arbitrary injustices [he] suffered in Russia."[61] Shimen Isaac Leon arrived in Philadelphia in 1912 from Ukraine and immediately dedicated himself to acquiring citizenship. While he was critical of the low level of Yiddish discourse in America (as exemplified by the constant use of English words in the Yiddish press and the Yiddish theater), he explained that America's rule of law and promise of equal rights made him realize that he could never return to Russia. In Russia, even with all the revolutionary efforts, all he could foresee was a future of persecution, despotic rule, and pain for himself and his family.[62] Lena Weinberger, a dedicated Bundist who left Vilna for Philadelphia in 1906, explained that her difficult decision to leave Russia was ultimately driven by her fear of arbitrary arrest and her heartfelt desire to participate fully in the political process, conduct open political meetings, and publicly express her political views.[63]

Others saw political integration as intertwined with economic normalization.[64] The father of "Ish Yehudi," E(liezer) Hanson, believed the greatest achievement of any Jew was to gain civic equality so that he could engage in economic activities similar to those of his fellow (non-Jewish) countrymen. Thus, he encouraged his son to immigrate to Calgary in 1906 together with four siblings so that they could set up a farm and work like the common man did in Russia.[65]

Parental concern for children's safety against the backdrop of counterrevolutionary Russia's new political reality also brought many young Jews to American shores. Several writers recount their desire to join the battle to overthrow the tsar, but their concerned parents, who wanted to protect them from arrest, forced them to move to America.[66] Yitzkhok "Charcher" Smith, from a small town in the region of Grodno, for example, exulted that the "happiest day of his life" was the day after "the constitution of the Duma was granted" and he "marched proudly through the streets of Pruzhany with the red flag."[67] His parents, apparently concerned that the authorities took notice of his exuberant joy, immediately paid his brother to take him to Chicago. Their ultimate goal of having their son become "a respectable man" in Russian Jewish society would never come to fruition in Russia, and they feared he would be sent to Siberia for his activities.[68] The counterrevolution in Lodz instilled so much fear in Aaron Cohen's pious hasidic father that he decided to pay for his son's passage to New Jersey. Despite America's impurities—"people did not fear god, worked on *shabes* and ate *treyf*"—he concluded that it was better than his "son being sent off to Siberia . . . or being executed."[69] Similarly, Noyekh Zeidman's hasidic father paid for his and his brother's passage from Minsk to London out of fear his sons would be arrested and exiled to Siberia and he would never see them again.[70]

Regardless of whether they arrived in the new world of their own volition or as a result of parental coercion, post-1905 Russian Jewish immigrants continued to pursue their revolutionary agenda, both by supporting the Bund in Russia and by strengthening the Jewish labor movement, be it in North or South America.[71] The Arbeter ring (Workmen's circle), founded in 1892, was mentioned by half of the post-1905 autobiographers as an important organization in their lives after arriving in America. A national organization with only four branches in the 1890s, the Arbeter Ring struggled to find support until 1905. Thereafter, the ranks of new arrivals quadrupled its membership and the organization expanded rapidly, growing to over eighty-five branches by 1910.[72] With the help of these new members, the Arbeter Ring became a powerful voice in the Jewish immigrant community, and the Jewish labor movement emerged as the central organ of that community and the cornerstone of socialist activism in New York.[73] In Argentina, where the Jewish community was significantly smaller, the arrival of post-1905 Russian Jewish migrants had an even greater impact as they founded and fueled the various the Jewish labor movements, forming the revolutionary General Jewish Workers' Society in 1909.[74]

Interestingly, even among those self-proclaimed socialist autobiographers, one finds a commitment to economic liberalism—defined as the pursuit of individual ownership, financial success, and economic mobility. One could be, as Aaron Cohen argued in his autobiography, firmly committed to supporting the Workmen's Circle and the Socialist Party in America but also "an exploiter" who ran a silk manufacturing business that employed a substantial number of workers and made him, as he boasted with pride, "a wealthy man."[75] A. Gumner, who arrived in Boston in 1906, was a dedicated socialist and revolutionary in Russia and Germany and sought to continue these pursuits in America. Working as an upholsterer, Gumner organized his fellow workers into a union in order to strike; the strike's failure, apparently, launched Gumner on a new quest in which he sought personal autonomy instead of collective security. Gumner opened his own furniture business, which, as he matter-of-factly recalled in his autobiography, made him into "a bit of an exploiter," with a worker and an assistant," toiling away for his benefit.[76] While his vocabulary and underlying sense of guilt clearly hint at the socialist sensibility molding his inner world, his actions and economic practices suggest that other ideological influences, inspired in part by the principles of Russian Jewish liberalism, informed his activities and economic decisions in America as well.

Other contestants, such as A(vrom) Beitani, who immigrated to America in 1906, focused on the liberal quest for education and professional recognition. While Russian Jews acted like other immigrant groups in America in their embrace of education, few groups dedicated themselves as passionately to the pursuit of higher education in the immigrant generation.[77] To be sure, in Russia education was an ideal advanced not only by liberals; socialists also adhered to enlightenment principles that emphasized the importance of education, but they attributed less significance to the aspect of professional training and more to its role in instilling a rational way of thinking. Self-described as an "enlightened" man, Beitani possessed a "thirst" for secular and professional education. This unquenchable thirst provoked many in his hometown of Romanovo, outside Minsk, to see him as an agent of heresy.[78] Stirred by the ideals of enlightenment and education inculcated in him in Minsk's Russian high school, Beitani adopted Russian middle-class dress, social conventions, and language as part of his effort to integrate himself in Russian society. Beitani then opened a modern "gymnasium" for Jews in his hometown. The Revolution of 1905 and its disappointing failure, however, made him feel intensely "alienated" and he "grew increasingly restless."[79] He realized he had to emigrate to pursue his dreams of furthering his education, acquiring a profession, and integration. Beitani ultimately did achieve his dream in Baltimore in 1912, when he earned a degree in dentistry. His firm belief in the ideal of education prompted him to conclude his 1934 biography with the emphatic assertion that education is critical for Jewish renewal and "wealth does not matter."[80]

The autobiography collection is replete with narratives similar to Beitani's, suggesting the pivotal role the hopes, ideals, and values espoused by the fin de siècle liberal Jewish intelligentsia, who first articulated the importance of the quest for professional status, played in driving many Russian Jews to America.[81] The experience of Beyle Peltzman is typical: devoted to seeing her five children acquire a secular education and professional credentials, Peltzman moved from Ukraine to New York ahead of her husband. She emphasizes in her autobiography that she made this drastic move alone because she could no longer tolerate the quota system in Russia that did not allow her children to enter the local high school even though they had passed the required exams. She realized she could not achieve her goal in Russia and wanted her children to live in a place where schools were free and open, everyone was "equal," and will and ability—not religion—were the most important prerequisites for success in education.[82] Similarly, Julius Baron, who immigrated to the United States in 1906 at the age of twenty from a small town outside Vilna, notes that after the "upheaval" of 1905 he did not envision a future for himself in Russia's educational system. He realized that he would never be able to achieve his dream of becoming a lawyer and began fantasizing about continuing his education in the United States.[83]

Even for those who did not have the opportunity to attend professional school in the United States as a result of the realities of immigrant life, the pursuit of education was a major theme shaping their lives. Samuel Dinerstein, whose attempts to attend school were twice stymied by his older siblings' illnesses, described in detail the ways in which he struggled his entire life to give his children the education he had always aspired to but had never been able to achieve because of his family obligations. He concludes his autobiography by celebrating his son's success as a "Harvard Ph. D." and his daughter's graduation from Brooklyn College (and marriage to a "Harvard-educated lawyer"). [84]

The "Progressive" New Landsmanshaftn of the Post-1905 Russian Jewish Immigration

Profoundly shaped by the ideals of education, professional status, civic emancipation, and economic integration, the cohort of Russian Jewish migrants who arrived in America after 1905 established a host of organizations that reflected their new needs and aspirations. To be sure, one finds among many different immigrant groups the formation of organizations to serve particular economic, social, and spiritual needs.[85] But post-1905 Russian Jews' establishment of new *landsmanshaftn* (hometown associations) is noteworthy, since there already existed hundreds of these types of societies to which Russian Jewish immigrants could turn to for help.[86] Their zeal to create new institutions can only be fully understood within the context of their experiences in fin de siècle Russia, where Jews distinguished themselves in the empire by forming more voluntary organizations than any other minority group. In 1898, as Adele Lindenmeyr points out, almost half of all the societies petitioning for recognition in the Russian Empire were Jewish charitable or voluntary associations.[87] Russian Jewry's passionate devotion to forming organizations, explains Natan Meir, was rooted in their "integrationist" desires to actively participate in Russia's burgeoning civil society. As "Jews' opportunities to enter public life were becoming even fewer," Meir continues, "with government restrictions block[ing] . . . the path to participation in municipal government, higher education and the bar, the voluntary sector offered an alternative—and a chance [for Jews] to be active in a nonsectarian quarter of society."[88] Once in America, these post-1905 immigrants did not abandon their vision of integration through institution building, forming a myriad of self-proclaimed "progressive" societies that embraced English, abandoning both Yiddish and Russian and choosing names that trumpeted their "progressive" nature.

Typical of such "progressive" post-1905 forward-looking Jews were the founders of the Bialystoker Young Men's Association. Coming together in 1906 to establish a new organization, these young men from Bialystok construed their former home as a social, cultural, and political center possessing all the traits esteemed by the Russian Jewish liberal intelligentsia.[89] Viewing themselves as *inteligentn*, these immigrants used depictions of Bialystok to demonstrate their "intellectual" approach to the world. They stressed that Bialystok had taught them "not to seek any immediate gains of a material order" but instead to seek intellectual stimulation that was defined by "good fellowship that follows the golden mean," of not adhering to either radicalism or zealous piety.[90] They described Bialystok, and themselves, in their 1906 charter in the following manner:

[We are] young men of good Bialystoker families . . . who were intellectuals and socially-minded men interested in the movements of the day. Our interests were of a different sort than what prevailed in the organizations that were already in existence . . . since we were not inclined to follow any extreme policy or political movement of the time. We were the children of Bialystok middle-class families that were endowed with the immense tolerance that would enable them to dwell in peace with both the religious Jew and the socialist.[91]

Considering tolerance and intellectual pursuits as central to their identities, these post-1905 newcomers established this association so that, despite their impoverished, unemployed immigrant status, they could still feel like members of the intelligentsia by being "active in social and cultural matters" and attending "lectures on learned topics."[92] Through their activity in their new organization, these post-1905 immigrants thus sought to bridge the chasm in their lives between their aspirations and their actual economic situation.

To this end, they also did something that was unprecedented among the two dozen Bialystoker societies already existing in the city: they chose an English name for their organization. The name they chose—the Bialystoker Young Men's Association—directly sought to imitate another Jewish institution in New York founded in the nineteenth century to promote Jewish integration through the ideals of middle-class respectability, the Young Men's Hebrew Association.[93] Like many other Russian Jewish immigrants in this era, these young Bialystoker men wanted to express their desire to integrate into American society and saw their new organization as holding the key to establishing themselves as respected and wealthy figures.

Like the Bialystoker Young Men's Association, the First Proskurover Young Men's Progressive Association (YMPA), which convened its initial meeting on October 4, 1904, aspired to help its members "assimilate more quickly into the mainstream of American life." With a membership comprising exclusively men between the ages of eighteen and twenty-four, this organization pursued an "Americanization" agenda that strove to help its constituents "build a place for themselves in America." Feeling alienated from other Jewish organizations, even those founded by men from their common hometown of Proskurov, these young men also deliberately chose an English name including the word "progressive" with the hope that such a move would help them (and their organization) become more thoroughly integrated into American society.[94]

The "Americanization" agendas of "progressive" landsmanshaft organizations founded in the United States by post-1905 Russian Jewish immigrants—embracing English, aspiring to further "progressive" goals such as integration and education, and abandoning Yiddish names—underscores the political legacy of Russian Jewish liberalism in the aftermath of 1905. To be sure, while many groups in America championed the process of "Americanization," they conceptualized and defined it in different ways.[95] As American writers and politicians summoned this phrase to question Russian Jews' place in the emerging "new" American nation on racial grounds, members of these "progressive" landsmanshaftn viewed the process of "Americanization" through a Russian Jewish liberal lens.[96] The twin pillars of their organizations' programs for Americanization—linguistic assimilation and education—bear a striking resemblance to the programs advocated by Russian Jewish liberals for Jewish integration in Russia through organizations such as the Union for the Attainment of Full Jewish Rights in Russia (Soiuz dlia dostizheniia polnopraviia evreiskogo naroda v Rossii) or the Society for the Promotion of Enlightenment among the Jews (Obshchestvo rasprostraneniia prosveshcheniia mezhdu evreiami).[97] While these immigrants may not have been members of these societies in Russia, they surely were familiar with each society's goals and its course of action from dozens of local branches scattered throughout the empire.[98] Thus, while the disturbing developments in Russia in the wake of 1905 may have motivated Jews to leave the Russian Empire, they did not abandon their dreams of integration nurtured within its bounds or the programs to achieve it.

Conclusion

Initially exuberant over the issuing of the October Manifesto, Jews saw their hopes rapidly dashed in the course of the general unraveling of the tsarist state and increased anti-Jewish violence in this revolutionary period. As Jews became painfully aware of tsarist Russia's irreparable shortcomings, they experimented with new strategies—such as migration or radical politics—in their search for the most effective and quickest way to achieve their dreams.[99] Scholarly analyses of the political clashes that consumed Russian Jewry following the revolution generally cast Russian Jewish liberalism as a peripheral intellectual and political movement in Russian Jewish life, particularly in comparison to Zionism or the Bund, which dominated the Jewish political arena.[100] Discussions of Russian Jewish liberalism, rather, focus on the limited success of notables such as Maxim Vinaver, Simon Dubnov, and Henry Sliozoberg in achieving the goal of Jewish emancipation. However, as immigrant autobiographers suggest, liberal ideology cannot be viewed as operating exclusively in the realm of "ideas and the endeavors of political activists" but must also be viewed, as Laura Engelstein persuasively argues, as "a configuration of attitudes" devoted to such ideals as education, rule of law, economic betterment, and attainment of professional status that influenced Russian Jews' pursuits not only within the Russian Empire's geographic borders but also when they ventured beyond them.[101]

Avowedly committed to economic integration, political emancipation, linguistic assimilation, and education, Russian Jews who made their way to America in the wake of 1905 left their mark in realms far beyond the meetings rooms of organizations such as the Bialystoker Young Men's Association. These immigrants and their descendants (who constituted the majority of American Jewry by 1924) remained staunchly committed to liberal ideals well into the late twentieth century. Defying widely held assumptions about American political culture, Milton Himmelfarb once famously observed that American Jews lived like Episcopalians but continued to vote like Puerto Ricans. American Jews did not embrace conservatism despite their rapid social and economic mobility, explains the historian Marc Dollinger, because they valued social, economic, and political inclusion. These values, Dollinger continues, were derived from their experiences of persecution in Russia, rather than their encounter with Russian Jewish liberalism.[102] But as post-1905 Russian Jews conveyed publicly in their organizations and privately through their autobiographies, their initial encounter with the ideals of Russian Jewish liberalism left an imprint on their lives long after they had left Russia.

The voices of post-1905 East European Jewish settlers in the United States gathered by YIVO in 1942 highlight the far-reaching legacy of the

1905 Revolution in its cultivation of attitudes that shaped the development of Jewish life in the New World. The intimate details provided by contestants in the YIVO autobiography competition belie the narrative crafted by most American Jewish historians concerning the "East European Jewish immigrant" that rarely acknowledges transformations taking place *within* Russia that altered the stream of immigrants to America. A Jew, for example, who arrived from Bialystok in 1878 did not have the same education, aspirations, or view of Russia and America as a person who emigrated from the same city in 1906. Precisely illustrating this point is the fact that Jews from Bialystok who found themselves in New York in 1878 founded Beys Knesses Anshei Bialystok, a religious congregation for Jews from Bialystok to serve their pressing religious needs, whereas those who arrived in 1906 felt compelled to establish a progressive, forward-looking intellectual club modeled after the icon of American Jewish respectability, the YMHA. Thus, if scholars hope to understand American Jewry's contradictory impulses and political leanings, they must examine the divergent attitudes and shifting political ideologies that fueled Russian Jewish migration over the course of the late nineteenth and early twentieth centuries.

The general bifurcation of scholarship on Russian Jewry in the United States and in Russia has obscured the dense web of financial, literary, political, and cultural entanglements that historically linked these two communities. By applying a transnational lens to Russian history and examining the 1905 Revolution through the reminiscences of post-1905 Russian Jewish immigrants in the United States, one sees Jews' vexing relationship with the Russian state with new eyes: Jews' visceral response to the failure of the 1905 revolution involved not only the creation of revolutionary political organizations to topple the empire but also a mass abandonment of the empire. Immigrants' voices, rarely considered in the study of late-imperial Russia, evocatively demonstrate that the 1905 Revolution, an event that has long been overshadowed by the events of 1917, was truly a watershed. The Revolution of 1905 may have failed in liberalizing tsarist Russia but it succeeded in igniting a mass wave of immigration that forever changed Jewish life in the United States.

Chapter 17

Democracy and Assimilation: The Jews, America, and the Russian Crisis from Kishinev to the End of World War I

Eli Lederhendler

The revolutionary events in Russia in 1905, coming hard on the heels of the Russo-Japanese War, marked a pivotal point in the dissolution of the Russian imperial state. How did this turn of events resonate in far-away America? Did it register merely as a seismic incident far removed from American reality, or did it initiate a historic confrontation between America's new society and the revolution in Russia? For the Jews of America, in particular, what lasting imprint did the events of 1905 leave?

The deteriorating conditions of civil life in Russia from 1903 through 1906 heralded the first stage of wholesale political collapse and widespread social dislocation. As such, this was also a fateful juncture for the Jews of Russia. Hopes for political amelioration through a parliamentary system were raised and then dashed again. The pogroms of 1903 in Kishinev and Gomel were followed in late 1905 by large-scale, systematic anti-Jewish outbreaks. Lasting for over a year and taking place in almost seven hundred separate locations, this wave of pogroms entailed massive violence on a new, horrendous scale.[1]

Although right-wing Russian nationalists fomented this vicious antisemitic campaign, the discourse over the role of minority nationalities in the political process was by no means limited to the political right. The issue agitated both the revolutionary left and the liberal democratic center. At the same time, the steady emigration of Jews from Russia attained a new, much higher level between 1903 and 1907, totaling over 480,000. This represented the historic high point of Russian Jewish migration to America on the basis of annual average immigration; at nearly 100,000 per year, this wave was nearly seven times the magnitude of the annual average attained in the 1880s.[2]

In the decade that followed, Russian Jews were shocked by a blood libel case—the Beilis affair. Soon thereafter, during World War I, entire Jewish communities in areas under Russian military occupation fell victim to expulsion and destruction—and the worst was yet to come. The revolutions of 1917, the depredations of the ensuing civil war, the Soviet-Polish war of 1920, and the atrocities in Ukraine of 1919–21 left a trail of devastation in their wake that had no modern parallel prior to the Holocaust. This onslaught of events spelled the end of Jewish life in Russia as it had crystallized over the previous century.

To gain footing on the treacherous surface of this historic upheaval, Jewish writers, cultural activists, scholars and intellectuals, communal figures, political movements and parties—by turns at odds with each other and collectively—sought to create the groundwork for a new existence. The vibrant world of Hebrew and Yiddish letters, the emerging, modern innovations in Jewish education, the fledgling politics of national autonomy, and the determined efforts to create self-defense groups and to coordinate Jewish parliamentary representation all went into high gear in this period.[3]

These efforts constituted a diverse and manifold attempt to integrate Jews and Jewish life into Russian society—or, to be more precise, to define a place for Jews within an envisioned, alternative Russian society. However, within fifteen years of the 1905 Revolution, twenty at the most, all these Jewish endeavors had been swept away by the Soviet state, which had its own ideas about democratic participation and the assimilation of minority nationalities into the new Russia.

Operating under vastly different conditions, the Jewish immigrant community in the United States was also engaged in coming to terms with democracy and assimilation in the period from Kishinev to World War I. In some critical areas of endeavor in which their counterparts in Russia found it most difficult to progress, they reaped the benefits of social integration.

The Jewish labor movement that developed mainly in the first decade of the twentieth century, for example, faithfully reflected the radical political leanings of Russian revolutionary socialism. Its folk-ethnic style—including the use of Yiddish—and its passion for forging a decent life for the least regarded members of society (Jews and non-Jews) were similarly anchored in the Jewish experience on both sides of the Atlantic. At the same time, this movement saw itself as forming an integral part of a wider American workers' organization and a fully integrated segment of a nationwide and multiethnic socialist party—precisely the policy pursued (with little success) by the Bund in Russia.

On the wider economic front, Russian Jewish immigrants did not immediately free themselves from the endemic poverty they had known in Russia; but by the end of World War I, if not earlier, the immigrants stood on the verge of an economic take-off that would bring economic security and even a reasonable prosperity to the majority of Jews in America. Studies indicate that within ten to fifteen years of their arrival in the country, Russian Jewish immigrants attained a standard of living comparable to that of native-born American industrial workers and petty tradesmen and that their economic progress surpassed that of fellow immigrants from the less developed parts of Europe.[4]

Equally distinctive were the cultural expressions of the Jewish immigrants' adjustment to an American way of life when compared to the tenor of Russian Jewish acculturation in the years before and after 1905. The most obvious and important difference, of course, was the rapidity with which not only Yiddish but also Russian were discarded in favor of English as the preferred high-status language of culture and communication.

Closely related to the language issue was the matter of schooling. In Russia itself many Jewish parents and their progeny had demonstrated their keen desire to take advantage of public educational opportunities, at every level from primary education through university, only to be rebuffed by *numerus clausus* regulations and other forms of discrimination. Whereas the modernizing sectors of Russian Jewry had failed in Russia, in America, immigrant Jews effortlessly succeeded: they sent their children en masse almost exclusively to American public schools, and they themselves took advantage of evening classes in English offered by public and Jewish educational institutions. Jews, unlike American Catholics, showed no fear or hesitation in exposing their offspring to Protestant-tinged public education and, with very few exceptions, did not promote separate, parochial religious education as an alternative.

In the realm of literature and the arts, it is worth noting that Jewish literary and artistic creativity in Russia in the last decade of tsarist rule—whether in Russian, Yiddish, or Hebrew—demonstrated an incandescent, intensely ideological, eleventh-hour brilliance. In stark contrast, Jewish immigrant poets and writers, only a few years in America, were more apt to prefer a quiet lyricism of individual character and sensibility, a fairly passive but forward-looking momentum, a sentimental nostalgia, or a comic voice.[5] If their works externalized their angst, this was, after all, an anxiety of displacement and transition; they were, mercifully, spared the revolutionary Sturm und Drang. And although the immigrant Hebrew and Yiddish writers eventually found themselves deprived of a second generation of readers, theatergoers, and successors, this did not come at the same staggering human cost that their colleagues in Russia paid as they fell victim to the Stalinist dictatorship.

Despite, or rather because, of these disparities in fundamental experience, the Russian crisis left a deep and abiding imprint upon American

Jewry, doing much to define American Jewry's sense of its own, separate destiny. It was not just the fact that imperial Russia, in its death throes, furnished the bulk of the immigration of Jews to America, creating a new Jewry in the United States, some three million strong by 1914. It was also the fact that, from Kishinev through to the end of 1917 and beyond, Jews in America, recent immigrants as well as long-established families and communal leaders, formulated the possibilities of life in America, under optimal conditions of democracy and assimilation, in terms of the gulf separating America from the Russia of autocracy and the Black Hundreds.[6] It was the Russian crisis, as well, that furnished Jews in America with a cause to champion in the White House and the halls of government, in Congress, in public opinion and the press, as well as in the internal ethnic politics of American Jewry. The issue thus contributed a great deal to the coalescence of organizations and institutions within the heterogeneous American Jewish population. As Jonathan Frankel has put it, "The concept of American-Jewish politics—the defense of Jewish interests in the world and in the United States—was now increasingly taken for granted, gained legitimacy."[7]

Under the impact of the events of 1905–6, prominent elements of American Jewry joined under the leadership of Judah L. Magnes to organize a Jewish Defense Association in order to support Jewish self-defense in Russia. This marked one of the first joint efforts linking Jews across the communal spectrum (with the notable exception of the socialist and anarchist left).[8] More crucially, the 1905 era also saw the establishment of two of America's longest-existing national Jewish organizations: the American Jewish Committee (AJC—founded in 1906) and the Hebrew Sheltering and Immigrant Aid Society (HIAS—established in 1909). Both of these were conceived as necessary steps toward organizing American Jewish affairs more effectively in light of the urgent crisis abroad, on the one hand, and the resulting wave of immigrants, on the other, and in response to the hitherto spontaneous, not to say chaotic, character of domestic Jewish political and communal activity.

In the case of HIAS, this was a dual effort on the part of established "downtown" leaders and leading "uptown" philanthropists (Jacob Schiff, in particular) to bring orderly and noncompetitive methods to bear on the reception and rapid integration of incoming Jewish immigrants. Its hallmarks were an emphasis on the self-help ethic of American voluntarism and the utilization of every opportunity, within the law, to facilitate and to maximize Jewish immigration from Eastern Europe.[9]

As for the AJC, the "uptown" Jewish *politburo* (so to speak), it emerged out of a concern that unrestrained and combustible elements in immigrant Jewry—symptomatic vestiges of the volatile "Russian" temperament—were liable to misinterpret both the opportunities of democracy

and the responsibilities that come with assimilation, unless more responsible elements took a firm hand in channeling Jewish political efforts. It
should be noted in this context that to the men at the top of the American Jewish pyramid, playing by American rules did not necessarily mean
the adoption of a culture of deference or a pusillanimous posture:
recall, for example, the banker Jacob Schiff's involvement in furnishing
credit to Japan during the Russo-Japanese War.[10] As we read in Naomi
Cohen's biography of Schiff, this leading capitalist also financed the
shipment of revolutionary literature to the fifty thousand Russian officers and soldiers held as prisoners of war in Japan in 1904. It is not
inconceivable that in so doing he made some small and indirect contribution to the Russian Revolution of 1905. In 1906, after the bloody
pogrom in Belostok, it was Schiff who pressed for public protest meetings. And in 1909, it was Schiff, again, who publicly rebuked U.S. President Taft at a White House meeting for his reluctance to adopt a more
forceful diplomatic position against Russia's Jewish policy.[11]

Jews in America had some success in popularizing the image of despotic Russia as inimical to American democratic values and universalist
ideals. This was a ubiquitous phenomenon, making it almost superfluous to single out specific cases. Yet a few prominent examples may illustrate the point. In 1904, the Jewish Publication Society published a
protest and denunciation of tsarist policies vis-à-vis Russian Jewry, edited
by the prominent Semitics scholar Cyrus Adler and titled *The Voice of
America on Kishineff.*[12] The Kishinev pogrom and the more devastating
anti-Jewish violence of 1905–6 also formed the backdrop to the most
prominent Jewish contribution to the American stage in the years before
World War I: Israel Zangwill's 1908 play *The Melting Pot.* The play not
only won the hearty approval of President Theodore Roosevelt (to
whom it was dedicated) but also remained a key text in the formulation
of American attitudes to European immigrants and their role in recons-
tituting American society as the first "universal nation." The play posed
the question of America's unique destiny in the following unsubtle,
melodramatic formula: Could American conditions of freedom and the
wisdom of toleration succeed in bringing together the son of Jews murdered in Kishinev and the enlightened daughter of a Russian official
who oversaw the bloodshed?[13]

Preferring a more explicitly anti-assimilationist model, some critics at
the time took Zangwill to task over his positive stance toward intermar-
riage and his implied support for the "melting" or fading of group dis-
tinctions as such. They essentially agreed, however, with his vision of
America as an ethnic and religious democracy, enabling Jews to live in
peace among their neighbors while remolding their own heritage as a
unique contribution to the American way of life.[14] The contrast with the

situation obtaining in Russia served as a natural point of reference, affording Americanizers of both the "melting pot" and cultural-pluralist varieties evidence of the superiority of the American idea.

The quasi-official *American Jewish Year Book* published a lengthy report on the Russian pogroms in its 1906–7 volume. Tracing a direct line "From Kishineff to Bialystok (Belostok)" (the latter having been the site of the major pogrom of 1906)—a title that was emblazoned on the cover of the volume as a special headline—the report included a detailed statistical table of casualties suffered. The editor, Henrietta Szold, took pains to state that such dry data alone could never fully convey what she described as the "terror by night . . . the pestilence that walketh in darkness, the destruction that wasteth at noonday, these cannot be confined in lists and columns." She further noted that appeals for aid to the victims elicited contributions from eight hundred communities in the United States, totaling $1.25 million.[15]

During those same years, Peter Wiernik, editor of the New York Yiddish daily *Morgen zhurnal*, wrote a full-length, English-language history of American Jewry, intended for the wider American public. There he compared "the treatment accorded to the Jews in our own times" in lands of persecution such as Russia to the "pillage, massacres, and expulsions" endured by Jews in the "dark ages."[16] He provided detailed information on "riots and massacres" in Russia, including the number of victims killed in outbreaks such as those at Gomel (September 1903) and Zhitomir (May 1905), which, in turn, were mere episodes compared with the large-scale attacks in late October and early November 1905, "with which the Russians inaugurated their quasi-constitutional regime." It was this that "aroused and united the Jews of the civilized world," initiating a new era in the organization of Jewish political defense, because, as he put it, "The time when the Alliance Israélite Universelle . . . could act for the Jewry of all countries was now past, and only a new organization in which each country was independently represented could answer the purpose."[17] As for America and its Jews, Wiernik wrote, "America became for the suffering Jews of Russia the Egypt of the time of the Patriarch Jacob"—that is, a place of refuge—and the Russian immigrant in America was "the prosperous brother Joseph whom God sent to the New World before them to preserve life."[18]

One Russian Jewish soul who sought to preserve his life in America at the time was the writer Sholem Aleichem. Desperately seeking an American connection, he contracted with the New York Yiddish daily *Tageblat* to furnish a regular column. From the end of November 1905, the paper printed forty-two of his detailed reports on the pogroms and the situation in Russia generally.[19] He himself subsequently arrived in America, where he stayed for the better part of a year (October 1906 to June

1907); he later returned to New York, where he lived from 1914 until his death in 1916. His experiences during the pogroms were highlighted by the *New York Times*, which identified him, quite inaccurately, as "the Jew whose house was the first to be destroyed in the Kief massacre."[20] Sholem Aleichem himself believed that the stillborn 1905 Revolution might yet inspire wholesale political change in Russia, with positive consequences for the Jewish condition, should the progressive forces find it possible to reunite, despite their recent fiasco.[21] Still, in his famous work *Motl payse dem khazns* (Motl, Peysi the cantor's son), he would write: "America was created by God . . . to protect and to serve as a haven for all who are harassed and persecuted, all who get pushed about and driven from the four corners of the earth."[22]

Americans appeared generally sympathetic to the plight of Russian Jews. As one observer put it at the time, "Americans dislike injustice," particularly when a foreign government appeared to sanction actual brutality.[23] In early 1906 both houses of Congress passed a unanimous joint resolution, "That the people of the United States are horrified by the reports of the massacre of Hebrews in Russia, on account of their race and religion," which received Theodore Roosevelt's presidential approval later that year.[24] It is also relevant in this context that Roosevelt had appointed Oscar Straus—the first U.S. Jew to hold a cabinet post—as secretary of the Commerce and Labor Department, with responsibility for immigration policy. It was Straus, apparently, who persuaded Roosevelt to write to Count Witte in 1905, communicating America's interest in matters related to Russia's Jewish policy that impinged on the two countries' commercial relations. This was the first step in a wider initiative that led, in 1911, to the abrogation of the American commercial treaty with Russia.[25]

The aggravated assault on the Jewish people perpetrated by the Russian autocracy's most brutal cohorts made a profound impression on American Jewry—immigrant and native-born alike. Such was the overwhelming power of the general feeling about the plight of Russian Jewry that, in 1913, when Simon Dubnov was working on a history of the Jews in Russia and Poland for the Jewish Publication Society,[26] Israel Friedlaender, Dubnov's English translator (and a prominent scholar in his own right), called on Dubnov to go beyond the standard lachrymose fare and to devote more space in his book to the internal life of the Jews. Friedlaender, among whose major concerns was the future spiritual development of the Jews in America, argued:

The external conditions of Russian Jewish life, and particularly the economic and political oppression which characterizes it, are known to [the American reader] in a general way. . . . The Jew outside of Russia who will read your book . . . will find in Russian Jewish history too little that will enlighten his mind or inspire his heart. To him the Russian Jews will appear not as active agents, but merely as passive objects . . . of the Russian Government. . . . Speaking personally, I should like to find in a book of this sort the key to that remarkable make-up of the Russian Jew, the traces of which manifest themselves in all the countries of their abode, and particularly in America: his intellectualism and greed of knowledge, his idealism and the lack of a practical sense on the one hand, and his materialism and the lack of a social sense on the other.[27]

Dubnov did not see it that way, insisting that the steady march of political change affecting the status of Russian Jewry was the defining and unifying theme of the book, while literary, spiritual, or cultural themes were noted insofar as they had developed, as he put it, "at points of contact with the basic changes in national life." He was therefore unwilling to digress into the "static" elements of culture and personality at the expense of the public, political realm.[28]

The dominant and lasting image of Russian Jewry within the American Jewish consciousness would remain, therefore, one of relentless persecution. Such depictions of Russia became a staple part of American Jewish consciousness because they were embedded within a truly wide-scale folk experience: the mass immigration of Russian Jews to America. Although it has been argued that the roots of that immigration lie primarily in the social, demographic, and economic crisis that plagued the Pale of Settlement—and this is an accurate perception[29]—there can be no doubt that pogroms and the Russian regime's repressive legislation multiplied and intensified the effects of underlying socioeconomic problems. The rate of Jewish emigration from Russia (the proportion of emigrants to total base population) far exceeded that of non-Jewish Russians and was more than twice the rate among Poles. In 1906 alone, emigrants accounted for 2.5 percent of all Russian Jews, over thirty times the share of emigrants among Russians, which stood at 0.07 percent.[30] The deteriorating political conditions in Russia beginning in the 1903–6 period confirmed and perpetuated the self-perception of the Jewish immigrants as exiles fleeing persecution. The Russian background lent the act of immigration the character of destiny or fate more than a spontaneous choice by migrants seeking a better quality of life.

This perception, in turn, had a profound effect on the immigrants' approach to America and its way of life. America was expected to offer an antithesis to the political barbarism of Russia. The Russian background—and the anticipation by Jews that, in America, things would be different—lent a fairly untypical alertness and even fervor to the political culture of American Jewry, a legacy that outlived the immigrant generation and, indeed, outlived the preoccupation with Russia and its Jews. The characteristics of the politics of East European Jews in America in the period before and after World War I were based on this expectation and ranged from a dyed-in-the-wool American patriotism to a utopian anticipation of new forms of egalitarian social relations, or, alternatively, to a stubborn, radical critique aimed at those areas of American life that did not live up to the democratic ideal.[31] Most socialists, however, distinguished between benighted Russia and capitalist America. At a meeting of radical sympathizers in New York in 1905, for instance, the Socialist Revolutionary leader Grigorii Gershuni, conducting a speaking tour in the United States, drew vocal protest from his audience when he alleged that America was not much better than Russia.[32]

Whereas a great deal of Jewish public activity, both before and after 1905, was intended to sway the American administration and American public opinion as a whole against the tsarist regime in Russia, ultimately it was within the Jewish community itself that the issue achieved its greatest resonance. Thus, the Russian problem and its lasting political effects became a marker of Jewish ethnic distinctiveness within American democracy—a sign, in effect, of their incomplete assimilation. The historian Zosa Szajkowski, who concurred in this assessment, cited the observation made at the time by Mark Twain. Twain was of the opinion that Americans, in general, remained apathetic to the situation in Russia and that the American government's role in Russian affairs was less than helpful to the revolutionary cause. President Roosevelt's peace mediation of 1905 to end the war between Russia and Japan, he argued, had "postponed the Russian nation's imminent liberation from its age-long chains indefinitely" by artificially resuscitating the tsarist regime. In response to a fund-raising tour of the United States on behalf of Russian revolutionaries conducted by Nikolai Chaikovskii in 1906, Twain warned:

His audiences would be composed of foreigners who have suffered so recently that they have not yet had time to become Americanized and their hearts turned to stone in their breasts; that these audiences will be drawn from the ranks of the poor, not those of the rich. . . . That money [collected in the United States] came not from Americans, it came from Jews. . . . Suffering can always move a Jew's heart and tax his pocket to the limit. He will be at your mass meetings. But if you find any Americans there put them in a glass case and exhibit them. It will be worth fifty cents a head to go and look at that show and try to believe in it.[33]

In later years, as well, it appears that American Jewish immigrants from Russia and their children were left peculiarly "spinning in the Russian turbulence," as Alfred Kazin put it.[34] It is undoubtedly relevant to the point in question that an entire generation of Jews in the ranks of the American radical left invested the mystique of the Russian Revolution with particular fervor, identified with its myths. and venerated its heroes as political saints and martyrs. As Russian autocracy had been the epitome of evil, the revolution that caused its downfall could be nothing less than the epitome of political virtue and the root of salvation. For Jewish communists in America, living under benign conditions of democracy and assimilation, it was their or their parents' Russian, pre-revolutionary background that fueled their desire to participate, if only vicariously, in the revolution. Their hatred and contempt for the "class enemies" of the revolution, whether Spanish fascists or American impe-rialists, were rooted in the historical rage against the perpetrators of "Bloody Sunday" and the anti-Jewish pogroms.[35]

Notes

Introduction

1. S. M. Dubnov, *Kniga zhizni: Vospominaniia i razmyshleniia. Materialy dlia istorii moego vremeni* (Moscow-Jerusalem, 2004), p. 297.

2. V. I. Lenin, *Polnoe sobranie sochinenii,* 5th ed. (Moscow, 1974), 31:39–40; 34:137–38, 195–96; 38:305–6; 41:8–10.

3. Outstanding examples include Olga Litvak, *Conscription and the Search for Modern Russian Jewry* (Bloomington, Ind., 2006); Kenneth Moss, "'A Time for Tearing Down and a Time for Building Up': Recasting Jewish Culture in Eastern Europe, 1917–1921" (Ph.D. diss., Stanford University, 2003); Ezra Mendelsohn, *Painting a People: Maurycy Gottlieb and Jewish Art* (Hanover, N.H., 2002); Iris Parush, *Nashim korot: Yitronah shel shuliyut bahevrah hayehudit bemizrah eiropah bameah hatesh'a-'esreh* (Tel Aviv, 2001); Michael Stanislawski, *Zionism and the Fin-de-Siècle: Cosmopolitanism and Nationalism from Nordau to Jabotinsky* (Berkeley, Calif., 2001).

4. Frankel, *Prophecy and Politics: Socialism, Nationalism, and the Russian Jews, 1862–1917* (1981; 2nd ed., Cambridge, 2003); translated into Hebrew as *Nevuah upolitikah: Sotzializm, leumiyut veyehudei rusiyah, 1862–1917* (Tel Aviv, 1989).

5. Frankel, *Prophecy and Politics,* p. 182. Close attention to individuals (i.e., identity) and interpersonal relations (i.e., experience) has been one of the hallmarks of Frankel's scholarship. An early example can be found in his essay on the Russian Marxist Vladimir Akimov, Lenin's antagonist in the controversy over "Economism." In its genesis, Frankel wrote, "the Economist crisis has to be seen as the last and most dramatic of those essentially personal disputes that since the 1880s had periodically ensnared Plekhanov's Group for the Emancipation of Labor." See Frankel, "The Polarization of Russian Marxism (1883–1893): Plekhanov, Lenin, and Akimov," in Frankel, ed., *Vladimir Akimov on the Dilemmas of Russian Marxism, 1895–1903* (Cambridge, 1969), p. 96.

6. Anita Shapira, review published in *Studies in Zionism* 5, no. 1 (1984): 145–50, quotation on p. 145.

7. *Prophecy and Politics,* p. 134.

8. Jonathan Frankel, *Jewish Politics and the Russian Revolution of 1905,* Spiegel Lectures in European Jewish History (Tel Aviv, 1982), p. 20.

9. Quoted by Vladimir Levin in his chapter in this volume, p. 116.

10. Quoted in Scott Ury's chapter in this volume, p. 107.

11. Frankel, "'Youth in Revolt': An-sky's *In Shtrom* and the Instant Fictionalization of 1905," in Gabriella Safran and Steven J. Zipperstein, eds., *The Worlds of S. An-Sky: A Russian Jewish Intellectual at the Turn of the Century* (Stanford, Calif., 2006), pp. 137–63.

12. Quoted in Hever's chapter in this volume, p. 156.

Chapter 1. Interpreting 1905

1. Lenin's comments on 1905 are scattered throughout his works. For a succinct statement by him on the upheaval, see his "Lecture on the 1905 Revolution," in Robert C. Tucker, ed., *The Lenin Anthology* (New York, 1975), pp. 278–92. For his view on the Revolution of 1905 as the "dress rehearsal," see ibid., pp. 555–56. In 1918 and 1920, he described the armed uprising as the "highest point in the development of the first workers' revolution against tsarism." See his *Sochineniia*, 3rd ed. (Moscow, 1926–37), 23: 451 and 26: 60.

2. Kommunisticheskaia Akademiia, *Pervaia russkaia revoliutsiia: Ukazatel' literatury* (Moscow, 1930).

3. See Edith Bloomfield, "Soviet Historiography of 1905 as Reflected in Party Histories of the 1920s" (Ph.D. diss., University of Washington, 1966).

4. L. Martov, P. Maslov, and A. Potresov, eds., *Obshchestvennoe dvizhenie v nachale XX-go veka*, 4 vols. (St. Petersburg, 1909–14).

5. Ibid., 2: 185.

6. *Istorik-Marksist*, no. 1(1926): 253.

7. Ibid.

8. M. N. Pokrovsky, *Brief History of Russia*, trans. D. S. Mirsky (London, 1933), 2:122.

9. Ibid.

10. See Vasil'ev-Iuzhin's comments in *Istorik-Marksist*, no. 1 (1926): 244.

11. Ibid., pp. 215–17.

12. See, for example, G. D. Kostomarov, *Moskovskii sovet rabochikh deputatov v 1905 godu* (Moscow, 1948); L. K. Erman, "Uchastie demokraticheskoi intelligentsii vo vserossiiskoi oktiabrskoi stachke," *Istoricheskie zapiski* 49 (1954): 352–90; E. D. Chermenskii, *Burzhuaziia i tsarizm v pervoi russkoi revoliutsii*, 2nd ed. (Moscow, 1970).

13. "Za glubokoe izuchenie istorii pervoi russkoi revoliutsii," *Voprosy istorii*, no. 1(1955): 3–10.

14. The most notable example is the book by U. A. Shuster, *Peterburgskie rabochie v 1905–1907 gg.* (Leningrad, 1976).

15. A. Pankratova et al., eds., *Revoliutsiia 1905–7 gg. v Rossii: Dokumenty i materialy*, 8 vols. in 17 parts (Moscow, 1955–65).

16. For additional details on the historical scholarship during the four periods, see Abraham Ascher, "Soviet Historians and the Revolution of 1905," in François-Xavier Coquin and Celine Gervais-Francelle, eds., *1905: La Première Revolution Russe* (Paris, 1886), pp. 475–96.

17. See, for example, Walter Sablinsky, *The Road to Bloody Sunday: Father Gapon and the St. Petersburg Massacre* (Princeton, N.J., 1976); Robert C. Weinberg, *The Revolution of 1905 in Odessa: Blood on the Steps* (Bloomington, Ind., 1993); John Bushnell, *Mutiny and Repression: Russian Soldiers in the Revolution of 1905–1906* (Bloomington, Ind., 1985); Laura Engelstein *Moscow, 1905: Working-Class Organization and Political Conflict* (Stanford, Calif., 1982); Gerald D. Surh, *1905 in St. Petersburg: Labor, Society, and Revolution* (Stanford, Calif., 1989); Robert Edelman, *Proletarian Peasants: The Revolution of 1905 in Russia's Southwest* (Ithaca, N.Y., 1987). For additional titles, see the bibliographies in Abraham Ascher, *The Revolution of 1905: Russia in Disarray* (Stanford, Calif., 1988), and *The Revolution of 1905: Authority Restored* (Stanford, Calif., 1992). The social historians have all benefited from a close reading of the magisterial four-volume work published by a number of Mensheviks mentioned above. This is not a systematic, chrono-

logical account of events during the revolution. It consists of detailed and scholarly studies of political parties, political developments, the working class, the bourgeoisie, the intelligentsia, and peasantry, to mention only some of the more important topics. Written from a Marxist and Menshevik perspective, the work is a gold mine of reliable information. The interpretive issues discussed in this essay became a central concern of activists and historians well after the appearance of the Menshevik oeuvre.

18. S. S. Oldenburg, *Last Tsar: Nicholas II, His Reign and His Russia*, trans. Leonid I. Mihalap and Patrick J. Rollins, 4 vols. (Gulf Breeze, Fla., 1975–77), 1: 55; 2: 161, 239, and passim.

19. Dominic Lieven, *Nicholas II: Twilight of the Empire* (New York, 1993), pp. 142–43 and passim. For additional, similar evaluations of 1905, see V. A. Maklakov, *Vtoraia Gosudarstvennaia Duma (Vospominaniia sovremennika)* (Paris, n.d.), pp. 5–17, and V. N. Kokovtsev, *Iz moego proshlogo* (Paris, 1933), 1: 257.

20. J. L. H. Keep, *The Rise of Social Democracy in Russia* (Oxford, 1963), p. 150.

21. For this interpretation of the revolution, I have drawn on my two works on 1905 cited above in note 17.

22. *Russkie vedomosti*, October 18, 1905, p. 1.

23. *Pravo*, no. 41 (October 25, 1905), columns 3397–3400.

24. A. A. Kizevetter, *Na rubezhe dvukh stoletii (Vospominaniia 1881–1914)* (Prague, 1929), p. 419.

25. The quote is from a dispatch sent by the Austro-Hungarian Embassy in St. Petersburg to Vienna, June 13, 1906, Haus-Hof-und-Staatsarchiv, Russland, Berichte, Vienna.

26. On the two dumas, see Ascher, *The Revolution of 1905*, 2: 81–110, 162–215, 292–368, and Alfred Levin, *The Second Duma: A Study of the Social Democratic Party and the Russian Constitutional Experiment* (New Haven, Conn., 1940).

27. The best study on the Russian rightists is Donald C. Rawson, *Russian Rightists and the Revolution of 1905* (Cambridge, 1995).

28. Alexander Gerassimoff, *Der Kampf gegen die erste Russische Revolution*, trans. Ernst Thälmann (Frauenfeld-Leipzig, 1934).

29. Victoria E. Bonnell, *Roots of Rebellion: Workers' Politics and Organizations in St. Petersburg and Moscow, 1900–1914* (Berkeley, Calif., 1983), pp. 320–21.

30. Francois-Xavier Coquin, "Un aspect méconnu de la révolution de 1905: Les 'motions paysannes,'" in Coquin and Gervais Francelle, *1905*, p. 196.

31. Andreas Kappeler, *The Russian Empire: A Multiethnic History*, trans. Alfred Clayton (London, 2001), p. 333. See pp. 329–43 for an excellent discussion of the national question in the Revolution of 1905.

32. Hugh Seton-Watson, *The Russian Empire, 1801–1917* (Oxford, 1967), pp. 610–11.

33. For more on the Jews in 1905, see Jonathan Frankel, *Prophesy and Politics: Socialism, Nationalism, and the Russian Jews* (Cambridge, 1981), passim, and Christoph Gassenschmidt, *Jewish Liberal Politics in Tsarist Russia, 1900–14: The Modernization of Russian Jewry* (New York, 1995), pp. 19–63.

34. Abraham Ascher, *P. A. Stolypin: The Search for Stability in Late Imperial Russia* (Stanford, Calif., 2001), pp. 164–72.

Chapter 2. Nicholas II and the Revolution

1. See *Scenarios of Power: Myth and Ceremony in Russian Monarchy*, vol. 2, *From Alexander II to the Abdication of Nicholas II* (Princeton, N.J., 2000), part 2.

2. On the "selective integration" of Jews in the second half of the nineteenth century and the setbacks during the 1880s, see Benjamin Nathans, *Beyond the Pale: The Jewish Encounter with Late Imperial Russia* (Berkeley, Calif., 2002).

3. On the shift from St. Petersburg to Moscow as the symbolic center of empire, see my article "Moscow and Petersburg: The Problem of Political Center in Tsarist Russia, 1881–1914," in Sean Wilentz, ed., *Rites of Power: Symbolism, Ritual and Politics since the Middle Ages* (Philadelphia, 1985), pp. 244–74.

4. *Tsarskoe prebyvanie v Moskve v aprele 1900 goda* (St. Petersburg, 1900), p. 56; "Pis'ma imp. Nikolaia II imp. Marii Fedorovne, 23 ianv. 1899–22 dekabria 1900," State Archive of the Russian Federation (hereafter GARF), 642-1-2326, pp. 56–57.

5. Francis William Wcislo, *Reforming Rural Russia: State, Local Society, and National Politics, 1855–1914* (Princeton, N.J., 1990), pp. 145–46.

6. Igor Vinogradoff, "Some Russian Imperial Letters to Prince V. P. Meshcherskii, (1839–1914)," *Oxford Slavonic Studies*, no. 11 (1962): 134.

7. "Dnevnik Nikolaia II" (May 19–December 31, 1903), GARF, 601-1-246, pp. 42–47.

8. A. A. Mosolov, *Pri dvore poslednego Rossiiskago Imperatora* (Moscow, 1993), pp. 119–21.

9. Andrew M. Verner, *The Crisis of Russian Autocracy: Nicholas II and the 1905 Revolution* (Princeton, N.J., 1990), pp. 124–29.

10. Ibid., p. 132.

11. Ibid., pp. 170–73.

12. *Polnoe sobranie rechei Imperatora Nikolaia II* (St. Petersburg, 1906), pp. 57–58; Verner, *The Crisis of Russian Autocracy*, pp. 195–96.

13. Verner, *The Crisis of Russian Autocracy*, pp. 213–14

14. N. A. Epanchin, *Na sluzhbe trekh imperatorov* (Moscow, 1996), pp. 324–25.

15. Verner, *The Crisis of Russian Autocracy*, pp. 239–41.

16. Ibid., pp. 299–300.

17. *Moskovskie vedomosti*, January 15, 1906, p. 2.

18. Verner, *The Crisis of Russian Autocracy*, p. 299.

19. For a valuable discussion of the juridical principles involved in these changes, see Hiroshi Oda, "The Emergence of Pravovoe Gosudarstvo (Rechtsstaat) in Russia," *Review of Central and East European Law* 25, no. 3 (1999): 395–97.

20. For the rules for the Duma elections, see Terence Emmons, *The Formation of Political Parties and the First National Elections in Russia* (Cambridge, Mass., 1982), pp. 12–14.

21. "Dnevnik v. kn. Konstantina Konstantinovicha, 10/8/05–11/6/06," GARF, 660-1-55, p. 90.

22. Abraham Ascher, *The Revolution of 1905: Authority Restored* (Stanford, Calif., 1992), pp. 83–84.

23. Henry W. Nevinson, *The Dawn in Russia: Or Scenes in the Russian Revolution* (New York, 1906), p. 322.

24. *Novoe vremia*, April 28, 1906, p. 1.

25. *Dnevniki Imperatora Nikolaia II* (Moscow, 1991), p. 312.

26. Verner, *The Crisis of Russian Autocracy*, p. 260.

27. A. S. Tager, *Tsarskaia Rossiia i delo Beilisa* (Moscow, 1933), pp. 39–40.

28. Ascher, *The Revolution of 1905*, p. 351; Polnoe sobranie zakonov (PSZ) 3, 29240, June 3, 1907.

29. The telegram was immediately printed in the party newspaper, *Russkoe znamia* (Ascher, *The Revolution of 1905*, pp. 357–58).

30. For a convincing analysis of Alexandra's ideas and their relationship to

Nicholas's, see Mark Steinberg, "Nicholas and Alexandra: An Intellectual Portrait," in Mark Steinberg and Vladimir M. Khrustalev, eds., *The Fall of the Romanovs: Political Dreams and Personal Struggles in a Time of Revolution* (New Haven, Conn., 1995), pp. 34–36.

31. "Zapisnaia knizhka imp. Aleksandry Fedorovny s vyskazyvaniiami Grigoriia Rasputina (1907–1916) s darstvennoi nadpis'iu Rasputina," GARF, 640-1-309, pp. 38–39, 52–54.

32. Andrei Maylunas and Sergei Mironenko, *A Lifelong Passion: Nicholas and Alexandra, Their Own Story* (London, 1996), pp. 296–97, 314, 320–22, 328–30, 341, 343, 350–74, 376; M. V. Rodzianko, *The Reign of Rasputin: An Empire's Collapse* (London, 1927), p. 11; Sir Bernard Pares, *The Fall of the Russian Monarchy* (New York, 1961), p. 143; A. Ia. Avrekh, *Tsarizm i IV Duma* (Moscow, 1981), p. 255.

33. Nathans, *Beyond the Pale*, pp. 296–301, 366; Hans Rogger, "The Beilis Case: Anti-Semitism and Politics in the Reign of Nicholas II," *Slavic Review* 25, no. 4 (December 1966): 615–29.

Chapter 3. A Note on the Jewish Press and Censorship

1. For greater detail on the history of the censorship of Jewish publications in the Russian Empire, see Dmitrii El'iashevich, *Pravitel'stvennaia politika i evreiskaia pechat' v Rossii, 1797–1917: Ocherki istorii tsenzury* (St. Petersburg-Jerusalem, 1999).

2. Russian State Historical Archive (RGIA), fond 821, opis' 8, ed. khr. 276, l. 136

3. RGIA, fond 776, opis' 9, ed. khr. 686.; opis' 17, ed. khr. 552.

4. RGIA, fond 776, opis' 2, ed. khr. 36, ll. 121–121 oborot.

5. This refers to translations of tractates of the Talmud by N. A. Pereferkovich that were published in St. Petersburg from 1899 to 1911; for further details, see V. E. Kel'ner and D. A. El'iashevich, eds., *Literatura o evreiakh na russkom iazyke, 1890–1947: Knigi, broshiury, ottiski statei, bibliograficheskii ukazatel'* (St. Petersburg, 1995).

6. See A. Lokshin, "'Formirovanie politiki' (Tsarskaia administratsiia i sionism v Rossii v kontse XIX-nachale XX v.)," *Vestnik evreiskogo universiteta v Moskve* 1 (1992): 42–56. The 1903 circular forbade any Zionist activity with the exception of that which was directed at the Jews' immediate departure from Russia.

7. RGIA, fond 776, opis' 14 (1903), ed. khr 16, l. 1.

8. See Saul Ginsburg, *Amolike peterburg: Forshungen un zikhroynes vegn yidishn lebn in der rezidents-shtot fun tsarishn rusland* (New York, 1944), pp. 184–238.

9. El'iashevich, *Pravitel'stvennaia politika*, pp. 366–67.

Chapter 4. The Russian Right Responds to 1905

1. For a treatment of visual images during 1905, see Sarah Abrevaya Stein, "Faces of Protest: Yiddish Cartoons of the 1905 Revolution," *Slavic Review* 61, no. 4 (Winter 2002): 732–61.

2. Hans Rogger, "The Formation of the Russian Right: 1900–06," and "Was There a Russian Fascism? The Union of the Russian People," in Hans Rogger, *Jewish Politics and Right-wing Politics in Imperial Russia* (Berkeley, Calif., 1986), pp. 188–211 and 212–32; V. Levitskii, "Pravye partii," in L. Martov, P. Maslov, and

A. Potresov, eds., *Obshchestvennoe dvizhenie v Rossii v nachale XX-go veka*, vol. 3, bk. 5 (St. Petersburg, 1914), pp. 347–469; Don Rawson, *Russian Rightists and the Revolution of 1905* (Cambridge, 1995); Heinz-Dietrich Lowe, *The Tsars and the Jews: Reform, Reaction, and Anti-Semitism in Imperial Russia, 1772–1917* (Chur, 1993), pp. 221–30; S. A. Stepanov, *Chernaia sotnia v Rossii (1905–1914 gg.)* (Moscow, 1992); Iu. I Kir'ianov, *Pravye partii v Rossii, 1911–1917 gg.* (Moscow, 2001); Iu. I. Kir'ianov, ed., *Pravye partii, 1905–1917: Dokumenty i materialy*, 2 vols. (Moscow, 1998).

3. Charles Press, *The Political Cartoon* (East Brunswick, N.J., 1981), p. 76.

4. Victoria Bonnell, *The Iconography of Power: Soviet Political Posters under Lenin and Stalin* (Berkeley, Calif., 1997), p. 14.

5. Ibid., p. 83.

6. Presumably, the Black Hundreds attacked Bobrinskii because he believed the Duma could contribute to the restoration of political stability and social order.

7. The quote is from Abraham Ascher, *The Revolution of 1905: Russia in Disarray* (Stanford, Calif., 1988), p. 241. See also Sidney Harcave, *Count Sergei Witte and the Twilight of Imperial Russia: A Biography* (Armonk, N.Y., 2004), pp. 42–43 and 46, and Rawson, *Russian Rightists and the Revolution of 1905*, pp. 69, 128, and 131–32.

8. In addition, the Trudoviki split on whether private landowners were entitled to compensation. Nevertheless, all Trudoviki agreed that the state—not the peasants—should be responsible for compensating the gentry.

9. Abraham Ascher, *The Revolution of 1905: Authority Restored* (Stanford, Calif., 1992), pp. 195–201.

10. Ibid., p. 89.

11. A similar drawing appeared virtually at the same time in an American publication. Titled "Gulliver Knickerbocker and the Lilliputians," the American version of Gulliver, shown as a descendant of the early Dutch settlers of New York, has been overwhelmed by hordes of Jews who have taken control of many branches of the local economy, including clothing, jewelry, real estate, and the theater. Money, not political influence, motivates the Jews in this depiction. See Richard Levy, ed., *Antisemitism in the Modern World: An Anthology of Texts* (Lexington, Mass., 1991), p. 140.

12. A variation on this theme of Jews' tending gardens appeared in the November 26, 1906, issue of *Veche*. Titled "A New Kike Garden," the drawing depicts a traditional Jew watering a crop of sprouting Jewish youths armed with guns and daggers.

13. See Andrea de Jorio, *Gesture in Naples and Gesture in Classical Antiquity* (Bloomington, Ind., 2000), pp. 214–15. De Jorio's book first appeared in 1832. Similarly, Black Hundred disdain for parliamentary politics is evidenced on the cover of issue no. 9 of *Knut* from 1907. In the drawing, labeled "The State Duma's Easter Egg for the Russian People," a Duma politician with a pointed head is dwarfed by an immense egg that has been dyed red. Six fists giving the *mano in fica* have punctured the egg's shell.

14. The cover of the first issue of the journal *Gudok* from 1906 shows two sinister-looking, devil-like hands giving the *mano in fica* to a rising sun that symbolizes the dawning of freedom in Russia. The caption reads, "The double-headed . . . *fica,*" a play on the double-headed eagle, emblem of the Romanov dynasty.

Chapter 5. The "Jewish Question" in the Tsarist Army

1. Thus, according to the order of the minister of war of December 12, 1891, Jewish volunteers who converted to Russian Orthodoxy before entering the army were permitted to take the officer's exam on the condition that they had passed an exam in theology; see Central Archives of the History of the Jewish People (hereafter CAHJP, Jerusalem), HM2/ 7912.3; original in the Rossiiskii gosudarstvennyi voenno-istoricheskii arkhiv (Russian State Military Historical Archive, hereafter RGVIA), f. 1859, op. 2, d. 287. See A. I. Denikin's memoirs: "Individuals of the Jewish faith had no access to the officers' ranks. But the officers' corps included officers and generals who had accepted Christianity before service and had then gone through military academies" (A. I. Denikin, *Put' russkogo ofitsera*, New York, 1953, p. 283). One of these generals was M. V. Grulev, who left interesting memoirs (*Zapiski generala-evreia*, repr. Orange, Conn., 1987).

2. CAHJP, Jerusalem, HM2/ 7912.3 (original in the RGVIA, f. 1859, op. 2, d. 287).

3. Ibid.

4. Ibid.

5. Order of the commander of the troops of the Warsaw military district from January 13, 1914, ibid.

6. See Hans Rogger, *Jewish Policies and Right-Wing Politics in Imperial Russia* (Berkeley-Los Angeles, 1986), pp. 33–39. Rogger provides examples of a similar "racial" approach back in the reigns of Alexander II and Alexander III, when Jewish converts to Christianity were not permitted to serve in the gendarmerie in the border regions or to be censors of publications in Jewish languages. In the elections to the Fourth Duma in 1912, the racial approach was confirmed in the Interior Ministry's instructions to register Jewish converts in the curia (a discrete group of voters entitled to elect a given number of representatives) of Jewish electors (according to the election law of 1907, the governor had the right, with confirmation from the Interior Minister, to establish national [ethnic] curiae in localities that selected more than one elector). The governors in the Pale of Settlement often used this right, setting up separate "Russian" and Jewish curiae of electors in order to guarantee the election of non-Jewish candidates (pp. 35, 36).

7. CAHJP, HM2/ 8279.6 (original in RGVIA, f. 400, op.19, d. 37). Perhaps a shortage of funds for military expenditures led the ministers to devise this plan. In any case, it was precisely in 1903 that the war ministry considered the issue of not permitting even Jewish converts to enter military academies.

8. Ibid.

9. Ibid.

10. Ibid.

11. Ibid.

12. Ibid.

13. Ibid.

14. Ibid.

15. Ibid. Note of the Chief of the General Staff Ia. G. Zhilinskii to War Minister V. A. Sukhomlinov presenting the results of the poll, published also by A. Litvin, "Generaly i evrei. Dokladnaia zapiska nachal'nika General'nogo Shtaba Ia. G. Zhilinskogo," in *Vestnik evreiskogo universiteta* 4, no. 22 (Moscow-Jerusalem 2000): 273–90. Iokhanan Petrovskii-Shtern considers that the poll of the top-

ranking commanders was related to the preparation of the new military regulations of 1912; see I. Petrovskii-Shtern, *Evrei v russkoi armii, 1827–1914* (Moscow, 2003), p. 343.

16. CAHJP, HM2/ 8279.6 (original in RGVIA, f. 400, op.19, d. 37).

17. Ibid. The Russian military command's negative attitude toward Jewish soldiers, which linked the Jewish soldiers' physical and moral qualities, can be analyzed with the help of the French critic Michel Foucault's concept of "biopower" as a form of control over the human body (Michael Donnely, "On Foucault's Uses of the Notion 'Biopower,'" in *Michel Foucault, Philosopher: Essays Translated from the French and German*, trans. Timothy J. Armstrong [New York, 1992], pp. 199–203). Although certainly interesting, such an analysis goes beyond the framework of this study. For attempts to apply Foucault's methods to an analysis of the disciplinary methods of imperial Russia, see the following works: A. Etkind, "Fuko i imperskaia Rossiia: Distsiplinarnye praktiki v usloviiakh vnutrennei kolonizatsii," in Oleg Charchordin, ed., *Mishel Fuko i Rossiia* (St. Petersburg-Moscow, 2001), pp. 166–91, and Laura Engelstein, "Combined Undevelopment: Discipline and the Law in Imperial and Soviet Russia," in Jan Goldstein, ed., *Foucault and the Writing of History* (Oxford-Cambridge, Mass., 1994), pp. 220–36.

18. CAHJP, HM2/ 8279.6 (original in RGVIA, f. 400, op.19, d. 37).

19. Ibid.

20. Ibid.

21. Ibid. At the same time, Ekk believed that even Jewish converts should be denied access to the officer corps.

22. Ibid.

23. Ibid. For Rittikh's opinion, see E. Iu. Sergeev, *"Inaia zemlia, Inoe nebo"*: *Zapad i voennaia elita Rossii (1900–1914)* (Moscow, 2001), p. 193.

24. The information gathered by Russian military agents about the Jews' service in foreign armies is not without interest. On this basis it would seem that the Italian and French armies had the most liberal attitude toward the Jews whereas the Romanian was the most antisemitic. The Russian military agent in Romania sympathetically described the Romanian army's attitude toward the Jews, whom it treated as a harmful "element in the practical and political sense" (CAHJP, HM2/ 8279.6 [original in RGVIA, f. 400, op.19, d. 37]).

25. Ibid.

26. Ibid.

27. D. A. Kotsubinskii, *Russkii natsionalizm v nachale XX stoletiia: Rozhdenie i gibel' ideologii vserossiiskogo natsional'nogo soiuza* (Moscow, 2001), pp. 32–34.

28. Ibid., p. 264.

29. Ibid., pp. 270–71.

30. Sergeev, "Inaia zemlia: Inoe nebo," p. 83. In other words, "the military-political elite of Russia associated the image of the Jews with attempts by the West to impose alien socio-political practices on Russia and to destroy the empire's armed forces" (p. 83).

31. Ibid.

32. After the start of World War I, this myth continued to work effectively under the new conditions (Rogger, *Jewish Policies and Right-Wing Politics*, pp. 54–55).

33. M. Howard, *War in European History* (London-Oxford-New York, 1976), pp.110–11.

34. Ibid., p. 112.

35. Peter Holquist, "To Count, to Extract, and to Exterminate: Population Statistics and Population Politics in Late Imperial and Soviet Russia," in Ronald Grigor Suny and Terry Martin, eds., *A State of Nations: Empire and Nation-Making in the Age of Lenin and Stalin* (New York, 2001), p. 115. The definition of statistics as "political arithmetic" can also be found in Michel Foucault, "The Political Technology of Individuals," in P. H. Hutton, H. Gutman, and L. H. Martin, eds., *Technologies of the Self: A Seminar with Michael Foucault* (Amherst, Mass., 1988), p. 151.

36. Holquist, "To Count, to Extract, and to Exterminate," p. 113.

37. Ibid., p. 115.

38. Sergeev, "*Inaia zemlia, Inoe nebo,*" p. 194.

39. See Foucault: "Since the population is nothing more than what the state takes care of for its own sake, of course, the state is entitled to slaughter it, if necessary" ("The Political Technology of Individuals," p. 160).

40. Holquist, "To Count, to Extract, and to Exterminate," p. 123.

Chapter 6. Victory from Defeat

1. E. Cherikower, *Istoriia obshchestva dlia rasprostraneniia prosveshcheniia mezhdu evreiami v Rossii* (St. Petersburg, 1913), p. 41.

2. Ibid., p. 45.

3. Ibid., pp. 40–45.

4. S. Zipperstein, "Transforming the Heder: Maskilic Politics in Imperial Russia," in A. Rapoport-Albert and S. Zipperstein, eds., *Jewish History: Essays in Honor of Chimen Abramsky* (London, 1988), pp. 88–89.

5. Kriticus (Simon Dubnov), "Itogi 'obshchestva prosveshcheniia evreev: Literaturnaia letopis'," *Voskhod* 10 (1891): 41.

6. "Prosveshchenie," *Evreiskaia entsiklopediia: Svod znanii o evreistve* (St. Petersburg, 1907–13), 13: 60.

7. Ibid., 61.

8. Ibid.

9. *Regesty i nadpisi: Svod materialov dlia istorii evreev v Rossii*, 3 vols. (St. Petersburg, 1897–1913), of which vols. 1 and 2 appeared in 1897 and 1899 respectively; *Sistematicheskii ukazatel' literatury o evreiiakh na russkom iazyke* (St. Petersburg, 1892); *Spravochnaia kniga po voprosam obrazovaniia evreev: Posobie dlia uchitelei i uchitel'nits evreiskikh shkol i deiatelei po narodnomu obrazovaniiu* (St. Petersburg, 1901).

10. B. Horowitz, "The Society for the Promotion of Enlightenment among the Jews of Russia, and the Evolution of the St. Petersburg Russian–Jewish Intelligentsia, 1893–1905," in Ezra Mendelsohn, ed., *Jews and the State: Dangerous Alliances and the Perils of Privilege, Studies in Contemporary Jewry* 19 (2004): 200–205.

11. *Protokol soveshchaniia komiteta s inogorodnimi chlenami obshchestva ot 25–27 dekabria, 1902 g.* (St. Petersburg, 1903).

12. Among OPE's traveling inspectors were such illustrious individuals as Dr. Lerner, P. Marek, A. Strashun, and D. Kantor. There is even a portrait of one of these inspectors, Chaim Fialkov, in Hirsz Abramowicz's *Profiles of a Lost World: Memoirs of East European Jewish Life before World War II*, trans. E. Z. Dobkin, ed. Dina Abramowicz and Jeffrey Shandler (Detroit, 1999), pp. 126–31.

13. In 1902, the OPE spent 3,332 rubles on library expansion. *Otchet OPE za 1902* (St. Petersburg, 1903), pp. 11–15.

14. *Spravochnaia kniga po voprosam obrazovaniia evreev,* pp. 81–82.

15. An-sky subtitled his play *The Dybbuk* (1914) with the words "Between Two Worlds," which was a metaphor for the so-called semi-intelligentsia (*polu-intelligenty*) who had left Orthodox Jewry but had not succeeded in adapting fully to Russian life.

16. Nevertheless, it must be said that OPE leaders were detached from the poverty and legal powerlessness that many Jews of the Pale experienced as bitter reality. It should also be mentioned that the Pale itself was changing and the image of the huddled masses must be juxtaposed against another image of urban culture, economic prosperity, and growing political confidence. For a discussion of progress as related to Jews in the Russian Empire, see Benjamin Harshav, *Marc Chagall and His Times: A Documentary Narrative* (Stanford, Calif., 2004), pp. 1–20.

17. For a more comprehensive picture of the OPE between 1880 and 1905, see Horowitz, "The Society for the Promotion of Enlightenment among the Jews of Russia," pp. 195–213.

18. The government's rules of March 4, 1906, permitted the legalization of societies and unions. These rules were reaffirmed in 1907.

19. "Prosveshchenie," p. 62.

20. Ibid.

21. T. Emmons, "Russia's Banquet Campaign," *California Slavic Studies* 10 (1977): 46.

22. "Protocols of general meetings of the members of the society, 1904–1909," Archive of the Society for the Promotion of Enlightenment among the Jews of Russia, Fond 1532-1-422, list 32. These papers are located in the Russian State Historical Archive (RGGU) in St. Petersburg, Russia. All further citations to archival material come from the same source.

23. Ibid., list 34.

24. For more than a decade Russian intellectuals had been clamoring for universal education for all Russian peasants of school age. See Ben Eklof, *Russian Peasant Schools: Officialdom, Village Culture and Popular Pedagogy, 1861–1914* (Berkeley, Calif., 1986), pp. 283–84.

25. Ibid.

26. Interestingly, in 1909 the tsarist government was going to arrest the original organizers of the meetings of the Union for the Attainment of Full Rights for the Jews, which took place in St. Petersburg November 22–25, 1905, but ultimately changed its mind. See R. M. Kantor, "'Razgrom' evreiskoi intelligentsii," *Evreiskaia letopis'* 2 (Petrograd-Moscow, 1923): 87–95.

27. The Kiev branch was established in 1897.

28. E. M., "Obshchee sobranie chlenov kievskogo otdeleniia obshchestva prosveshcheniia," *Nedel'naia khronika Voskhoda* 25 (June 13, 1905): 11.

29. Ibid. Cooperative members paid dues of only 50 kopeks.

30. "A. Izr[ailitin], "Obshchee sobranie 'Obshchestva rasprostranenia prosveshcheniia mezhdu evreiami,'" *Nedel'naia khronika Voskhoda* 49–50 (December 16, 1905): 37.

31. "Protokoly Obshchestva dlia rasprostraneniia prosveshcheniia za 1905," 1532-1-492, list 51.

32. Ibid.

33. Ibid.

34. "Protokol obshchego sobraniia chlenov obshchestva za 1906–07," 1532-1-633, list 13.

35. A somewhat different view of the OPE during 1905 with particular use of Yiddish sources can be found in David Fishman's insightful book, *The Rise of Modern Yiddish Culture* (Pittsburgh, 2005), pp. 33–47.

36. "Protokoly Obshchestva dlia rasprostraneniia prosveshcheniia za 1905," 1532-1-492, list 48.

37. Although scholars now differ as to whether the government fomented pogroms in 1905, Jews at the time believed that the government was behind them. For more, see Shlomo Lambroza, "Jewish Responses to Pogroms in Late Imperial Russia," in Jehuda Reinharz, ed., *Living with Antisemitism: Modern Jewish Responses* (Hanover, N.H., 1987), pp. 253–74.

38. The failure to democratize the OPE can be compared to the stalled process of democratic change reflected in the closing of the first two Dumas.

39. "Protokol OPE za 1906–1908," 1532-1-634, list 37.

40. Ibid., list 39.

41. C. Gassenschmidt, *Jewish Liberal Politics in Tsarist Russia, 1900–1914: The Modernization of Russian Jewry* (New York, 1995), pp. 55–75.

42. See S. Dubnov, *Pis'ma o staron i novom evreistve* (St. Petersburg, 1907).

43. *Otchet Obshchestva dlia rasprostraneniia prosveshcheniia za 1907* (St. Petersburg, 1908), p. 8.

44. *Otchet Obshchestva dlia rasprostraneniia prosveshcheniia za 1912* (St. Petersburg, 1913), pp. 58–69. There is a list of the branches and summaries of their activities.

45. *Otchet Odesskogo otdeleniia za 1913–1914* (Odessa, 1915), p. 9.

46. *Otchet Moskovskogo otdeleniia obshchestva dlia rasprostraneniia prosveshcheniia mezhdu evreiami v Rossii za 1909* g. (Moscow, 1910), p. 7

47. *Otchet Kievskogo otdeleniia obshchestv dlia rasprostraneniia prosveshcheniia mezhdu evreiami v Rossii za 1908* (Kiev, 1909), p. 9.

48. Ibid., p. 30.

49. Ibid., p. 7.

50. It is possible to get a sense of what was happening in the remote areas of the Pale by reading the *Vestnik Obshchestva dlia rasprostraneniia prosveshcheniia mezhdu evreiami v Rossii*, which devoted a section of the journal to Jewish education in the provinces. In addition, many cities did fulfill their obligations to send St. Petersburg an annual report of their activities. Some of these were published. An example is *Otchet akkermanskogo otdeleniia obshchestva dlia rasprostraneniia prosveshcheniia mezhdu evreiami v Rossii za 1910–1911 gg.* (Akkerman, 1913).

51. Iris Parush, *Reading Jewish Women: Marginality and Modernization in Nineteenth-Century Eastern European Jewish Society* (Waltham, Mass., 2004), pp. 61–70, 77–80.

52. Azriel Shohet, *Mosad "harabanut mi-ta'am" berusiyah: Parashah bema'avakhatarbut ben haredim leven maskilim* (The "Crown Rabbinate" in Russia: A Chapter in the Cultural Struggle between Orthodox Jews and Maskilim) (Haifa, 1975), pp. 93–94

53. "Perepiska s sovetom Peterburgskoi vol'noi vysshei shkoly o vvedenii lektsii po evreiskoi istorii i podbore lektury v 1906 g.," 1532-1-676, list 3. Dubnov describes his meeting with the head of the Free Advanced School this way: "On one of the first days following my arrival, I went to see the director of the Free Advanced School, Professor Lesgaft, that wonderful old man. A popular anatomist in Petersburg, he had left the medical academy as a result of a political conflict with the administration (Lesgaft sympathized with the leftist radicals) and established his own private courses in the natural sciences where women

(lesgaftchiks) studied. During the year of revolution these courses were opened to both sexes and were legalized as the Free Advanced School with three departments, biology, pedagogy, and sociology. The new institution attracted the best, for the most part radical, professors and a great mass of students, predominantly from among the revolutionary youth." S. M. Dubnov, *Kniga zhizni: Vospominaniia i razmyshleniia, materialy dlia istorii moego vremeni*, 3 vols. (Vilna, 1937; reissued St. Petersburg, 1988), p. 282.

54. The administration, nevertheless, demanded the right to have their own faculty vote on the appointment of all lecturers ("Perepiska s sovetom Peterburgskoi vol'noi vysshei shkoly o vvedenii lektsii po evreiskoi istorii i podbore lektury v 1906 g.," 1532-1-676, list 6).

55. Dubnov, *Kniga zhizni*, p. 283. In his version of events, he stopped because of an insufficient number of students, whereas according to OPE documents, the government prohibited further lectures.

56. Ibid., p. 282. According to Dubnov, the "government did not want the Advanced School to have a Jewish name and therefore covered this sin with the epithet 'Oriental Studies,' which Baron [David Gintsburg] suggested, having been a former student of the Oriental faculty [of St. Petersburg University] and a student of the orientalist Chwolson" (p. 292).

57. To increase the prestige and visibility of the school, an advisory committee was selected that included individuals from as many as eighteen cities, including London, New York, Berlin, and Frankfurt. Friends from Moscow were generous with donations.

58. 1532-1-676, listy 5–6. The endowment came from private donations to honor Baron Horace Gintsburg on his seventy-fifth birthday.

59. Dubnov, *Kniga zhizni*, pp. 292–93.

60. 5312-1-952, listy 7–9. Dubnov had difficulties in getting a permanent permit to live in the capital (see *Kniga zhizni*, p. 290).

61. Dubnov, *Kniga zhizni*, p. 293.

62. The term "amateur" does not seem appropriate. Universities in tsarist Russia did not have departments of Jewish literature and history, and many of the major scholars were self-taught (Zinberg had a degree in chemistry). Rather than discount them for their lack of institutional training, one should acknowledge the amazing contributions of this group. For example, *Regesty i nadpisi: Svod materialov dlia istorii evreev v Rossii (80 g.–1900 g.)* (Decrees and inscriptions: A collection of materials on the history of the Jews in Russia [from the Year 80 to 1900]) (1899–1913); the sixteen-volume Jewish Encyclopedia, *Evreiskaia entsiklopediia: Svod znaniia o evreistve* (1907–13); and the extraordinary scholarly articles in the quarterly journal *Evreiskaia starina* (Jewish antiquity) (1908–24) represented a renaissance of major significance to Jewish culture worldwide.

63. Women tended to be strongest precisely in secular subjects that were prohibited to religiously observant men. Because women held a marginal position in traditional Jewish society, argues Iris Parush, they had distinct advantages over men in acquiring nonreligious secular knowledge. See Parush, *Reading Jewish Women*, pp. 73–97.

64. Goldberg, "O podgotovke uchitelei dlia nachal'nykh shkol," *Vestnik Obshchestva dlia rasprostraneniia prosveshcheniia mezhdu evreiami v Rossii* 2 (1910): 22.

65. Ibid., p. 23.

66. 1532-1-494, list 29. Although the OPE earmarked 50,000 rubles for the institution for its first three years, the annual budget turned out to be higher—

27,300 rubles annually. Money was provided from Baron Gintsburg's School Fund, the OPE's general budget, and local donations from Grodno ("Protokoly zasedanii komiteta i obshchego sobraniia chlenov obshchestva za 1908," 1532-1-944).

67. "Grodnenskie pedagogicheskie kursy Obshchestva rasprostraneniia prosveshcheniia mezhdu evreiami v Rossii," *Vestnik OPE* 1 (1910): 95–96.

68. Ibid., p. 96.

69. Ibid., p. 97.

70. Ia. Eiger, "Normal'nyi tip evreiskoi shkoly (doklad, chitannyi v soveshchanii Komiteta Obshchestva dlia rasprostraneniia prosveshcheniia mezhdu evreiami v Rossii s predstaviteliami otdelenii v marte 1910 g.," *Vestnik Obshchestva dlia rasprostraneniia prosveshcheniia mezhdu evreiami v Rossii* 1 (1910): 6.

71. These statistics are for 1898–1900 and are taken from Steven Rappaport, "Jewish Education and Jewish Culture in the Russian Empire" (Ph.D. diss., Stanford University, 2000), p. 52.

72. *Otchet o soveshchanii Komiteta OPE s predstaviteliami otdelenii, 11–14 aprelia 1911 g.* (St. Petersburg, 1912).

73. "Protokoly zasedanii Kovenskogo evreiskogo soveshchaniia za 19–22 noiabria, 21–23 dekabria 1909 g. i 17 ianvaria 1910 g.," 1532-1-1110.

74. In his article "Russian Jewry and the Duma Elections, 1906–1907," Vladimir Levin argues that it was not only the curtailment of voting rights but also bad political decisions and an inability to form coalitions that led to the drastic diminution of Jewish representatives in the Duma: from twelve in the first to four in the second, two in the third, and three in the fourth. The article appears in W. Moskovich, L. Finberg, and M. Feller, eds., *Jews and Eastern Slavs: Essays on Intercultural Relations* (Jerusalem, 2000), 7: 233–64.

75. "Obzor deiatel'nosti obshchestva za vremia 1-oi imperialisticheskoi voiny, 1914–1916 gg. i kassovoi otchet za 1915 g.," 1532-1-1415, list 17.

Chapter 7. The Generation of 1905 and the Politics of Despair

Research for this article was supported, in part, by an East European Studies Doctoral Dissertation Grant from the American Council of Learned Societies (ACLS), a Doctoral Dissertation Fellowship from the National Foundation for Jewish Culture, the Memorial Foundation for Jewish Culture, and a George L. Mosse Fellowship at the University of Wisconsin-Madison.

1. D. Y. Green to Shmuel Fuchs, Warsaw, July 8, 1904, in Yehuda Erez, ed., *Igrot David Ben-Gurion, 1904–1919*, vol. 1 (Tel Aviv, 1971), p. 20. All further citations of *Igrot David Ben-Gurion* are to volume 1.

2. On cities and strangers, see Georg Simmel, "The Metropolis and Mental Life," and "The Stranger," in Kurt H. Wolff, ed. and trans., *The Sociology of Georg Simmel* (Glencoe, Ill., 1950), pp. 402–8 and 409–24. On anonymity, alienation, and invisibility as leitmotifs of the modern experience, see Hannah Arendt, *The Origins of Totalitarianism* (London, 1973), pp. 305–26 and pp. 474–79; E. J. Hobsbawm, *Nations and Nationalism since 1780: Programme, Myth, Reality* (Cambridge, 1990), pp. 91, 109, 124, 173, and 177; and Homi K. Bhabha, "Dissemination: Time, Narrative and the Margins of the Modern Nation," in Bhabha, *The Location of Culture* (London-New York, 1994), pp. 139–70, esp. pp. 169–70. See also Ralph Ellison, *The Invisible Man* (New York, 1952), p. 7.

3. Not surprisingly, David Ben-Gurion's later recollections of this early period in Warsaw vary significantly from the account detailed in the different letters

sent by the young David Yosef Green to his role model, confidant, and *landsman* Shmuel Fuchs. See, for example, David Ben-Gurion, *Beit Avi* (Tel Aviv, 1974), pp. 37–40; and David Ben-Gurion, *Zikhronot*, (Tel Aviv, 1971), 1:11–18. For a similarly romantic panegyric of "the Old Man" as a young man, see Amos Oz, "David Ben-Gurion," *Time*, April 13, 1998, pp. 134–36.

4. A convincing argument regarding the fate of the Jewish enlightenment (haskalah) in the era of mass society is made by Shmuel Feiner, "'Keyonek hanosheh shedei imo': Post-haskalah beketz hameah hatesh'a-'esreh," *Alpayim* 21 (2000): 59–94. I am indebted to Philip Hollander for bringing this article to my attention.

5. See, for example, Roger Weiss, ed., *Arcadius Kahan: Essays in Jewish Social and Economic History*, introduction by Jonathan Frankel (Chicago-London, 1986), pp. 1–81.

6. Shaul Stampfer, "Patterns of Internal Jewish Migration in the Russian Empire," in Yaacov Ro'i, ed., *Jews and Jewish Life in Russia and the Soviet Union* (Ilford, Essex, 1995), pp. 28–47. For more on Jewish migration at this time, see Arthur Ruppin, *Hasotziologiyah shel hayehudim: Hamivneh hasotziali shel hayehudim*, vol. 1, bk. 1 (Berlin-Tel Aviv, 1934), pp. 83–138. On internal migration within the Russian Empire, see Barbara A. Anderson, *Internal Migration during Modernization in Late Nineteenth-Century Russia* (Princeton, N.J., 1980); Joseph Bradley, *Muzhik and Muscovite: Urbanization in Late Imperial Russia* (Berkeley-Los Angeles, 1985); and Diane Koenker, *Moscow Workers and the 1917 Revolution* (Princeton, N.J., 1981), pp. 47–53.

7. On the history of Jews in Odessa, see Steven J. Zipperstein, *The Jews of Odessa: A Cultural History, 1794–1881* (Stanford, Calif., 1985).

8. See Stephen D. Corrsin, "Warsaw: Poles and Jews in a Conquered City," in Michael F. Hamm, ed., *The City in Late Imperial Russia* (Bloomington, Ind., 1986), p. 128.

9. Daniel R. Brower, "Urban Revolution in Late Imperial Russia," in Hamm, ed., *The City in Late Imperial Russia*, p. 327.

10. In light of the suggestive power of memory and the reconstruction of personal narratives, I have refrained from relying too heavily on memoirs as historical sources for this period and have, instead, concentrated on personal letters and other sources. For more on the power of persuasion and the reconstruction of the painful path of modern Jewish politics, see Michael Stanislawski, *Zionism and the Fin-de-Siècle: Cosmopolitanism and Nationalism from Nordau to Jabotinsky* (Berkeley-Los Angeles, 2001), pp. 121 and 135; and Stanislawski, *Autobiographical Jews: Essays in Jewish Self-Fashioning* (Seattle-London, 2004), esp. pp. 3–17. On the construction of personal biographies in another context, see Igal Halfin, *Terror in My Soul: Communist Autobiographies on Trial* (Cambridge, Mass., 2003).

11. On the making of the Second Aliyah, see, for example, Bracha Habas, ed., *Sefer ha'aliyah hashniyah* (Tel Aviv, 1947). Also see Jonathan Frankel, "The 'Yizkor' Book of 1911—A Note on National Myths in the Second Aliya," in Jehuda Reinharz and Anita Shapira, eds., *Essential Papers on Zionism* (New York-London, 1996), pp. 422–53; Benjamin Harshav, *Language in Time of Revolution* (Stanford, Calif., 1993); as well as Ya'akov Sharet and Nahman Tamir, eds., *Anshei ha'aliyah hashniyah: Pirkei zikhronot*, 6 vols. (Tel Aviv, 1971–74); and Israel Bartal, Ze'ev Zahor, and Yehoshua Kaniel, eds., *Ha'aliyah hashniyah*, 3 vols. (Jerusalem, 1997).

12. For more on the intellectual climate at the time, see George L. Mosse, *The Image of Man: The Creation of Modern Masculinity* (New York-Oxford, 1996), pp.

77–106; Carl E. Schorske, *Fin-de-Siècle Vienna: Politics and Culture* (New York, 1981); and Stanislawski, *Zionism and the Fin-de-Siècle*. On alienation, see Nathan Rotenstreich, *Alienation: The Concept and Its Reception* (Leiden-New York, 1989), esp. pp. 77–80.

13. On hybridity, influence, and Jewish society, see David Biale, ed., *Cultures of the Jews: A New History* (New York, 2002). Also see David Roskies's critique of *Cultures of the Jews*, "Border Crossings," *Commentary* (February 2003): 62–66.

14. Despite a rather powerful tendency to refer to him by his better-known Hebrew name of David Ben-Gurion, I will refer to Green throughout this essay exactly as he referred to himself in this period, David Yosef Green. Note the similarly apologetic comment by the editor of Ben-Gurion's published letters justifying his own decision to leave the published sources signed D. Y. Green: "In the letters that he wrote before he made aliyah to Israel, he signed his full name, David Yosef Green" (*Igrot David Ben-Gurion*, p. 10).

15. D. Y. Green to Shmuel Fuchs, Płońsk, June 2, 1904, in *Igrot David Ben-Gurion*, p. 3. Like many other young Jewish migrants, Green often traveled back and forth between the city, in this case Warsaw, and his hometown, Płońsk, especially for holidays or when he felt particularly ill.

16. D. Y. Green to Shmuel Fuchs, Płońsk, September 24, 1904, in *Igrot David Ben-Gurion*, p. 28. Also see D. Y. Green to Shmuel Fuchs, Warsaw (?), June 28, 1904, in *Igrot David Ben-Gurion*, p. 18: "Only my soul remains unsettled. I don't exactly know why, but from time to time I'm so sad here. I feel this gaping hole deep within my heart. . . . I have these tremendous longings for something that I can't quite describe." And D. Y. Green to Shmuel Fuchs, Płońsk, July 22, 1904, in *Igrot David Ben-Gurion*, p. 25: "I know how deep and bitter the feeling of loneliness can be and how sharp it can sting. . . . I won't be long this time as a certain sadness has overcome me today. I, myself, don't know exactly why this is the case."

17. D. Y. Green to Shmuel Fuchs, Płońsk, June 2, 1904, in *Igrot David Ben-Gurion*, p. 8. Also see D. Y. Green to Shmuel Fuchs, Warsaw (?), June 15, 1904, in *Igrot David Ben-Gurion*, p. 16; and D. Y. Green to Shmuel Fuchs, Warsaw, November 6, 1904, in *Igrot David Ben-Gurion*, p. 31.

18. Shmarya Levin, "Youth in Revolt," *Forward from Exile: The Autobiography of Shmarya Levin*, trans. Maurice Samuel (Philadelphia, 1967), p. 219. Nor were such experiences limited to urban metropolises. Even medium-sized cities such as Dvinsk were foreign enough to bewilder the new arrival. Note Levin's own comments: "Dvinsk was the first big city that I had ever really seen. With its population of 100,000, its seemingly endless streets of stone houses, massive and unshakable, it made me breathless with wonder. Even Berezino, which had made such a prodigious impression on me, was a village in comparison. I walked the streets for hours, drinking in the atmosphere of power and permanence. This was a revolution indeed. The old world had been softer, weaker, more yielding; against this new world axes, hammers and saws would be of no effect: nothing short of bombs and heavy guns could do anything here. The stone walls of the great fortress were a human symbol too; in such a city the people were harder and firmer" ("Youth in Revolt," p. 213).

19. Y. H. Brenner to Shimon Bichovski, Gomel, December 27, 1899, in *Kol kitvei Y. H. Brener* (Tel Aviv, 1967), 3: 221; Y. H. Brenner to Dr. Joseph Klausner, London, December 10, 1906, in *Kol kitvei Y. H. Brener*, 3: 289; and Y. H. Brenner to L. Shofman, London, July 16, 1907, in *Kol kitvei Y. H. Brener*, 3: 313. All further citations of *Kol kitvei Y. H. Brener* are to volume 3.

20. See, for example, the two-part letter that Brenner sent to Ginzburg and Gnessin. Brenner to Gershon Ginzburg and Uri Nissan Gnessin, Gomel, January 12, 1900, in *Kol kitvei Y. H. Brener*, p. 222.

21. Brenner to Gershon Ginzburg and Uri Nissan Gnessin, Gomel, January 12, 1900, in *Kol kitvei Y. H. Brener*, p. 222. For additional observations on the state of Jewish youth at the time, see Chaim Weizmann to Theodor Herzl, Geneva, May 6, 1903, in Meyer W. Weisgal, ed., *The Letters and Papers of Chaim Weizmann* (London, 1971), 2:301–22.

22. U. N. Gnessin to Sh. Bichovski, Potchep, August 11, 1898, in *Kitvei Uri Nisan Gnesin*, vol. 3 (Merhavia, 1946), pp. 11–12 (ellipses in original). All further citations of *Kitvei Uri Nisan Gnesin* are to volume 3.

23. U. N. Gnessin to Z. Y. Anokhi, Borisoglebsk, May-June 1902, in *Kitvei Uri Nisan Gnesin*, pp. 29–30.

24. George L. Mosse, *Nationalism and Sexuality: Respectability and Abnormal Sexuality in Modern Europe* (New York, 1985), p. 89. For more on friendship circles and informal networks among Jews in Eastern Europe, see Avner Holtzman, *Temunah leneged 'aynei* (Tel Aviv, 2002), pp. 72–74. In his discussion of friendship and the Jewish enlightenment, Biale arrives at similar conclusions regarding the need for friendship and community in transitional periods: "Small wonder that the maskilim should turn to male friendships for comfort in their shattered personal lives." David Biale, *Eros and the Jews: From Biblical Israel to Contemporary America* (New York, 1992), p. 158.

25. See *Songs from Bialik: Selected Poems of Hayim Nahman Bialik*, ed. and trans. Atar Hadari (Syracuse, N.Y. 2000), pp. 119–20. For an additional discussion of this poem, see Hamutal Bar-Yosef, *Maga'im shel dekadans: Bialik, Berdichevski, Brener* (Jerusalem, 1997), pp. 196–98.

26. For a description of this encounter, see Holtzman, *Temunah leneged 'aynei*, pp. 85–91. I am indebted to the author for generously sharing and discussing this material with me.

27. On Gnessin's life and death, see Holtzman, *Temunah leneged 'aynei*, pp. 93–133.

28. "Uri Nisan: Milim ahadot," in *Yosef Haim Brener, ketavim* (Tel Aviv, 1985), 3:157.

29. Y. H. Brenner to Z. Y. Anokhi, Orel, April 27, 1903, in *Kol kitvei Y. H. Brener*, p. 227. Also see Y. H. Brenner to Z. Y. Anokhi, Orel, August 10, 1903, in *Kol kitvei Y. H. Brener*, p. 228.

30. On Brenner's fiction, see Ariel Hirshfeld, "Retet zamarot vedagim meluhim," in Yehudit Bar-El, Yigal Schwartz, and Tamar S. Hess, eds., *Sifrut vehevrah batarbut ha'ivrit hahadashah* (Tel Aviv, 2000), pp. 71–81, esp. 78–79. Also see Dana Olmert, "Shama halo lo po'—Kriyah beshnei sipurim mukdamim shel Yosef Haim Brener," *Mehkerei Yerushalayim besifrut 'ivrit* 19 (2003): 123–41. I would like to thank Tamar Hess and Dana Olmert for sharing these and other sources with me. For more on Brenner's relationship with Gnessin and others, see Ariel Hirshfeld, "Diyokan 'atzmi o hadiyokan baderekh el ''atzmi,'" *Helikon* 5 (Winter 1992): 30–54; and Haim Be'er, *Gam ahavatam, gam sinatam: Bialik, Brenner, Agnon—Ma'arkhot yahasim* (Tel Aviv, 1992), p. 107. The latter two sources are originally cited in Holtzman, *Temunah leneged 'aynei*, p. 87, n. 68, and p. 91, n. 72, respectively.

31. Dan Miron, *Bodedim bemo'adam: Lediyokanah shel harepublikah hasifrutit ha-'ivrit betehilat hameah ha'esrim* (Tel Aviv, 1987), pp. 422, 420. Also note Biale's observation regarding the elusive nature of love in turn-of-the-century Hebrew

literature. "Love was the goal, but it could never be achieved and the male anti-heroes of this literature were trapped in a kind of perpetual adolescence. Presented with the possibility of an actual sexual relationship, the protagonists flee back into their books or, in some other way, abort the erotic encounter" (Biale, *Eros and the Jews*, p. 171).

32. Miron's *Bodedim bemo'adam* was given the English title of *When Loners Come Together*.

33. D. Y. Green to Shmuel Fuchs, Plonsk, June 2, 1904, in *Igrot David Ben-Gurion*, p. 6. In another letter, Green again admonished Fuchs for not adequately carrying out his obligations as a friend. Here, too, one can get a glimpse of Green's own dependence upon Fuchs and others. "Today I received your letter . . . and I read it with a thirst no less than your own; however, that which I had prayed to find in it—I did not find. The limited details about your life were filled in with information from your letter to Yitzhak and Shlomo. . . . It seems to me that due to repeated use you have forgotten the meaning of the word 'detailed letter.' . . . Because, if you have already written a letter—you could have included a few more details" (Green to Shmuel Fuchs, Warsaw, June 14, 1904, in *Igrot David Ben-Gurion*, p. 11).

34. See Green's reference to Fuchs as "my older brother": D. Y. Green to Shmuel Fuchs, Warsaw, December 18, 1904, in *Igrot David Ben-Gurion*, p. 39.

35. D. Y. Green to Shmuel Fuchs, Warsaw, July 16, 1904, in *Igrot David Ben-Gurion*, p. 23. Also see D. Y. Green to Shmuel Fuchs, Warsaw, November 20, 1904, in *Igrot David Ben-Gurion*, pp. 33–34; and D. Y. Green to Shmuel Fuchs, Warsaw, July 8, 1904, in *Igrot David Ben-Gurion*, p. 20. Cf. D.Y. Green to Shmuel Fuchs, Płonsk, June 2, 1904, in *Igrot David Ben-Gurion*, p. 3; D. Y. Green to Shmuel Fuchs, Warsaw, July 8, 1904, in *Igrot David Ben-Gurion*, p. 20; and Green to Shmuel Fuchs, Warsaw, July 16, 1904, in *Igrot David Ben-Gurion*, p. 23.

36. While some observers may doubt the earnestness of such comments, there is no reason why such expressions of intimacy between men should be treated any less seriously than other, more politically conscious (and politically correct) comments made by the same individuals. For a discussion of similar methodological dilemmas, see Katherine O'Donnell, " 'Dear Dicky,' 'Dear Dick,' 'Dear Friend,' 'Dear Shackleton': Edmund Burke's Love for Richard Shackleton," *SEL: Studies in English Literature, 1500–1900* 46, no. 3 (Summer 2006): 635.

37. D. Y. Green to Shmuel Fuchs, Płonsk, June 2, 1904, in *Igrot David Ben-Gurion*, p. 3; D. Y. Green to Shmuel Fuchs, Warsaw, November 16, 1904, in *Igrot David Ben-Gurion*, p. 21; D. Y. Green to Shmuel Fuchs, Płonsk, July 22, 1904, in *Igrot David Ben-Gurion*, p. 25; and D. Y. Green to Shmuel Fuchs, Płonsk, September 27, 1904, in *Igrot David Ben-Gurion*, p. 29.

38. D. Y. Green to Shmuel Fuchs, Warsaw, July 8, 1904, in *Igrot David Ben-Gurion*, p. 20.

39. D. Y. Green to Shmuel Fuchs, Warsaw, December 18, 1904, in *Igrot David Ben-Gurion*, p. 39.

40. D. Y. Green to Shmuel Fuchs, Warsaw, July 8, 1904, in *Igrot David Ben-Gurion*, p. 20.

41. Y. H. Brenner to Uri Nissan Gnessin, Orel, February 1, 1902, in *Kol kitvei Y. H. Brener*, p. 224.

42. Y. H. Brenner to Z. Y. Anokhi, Orel, April 27, 1903, in *Kol kitvei Y. H. Brener*, p. 227.

43. Y. H. Brenner to H. N. Bialik, London, July 22, 1904, in *Kol kitvei Y. H. Brener*, p. 233.

44. Y. H. Brenner to H. N. Bialik, London, August 14, 1904, in *Kol kitvei Y. H. Brener*, p. 234.

45. Y. H. Brenner to Shimon Bichovski, London, January 28, 1907, in *Kol kitvei Y. H. Brener*, p. 298.

46. Gnessin to Y. H. Brenner, Potchep, April 1904, in *Kitvei Uri Nisan Gnesin*, p. 46; Gnessin to Y. H. Brenner, Kiev, June 2, 1906, in *Kitvei Uri Nisan Gnesin*, p. 111; and Gnessin to Y. Z. Anokhi, Borisoglebsk, May–June 1902, in *Kitvei Uri Nisan Gnesin*, p. 30.

47. Biale, *Eros and the Jews*, p. 158. In a piece on male friendship among Russian university students, Friedman similarly notes: "Young Russian boys no doubt enthusiastically absorbed, at least partially, an aesthetic of friendship from these [German Romantic] philosophers and most especially from Schiller" (Rebecca Friedman, "Romantic Friendship in the Nicholaevan University," *Russian Review* 62, no. 2 [April 2003]: 266, 268). For more on male friendship in the broader European and North American context, see, for example, Alan Bray, *The Friend* (Chicago, 2003); Scott Herring, "Catherian Friendship; or, How Not to Do the History of Homosexuality," *MFS: Modern Fiction Studies* 52, no. 1 (2006): 66–91; Stefan-Ludwig Hoffmann, "Civility, Male Friendship, and Masonic Sociability in Nineteenth-Century Germany," *Gender and History* 13, no. 2 (August 2001): 224–48; Jeffrey Merrick, "Male Friendship in Prerevolutionary France," *GLQ: A Journal of Lesbian and Gay Studies* 10, no. 3 (2004): 407–32; and Katherine O'Donnell, "'Dear Dicky,' 'Dear Dick,' 'Dear Friend,' 'Dear Shackleton,'" pp. 619–40.

48. For more on the tension between homosocial behavior, homosocial desire, and homosexuality, see Eve Kosofsky Sedgwick, *Between Men: English Literature and Male Homosocial Desire* (New York, 1985).

49. Judith Walkowitz, *City of Dreadful Delight: Narratives of Sexual Danger in Late-Victorian London* (Chicago, 1992).

50. Dan Miron, *Imahot meyasdot, ahayot horgot*, pp. 43–85.

51. On this sense of crisis, see Daniel Boyarin, *Unheroic Conduct: The Rise of Heterosexuality and the Invention of the Jewish Man* (Berkeley, 1997); and Michael Gluzman, "Hakemihah leheteroseksualiyut: Tziyonut uminiut bealteneuland," *Teoriyah vebikoret* 11 (Winter 1997): 145–62.

52. Sedgwick, *Between Men*, p. 207.

53. See ibid., esp. pp. 1–27.

54. On these points, see, for example, Herring, "Catherian Friendship," p. 70.

55. I have, admittedly, reduced this fascinating and unexplored issue to a few simple paragraphs. I do, however, plan to address many of these questions in a future piece.

56. George L. Mosse, *Nationalism and Sexuality: Respectability and Abnormal Sexuality in Modern Europe* (New York, 1985), p. 80. Also see Biale's comment that "the sublimation of sexual desire in the service of the nation was a common theme in the ideologies of the Second and Third Aliyot and it was often expressed in the notion that the *halutzim* were creating a new family in which all were brothers and sisters" (Biale, *Eros and the Jews*, p. 193).

57. Note Biale's observation: "While the Haskalah did not share this aggressive form of male camaraderie, it did make a similar connection between friendship and the creation of an incipient form of modern nationalism" (*Eros and the Jews*, p. 158). The literature on Zionism and Jewish masculinity is rich and growing. See, for example, Biale, *Eros and the Jews*, pp. 176–203; Boyarin, *Unheroic Con-*

duct; and Gluzman, "Hakemihah leheteroseksualiyut." I would like to thank Galit Hasan-Rokem for bringing these sources to my attention. For more on these issues, see Israel Bartal, "'Onut' ve'ain-onut'—Bein masoret lehaskalah," in Israel Bartal and Isaiah Gafni, eds., *Eros, isurin veirosim: Miniut vemishpahah behistoriyah* (Jerusalem, 1998), pp. 225–37; and Philip Abraham Hollander, "Between Decadence and Rebirth: The Fiction of Levi Aryeh Arieli" (Ph.D. diss., Columbia University, 2004), pp. 157–378. Perhaps it should come as no surprise that Brenner is buried in a common grave in Tel Aviv's Old Cemetery on Trumpeldor Street, a stone's throw from Bialik's tomb.

58. For an engaging discussion of the turn to action in the Polish political sphere, see Brian Porter, *When Nationalism Began to Hate: Imagining Modern Politics in Nineteenth-Century Poland* (Oxford, 2000).

59. D. Y. Green to Shmuel Fuchs, Warsaw (?), June 28, 1904, in *Igrot David Ben-Gurion*, p. 17. Also see D. Y. Green to Shmuel Fuchs, Warsaw, November 6, 1904, in *Igrot David Ben-Gurion*, p. 32; and David Ben-Gurion, *Zikhronot*, 1:11.

60. Brenner to Z. Y. Anokhi, Orel, August 10, 1903, in *Kol kitvei Y. H. Brener*, p. 228. On Brenner's repeated attempts to master Russian, see Holtzman, *Temunah leneged 'aynei*, p. 69.

61. Berl Katznelson to Haim Katznelson, Bobroisk, September 5, 1908, in Yehuda Sharet, ed., *Igrot B. Katznelson, 1900–1914* (Tel Aviv, 1961), 1: 69–70.

62. As Shmarya Levin recalled of his own arrival in Warsaw: "I was not equipped with means or a profession" (Levin, "The Arena," in *Forward from Exile*, p. 306).

63. See the earlier citation of Brenner's two-part letter to Gnessin and Ginzburg in note 20. For an alternative view of Brenner's interpretation of the delicate balance between the nation, the "National Subject," and "the construction of the national collective in the free individual," see Hannan Hever, *Producing the Modern Hebrew Canon: Nation Building and Minority Discourse* (New York-London, 2002), pp. 27–32.

64. U. N. Gnessin to G. Ginzburg, Warsaw, August 25, 1900, in *Kitvei Uri Nisan Gnesin*, p. 24.

65. D. Y. Green to Menahem Ussishkin, Warsaw, 13th of Adar bet (March 20) 1905, in *Igrot David Ben-Gurion*, p. 52.

66. D. Y. Green to Shmuel Fuchs, Płońsk, May 9, 1905, in *Igrot David Ben-Gurion*, p. 57. Also see D. Y. Green to Shmuel Fuchs, Warsaw, December 18, 1904, in *Igrot David Ben-Gurion*, p. 39.

67. For more on Zionism and self-sacrifice, see Biale: "The notion prevailed that one must sacrifice family life and erotic relations for the fulfillment of national goals" (*Eros and the Jews*, p. 192, and pp. 192–96).

68. See, for example, Jonathan Frankel, *Prophecy and Politics: Socialism, Nationalism and the Russian Jews, 1862–1917*, and idem, *The Damascus Affair: "Ritual Murder," Politics, and the Jews in 1840* (Cambridge, 1997). Also see Frankel, "Crisis as a Factor in Modern Jewish Politics, 1840 and 1881–1882," in Jehuda Reinharz, ed., *Living with Antisemitism* (Hanover, N.H., 1987), pp. 43–58; and Frankel, "Demanding Leadership: The Russian-Jewish Question and the Board of Deputies of the British Jews, July 1842–February 1846," in Shmuel Almog, Israel Bartal, Michael Graetz, et al., eds., *Temurot bahistoriyah hayehudit hahadashah* (Jerusalem, 1987), pp. xxxi–lxxi. For a dissenting voice from what should already be recognized as "the Frankel School of Jewish history," see Benjamin Nathans, *Beyond the Pale: The Jewish Encounter with Late Imperial Russia* (Berkeley-Los Angeles, 2002), pp. 7–9.

69. Arendt writes: "Selflessness in the sense that oneself does not matter, the feeling of being expendable, was no longer the expression of individual idealism but a mass phenomenon"; and "It soon became apparent that highly cultured people were particularly attracted to mass movements and that, generally, highly differentiated individualism and sophistication . . . sometimes encouraged the self-abandonment into the mass for which mass movements provided" (Hannah Arendt, *The Origins of Totalitarianism* [New York-London, 1973], pp. 315, 316). Mosse describes nationalism as "the mobilization of private discontent into collectivities that promised to transcend the anxieties of the modern age" and also contends that "the individual fulfilled himself in the collectivity, which alone really mattered; the virtues of tolerance and compassion were not abolished but annexed and monopolized by the nation" (George L. Mosse, *Masses and Man: Nationalist and Fascist Perceptions of Reality* [New York, 1980], pp. 1 and 9, 1–18). Also see Fritz Stern, *The Politics of Cultural Despair: A Study in the Rise of the Germanic Ideology* (Berkeley-Los Angeles, 1961), pp. xi–xii, and pp. 274–75. Biale similarly claims that the "ascetic streak in Zionism was overtly the product of a nationalist ideal of self-sacrifice, part and parcel of a pioneering philosophy that called for renunciation of the pleasures of the present in favor of a utopian future" (*Eros and the Jews*, p. 196).

70. See, for example, Porter's discussion of this issue in the Polish context: Porter, *When Nationalism Began to Hate*, pp. 77–80.

71. On the tension between the place of the individual and the role of the nation in European Enlightenment thought, see Zeev Sternhell, "From Counter-Enlightenment to the Revolutions of the Twentieth Century," in Shlomo Avineri and Zeev Sternhell, eds., *Europe's Century of Discontent: The Legacies of Fascism, Nazism, and Communism* (Jerusalem, 2003), pp. 3–22. Note Sternhell's observation: "The men of the eighteenth century saw the process of the liberation of the individual from the shackles of history as the essence of the Enlightenment and the birth of modernity. For them, the autonomy of the individual was the final objective of all social and political action" (p. 11). Also see Sternhell, "Modernity and Its Enemies: From the Revolt against the Enlightenment to Undermining Democracy," in Sternhell, ed., *The Intellectual Revolt against Liberal Democracy, 1870–1945* (Jerusalem, 1986), pp. 11–29. Also see Keith Michael Baker, "Representation," in Keith Michael Baker, ed., *The Political Culture of the Old Regime*, vol. 1 of *The French Revolution and the Creation of Modern Political Culture* (New York-Oxford, 1987), p. 478.

72. Czesław Miłosz, "The Pill of Murti-Bing," in *The Captive Mind*, trans. Jane Zielonko (New York, 1981), p. 8. Mosse similarly observed: "We find men and women wanting to make their life whole again and using national collectivity to achieve this purpose" and: "The longing for totality and for immutability helped integrate man with the masses" (Mosse, *Masses and Man*, p. 12).

Chapter 8. The Jewish Socialist Parties in Russia in the Period of Reaction

The preparation of this article was made possible by a grant from the Memorial Foundation for Jewish Culture

1. Hersh Mendl, *Zikhroynes fun a yidishn revolutsioner* (Tel Aviv, 1959), p. 43.

2. Jonathan Frankel, *Prophecy and Politics: Socialism, Nationalism, and the Russian Jews, 1862–1917* (Cambridge, 1981), p. 557.

3. On the Jewish parties in the elections to the Second Duma, see Vladimir Levin, "Russian Jewry and the Duma Elections, 1906–1907," in W. Moskovich,

L. Finberg, and M. Feller, eds., *Jews and Slavs: Essays on Intercultural Relations,* (Jerusalem-Kiev, 2000), 7:233–64.

4. On the perception of the elections and their influence on the activities of the Jewish political parties, see Vladimir Levin, "Politics at the Crossroads— Jewish Parties and the Second Duma Elections, 1907," *Leipziger Beiträge zur jüdischen Geschichte und Kultur* 2 (2004): 129–46.

5. Yisroel Efroikin, "Unparteyshe arbeter-komitetn," *Folks-shtime,* no. 14, August 3, 1907, p. 27.

6. *Der "Bund" in der revolutsye fun 1905–1906* (Warsaw, 1930), p. 130; M. Liadov, "Londonskii s'ezd R.S.-D.R. Partii v tsifrakh," in *Itogi Londonskogo s'ezda* (St. Petersburg, 1907), p. 84; A. Kirzhnits, *Der yidisher arbeter: Khrestomatie tsu der geshikhte fun der yidisher arbeter revolutsionerer un sotsialistisher bavegung in rusland,* vol. 2, part 2 (Moscow, 1925), p. 338.

7. Circulars nos. 8 and 9 of the Central Committee of the Jewish Socialist Workers' Party, State Archive of the Russian Federation (hereafter GARF), fond 102, opis' 1907, delo 353, ll. 108v, 126 (Microfilm in the Central Archives for the History of the Jewish People [hereafter CAHJP], HMF221).

8. Sonia Syrkin to Nahman Syrkin, November 7, 1907, Arkhiyon Ha'avodah, IV-104-94-75.

9. *Bericht über die Tätigkeit des Allgemeinen Jüdischen Arbeiterbundes in Litauen, Polen und Russland ("Bund") an den Internationalen Sozialistischen Kongress in Kopenhagen* (Geneva, 1910), p. 43.

10. M. Vinitski (V. Medem), "Tsayt-fragn," *Folks-tsaytung,* no. 414, July 26, 1907, pp. 1–2.

11. Matityahu Mintz, *Ve'idat krakov shel mifleget hapo'alim hasotzial-demokratit hayehudit po'alei-tzion berusiah (ogust 1907)* (Tel Aviv, 1979), p. 86.

12. In the second half of 1907 those who emigrated included Vladimir Kossovsky from the Bund, Haim Zhitlovsky and Mark Ratner from the Seimist party, Nahman Syrkin from the Zionist-Socialists, Ber Borochov, Leon Khazanovich (Katriel Shub), and Zelig Abramovich-Rabinovich (Zar) from Poale Zion.

13. Circular no. 1 of the Central Committee (December 1907), Arkhiyon Ha'avodah, IV-104–7-66B; Mintz, *Ve'idat krakov,* p. 203; Israel Raikhman-Vesher, *Dvarim me'izvono, zikhronot veha'arakhot* (Tel Aviv, 1942), p. 71.

14. N. K. Loevsky, "Di drite s.s. konferents in rusland," *Dos folk* (New York), no. 4, February 15, 1908, p. 16; *Rassvet,* no. 2, January 12, 1908, p. 35.

15. Yehuda Beiner, "Fun poyle-tsien tsu seimovtses," in Grigori Aronson, Yankev Leshtsinski, and Avraham Kihn, eds., *Vitebsk amol: Geshikhte, zikhroynes, khurbm* (New York, 1956), pp. 345–47.

16. *Fun partey-lebn,* March 1908, p. 1; *Golos Sotsial-Demokrata,* nos. 4–5, April 1908, p. 31.

17. A. Litvak, *Vos geven: Etiudn un zikhroynes* (Vilna, 1925), p. 248.

18. *VII-oi s'ezd Ob"edinennoi organizatsii rabochikh fereinov i grupp sodeistviia Bundu zagranitsei* (Geneva, 1909), p. 11; *Kurtser barikht vegn VII tsuzamenfor fun der fareynikter organizatsye fun di arbeter fareynen un mithilfs-grupn fun bund in oysland* (Geneva, 1909), p. 4.

19. *Barikht fun der VIII konferents fun bund* (Geneva, 1910), p. 3.

20. Zerubavel, *Bleter fun a lebn* (Tel Aviv, 1956), pp. 134–49; idem, *Alei hayim* (Tel Aviv, 1960), pp. 154–65. See also the report of the *okhranka*—GARF, fond 102, opis' 1908, delo 55, lit. A, l. 30 (Microfilm in CAHJP, HMF223). Bezalel Yaffe to Yitzhak Grünbaum, August 17, 1909, Central Zionist Archive, A127/60/5.

21. Henry J. Tobias and Charles E. Woodhouse, "Primordial Ties and Political Process in Pre-Revolutionary Russia: The Case of the Jewish Bund," *Comparative Studies in Society and History* 8 (April 1966): 331–60.

22. Beiner, "Fun poyle-tsien tsu seimovtses," p. 349.

23. Raphael Abramovich, *In tsvey revolutsyes: Di geshikhte fun a dor* (New York, 1944), 1: 318–38. Cf. discussion at the Eighth Conference of the Bund, *Barikht fun der VIII konferents fun bund*, pp. 21–26.

24. The Bund's report to the Vienna Congress of the International that was planned for August 1914, published in Eduard Savitskii, *Bund v Belarusi, 1897–1921: Dokumenty i materialy* (Minsk, 1997), pp. 388, 391 (I am grateful to Dr. Arkadii Zeltser for bringing this publication to my attention); Aleksandr Svalov, "Bund—Venskomu mezhdunarodnomu sotsialisticheskomu kongressu 1914 goda," *Vestnik evreiskogo universiteta*, no. 8 (26) (2003): 233, 237.

25. The commission of the Bund was established in June 1907 (*Folks-tsaytung*, no. 393, June 29, 1907, pp. 3–4); the commission of the SSRP was established two weeks later (*Dos vort*, no. 7, July 12, 1907, pp. 21–23); the commission of the Poale Zion was established at the Cracow congress at the end of July (Mintz, *Ve'idat krakov*, pp. 160, 167).

26. The Bund's *Fun profesioneln lebn* first appeared in July 1907 as a supplement to *Folks-tsaytung* and later to *Di hofnung* and ceased publication in October 1907; the SSRP's *Di profesionele bavegung* was started in September 1907 as a supplement to *Unzer veg* and stopped in November 1907.

27. The Bund organized central bureaus in Vilna, Kovno, Vinnitsa, Mogilev, Lodz, Berdichev, Dvinsk, Vitebsk, Belaia Tserkov', Bobruisk, Warsaw, Minsk, and Polotsk; the SSRP established central bureaus in Vitebsk (parallel to the Bund's), in Bendin together with Sosnowiec, in Czestochowa, and in Pinsk.

28. Mintz, *Ve'idat krakov*, p. 157; Ber Borochov, *Ketavim* (Tel Aviv, 1958), 2: 414.

29. *Di shtime fun bund*, no. 1 (December 1908): 11; cited also in *Otkliki Bunda*, no. 1 (March 1909): 33.

30. *Di shtime fun bund*, no. 1 (December 1908): 10; *Otkliki Bunda*, no. 1 (March 1909): 32.

31. Sofie Dubnov-Erlikh, *Garber-bund un bershter-bund* (Warsaw, 1937), p. 123.

32. *Di shtime fun bund*, no. 1 (December 1908): 11; cited also in *Otkliki Bunda*, no. 1 (March 1909): 33.

33. Blekhman, *Bleter fun mayn yugnt*, pp. 286–88.

34. *Otkliki Bunda*, no. 1 (March 1909): 33.

35. Savitskii, *Bund v Belarusi*, p. 382; Svalov, "Bund," pp. 226–27.

36. About the Bund's educational and cultural activities before the revolution, see Ezra Mendelsohn, *Class Struggle in the Pale: The Formative Years of the Jewish Worker's Movement in Tsarist Russia* (Cambridge, 1970), pp. 116–25. On the shift from "propaganda," i.e., workers' education, to agitation, see ibid., pp. 45–62; Moshe Mishkinsky, *Reshit tenu'at hapo'alim hayehudit berusiah: Megamot yesod* (Tel Aviv, 1981), pp. 122–60; Henry J. Tobias, *The Jewish Bund in Russia: From Its Origin to 1905* (Stanford, Calif., 1972), pp. 122–60; Frankel, *Prophecy and Politics*, pp. 172–73.

37. *Protokoly Tsentral'nogo komiteta Konstitutsionno-demokraticheskoi partii* (Moscow, 1994),1:235–36, 242, 245–46.

38. M. N., "Velkhe bildungs-khevres zeynen far unz noytik?" *Folks-tsaytung*, no. 418, July 31, 1907, p. 1; Mikhalevich, "Der politisher shtilshtand un unzere oyfgabe: Di kultur-arbet un di organizatsions-formn," *Di hofnung*, no. 12, Sep-

tember 23, 1907, p. 2. See also the decision of the Lodz Committee of the Bund to discuss the question about party affiliation of the cultural associations at the planned Eighth Bund Convention (Yankev-Shmuel Herts, *Di geschichte fun bund in lodzh* [New York, 1958], p. 205).

39. M. N., "Velkhe bildungs-khevres zeynen far unz noytik?" p. 1; "Tsu der bildungs-frage," *Di hofnung*, no. 14, September 25, 1907, p. 1; M. K. (Moyshe Kats), "Arbeter bildung," *Unzer veg*, nos. 8–9, November 1, 1907, supplement *Di profesionele bavegung*, pp. 60–64.

40. Dovid M. (Myer), "Di varshaver ovnt-shuln," *Di hofnung*, no. 32, October 17, 1907, p. 4.

41. It is difficult to assess the relationship between the cultural associations and the socialist parties that founded them because the parties' illegal publications usually did not mention the name of the legal cultural associations affiliated with them; similarly, the publications of the associations did not mention their party connections. Therefore, a historian can rely only on memoirs, legal party periodicals, and the names of the associations' activists.

42. A. L. (A. Litvak?), "Vegn di yekaterinoslaver rezolutsye vegn bildungs khevres," *Folks-tsaytung*, no. 397, July 4, 1907, p. 1; correspondence from Vilna, ibid., no. 411, July 23, 1907, p. 4.

43. Itshok Gordin, *Yorn fargangene, yorn umfargeslekhe* (Warsaw, 1960), p. 110.

44. Herts, *Di geshikhte fun bund in lodzh*, pp. 208–9, 215–16; Sofie Dubnov-Erlikh, "In di yorn fun reaktsye," *Di geshikhte fun bund* (New York, 1962), 2: 557; Joshua D. Zimmerman, *Poles, Jews, and the Politics of Nationality: The Bund and the Polish Socialist Party in Late Tsarist Russia, 1892–1914* (Madison, Wisc., 2004), pp. 241–42.

45. P. Libmai (Pesah-Libman Hersch), "Der 'universitet far alemen' in varshe," *Di naye tsayt* 2 (1908): 87–89; Dovid M. (Myer), "Di kulturele tetykayt in varshe," *Di naye tsayt* 5–6 (1909): 122–24. See also Zimmerman, *Poles, Jews, and the Politics of Nationality*, pp. 239–44.

46. On the Warsaw branch of the Jewish Literary Society, see Zimmerman, *Poles, Jews, and the Politics of Nationality*, p. 239.

47. Litvak, *Vos geven*, p. 270; *Otchet evreiskogo musykal'no-dramaticheskogo i litera-turnogo obshchestva "Karmel" v g. Rige za 1910 god* (Riga, 1911).

48. Beiner, "Fun poyle-tsien tsu seimovtses," p. 349.

49. Moisei Galinskii, "Vilna," *Rassvet*, no. 3, January 18, 1908, p. 23.

50. On both institutions, see Vladimir Medem, *The Life and Soul of a Legendary Jewish Socialist*, trans. Samuel A. Portnoy (New York, 1979), p. 445; Litvak, *Vos geven*, p. 270; Abramovich, *In tsvey revolutsyes*, 1: 320–21.

51. *Di shtime fun bund*, no. 1 (December 1908): 11; cited also in *Otkliki Bunda*, no. 1 (March 1909): 33.

52. Litvak, *Vos geven*, p. 269.

53. Abramovich, *In tsvey revolutsyes*, 1: 322.

54. From the very beginning the Bund's leadership regarded the Jewish Literary Society as a suitable framework for the Bund's goals. Therefore the society's appeal to establish local branches that was published in the Bund's legal publication *Di naye tsayt*. (7 [1909]: 96) should be understood as a call to Bundist activity within the framework of this institution.

55. Levin, "Politics at the Crossroads," pp. 140–45.

56. Sanago (Vladimir Medem), "Itogi i vyvody," *Nasha tribuna*, no. 12 (February 1907): 10–11.

57. Ibid., p. 15.

58. *Folks-shtime*, no. 5, March 16, 1907, p. 80.

59. *Folks-tsaytung*, no. 422, August 5, 1907, p. 4 (correspondence from Rossieny); *Di hofnung*, no. 13, September 24, 1907, p. 3 (correspondence from Svisloch); A. Litovski (Isroel Efroikin), "Vitebsker brif," *Folks-shtime*, no. 7, June 12, 1907, pp. 39–45.

60. Bazin (Moyshe Zilberfarb), "Di arbeter-politik in der yidishe gemeinde," *Folks-shtime*, nos. 12, 13, 15, 16 (July–August 1907); Beynish Mikhalevich, "Di yidishe kehiles un unzer batsyung tsu zey," *Der morgenshtern*, no. 2, November 23, 1907, pp. 4–7; V. Medem, "Di yidishe kehile," *Tsayt-fragn* 2 (March 1910): 24–37; A. Litvak, "Fragn fun der yidisher kehile," *Tsayt-fragn* 3–4 (August 1910): 47–59. In the Bund it was Vladimir Medem who initially supported the idea of communal work and who solicited several articles for the periodicals that he edited: Beynish Mikhalevich, "Di yidisher kehiles"; B. Borisov (Moyshe Rafes), "Di yidishe kehile," *Di naye tsayt* 1 (1908): 14–26; Dr. Mikhol Rafes (the brother of Moyshe), "Vegn di yidishe shtayern," *Tsayt-fragn* 3 (1908): 47–66. Cf. Vladimir Medem's memoirs, *The Life and Soul*, pp. 444–45.

61. The central committee decision to participate in the Kovno conference was published in *Otkliki Bunda*, no. 3 (November 1909): 21. The Bund was represented in Kovno by the central committee members Mark Liber and Rakhmiel Vainstein and by a leading publicist, Haim-Yankel Litvak, elected by legal associations in Vilna, Minsk, and Riga. The fourth Bundist was I. Zastenkin from Riga. According to Litvak, three additional Bundists were elected by "cultural associations" but did not arrive. See A. Litvak, "Der kovner tsuzamenfor," *Tsayt-fragn* 1 (November 1909): 9, 12; *Soveshchanie evreiskikh obshchestvennykh deiatelei v g. Kovne 19–22 noiabria 1909 g.* (St. Petersburg, 1910), pp. 7–8, 113; Yankev-Shmuel Herts, ed., *Doyres bundistn* (New York, 1956), 1: 214.

62. *Soveshchanie*, p. 113; Litvak, "Der kovner tsuzamenfor," p. 12.

63. Litvak, "Der kovner tsuzamenfor," p. 13.

64. *Soveshchanie*, pp. 177–83; Litvak, "Der kovner tsuzamenfor," p. 7. See also Medem, "Di yidishe kehile," pp. 28–29; Litvak, "Fragn fun der yidisher kehile," pp. 53–54.

65. Medem, "Di yidishe kehile," pp. 24–37; *Barikht fun der VIII konferents fun bund*, p. 58.

66. Litvak, "Fragn fun der yidisher kehile," pp. 47–59; *Barikht fun der VIII konferents fun bund*, pp. 60–61.

67. *Barikht fun der VIII konferents fun bund*, pp. 67, 77.

68. Borokhov, *Ketavim*, 2: 424.

69. *Izvestiia zagranichnogo komiteta S.E.R.P.*, no. 1 (August 1911): 11–12.

70. The decisions of the Fourth Conference in a circular of the *okhranka*, August 9, 1911, CAHJP, HM2/8257.2, fol. 34v.

71. *Di naynte konferents fun bund: Barikht* (Geneva, 1912), p. 15; Litvak, *Vos geven*, p. 286.

Chapter 9. 1905 as a Watershed in Polish-Jewish Relations

1. Theodore R. Weeks, "The Best of both Worlds: Creating the *Żyd-Polak*," *East European Jewish Affairs* 34, no. 2 (Winter 2004): 1–20.

2. This is one of my main arguments in Theodore R. Weeks, *From Assimilation to Antisemitism: The "Polish Question" in Poland, 1850–1914* (DeKalb, Ill., 2006).

3. See, for example, *Kraj*, no. 3 (January 21/February 3, 1905): 18–20, which claimed that the recent disturbances in Warsaw were the work not of "Poles"

but of socialists. Similarly, an article in *Izraelita* claimed that few Jews would support the socialists because Jews are primarily petty traders and industrialists (Józef Kirszrot, "Stronnictwa krajowe," *Izraelita* 40, no. 23 [June 3/16, 1905]: 262).

4. On the threat of pogroms and the Russian authorities' response to it, see Theodore R. Weeks, "Polish-Jewish Relations, 1903–1914: The View from the Chancellery," *Canadian Slavonic Papers* 40, no. 3–4 (September–December 1998): 240–43; and Shlomo Lambroza, "The Tsarist Government and the Pogroms of 1903–06," *Modern Judaism* 7, no. 3 (October 1987): 287–96. The provinces of the former Kingdom of Poland (now known officially as the "Vistula region") were not subject to the legal restrictions of the Pale. These ten provinces of the Russian Empire stretched from Kalisz in the west to Lublin in the east, including such large cities as Warsaw and Lodz.

5. "Z ostatnich dni," *Tygodnik Ilustrowany*, no. 29 (July 21, 1906): 565.

6. "Krwawe dnie Siedlec," *Tygodnik Ilustrowany*, no. 38 (September 22, 1906): 745–47.

7. Liberum Veto, "Wobec pogromu [in Belostok]," *Prawda* 26, no. 25 (June 23, 1906): 305–6 (quotation). For other reactions, see *Izraelita* 41, no. 24 (June 22, 1906), passim; and "Białystok," *Tygodnik Ilustrowany*, no. 25 (June 23, 1906): 485–86.

8. On the pogroms, see "From Kishineff to Bialystok: A Table of Pogroms from 1903 to 1906," *American Jewish Yearbook* (5667/1907): 34–89; and Shlomo Lambroza, "The Pogroms of 1903–1906," in John Klier and Shlomo Lambroza, eds., *Pogroms: Anti-Jewish Violence in Modern Russian History* (Cambridge, 1992), pp. 195–247.

9. Jews made up around 15 percent of the total population of the Kingdom of Poland, and there were also sizeable numbers of Lithuanians (in Suwalki province) and Ukrainians (in eastern Siedlce and Lublin provinces).

10. "Żydzi wobec autonomii Królestwa," *Nowa Gazeta*, May 16, 1907, morning edition, pp. 3–4.

11. *Głos* quoted a police communiqué asserting that the Bund was behind much of the agitation and disorders in the Polish Kingdom and had lately formed armed squads (*drużyny bojowe*). ("Komunikat departamentu policji o ruchach w Królestwie Polskiem," *Głos* 20, no. 36 [August 27/September 9, 1905]: 545–49.)

12. A. J. Cohn, "Nasze stanowisko," *Izraelita* 40, no. 5 (January 18/ February 10, 1905): 49–50. (A literal translation would read: "go forward with the living" [*z żywymi naprzód iść*].)

13. Józef Kirszrot, "Równouprawnienie," *Izraelita* 40, no. 39 (September 23/ October 6, 1905): 453–54.

14. A. J. Cohn, "O posła żyda," *Izraelita* 40, no. 42 (October 14/27, 1905): 489–90. Nowadays we would probably use the term "acculturated" where *Izraelita* used "assimilated."

15. Józef Kirszrot, "Związek polaków wyznania mojżeszowego," *Izraelita* 40, no. 45 (December 1, 1905): 517–18.

16. For attempts by Endeks to explain and justify their nonrevolutionary program during this revolutionary year, see Z. Balicki, "Czynniki zachowawcze i postępowe w dobie ostatniej," in R. Dmowski, ed., *Dziesięciolecie Przeglądu Wszechpolskiego* (Cracow, 1905), pp. 63–78; and Dmowski's articles "Wobec wojny rosyjsko-japońskiej" (June 1904), "Nasze cele i nasze drogi" (January 1905), "Polityczna konieczność" (February 1905), and "Chwila obecna w naszej poli-

tyce" (April–June 1905) in *Pisma* (Częstochowa, 1937), 3: 358–405. See also Adam Próchnik, "Stanowisko Narodowej Demokracji wobec wojny japońsko-rosyjskiej," *Kwartalnik Historyczny*, no. 3 (1957): 21–43.

17. Roman Dmowski, *Polityka polska i odbudowanie państwa* (Warsaw, 1925), pp. 60–62.

18. *Gazeta Warszawska*, no. 258 (November 21, 1905): 1 (lead article).

19. GARF (Moscow), f. 579, op. 1, 1905, d. 1893 ("Soobshchenie pol'skoi delegatsii o polozhenii Tsarstva Pol'skogo i o nuzhdakh kraia"). Also among the signatories was M. L. Bergson, chairman of the Warsaw Jewish community.

20. It is noteworthy that even much later Dmowski felt the need specifically to deny such rumors. According to Dmowski, at this meeting he pointed out to Witte that calm would be restored in Russian Poland only when power (*władza*) was given back to the Poles (Dmowski, *Polityka polska*, p. 67).

21. For a relatively objective though thoroughly anti-endek analysis (and party history) by an independent socialist, see Ludwik Kulczycki, *Narodowa Demokracja* (Warsaw, 1907). Later Polish historiography sometimes reflected these accusations; see, for example, the "Leninist" but at times useful Stanisław Kalabiński, *Antynarodowa polityka endecji w rewolucji 1905–1907* (Warsaw, 1955).

22. "Komunikat departamentu policji o ruchach w Królestwie Polskiem," *Głos* 20, no. 36 (August 27/ September 9, 1905): 545.

23. *List otwarty Polaka do ministra rosyjskiego* (Lwów, 1905). While the pamphlet was published anonymously, it was an open secret that Sienkiewicz was the author.

24. Szczerbiec (pseud.), "W naszych sprawach," *Kraj* 24, no. 48 (December 2/15, 1905): 17–18.

25. Jan Jeleński, "Bóg, Wiara, Ojczyzna!" *Rola* 23, no. 45/46 (November 5/18, 1905): 693–94.

26. Jan Jeleński, *Robotniku polski! (Głos swojego do swoich)* (Warsaw, 1905), p. 11. The brochure is a reprint from *Dziennik dla wszystkich*.

27. On the Polish progressives just before and during the 1905 Revolution, see Tadeusz Stegner, "Grupa 'Kuźnicy' i jej działalność," *Dzieje najnowsze* 12, no. 1 (1980): 47–62; Barbara Petrozolin-Skowronska, "Z dziejów liberalizmu polskiego: Partie liberalno-demokratyczne inteligencji w Królestwie Polskim, 1905–1907," *Dzieje Najnowsze* 3, no. 3 (1971): 3–38. More generally on Polish liberalism, see Tadeusz Stegner, *Liberałowie Królestwa Polskiego* (Gdańsk, 1990), and Maciej Janowski, *Polska myśl liberalna do 1918 roku* (Cracow, 1998). On the connection with the Russian Constitutional Democrats (Kadets), see "Do narodu rosyjskiego," *Prawda* 25, nos. 45/46 (November 30, 1905): 517–18, and Pavel Miliukov, *Aleksander Lednicki jako rzecznik polsko-rosyjskiego porozumienia* (Warsaw, 1939).

28. The numerous splits and "reconciliations" within the liberal camp from 1904 onward prove that factional infighting was no monopoly of the socialists. See Stegner, *Liberałowie*, pp. 29, 152, 163–64. To simplify somewhat: The *Pedecja* (Związek Postępowo-Demokratyczny or Postępowa Demokracja) was founded in December 1904. In 1906 the right wing of the ZP-D. split away to form Polska Partia Postępowa (PPP), which in the following year rejoined the ZP-D., creating the Polskie Zjednoczenie Postępowe (PZP). In 1909, the PPP once again left the PZP.

29. Janowski points out that Stanisław Kempner's *Zarysy ekonomii społecznej* (Warsaw, 1906) explicitly advocated state intervention in the economy and that this position was written into the progressives' economic program (Janowski, *Polska myśl liberalna*, pp. 232–35).

30. *Zasady programu: Związek Postępowo-Demokratyczny* (Warsaw, 1905). For a sympathetic discussion of the party's program by a contemporary man of the left, see Ludwik Kulczycki, *Związek Postępowo-Demokratyczny jako stronnictwo polityczne* (Warsaw, 1907).

31. For a general discussion of the "Jewish Question" as seen in the views and programs of Polish progressives, see Tadeusz Stegner, "Liberałowie Królestwa Polskiego wobec kwestii żydowskiej na początku XX wieku," *Przegląd Historyczny* 80, no. 1 (1989): 69–88. The rather different situation in Galicia is discussed in Maciej Janowski, *Inteligencja wobec wyzwań nowoczesności: Dylematy ideowe polskiej demokracji liberalnej w Galicji w latach 1889–1914* (Warsaw, 1996). 93–120.

32. Liberum Veto, "Wybierać albo nie wybierać?" *Prawda* 26, no. 3 (January 20, 1906): 30–31; "A. Świętochowski o wyborach do Dumy," *Tygodnik Ilustrowany*, no. 5 (February 10, 1906): 92–93.

33. On the actual elections to the First Duma in the Kingdom of Poland and especially in Warsaw, see Blobaum, *Rewolucja*, pp. 226–30; Petrozolin-Skowrońska, "Z dziejów liberalizmu," pp. 21–23; and Halina Kiepurska, *Warszawa w rewolucji 1905–1907* (Warsaw, 1974), pp. 284–91.

34. Kiepurska, *Warszawa w rewolucji*, p. 290.

35. A broad view of Jewish participation in the first two Duma elections is provided in Vladimir Levin, "Russian Jewry and the Duma Elections, 1906–1907," in Wolf Moskovich, L. Finberg, and M. Feller, eds., *Jews and Slavs: Essays on Intercultural Relations* (Jerusalem-Kiev, 2000), 7: 233–64.

36. This is the main conclusion of Yisrael Oppenheim, "Haktzanat hakav haanti-yehudi shel haendetsiah biyemei mahapekhat 1905–1907 uveikvotehah" *Gal-Ed* 15–16 (1997): 96–119. On the National Democrats and the First Duma, see Kalabiński, *Antynarodowa polityka endecji*, pp. 359–95.

37. On Endek antisemitic rhetoric (and attacks on the progressives) in the First Duma campaign, see Ad. J. Cohn, "Żyd idzie!" *Izraelita* 41, no. 16 (April 27, 1906): 185–86.

38. See, for example, the following articles in *Gazeta Polska* criticizing calls for boycotting the Duma and pointing out that the Jews were organizing to get the vote out: "Żydzi a my wobec wyborów," no. 9 (January 11, 1906); "Przed wyborami," no. 14 (January 16, 1906); "Zigzagi," no. 21 (January 23, 1906); and "Walka opinii," no. 28 (January 30, 1906).

39. Władysław Studnicki, "Wybory a Żydzi," *Gazeta Polska* 75, nos. 41 and 44 (February 12 and 15, 1906). Studnicki cannot, however, be considered typical of the National Democrats, and the editorial comment (in no. 44), while allowing for a Jewish representative, specifically rejected Studnicki's argumentation.

40. "Kronika miesięczna: Wybory w Warszawie i ich rezultat," *Biblioteka Warszawska* (May 1906), pp. 392–97, quotation from p. 395.

41. Ad. J. Cohn, "Epilog," *Izraelita* 41, no. 17 (May 4, 1906): 197–98.

42. See, for example, Łukawski, *Koło Polskie*, and the rather shorter treatment in Edward Chmielewski, *The Polish Question in the Russian State Duma* (Knoxville, Tenn., 1970), esp. pp. 33–43. A special supplement to *Kraj* described the first day of the Duma's deliberations (no. 17 [May 11/April 28, 1906]).

43. On the First Duma and the strains between government and Duma, see Vasilii A. Maklakov, *The First State Duma: Contemporary Reminiscences*, trans. Mary Belkin (Bloomington, Ind., 1964); and Abraham Ascher, *The Revolution of 1905*, vol. 2: *Authority Restored* (Stanford, Calif., 1992), pp. 42–110, 162–215.

44. RGIA, f. 1284, op. 194, 1907, d. 62, l. 7.

45. Ascher, *Revolution of 1905*, 2: 275; RGIA, f. 1327, op. 3, 1906, d. 65 (on

elections to the Second Duma in Warsaw province); f. 1327, op. 2, 1906, d. 36, ll. 33–39 ("Russian society in Warsaw" demands its own Duma representative); Archiwum Główne Akt Dawnych, Warsaw (AGAD), GGW 8970 (Results of elections to the Second Duma). For a very detailed account of the election laws and results for the Second Duma in Warsaw, see Ignacy Chabielski, "Wybory do drugiej Dumy w Warszawie: Uwagi i cyfry," *Praca* (supplement to *Biblioteka Warszawska*), no. 8 (August 1907): 1–35.

46. Kmiecik, *Prasa polska w rewolucji*, pp. 141–42.

47. On these issues, see the following articles in *Prawda*: "Autonomia jako konsekwencja samorządu," 27, no. 1 (January 5, 1907): 1; and A. Świętochowski's series, "O prawach mniejszości" (in nos. 1, 2, 3, and 4).

48. "Współdzialający," *Prawda* 27, no. 5 (February 2, 1907): 49–50.

49. "Materiały do sprawy żydowskiej" appeared in the following issues of *Nowa Gazeta* in 1907: nos. 15, 21, 25, 31, 33, 35, 37, 39, 79, 87. The comments on Jews and autonomy appeared in "Żydzi obec autonomii Królestwa: (Referat z wczorajszego posiedzenia w 'Żydowskim klubie narodowym')," *Nowa Gazeta* 2, no. 22, May 16, 1907, morning edition, pp. 3–4.

50. The term used for this process was "unarodowienie"—the Jews were becoming "nationalized" (into Poles). "Materyały do sprawy żydowskiej," *Nowa Gazeta* 2, no. 15, May 11, 1907, evening edition, p. 2.

51. On the Duma elections, see the following articles in *Izraelita* 42 (1907): Civis, "Żydzi wobec 'Koncentracji Narodowej,'" no. 1 (January 4): 1–3; R. Lipski, "Kandydatura żydowska do Dumy: (Uwagi historyczno-porównawcze)," no. 2 (January 11, 1907): 13–14; (and after the actual elections) "Kwestya żydowska w Dumie," no. 12 (March 22, 1907): 133–34.

52. Jeleński, *Precz z wrogami Ojczyzny!* The pamphlet ends by denouncing (p. 16) Jews as "enemies of the Cross and Poland, in whom Talmudism and cosmopolitanism are united."

53. Kamienny, "Na posterunku: Baczność! Albowiem zło i hańba nam grożą!" *Rola* 25, no. 3 (January 19, 1907): 35–37.

54. On the Endeks and elections to the Second Duma, see Kalabiński, *Antynarodowa polityka Endecji*, pp. 436–49.

55. Beylin, *W Warszawie*, pp. 239–41.

56. "Świętne zwyczięstwo stolicy Polski!" *Rola* 25, no. 8 (February 23, 1907): 113.

57. On the Second Duma, see Ascher, *Revolution of 1905*, 2:292–336, and A. L. Tsitron, *Sto tri dnia Vtoroi Dumy* (St. Petersburg, 1907). On the Poles in the Second Duma, see "Poslowie Królestwa Polskiego, Litwy i Rusi," *Kraj*, no. 3 (February 23/March 8, 1907): 3–4; and Henryk Dymsza, *Polacy w drugiej Dumie* (Warsaw, 1909).

58. Aleksy, "Koniec drugiej Dumy," *Przegląd spoleczny* 2, no. 25 (June 21, 1906): 251–52.

59. "Manifest Najwyższy," *Kraj*, no. 18 (June 8/21, 1907): 1.

60. For the Manifesto and the new electoral law, see *Sobranie uzakonenii i rasporiazhenii pravitel'stva* (June 3, 1907), no. 94, otdel pervyi, st. [article] 845.

61. On the Lodz lockout, see W. L. Karwacki, *Łódź w latach Rewolucji 1905– 1907* (Lodz, 1975), pp. 275–84.

62. GARF, f. 102, 4 d-vo, 1907, d.8, ch. 9. On the activities of the Macierz Szkolna and the difficulties presented by suspicious Russian officials, see *Memoryal Antoniego Osuchowskiego Prezesa Towarzystwa 'Polskiej Macierzy Szkolnej' przeslany Kolu Polskiemu w Petersburgu w kwietniu 1907* (Warsaw, 1907) and Józef Stemler,

Polska Macierz Szkolna: Rys informacyjny o dwudziesto-leciu dzialalności 1905–1925 (Warsaw, 1926).

63. On the anti-Jewish boycott that began in late 1912, see Robert Blobaum, "The Politics of Antisemitism in Fin-de-Siècle Warsaw," *Journal of Modern History* 73, no. 2 (2001): 275–306.

Chapter 10. Polish Literature's Portrayal of Jewish Involvement in 1905

1. Jan Jakóbczyk, *O tym, jak Młoda Polska posiwiala* (Katowice, 1992), p. 8.
2. Krzysztof Stępnik, "Metafory rewolucji w literaturze polskiej, 1905–1914," *Pamiętnik Literacki* 83, no. 2 (1992): 59.
3. Iza Moszczeńska (1863–1941) was a political activist and journalist. She worked for the Warsaw *Głos*. She was a supporter of Niemojewski's "progressive antisemitism." See Tadeusz Stegner, *Liberałowie Królestwa Polskiego, 1904–1915* (Gdańsk, 1990), pp. 125–26.
4. Iza Moszczeńska, "Kwestia żydowska w Królestwie Polskim," *Izraelita* (1906). In Andrzej Żbikowski, *Dzieje Żydów w Polsce: Ideologia antysemicka, 1848–1914: Wybór tekstów źródłowych* (Warsaw, 1994), p. 131.
5. Julian Unszlicht (1883–1944) was a journalist of Jewish origin who fought against the socialist movement in general and especially against Jewish involvement in it. In later years he converted to Catholicism, and in 1924 he joined the priesthood.
6. Unszlicht, *O pogromy ludu polskiego (Rola Socjal-Litwactwa w niedawnej rewolucji)* (Cracow, 1912), p. 8.
7. Jakóbczyk, *O tym, jak Młoda Polska posiwiała*, p. 7; Krzysztof Stępnik, "Metafory rewolucji w literaturze polskiej," pp. 59–82.
8. It should be noted that it was very rare, in general, to find a Jew as a prominent character in Polish literature at that time.
9. Andrzej Niemojewski (1864–1921) was one of the most influential Polish journalists. From 1906 to 1921 he edited *Myśl Niepodległa* (Independent thought), which was a progressive and anti-Catholic journal supporting freemason ideas. After the revolution, he broke with socialism and started a campaign against Judaism and Jews, developing the idea of "progressive antisemitism." See Irena Maciejewska, "Andrzej Niemojewski," in *Literatura okresu Młodej Polski* (Warsaw, 1968), 1:391–409.
10. Halina Kiepurska, *Warszawa, 1905–1907* (Warsaw, 1991), pp. 205–6.
11. Andrzej Niemojewski, "Boruch," in *Ludzie rewolucji i inne opowiadania* (Warsaw, 1961), p. 281.
12. Ibid., p. 282.
13. Stępnik, "Metafory rewolucji w literaturze polskiej," pp. 68–69.
14. Andrzej Strug (real name Tadeusz Gałecki,1871–1937), besides being one of the leading figures of the PPS (Polish Socialist Party), was also a popular writer. An active fighter in 1905, in his novels and short stories he depicted socialist activists involved in moral dilemmas. See Janusz Rohoziński, "Andrzej Strug," in *Literatura okresu Młodej Polski*, vol. 3 (Warsaw, 1968).
15. Andrzej Strug, *Dzieje jednego pocisku* (Warsaw, 1957), p. 194.
16. Bolesław Prus (1847–1912) is regarded as one of Poland's leading writers. His novel *Lalka* (A Doll) is considered the best Polish novel of the nineteenth century. See Józef Bachórz, "Wstęp" (Introduction), in Bolesław Prus, *Lalka* (Wrocław-Warsaw-Cracow, 1986). See also Harold B. Segel, ed., *Poles and Jews: Myth and Reality in the Historical Context* (New York, 1986), p. 310. Prus was also a

prominent publicist whose writings were very well known in his time and had a great impact on his contemporaries. Prus tried to be politically neutral and independent.

17. Bolesław Prus, *Dzieci*, in Z. Szweykowski, ed., *Pisma* (Warsaw, 1952), 21:205.

18. Teodor Jeske-Choiński (1854–1920) was a writer and publicist. A pugnacious conservative and outspoken antisemite, he opposed socialist ideas. Jeske-Choiński was a pen friend of Jan Jeleński, editor-in-chief of the antisemitic *Rola* (The field) and he published many articles in this magazine. See Andrzej Jaszczuk, *Spór pozytywistów z konserwatystami o przyszłość Polski, 1870–1903* (Warsaw, 1986); Brian Porter, *When Nationalism Began to Hate: Imagining Modern Politics in Nineteenth-Century Poland* (Oxford-New York, 2000), pp. 46, 76, 166.

19. Tomasz Weiss, "Teodor Jeske-Choiński," in: *Literatura polska w okresie realizmu i naturalizmu* (Warsaw, 1969), 3: 482.

20. In his time Józef Weyssenhoff (1860–1932) was a well-known writer. His first novel, *Żywot i myśli Zygmunta Podfilipskiego* (The life and opinions of Zygmunt Podfilipski), published in 1898, was extremely popular. During the Revolution of 1905 and soon after it, his literary output served the goal of political agitation in favor of the National Democrats (the Endeks). He strongly believed that there were Jews who were organizing the revolutionary movement for their personal interests. On the development of this right-wing movement, see Porter, *When Nationalism Began to Hate*, pp. 219–27. For the attitude of National Democracy toward Jews, see ibid., pp. 227–32.

21. Józef Weyssenhoff, *Hetmani: Powieść współczesna* (Warsaw, n.d.), p. 182.

22. Józef Weyssenhoff, *W ogniu* (Warsaw, 1908), pp. 10–11.

23. Ibid., p. 102.

24. During his lifetime Marian Gawalewicz (1852–1910) was a famous journalist, writer, and theater critic. He is now regarded as a minor nineteenth-century writer with a predominantly tendentious style. For further information, see Tomasz Sobieraj, *O prozie Mariana Gawalewicza* (Poznań, 1999).

25. Tomasz Sobieraj, *O prozie Mariana Gawalewicza*, pp. 94, 206.

26. Andrzej Niemojewski, "Jur," in *Ludzie rewolucji*, p. 232.

27. Maria Konopnicka (1842–1910) is one of the famous writers of nineteenth-century Polish literature. She was also a journalist involved in women's emancipation and editor-in-chief of *Świt* (The dawn). During 1905 she helped political prisoners although she was politically unengaged. She is the author of a famous short story "Mendel Gdański," based on the Warsaw pogrom of 1881.

28. Niemojewski, "Jur," p. 239.

29. Interesting comments on the idea of "a true revolutionary" are included in Wilhelm Feldman's review. See Feldman, "Dwa światy," *Krytyka* 13, no. 3 (1911).

30. Weyssenhoff, *Hetmani*, p. 133.

31. Marian Gawalewicz, *Wir* (Warsaw, 1908), pp. 50–51.

32. Jan Jeleński, *Siła przed prawem albo jak kto woli: Wolność socjalistyczna* (Warsaw, 1906), p. 14; Weyssenhoff, *W ogniu*, p. 9.

33. Teodor Jeske-Choiński, *Żyd w powieści polskiej: Studium* (Warsaw, 1914), p.105.

34. Ibid.

35. Władysław Stanisław Reymont (1867–1925) was a famous Polish writer, the author of *Ziemia obiecana* and *Chłopi* (Peasants), for which he was awarded the Nobel Prize in 1924.

36. Henryk Sienkiewicz (1846–1916) was ranked by his contemporaries as the most popular Polish writer. He received the Nobel Prize in 1905. His opposition to the socialist movement was reflected in his novel about the Revolution of 1905, *Wiry*. He sympathized with National Democracy.

37. Eliza Orzeszkowa (1841–1910) was one of the most famous Polish writers of her time. During the Revolution of 1905, confused by the events, she suspended her writing. She is also well known from her abundant correspondence with influential contemporaries. She is the author of a popular novel about Jews, *Meir Ezofowicz*. On *Meir Ezofoficz*, see Segel, "Polish Literature and the Jew," *Poles and Jews*, pp. 312–14. For more general information on Jewish topics in Orzeszkowa, see Irena Butkiewiczówna, *Powieści i nowele żydowskie Elizy Orzeszkowej* (Lublin, 1937).

38. It is worth adding that the problem of revolution appears only in her correspondence. See, for example, "Orzeszkowa do Posnera," a letter from March 25, 1905, in E. Orzeszkowa, *Listy zebrane* (Wrocław, 1954), 1:279, or "Orzeszkowa do Nusbauma," a letter from December 14, 1905, in E. Orzeszkowa, *Listy zebrane* (Wrocław, 1956), 3:164–65.

Chapter 11. Rebellion in Writing

1. Yitzhak Bakon, *Brener belondon, tekufat hame'orer (1905–1907)* (Beersheva, 1990), p. 11; idem, *Brener hatza'ir, hayav veyitzirotav shel brener 'ad lehofa'at hame'orer belondon*, vol. 1: *Biografiyah* (Tel Aviv, 1975), pp. 174–83.

2. There is another opinion regarding Brenner's affiliation to the Socialist Revolutionaries. See Jonathan Frankel, "Yosef Haim Brenner: The 'Half-Intelligentsia' and Russian Jewish Politics," in Benjamin Nathans and Gabriella Safran, eds., *Culture Front: Representing Jews in Eastern Europe* (Philadelphia, 2007).

3. Bakon, *Brener hatza'ir*, 1: 130–31, 183–97.

4. Ibid., pp. 221–37.

5. Yizhak Ma'or, *Hatenu'ah hatziyonit mereishitah ve'ad yameinu* (Jerusalem, 1986), p. 304.

6. Ibid.

7. Ibid., p. 313.

8. Ibid., pp. 311–12; Jonathan Frankel, *Prophecy and Politics: Socialism, Nationalism, and the Russian Jews, 1862–1912* (Cambridge, 1981), p. 189.

9. Ma'or, *Hatenu'ah hatziyonit mereishitah ve'ad yameinu*, p. 307; Frankel, *Prophecy and Politics*, p. 136.

10. Frankel, *Prophecy and Politics*, p. 143.

11. Ibid., p. 167.

12. During the course of his military service, Brenner became attached to Chaya Wolfson; they were both in the town of Orel in 1903–4. A member of the Socialist Revolutionary party, she helped to engineer his flight from the Russian army in 1904. She was killed in the course of the pogrom in Simferopol late in 1905.

13. Quoted in Yizhak Kafkafi and Uri Brenner, eds., *'Al Y. H. Brener, 'od zikhronot* (Tel Aviv, 1991), p. 43.

14. *Lo-khlum* (New York, 1907).

15. Rabi Binyamin, "Shnatayim," quoted in Bakon, *Brener hatza'ir*, 1:215. Rabi Binyamin was confusing Chaya with Chava, her image in *Misaviv lanekudah*.

16. Ibid.

17. Bakon, *Brener hatza'ir*, 1: 219.

18. Ibid., 1:102; see also Frankel, "Yosef Haim Brenner."

19. Bakon, *Brener hatza'ir*, 1: 104–6.

20. In this context Bakon mentions Brenner's article "Shanim" (ibid., p. 107).

21. Ibid., p. 140.

22. Frankel, *Prophecy and Politics*, p. 166.

23. Brenner, *Yosef Haim Brener, ketavim*, vol. 3, *Publitzistikah, bikoret* (Tel Aviv, 1985), p. 121.

24. Frankel, *Prophecy and Politics*, p. 150.

25. Yoseh Haim Brenner, *Yosef Haim Brener, ketavim*, vol. 1, *Sipurim, romanim, mahazot* (Tel Aviv, 1978), p. 608.

26. Cited in Bakon, *Brener hatza'ir*, 1: 214.

27. Brenner, *Ketavim*, 1: 637–38.

28. Ibid., p. 638.

29. Ibid., pp. 640–41.

30. Ibid., p. 656.

31. Ibid., p. 679.

32. Ibid., pp. 680–81 (the Zionist Socialists mentioned here were members of the Zionist Socialist Labor Party, established early in 1905).

33. Ibid., p. 682.

34. Bakon, *Brener belondon*, p. 25.

35. Bakon, *Brener hatza'ir*, 1: 216.

36. "El hahotmim vehakorim," 1906, in Brener, *Ketavim*, 3: 144.

37. Bakon, *Brener hatza'ir*, 1: 211.

38. Frankel, *Prophecy and Politics*, p. 161.

39. "Mikhtavei sofer," in Brenner, *Ketavim*, 3: 137.

40. Ibid., p. 129.

41. Bakon, *Brener belondon*, pp. 32–34, 46–47. (The reference is specifically to "Klayner felyeton" [A small feuilleton] and "Dapim" [Pages].)

42. Bakon, *Brener belondon*, p. 31.

43. Brenner, *Ketavim*, 3: 76–78.

44. London, January 11, 1907; in *Igrot Y. H. Brener*, ed. Menahem Poznanski (Tel Aviv, 1941), 1:322; the word "comical" is deleted in the manuscript.

45. Ibid., p. 360.

46. Ibid., p. 382.

47. Brenner, *Ketavim*, 3: 125.

48. Ibid., pp. 126–27.

49. Ibid., p. 129.

50. Quoted in Y. Bakon, ed., *Y. H. Brener: Haketavim hayidiim* (Beersheva, 1985), p. 177.

51. Brenner, *Ketavim*, 3: 132.

52. Ibid., 1: 529–30.

53. Gayatry Spivak, "Can the Subaltern Speak?" in Patrick Williams and Laura Chrisman, eds., *Colonial Discourse and Post-Colonial Theory, A Reader* (New York, 1993), pp. 66–111.

54. Edith Wyschogrod, "Derrida, Levinas, and Violence," in Hugh J. Silverman, ed., *Derrida and Deconstruction* (New York-London, 1989), pp. 193–94.

55. Brenner, *Ketavim*, 1: 713.

56. Jacques Derrida, "The Voice That Keeps Silence," in *Speech and Phenomenon and Other Essays on Husserl's Theory of Signs*, trans. David Allison (Evanston, Ill., 1972).

57. Bakon, *Brener hatza'ir*, 1: 201.
58. Kafkafi and Brenner, eds., *'Al Y. H. Brener*, p. 32.
59. Ibid.
60. Brenner, *Ketavim*, 1: 713–14.
61. Ibid., p. 714.
62. Brenner, *Ketavim*, 3: 132.
63. Rabi Binyamin, *Ba'al hagevulin* (Setter of limits), quoted in Bakon, *Brener hatza'ir*, 1:214.
64. Brenner, *Ketavim*, 1: 716.
65. Ibid., pp. 717–18.
66. Ibid., p. 719.
67. Ibid., p. 720.
68. Brenner, *Ketavim*, 1: viii.
69. Brenner, *Igrot*, 1: 164.
70. Bakon, *Brener belondon*, p. 25.
71. Brenner, *Ketavim*, 1: 599.
72. The reference is clearly to the pogroms of 1881–82, with twenty-five years to be understood as a round, not an exact, number.
73. Brenner, *Ketavim*, 1: 599.
74. Ibid., p. 601.
75. Previous editions mistakenly gave this story the title of the anthology in which it appeared, *Lo-khlum* (Nothing), Bakon, *Brener belondon*, p. 172.
76. Brenner, *Ketavim*, 1: 706.
77. Ibid.
78. Ibid., p. 707.
79. Ibid.
80. Brenner, *Igrot*, 1: 282.
81. Bakon, *Brener belondon*, p. 177.
82. Brenner, *Ketavim*, 1: 708.
83. Ibid., p. 710.
84. Ibid., p. 711.
85. Brenner, *Ketavim*, 3: iv.
86. Ibid., p. 75.
87. Ibid., p. 79.
88. Ibid., p. 80.
89. Ibid., p. 83.
90. Bakon, *Brener belondon*, p. 91.
91. Walter Benjamin, *The Origin of German Tragic Drama*, trans. John Osborne (London, 1985), p. 166.
92. Jacques Derrida, *The Work of Mourning*, ed. Pascale-Anne Brault and Michael Naas (Chicago-London, 2003), p. 35.
93. Ibid., p. 176.
94. Brener, *Ketavim*, 3: 91.
95. Ibid., pp. 91–92. My emphasis.
96. Ibid., p. 88.
97. Ibid., p. 99.
98. Ibid., p. 100.
99. Ibid., p. 102. My emphasis.
100. Brenner, *Igrot*, 1: 312–13.
101. Ibid., p. 313.
102. Ibid., p. 315.

103. Brenner, *Ketavim,* 1: 772.
104. Ibid., p. 773.
105. Ibid., p. 777.
106. See, for example, ibid., p. 795.
107. Ibid., p. 783.
108. Ibid., pp. 778–79.
109. Ibid.
110. Ibid., p. 819.
111. Ibid., p. 821.
112. Ibid., p. 824.

Chapter 12. The Revolutionary Origins of Yiddish Scholarship

1. Jonathan Frankel, *Prophecy and Politics: Socialism, Nationalism, and the Russian Jews, 1862–1917* (Cambridge, 1981), p. 329.
2. The term "architects" is Emanuel Goldsmith's. See *Architects of Yiddishism at the Beginning of the Twentieth Century: A Study in Jewish Cultural History* (Rutherford, N.J., 1976).
3. Literally, "Yiddish science."
4. The full title was *Der pinkes: Yorbukh far der geshikhte fun der yidisher literatur un shprakh, far folklor, kritik un bibliografye* (Vilna, 1913).
5. See Dovid Katz, "On Yiddish, in Yiddish, and for Yiddish: Five Hundred Years of Yiddish Scholarship," in Mark H. Gelber, ed., *Identity and Ethos: A Festschrift for Sol Liptzin on the Occasion of His 85th Birthday* (New York, 1986), pp. 23–36.
6. David E. Fishman, "The Politics of Yiddish in Tsarist Russia," in Jacob Neusner, et al., eds., *From Ancient Israel to Modern Judaism, Intellect in Quest of Understanding: Essays in Honor of Marvin Fox* (Atlanta, 1989), 4: 155–71.
7. Frankel, *Jewish Politics and the Russian Revolution of 1905*, Spiegel Lectures in European Jewish History 4 (Tel Aviv, 1995), p. 20.
8. For a concise discussion of these three parties, see Jack Jacobs, *On Socialists and "the Jewish Question" after Marx* (New York, 1992).
9. *Der nayer veg* changed its name twice, to *Dos vort* (The word) and then *Unzer vort* (Our word) as a way of circumventing press restrictions. (A. Kirzshnits, *Di yidishe prese in der gevezener ruslendisher imperye (1823–1916)* [Moscow, 1930], p. 27.)
10. On the Czernowitz conference, see [Anonymous], *Di ershte yidishe shprakh-konferents* (Vilna, 1931); Goldsmith, *Architects of Yiddishism*; and Joshua A. Fishman, *Ideology, Society, and Language: The Odyssey of Nathan Birnbaum* (Ann Arbor, Mich., 1987). On *Di literarishe monatsshriften*, see Kenneth Moss, "Jewish Culture between Renaissance and Decadence: *Di Literarishe Monatsshriften* and Its Critical Reception," *Jewish Social Studies* 8, no. 1 (2001): 153–98.
11. Following Eliyohu Shulman, in describing these journals I use the Yiddish term *gezelshaftlekh*, which, like its German cognate *gesellschaftlich*, signifies something more inclusive than its English equivalent, "societal." In this case, the term not only implies an interest in community affairs but also incorporates all aspects of Jewish communal life, including politics, news, culture, language, education, and science. See Eliyohu Shulman, "Di tsaytshrift di yidishe velt," *Pinkes fun der forshung fun der yidisher prese* (New York, 1965), pp. 122–70.
12. Meyer Waxman, *A History of Jewish Literature: From the Close of the Bible to Our Own Days* (New York, 1945), 3: 158.

13. Noyekh Prilutski, "Materialen far yidisher gramatik un ortografye," *Lebn un visnshaft* 5 (September 1909): 61.

14. A. Litvin, "Tsu di lezer," *Lebn un visnshaft* 1 (1909): 3.

15. Ibid., p. 2.

16. Ibid.

17. Imported words from modern German that have a Yiddish equivalent.

18. Zalmen Reisen, *Yidishe gramatik* (Warsaw, 1908), p. 3. Emphasis in the original.

19. For an extended discussion of the range of Prilutski's efforts in the post-1905 revolutionary period (which included philology, theater criticism, folklore, and poetry in Yiddish), see Keith Ian Weiser, "The Politics of Yiddish: Noyekh Prilutski and the Folkspartey in Poland, 1900–1926" (Ph.D. diss., Columbia University, 2001), pp. 131–89.

20. Noyekh Prilutski, *Noyekh prilutski's zamelbikher far yidishen folklore, filologye, un kulturgeshikhte* 1 (Warsaw, 1912), pp. 7–8.

21. Zalmen Reisen, *Leksikon fun der yidisher literatur un prese*, ed. Shmuel Niger (Warsaw, 1914).

22. For example, see Max Weinreich, *History of the Yiddish Language*, trans. Shlomo Noble (Chicago, 1980), p. 298; Dovid Katz, "On Yiddish, in Yiddish, and for Yiddish," pp. 33–35; and Dovid Katz, "Preface: On the First Winter Symposium," in Dovid Katz, ed., *Origins of the Yiddish Language* (Oxford, 1987), p. 1; Cecile Kuznitz, "The Origins of Yiddish Scholarship and the YIVO Institute for Jewish Research" (Ph.D. diss, Stanford University, 2000), p. 26.

23. Borochov, "Di oyfgabn."

24. Niger, "Fun der redaktsye," *Der pinkes*, p. 2

25. Ibid., p. 1.

26. See, for instance, the value that Shtif placed on *Der pinkes* in his essay "Vegn a yidishn akademishn institut," *Di organizatsye fun der yidisher visnshaft* (Vilna, 1925), p. 9.

27. For example, Niger's own "Shtudyes: Tsu der geshikhte fun der yidisher literatur" continues to be cited as a pioneering work in the area of gender and Yiddish publishing. See Chava Weissler, *Voices of the Matriarchs: Listening to the Prayers of Early Modern Jewish Women* (Boston, 1999); Naomi Seidman, *A Marriage Made in Heaven: The Sexual Politics of Hebrew and Yiddish* (Berkeley, Calif., 1997); and Sheva Zucker's summarized translation of Niger's essay in Judith R. Baskin, ed., *Women of the Word: Jewish Women and Jewish Writing* (Detroit, 1994), pp. 70–90. On Hurvits's contribution, "Unzer ershte teglikhe tsaytung," see Sarah Abrevaya Stein, *Making Jews Modern: The Yiddish and Ladino Press in the Russian and Ottoman Empires* (Bloomington, Ind., 2003), pp. 31–36.

Chapter 13. 1905 as a Jewish Cultural Revolution?

1. See Mikhail Krutikov, *Yiddish Fiction and the Crisis of Modernity, 1905–1914* (Stanford, Calif., 2001); Nahman Mayzl, "Tsen yor," *Noente and vayte*, 2nd ed. (Vilna, 1927), 1:5–26.

2. John Bowlt, "From the Pale of Settlement to the Reconstruction of the World," in Ruth Apter-Gabriel, ed., *Tradition and Revolution: The Jewish Renaissance in Russian Avant-Garde Art, 1912–1928* (Jerusalem, 1988), pp. 43–60; Albert Weisser, *The Modern Renaissance of Jewish Music* (New York, 1954); Michael Steinlauf, "Fear of Purim: Y. L. Peretz and the Canonization of Yiddish Theater," *Jew-

ish Social Studies, n.s., 1, no. 3 (1995): 44–65; Vladislav Ivanov, *Russkie sezony: Teatr Gabima* (Moscow, 1999), pp. 11–12 and sources cited therein.

3. See especially Chone Shmeruk, *Peretses yiesh-vizye* (New York, 1971), chap. 1, and Kenneth B. Moss, "Jewish Culture between Renaissance and Decadence: *Di Literarishe Monatsshriften* and Its Critical Reception," *Jewish Social Studies*, n.s., 8, no. 1 (2001): 153–98 and sources cited therein.

4. H. D. Nomberg, "Unzere kunstferaynen," *Romantsaytung* (Warsaw), July 2, 1908; *Evreiskoe literaturnoe obshchestvo* (St. Petersburg, 1910), pp. 10–12; Kh. Sh. Kazdan, *Fun kheyder un shkoles biz tsysho* (Mexico, 1956), p. 231.

5. Shmeruk, *Peretses yiesh-vizye*, chap. 1; Moss, "Jewish Culture."

6. Shmeruk, *Peretses yiesh-vizye*, chap. 1; Moss, "Jewish Culture."

7. See, among many others, Sofie Dubnov-Erlikh, "In di yorn fun reaktsie," in G. Aronson et al., eds., *Di geshikhte fun bund* (New York, 1962), 2: 539–63; Shmuel Niger, "Mit draysik yor tsurik un itst," in Y. Kh. Pomerants and A. Pravotiner, eds., *L. M. Shteyn yoyvl-bukh* (Chicago, 1938), pp. 82–85; A. Litvak, "In di finstere yorn," *Vos geven: Etyudn un zikhroynes* (Vilna, 1925), pp. 249–58; Donyel Tsharni, *Vilna: Memuarn* (Buenos Aires, 1951), pp. 126–39; Peretz Hirshbayn, *In gang fun lebn: Zikhroynes* (New York, 1948). This narrative is so universally accepted for members of that generation that it is also often "activated" through mere partial invocation; see, e.g., the character sketch of Z. Anokhi (Zalman Yitzhak Aronson) in Natan Goren, *Demuyot besifruteinu* (Tel Aviv, 1953), pp. 77–80. Moreover, even writers whose own memoirs complicate or contradict the narrative sometimes recur to the same master narrative. See Nahman Mayzl, *Doyres un tekufes in der yidisher literatur* (New York, 1942), p. 30.

8. Niger, "Mit draysik yor tsurik," p. 85.

9. Dubnov-Erlikh, "In di yorn fun reaktsie."

10. Mechtatel' (Shtif), "Literaturnye zametki," *Rassvet* (St. Petersburg), March 8, 1908, pp. 9–13.

11. Krutikov, *Yiddish Fiction*, pp. 115–18.

12. Jonathan Frankel, *Prophecy and Politics: Socialism, Nationalism, and the Russian Jews, 1862–1917* (Cambridge, 1981), chap. 4.

13. Dan Miron, *Bodedim bemo'adam* (Tel Aviv, 1987), pp. 1–83.

14. See Litvak's sour comments on "the folksong mitzvah" in idem, "Di finstere yorn," p. 253.

15. Mark Kiel, "A Twice Lost Legacy: Ideology, Culture, and the Pursuit of Jewish Folklore in Russia until Stalinization (1930–1931)" (Ph.D. diss., Jewish Theological Seminary, 1991), pp. 151ff.

16. See M. Borisov (M. B. Ratner), "Nashi zadachi," *SERP* 1 (1907): 35–54, translated and reprinted in A. Greenbaum, ed., *Tenuat "hatehiyah" (vozrozhdenie) umifleget hapo'alim hayehudit-sotzialistit (MPY"S): Mivhar ketavim* (Jerusalem, 1989), p. 65.

17. See Moss, "Jewish Culture."

18. I take these commitments to be manifest in Klausner's insistence in his editorial foreword to *Hashiloah* that Hebrew writers must be free to explore any realm of human experience and that art as such is an individual and national value ("beauty, like thought and ethics, has great value in itself") (Yosef Klausner, "Megamateinu: davar meet haorekh hehadash," *Hashiloah* 11 [1902]: 6–7). On Gnessin's convictions concerning the sovereignty of art, see Miron, *Bodedim*, pp. 335–36.

19. See the translation of "Fun partey-leben: Berikht fun der ershter vilner rayoner konferents," *Folks-shtime* 6 (1907): 76–79, in Greenbaum, ed., *Tenu'at "hatehiyah" (vozrozhdenie)*, pp. 82–83.

20. Henry J. Tobias and Charles E. Woodhouse, "Political Reaction and Revolutionary Careers: The Jewish Bundists in Defeat, 1907–10," *Comparative Studies in Society and History* 19, no. 3 (1977): 370.

21. Nahman Mayzl, *Onhoybn—Dovid Bergelson* (Kibbutz Alonim, 1977), p. 14.

22. Anonymous biography of Osher Shvartsman, Literature and Writers Collection, RG 3, file 2976, YIVO, pp. 7–8.

23. See Gennady Estraikh, "From Yehupets Jargonists to Kiev Modernists," *East European Jewish Affairs* 30 (2000): 26ff.

24. Frankel, *Prophecy and Politics*, pp. 271–75.

25. See Ben-Adir's piece "Smelost' slova i trusost' mysli" in *Vozrozhdenie* 1–2 (1904) in Hebrew translation in Greenbaum, ed., *Tenu'at "hatehiyah" (vozrozhdenie)*, p. 57.

26. Editorial announcement in *Dos yudishe vort* 1–2 (Cracow), January 3, 1905.

27. Y. D. Berkovitsh, *Unzere rishoynim* (Tel Aviv, 1966), 2: 149; cited in Yona Altschuler, "Y. D. Berkowitz, the Bilingual Writer," in Yitzhak Dov Berkowitz, *Yidishe dertseylungn, 1906–1924*, ed. Y. A. Altschuler (Jerusalem, 2003), p. xi.

28. Frankel, *Prophecy and Politics*, pp. 160–68; Alexander, "Y. D. Berkowitz," p. xiii.

29. Alexander, "Y. D. Berkowitz," p. xi.

30. "Luria, Yosef," in *Leksikon fun der nayer yidisher literatur* (New York, 1963).

31. Ruth Wisse, "Not the 'Pintele Yid' but the Full-Fledged Jew," *Prooftexts* 15 (1995): 33–61.

32. Krutikov, *Yiddish Fiction*, pp. 115–18.

33. Hirshbayn, *In gang fun lebn*, p. 173.

34. Hamutal Bar-Yosef, *Mag'aim shel dekadens: Bialik, Berditsevski, Brener* (Beersheva, 1997).

35. Shmeruk, *Peretses yiesh-vizye*, chap. 1.

36. Peretz to Propus, undated, in Nahman Mayzl, ed., *Briv un redes fun Y. L. Peretz*, (New York, 1944), p. 199. See also see Avrom Reyzen on his prerevolutionary encounter with Bialik, in Reyzen, *Epizodn fun mayn lebn* (Vilna, 1935), 2:156.

37. Reference to the Russian Jewish liberal and liberal-Zionist politicians of St. Petersburg associated with the Union for the Attainment of Full Rights for the Jewish People in Russia, known popularly as the Attainers (di dergreykher) (Frankel, *Prophecy and Politics*, pp. 161–63).

38. See Abraham Novershtern, "Between Dust and Dance: Peretz's Drama and the Rise of Yiddish Modernism," *Prooftexts* 12 (1992): 71–90.

39. Y. Grinboym (Grünbaum), "Yitzhok Leybush Peretz," in Sh. Meltzer, ed., *Y. L. Peretz veyetzirato: 'Al Y. L. Peretz: Divrei soferim 'ivrim* (Tel Aviv, n.d.), p. 128.

40. Shmeruk, *Peretses yiesh-vizye*, pp. 3–11; Dan Miron, *Der imazh fun shtetl* (Tel Aviv, 1981), pp. 103–16.

41. David Roskies, *A Bridge of Longing* (Cambridge, Mass., 1995), pp. 99–100, 142–43.

42. See Avraham Novershtern's suggestive comments in idem, ed., "Igerotav shel Der Nister el Shmuel Niger," *Hulyot* 1 (1993): 237, n. 3.

43. Ibid., pp. 169–71.

44. Nomberg, "Unzere kunstferaynen," p. 707.

45. Anokhi to Niger (late 1908), Shmuel Niger Collection, RG 360, file 166, YIVO, letter 7.

46. Moyshe Olgin, "Di yidishe shprakh in undzer privat-lebn," repr. in Joshua A. Fishman, ed., *Never Say Die! A Thousand Years of Yiddish in Jewish Life and Letters* (The Hague, 1981), pp. 551–63.

47. D. A. El'iashevich, *Pravitel'stvennaia politika i evreiskaia pechat' v Rossii, 1797–1917* (St. Petersburg-Jerusalem, 1999), pp. 454–55.

48. Nomberg's article cited in note 4 and the journal in which it appeared is a key place to start a detailed analysis of this phenomenon, which has not yet received adequate conceptualization and attention. Michael Steinlauf stands out as one of the few pioneering students of this issue with special attention to drama (see Steinlauf, "Fear of Purim," and "Jewish Theater in Poland," *Polin* 16 [2003]: 79–81). See also the valuable references in Estraikh, "From Yehupets Jargonists," p. 30. A fascinating text testifying to this new formation is a book-length step-by-step introduction to what "literature" is, written in high Warsaw *daytshmerish* but with clear general Yiddishist commitments: A. B. Rozenshteyn, *Literatur-visenshaft: Lehrbukh far di yidishe un algemeyne literatur-teorye mit a groyse zamlung mustern fun di beste yidishe poezye un prozaiker*, ed. M. Krinski, vol. 1 (Warsaw, 1907–8). A useful model would be Beth Holmgren, *Rewriting Capitalism: Literature and the Market in Late Tsarist Russia and the Kingdom of Poland* (Pittsburgh, 1998).

49. David Fishman, "The Bund and Modern Yiddish Culture," in Zvi Gitelman, ed., *The Emergence of Modern Jewish Politics* (Pittsburgh, 2003), p. 115.

50. Mayzl, "Tsen yor," p. 11.

51. Steinlauf, "Jewish Theater," pp. 80–81.

52. "Tsu di lezer," *Literarishe monatsshriften* 1 (Vilna, January 1908): 1–3.

53. See discussion in Moss, "Jewish Culture"; major sources include Mechtatel', "Literaturnye zametki"; Dreamer (in Latin letters; presumably Shtif), "In shvere tsayten," *Dos yudishe folk* (Vilna), February 20, 1908, pp. 5–6; Zerubovel, "Shtrikhen un gedanken," *Peysekh-blat: A literarishe zamlung*, ed. Zerubovel (Nisan 1908), pp. 28–29; A. Litvak, "Di yudishe velt: Shtrikhen," *Di naye tsayt* (Vilna) 5 (1908): 77–90; M. L-r (Mark Liber), "***" [addendum to B-ch (Latin letters), "Bibliografishe notitsen: 'Literarishe monatsshriften' Februar-Marts"], *Di naye tsayt* 3 (1908): 92.

54. Sh. An-sky, "A nayer yudisher zhurnal ('Literarishe monatsshriften': Ershtes bukh, Februar 1908)," *Di shtime: Zamelbukh* (Vilna, 1908), 2: 190ff.

55. Dovid Mayer, "Di varshever opteylung fun der peterburger yidisher literarisher gezelshaft (a bisl zikhroynes)," Bund Collection, RG 1400, ME16-41, YIVO; but compare Mark Shvayd, *Mit Perets'n* (New York, 1923), p. 30. On Lodz, compare Dubnov-Erlich, "In di yorn," p. 557, with Moyshe Zilberfarb to Niger, 15/28 April 1908, RG 360:194, YIVO. On Vilna, see Dubnov-Erlich, "In di yorn," pp. 555–56.

56. Wisse, "Not the 'Pintele Yid'"; Fishman, "The Bund and Modern Yiddish Culture."

57. Moss, "Jewish Culture," pp. 176–77.

58. On the 1917–19 period as a further watershed for the "culture-politics" issue, see Kenneth Moss, "'A Time for Tearing Down and a Time for Building Up': Recasting Jewish Culture in Eastern Europe, 1917–1921" (Ph.D. diss., Stanford University, 2003), chaps. 1, 3, 4. On the interwar period, see Natan Cohen, *Sefer, sofer, ve'iton: Merkaz hatarbut hayehudit bevarshah, 1918–1942* (Jerusalem, 2003), chaps. 1–2 and infra.

Chapter 14. Jewish Cultural Associations in the Aftermath of 1905

1. See, for instance, Louise McReynolds, *Russia at Play: Leisure Activities at the End of the Tsarist Era* (Ithaca, N.Y., 2003), and Richard Stites, *Russian Popular Culture: Entertainment and Society since 1900* (Cambridge, 1992).

2. Jürgen Habermas, *The Structural Transformation of the Public Sphere: An Inquiry into a Category of Bourgeois Society* (Cambridge, Mass., 1991).

3. For more on the development of a public sphere within Russia, see Joseph Bradley, "Subjects into Citizens: Societies, Civil Society, and Autocracy in Tsarist Russia," *American Historical Review* 107, no. 4 (October 2002): 1094–1123; Louise McReynolds, *The News under Russia's Old Regime: The Development of a Mass-Circulation Press* (Princeton, N.J., 1991); David Wartenweiler, *Civil Society and Academic Debate in Russia, 1905–1914* (Oxford, 1999); and Edith W. Clowes, Samuel D. Kassow, and James L. West, eds., *Between Tsar and People: Educated Society and the Quest for Public Identity in Late Imperial Russia* (Princeton, N.J., 1991).

4. Wartenweiler, *Civil Society and Academic Debate*, p. 4.

5. Clowes, Kassow, and West, eds., *Between Tsar and People*, p. 6.

6. S. M. Dubnov, *Kniga zhizni: Vospominaniia i razmyshleniia: materialy dlia istorii moego vremeni*, ed. V. E. Kel'ner. (St. Petersburg, 1998), pp. 296–97.

7. Christoph Gassenschmidt, *Jewish Liberal Politics in Tsarist Russia, 1900–1914: The Modernization of Russian Jewry* (New York, 1995); and Heinz-Dietrich Löwe, "From Charity to Social Policy: The Emergence of Jewish 'Self-Help' Organizations in Imperial Russia, 1800–1914," *East European Jewish Affairs* 27, no. 2 (1997): 53–75. See also Brian Horowitz, "The Society for the Promotion of Enlightenment among the Jews of Russia, and the Evolution of the St. Petersburg Russian-Jewish Intelligentsia, 1893–1905," in Ezra Mendelsohn, ed., *Jews and the State, Studies in Contemporary Jewry* 19 (2004): 195–213. For work on the impact of mutual aid societies outside of Russia, see Derek Penslar, *Shylock's Children: Economics and Jewish Identity in Modern Europe* (Berkeley-Los Angeles, 2001), especially pp. 219–22.

8. See Wartenweiler, *Civil Society and Academic Debate*.

9. Tsentralnyi gosudarstvennyi istoricheskii arkhiv sankt-peterburga (TsGIAP), f. 2129, op. 1, d. 1. "Ustav evreiskogo istoriko-etnograficheskogo obshchestva."

10. M. Vinaver, "Kak my zanimalis' istoriei," *Evreiskaia starina* 1 (1909): 49.

11. Ibid., p. 52.

12. Dubnov, *Kniga*, pp. 153–54.

13. *Evreiskaia starina* 1 (1909): 154–58.

14. "Uchreditel'noe sobranie i publichnoe zasedanie evreiskogo istoriko-etnograficheskogo obshchestva," *Evreiskaia starina* 1 (1909): 154–157.

15. *Otchet evreiskogo istoriko-etnograficheskogo obshchestva za 1910 god* (St. Petersburg, 1911).

16. *Evreiskaia starina* 10 (1918): 318–20.

17. TsGIAP f. 2129, op. 1, d. 54, l. 12–13.

18. *Otchet evreiskogo istoriko-etnograficheskogo obshchestva za 1915 god*. The minute book was later released as an independent volume as S. Dubnov, ed., *Pinkas hamedinah o pinkas va'ad hakehilot harashiyot bemedinat lita* (Berlin, 1925).

19. M. Vinaver, ed., *Regesty i nadpisi: Svod materialov dlia istorii evreev v Rossii, 80 g.–1800 g.* (St. Petersburg, 1913). The JHES also planned on adding a fourth and fifth volume to Bershadskii's *Russko-evreiskii arkhiv* but was unable to complete the project.

20. In 1912 the JHES gave a hundred-ruble subsidy to the Riga department of the JHES in order to advance the publication of the *Regesty* of the Jews of Riga and Courland, which was being edited by I. Joffe. See *Otchet evreiskogo istoriko-etnograficheskogo obshchestva za 1912 god* (St. Petersburg, 1913).

21. *Otchet evreiskogo istoriko-etnograficheskogo obshchestva za 1911 god* (St. Peters-

burg, 1912). The book was published as L. A. Sev and M. I. Kulisher, eds., *Ocherki po evreiskoi istorii i kul'ture: Istoricheskaia khrestomatiia* (St. Petersburg, 1912).

22. TsGIAP f. 2129, op. 1, d. 60, l. 17 contains reports of extensive remainders from the first volume.

23. *Evreiskaia starina* 1 (1909): 159.

24. Ibid., p. 160.

25. *Evreiskaia starina* 6 (1913): 188.

26. TsGIAP, f. 2129, op. 1, d, 54, l. 120, and *Evreiskaia starina* 5 (1912): 476.

27. *Otchet evreiskogo istoriko-etnograficheskogo obshchestva za 1912 god.*

28. Aaron Shuster, "Melamdim un lerers," in M. Silon-Silberman, ed., *Kehilat Lipkany* (Tel Aviv, 1963), p. 60.

29. Dovid Roykhl, "Vi m'hot amol farshpreyt yidishe literatur," in Abraham Samuel Stein, ed., *Pinkas Kremenets* (Tel Aviv, 1954), pp. 376–78.

30. Avraham Yitskhak Slutski, "Der kulturelekh matsev in unzer shtetl," in M. Tamari, ed., *Kehilat Lenin: Sefer zikaron* (Tel Aviv, 1956 or 1957), p. 253.

31. Moshe Reuveni (Rostovski), "Hasifriyah," in N. Blumenthal, ed., *Sefer Mir* (Jerusalem, 1962), pp. 227–32.

32. For some of the difficulties in obtaining permission, see A. I. Izrailitin, "O merakh k razvitiiu obshchedostupnykh bibliotek sredi evreiskogo naseleniia v Rossii," *Knizhki voskhoda* 6, no. 2 (February 1905): 99–113.

33. A. I. Izrailitin, "O merakh k razvitiiu obshchedostupnykh bibliotek," p. 104. See also the entry under "Obshchestvo dlia rasprostraneniia prosveshcheniia mezhdu evreiami v Rossii," in *Spravochnik po evreiskomu bibliotechnomu delu* (St. Petersburg, 1914).

34. Aaron Shuster, *Lipkan fun amol* (Montreal, 1957), pp. 62–64.

35. A. D. Kirzhnits, "Bibliotechnoe delo u evreev i zadachi obshchestva prosveshcheniia," *Vestnik obshchestva rasprostraneniia prosveshcheniia mezhdu evreiami v Rossii*, no. 11 (January 1912): 12–13.

36. Ibid., pp. 19–21.

37. N. Kroshinksi, "Unter der rusish-tsarisher hershaft," in A. Sh. Shtain, *Baranovits: Sefer zikaron* (Tel Aviv, 1953), p. 71.

38. Jacob Plot, "Di arlozorov bibliotek," in A. Sh. Shtain, ed., *Sefer hazikaron lekehilat kamin koshirskii vehasevivah* (Tel Aviv, 1965), pp. 487–90.

39. Dvoyre Kutnik, "Di ershte yidishe bibliotek," *Yizkor kehilot luninets/kozanhorodok* (Tel Aviv, 1952), pp. 146–47.

40. Hayim Rabinovits, "Haskole, bund, zelbshuts," in *Sefer deretsin* (Tel Aviv, 1971 or 1972), pp. 81.

41. Kutnik, "Di ershte yidishe bibliotek," pp. 146–47.

Chapter 15. Writing between the Lines

1. Mendele Moykher Seforim, *The Mare*, in *Yenne Velt: The Great Works of Jewish Fantasy*, comp., trans., and introd. Joachim Neugroschel (London, 1978), p. 557.

2. Quoted in Nakhmen Mayzil, *Dos yidishe shafn un der yidisher shrayber in sovetnfarband* (New York, 1959), p. 28, originally published in *Yidishe kultur* 11–12 (1940).

3. For an analysis of *Baym Dniepr*, see Susan Ann Slotnik, "The Novel Form in the Works of David Bergelson" (Ph.D. diss., Columbia University, 1978), and Dafna Clifford, "Dovid Bergelson's *Baym Dnieper*: A Passport to Moscow," in Dov-Ber Kerler, ed., *The Politics of Yiddish: Studies in Language, Literature, and Society* (Walnut Creek, Calif., 1998), pp. 157–70.

4. The author used the pen name Lipman-Levin, which is made up of his first name and family name.

5. Sholem Aleichem, *Tevye the Dairyman and The Railroad Stories,* trans. and introd. Hillel Halkin (New York, 1987), p. 153.

6. For a more detailed analysis of the representations of 1905 in contemporary Yiddish fiction, see the article by Jonathan Frankel, "Youth in Revolt: Ansky's *In Shtrom and the Instant Fictionalization of 1905,*" in Gabriella Safran and Steven Zipperstein, eds., *The Worlds of S. An-sky: A Russian Jewish Intellectual at the Turn of the Century* (Stanford, Calif., 2006), and Mikhail Krutikov, *Yiddish Fiction and the Crisis of Modernity, 1905–1914* (Stanford, Calif., 2001), pp. 67–117.

7. Leo Strauss, *Persecution and the Art of Writing* (Chicago, 1988), p. 32.

8. The available biographical information on Lipman-Levin is scarce, incomplete, and somewhat contradictory: it remains to be explained how his seventieth anniversary could be celebrated in 1946 when he was only sixty-nine. The main sources on him are Zalmen Reyzen, *Leksikon fun der yiddisher literature, prese un filologye,* vol. 2 (Vilna, 1930), cols. 229–31, and *Leksikon fun der nayer yidisher literatur,* vol. 5 (New York, 1963), cols. 286–88.

9. Lipman-Levin, *Dem shturem antkegn* (Moscow, 1938), pp. 288–94.

10. Benjamin Nathans, *Beyond the Pale: The Jewish Encounter with Late Imperial Russia* (Berkeley, Calif., 2002), pp. 286–87.

11. Simon Dubnov, *History of the Jews in Russia and Poland,* trans. I. Friedlaender (New York, 1975), 3: 38.

12. Nathans, *Beyond the Pale,* p. 292.

13. Lipman-Levin, *Dem shturem antkegn,* p. 289. "Shir-hama'alot" (Songs of ascent), part of the Book of Psalms read or sung on festive occasions.

14. Ibid., p. 43.

15. Der Nister, "Fun finftn yor," *Sovetish heymland* 1 (1964): 3–73.

16. Chone Shmeruk, "Der Nister's 'Under a Fence': Tribulations of a Soviet Yiddish Symbolist," in Uriel Weinreich, ed., *The Field of Yiddish: Studies in Language, Folklore, and Literature,* second collection (London, 1965), p. 286.

17. Eliezer Podryatshik, "Genize-shafungen in der yidish-sovetisher literature," in his collection *In profil fun tsaytn* (Tel Aviv, 1978), pp. 103–6.

18. Shmeruk, "Der Nister's 'Under a Fence,'" p. 287.

19. Zerubovel, "Di grindungs-peryod fun der YSDAP-poyle tsien," *Royter pinkes* 1 (1925): 121–51; Rahel Yanait (Ben Zvi), *Anu olim: Pirke hayim* (Tel Aviv, 1960), pp. 286–87, quoted in Podryatshik, "Genize-shafungen," pp. 105–6.

20. Der Nister, "Fun finftn yor," p. 28.

21. Jonathan Frankel, *Prophecy and Politics: Socialism, Nationalism, and the Russian Jews, 1862–1917* (Cambridge, 1981), p. 344.

22. Strauss, *Persecution and the Art of Writing,* p. 36.

23. The American left-wing critic Nahman Mayzl included Lipman-Levin, Der Nister, and Bergelson in the oldest generation of Soviet Yiddish writers who began their literary career around 1905 and were, therefore, especially interested in that period. See Nahman Mayzl, *Dos yidishe shafn un der yidisher shrayber in sovetnfarband* (New York, 1959), p. 34.

Chapter 16. The 1905 Revolution Abroad

I would like to thank Jonathan Frankel, Stefani Hoffman, Tony Michels, Benjamin Nathans, and all those at the "The Revolution of 1905: A Turning Point in Jewish History?" conference who gave me valuable feedback for this essay. It should be noted that although the transliteration scheme of the YIVO Institute for Jewish Research is followed as a rule, many YIVO autobiographers transliterated their names at the time of submission, and they did not follow these guidelines. Although this book uses the Russian spelling of place names, in this essay, when referring to Jewish natives of a particular place, I use the Yiddish form (e.g., Bialystoker for a person from Bialystok [Belostok]). I have used the spelling of organizational names as they appear in English in *Di yidishe landsmanshaften fun Nyu York* and *From Alexandrovsk to Zyrardow: A Guide to YIVO's Landsmanshaftn Archive*.

1. Samuel Dinerstein (Der shtumpiker shrayber), Autobiography 159, pp. 33–34, RG 102 YIVO Archives, New York. Hereafter all autobiographies will be listed by their number (e.g., Autobiography 159); all autobiographies can be found in Collection RG 102 of the YIVO Archives.

2. Abraham Ascher, *The Revolution of 1905*, vol. 1 (Stanford, Calif., 1988), p. 218.

3. Dinerstein, p. 35.

4. Ibid., p. 36.

5. Hirsch Liebman, "Jewish Migrations during the Last Hundred Years," *The Jewish People: Past and Present* (New York, 1946), 1: 409; Arthur Ruppin, *The Jew in the Modern World* (London, 1934), p. 52. For more statistical information on the mass population shift, see Jacob Lestschinsky, *Przesiedlenie i przewarstowienie Żydów ostatniem stuleciu* (Warsaw, 1933), which he expanded in his *Jewish Migration for the Past Hundred Years* (New York, 1944).

6. Many scholars have written extensively on Russian Jewish migration and the pivotal role the crisis of 1881 played in shaping this mass population shift, but the limits of space allow me to mention only several works. The central premise of David Berger, ed., *The Legacy of Jewish Migration: 1881 and Its Impact* (Brooklyn, 1983) is that the crisis of 1881 sparked mass Jewish migration. See in particular Jonathan Frankel's arguments in his "The Crisis of 1881–82: A Turning Point in Jewish History," in that volume, pp. 9–22, as well as his discussion of this period in his pioneering work *Prophecy and Politics: Socialism, Nationalism, and the Russian Jews, 1862–1917* (Cambridge, 1981). A 1981 issue of *American Jewish History* 71, no. 2 (1981), titled "Centennial of Eastern European Jewish Immigration, 1881–1981," also advances the argument that the crisis of 1881 sparked Russian Jewish emigration. See also Bernard Johnpoll, "Why They Left: Russian-Jewish Mass Migration and Repressive Laws, 1881–1917," *American Jewish Archives* 47, no 1 (1995): 17–54.

7. John Klier, "Emigration Mania in Late-Imperial Russia: Legend and Reality," in A. Newman, ed., *Patterns of Migration, 1850–1914* (London, 1996), p. 24.

8. These numbers are based on U.S. immigration records for the period between 1881 and 1948 that can be found in Mark Wischnitzer, *To Dwell in Safety: The Story of Jewish Migration since 1800* (Philadelphia, 1948), p. 289. Slightly different figures appear in Simon Kuznets, "Immigration of Russian Jewry to the United States: Background and Structure," *Perspectives in American History* 9 (1975): 39–41.

9. Wischnitzer, *To Dwell in Safety*. This reflects statistics for the years 1903–10. For statistics regarding Argentina, see Judith Elkin, *The Jews of Latin America* (New York, 1998), pp. 52, 55.

10. Frankel, *Prophecy and Politics*, pp. 134–278. Also see Tony Michel's close analysis of the impact of Chaim Zhitlovsky on Jewish immigrant politics in New York in *A Fire in Their Hearts: Yiddish Socialists in New York* (Cambridge, Mass., 2005), pp. 125–78.

11. Marc Dollinger, *Quest for Inclusion: Jews and Liberalism in Modern America* (Princeton, N.J., 2000), pp. 8–9. Similarly, Ira Katznelson's discussion of the Jews' uneasy encounter with American liberalism ignores Russia, casting it as a "menacing pre-emancipation situation." See Ira Katznelson, "Jews on the Margins of American Liberalism," in Pierre Birnbaum and Ira Katznelson, eds. *Paths of Emancipation: Jews, States, and Citizenship* (Princeton, N.J., 1995), p. 186; and Benjamin Nathans, "The Other Modern Jewish Politics: Integration and Modernity in Fin de Siècle Russia," in Zvi Gitelman, ed. *Modern Jewish Politics: Bundism and Zionism in Eastern Europe* (Pittsburgh, 2003), p. 33.

12. The one major exception is Ezra Mendelsohn's *On Modern Jewish Politics* (New York, 1993), which includes an insightful transnational discussion of "integrationist Jewish politics," a political ideology that overlaps in many areas with the ideals of Russian Jewish liberalism (pp. 6–17). Otherwise, there is a general paucity of transnational studies of East European Jewry even though many scholars acknowledge that the nation-state is not the best framework for the study of Jewish life in this region: not only did state borders rarely coincide neatly with the boundaries of East European Jews' cultural identities but also the Jews' proclivity to constantly uproot themselves and venture to new locales caused few to see their life experiences circumscribed by the boundaries of a single nation-state. Other notable exceptions include Todd Endelman, ed., *Comparing Jewish Societies* (Ann Arbor, Mich., 1997); Nancy Green, ed., *Jewish Workers in the Modern Diaspora* (Berkeley, Calif., 1998), as well as her monograph (which addresses East European Jews and other groups) *Ready-to-Wear and Ready-to-Work: A Century of Industry and Immigrants in Paris and New York* (Durham, N.C., 1997).

13. Frankel, *Prophecy and Politics*, pp. 453–551.

14. For a discussion of socialism's impact on Jewish politics in Russia and America in the aftermath of 1905, see Frankel's *Prophecy and Politics*, pp. 171–257, 453–547.

15. Daniel Soyer, "Class Conscious Workers as Immigrant Entrepreneurs: The Ambiguity of Class among Eastern European Jewish Immigrants to the United States at the Turn of the Twentieth Century," *Labor History* 42, no.1 (2001): 45.

16. Benjamin Nathans, *Beyond the Pale: The Russian-Jewish Encounter in Late Imperial Russia* (Berkeley, 2002); Christoph Gassenschmidt, *Jewish Liberal Politics in Tsarist Russia, 1900–1914* (New York, 1995). Nathans provides an insightful discussion of why Russian Jewish liberalism has been "consigned to the dustbin of modern Jewish politics" in his "The Other Modern Jewish Politics,"p. 24. Prior to these discussions, glimpses of Russian Jewish liberalism could be found in works concerning organizations such as the Society for the Promotion of Enlightenment among the Jews of Russia (commonly referred to by its Russian acronym OPE). See I. M. Cherikover, *Istoriia Obshchestva dlia rasprostraneniia prosveshcheniia mezhdu evreiami v Rossii, 1863–1913* (St. Petersburg, 1913). See also the chapter by Brian Horowitz in this volume.

17. Andrzej Walicki, *Legal Philosophies of Russian Liberalism* (Oxford, 1987).

18. Richard Pipes, *Russian Conservatism and Its Critics: A Study in Political Culture* (New Haven, Conn., 2005), pp. 154–55. On the larger ideals of Russian liberalism, see Walicki, *Legal Philosophies of Russian Liberalism*. An informative overview of Russian liberalism's values beyond the realm of politics can be found in Laura Engelstein's *The Keys to Happiness: Sex and the Search for Modernity in Fin-de-Siècle Russia* (Ithaca, N.Y., 1992), pp. 6–8.

19. Nathans, "The Other Modern Jewish Politics," pp. 24–30.

20. Soyer, "Class Conscious Workers as Immigrant Entrepreneurs, p. 45.

21. Ibid. p. 59.

22. Virginia Woolf, "The Lives of the Obscure" *The Dial 78* (1925): 381–82.

23. James Olney, ed., *Autobiography: Essays Theoretical and Critical* (Princeton, N.J., 1980). For a taste of these debates, see William Spengemann, *The Forms of Autobiography* (New Haven, Conn., 1980), and Karl Joachim Weintraub, *The Value of the Individual: Self and Circumstance in Autobiography* (Chicago, 1978).

24. Alan Mintz, *Banished from Their Father's Table: Loss of Faith and Hebrew Autobiography* (Bloomington, Ind., 1989), p. 22.

25. Michael Stanislawski, *Autobiographical Jews: Essays in Jewish Self-Fashioning* (Seattle, 2004), p. 9.

26. An extensive discussion of the efforts made by Max Weinreich to encourage the participation of the widest possible contestant pool can be found in Jeffrey Shandler, ed., *Awakening Lives: Autobiographies of Jewish Youth in Poland before the Holocaust* (New Haven, Conn., 2002), pp. xxii–xxvi; Jocelyn Cohen, "Discourses of Acculturation: Gender and Class in East European Jewish Immigrant Autobiography, 1942" (Ph.D. diss., University of Minnesota, 2000), pp. 53–85.

27. Cohen, "Discourses of Acculturation," p. 176. An excellent discussion of the place of the YIVO autobiographies in the larger corpus of Jewish autobiography can be found in Marcus Moseley's *Being for Myself Alone: Origins of Jewish Autobiography* (Stanford, Calif., 2006), pp. 442–45.

28. For more on the haskalah in Western Europe, see Michael Meyer's excellent overview in *Jewish Identity in the Modern World* (Seattle, 1990) and David Sorkin, *The Transformation of German Jewry, 1780–1840* (Oxford, 1987). In Eastern Europe, the haskalah followed different patterns. See Immanuel Etkes, ed., *Hadat vehahayim: Tenu'at hahaskalah hayehudit bemizrah eropah* (Jerusalem, 1993); Shmuel Feiner, *The Jewish Enlightenment* (Philadelphia, 2003); Mordechai Zalkin, *Ba'alot hashahar: Hahasklah hayehudit baimperiyah harusit bameah hatesh'a-'esreh* (Jerusalem, 2000). For more on the haskalah in Western and Eastern Europe, see Shmuel Feiner and David Sorkin, eds., *New Perspectives on the Haskalah* (London, 2000). In American culture, the nineteenth-century myth of Horatio Alger, an orphan who rose out of poverty and was able to assume a position of respect and power in American society because of his hard work, dominates early twentieth-century immigrants' writings. See Andrew Carnegie, *The Autobiography of Andrew Carnegie* (Boston, 1920). Also see John Cawelti, *Apostles of a Self-Made Man* (Chicago, 1965), pp. 101–20.

29. Solomon Maimon, *Lebensgeschichte, von ihm selbst geschrieben* (Berlin, 1793); D. Kaufman, ed., *Die Memoiren der Glückel von Hameln* (Frankfurt, 1896); Alan Mintz, "Guenzburg, Lilienblum, and the Shape of Haskalah Autobiography," *AJSR 4* (1979): 71; S. Werses, "Darkhei haautobiografiyah betekufat hahaskalah," *Gilyonot 17* (1945): 175–83.

30. Moseley's *Being for Myself Alone* provides an informative and detailed overview of the entire corpus of Jewish autobiography. For a specific discussion of East European Jewish autobiographers, see pp. 333ff. It is also illuminating to look at the autobiographies of M. Guenzberg, *Avi'ezer* (Vilna, 1864); Moses Lieb Lilienblum, *Hatot ne'urim*, in his *Ketavim otobiografiyim*, ed. Shlomo Breiman (Jerusalem, 1970); and Mordecai Ze'ev Feierberg, *Le'an* (1899), in English translation in Hillel Halkin's *Whither? and Other Stories* (Philadelphia, 1972), for examples of the models that East European Jewish writers may have followed.

31. Carnegie, *The Autobiography of Andrew Carnegie* (Garden City, N.Y., 1920).

32. A concise history of YIVO can be found in Fruma Mohrer and Marek

Web, eds., *The Guide to the YIVO Archives* (Armonk, N.Y., 1998), pp. xi–xxi. For a longer discussion of this institution and its place in the intellectual world of East European Jewry, see Cecile Kuznets, "The Origins of Yiddish Scholarship and the YIVO Institute for Jewish Research" (Ph.D. diss., Stanford University, 2000).

33. Barbara Kirschenblatt-Gimblett, Marcus Moseley, and Michael Stanislawski, "Introduction," in Shandler, ed., *Awakening Lives.*

34. For more on the YIVO autobiography competitions in America and Eastern Europe, see Jocelyn Cohen and Daniel Soyer, "Introduction," in *My Life Is in America.* I would like to thank the authors for allowing me to see the manuscript of their introduction. Shandler, ed., *Awakening Lives*; Daniel Soyer, "Documenting Immigrant Lives at an Immigrant Institution: YIVO's Autobiography Contest of 1942," *Jewish Social Studies* 5, no. 3 (Spring/Summer 1999): 218–43.

35. "A konkurs af oytobiografyes fun imigrantn," *Yivo bleter* 19, no. 2 (March-April 1942): 281–82. See also the draft English-language version, American-Jewish Autobiographies Collection, unsorted materials, RG 102, YIVO.

36. Max Weinreich, "Proyekt fun a kunkurs tsvishn der idisher bafelkerung in amerike: 'Farvos bin ikh avek fun der alter heym un vos hob ikh dergreykht in der nayer heym,' " RG102, Folder 255, YIVO.

37. "Der kontest af oytobiografyes fun yidishe imigrantn in amerike," and "The Yivo Contest for the Best Autobiographies of Jewish Immigrants to America," *Yedyes fun Yivo/Newsletter of the Yivo* 1 (September 1943): 3, 4. Approximately a dozen entries were composed by Central European immigrants who had arrived as refugees in the late 1930s and wrote in German. For an overview of the contestants, see Archival Guide, Collection RG 102, YIVO.

38. By contrast, only forty entrants had left Russia before 1903 and fifty-two emigrated following World War I. See Archival Guide, Collection RG 102, YIVO.

39. For example, few hasidic Jews, who made up a large segment of the Jewish community in certain areas of Eastern Europe, lived in America in 1942; moreover, because the contest was enthusiastically promoted by the socialist Workmen's Circle, some immigrant Jews with different political leanings may have felt less enthusiastic about submitting their entries.

40. On the American steamship industry, see Lorraine Coons and Alexander Varias, *Tourist Third Cabin: Steamship Travel in the Interwar Years* (New York, 2003). On its relationship to the growth of the garment industry, see Egal Feldman, *Fit for Men: A Study of New York's Clothing Trade* (Washington, D.C., 1960); Joel Seidman, *The Needle Trades* (New York, 1942).

41. Pam Nadell, "East European Jewish Emigrants and the Agents System, 1868–1914," in Jacob Rader Marcus and Abraham J. Peck, eds., *Studies in the American Jewish Experience 2: Contributions from the Fellowship Programs of the American Jewish Archives* (Lanham, Md., 1984), pp. 49–78.

42. Pam Nadell, "En Route to the Promised Land," in K. Olitzky, ed., *We Are Leaving Mother Russia* (Cincinnati, 1990), p. 12.

43. Solomon Horowitz (Sholem Yitzkhok), Autobiography 120. Horowitz's is one of the over forty autobiographies of the 104 I examined that mention money being "sent" from America to pay for migration. On the increased ease of transferring money from America to Europe, see Gary Magee and Andrew Thompson, "The Global and the Local: Explaining Migrant Remittance Flows in the English-Speaking World, 1880–1914," *Journal of Economic History* 66, no. 1 (March 2006): 177–202.

44. Sara Abrevaya Stein, *Making Jews Modern: The Yiddish and Ladino Press in the Russian and Ottoman Empires* (Bloomington, Ind., 2004); Alexander Orbach,

New Voices of Russian Jewry: A Study of the Russian-Jewish Press of Odessa, 1860–1871 (Leiden, 1980); Keith Weiser, "The Politics of Yiddish: Noyekh Prilutski and the Folkspartey in Poland, 1900–1926" (Ph.D. diss., Columbia University, 2001). For the broader context of politics and the press in Russia, see Daniel Balmuth, *The Russian Bulletin, 1863–1917: A Liberal Voice in Tsarist Russia* (New York, 2000).

45. Orbach, *New Voices of Russian Jewry.*

46. Klier, "Emigration Mania in Late-Imperial Russia," pp. 26–28.

47. Stein, *Making Jews Modern,* p. 31.

48. "Vegn emigratsya kongress," *Vuhin,* no. 1 (1911): 20; "Tsu der geshikhte fun der galvestaner emigratsya," *Vuhin,* no. 2 (1911): 15–18; "Di aynvanderung frage in amerike," *Vuhin,* no. 2 (1911): 40–44.

49. *Vuhin,* no. 2 (1911): 59–60.

50. "Yidishe emigratsya-gezelshaft in kiev: Reshima 1–9," Folder RU/83, Central Archives for the History of the Jewish People, Jerusalem.

51. Jonathan Sarna, "The Myth of No Return: Jewish Return Migration to Eastern Europe, 1881–1914," *American Jewish History* 71 (December 1981): 256–68; Thomas Kessner, "Jobs, Ghettos, and the Urban Economy, 1880–1935," *American Jewish History* 71 (December 1981): 220–21.

52. Solomon Horowitz, Autobiography 120, 12–15.

53. Approximately one-third of the post-1905 autobiographies describe the pogroms that swept through the Russian Empire between 1903 and 1906. See J. Dudnik, Autobiography 26; Brukhe Steuer, Autobiography 212; Samuel Dinerster, Autobiography 159, Bella Lewis Autobiography 80, Israel Kerdman, Autobiography 105.

54. Stampfer, "Internal Jewish Migration in the Russian Empire," p. 42.

55. Jacob Sholtz, Autobiography 5, p. 1.

56. Ibid., p. 4.

57. Ibid., p. 6.

58. Anon. (Ish Ikor), Autobiography 162, pp. 5–6.

59. S. Rubin (Der Nister [pseudonym chosen by the author]), Autobiography 127, pp. 16–17.

60. B. Rosen (Yod-Beys-Resh), Autobiography 215, pp. 17–24.

61. Anon (Ish Ikor), Autobiography 162, p. 18.

62. Shimen Isaac Leon, Autobiography 181, n.p.

63. Lena Weinberger, Autobiography 160, pp. 8–9.

64. Economic factors are often discussed by immigrants when identifying their reasons for emigrating. Several fine examples can be seen in the following autobiographies: Max Feigan, Autobiography 4; Klara Varbalov, Autobiography 8; Harry Sprecher, Autobiography 20; J. Spievak, Autobiography 35; Abe Pachter, Autobiography 39; M. Timan, Autobiography 54; Barukh ben Shlome, Autobiography 58; Brukhe Steuer, Autobiography 61; Aleph-kuf, Autobiography 212 .

65. E. Hanson (Ish Yehudi), Autobiography 65.

66. This dedication to overthrowing the tsar reflects how these immigrants were molded by another stream in Russian Jewish politics: the principle known in the Jewish political lexicon as *doikeyt,* the Yiddish word for "hereness." Although *doikeyt* was not opposed to emigration, it was often adduced by revolutionaries to stress that Jews were rooted in Russia and to advance the notion that the Jewish problem should be solved in the Russian Empire and not some other region. See Ezra Mendelsohn, *On Modern Jewish Politics* (New York, 1993), pp. 10–11.

67. P. Smith (Yitskhok Charcher), Autobiography 76, pp. 54–56.

68. Ibid.

69. Aaron Cohen, "Der lodzer fun patterson, New Jersey," Autobiography 108.

70. M. (Noyekh) Zeidman, Autobiography 36.

71. Many contestants discussed their activities in the Arbeter Ring and how they founded new socialist organizations in America. See Anon, Autobiography 84; Shin Tess, Autobiography 87; Morris Freeman, Autobiography 94; Aleph-kuf, Autobiography 212.

72. A discussion of the Arbeter Ring's impressive growth and its implications can be found in Michels, *A Fire in Their Hearts*, p. 167.

73. Joseph Brandes, "From Sweatshop to Stability: Jewish Labor between the Two World Wars," *YIVO Annual of Jewish Social Science* 16 (1976): 16. Charles Leinenweber, "The Class and Ethnic Bases of New York City Socialism, 1904–1915," *Labor History* 22 (Winter 1981): 43.

74. Perla Reicher, "Tzmihatam shel zarmei-hasmol hasotzialisti bakehilah hayehudit beargentina (1905–1910)," *Asophot* 3, no. 16 (October 1972): 61–70; Haim Avni, *Argentina and the Jews* (Tuscaloosa, Ala., 1991), pp. 71–72.

75. Cohen, "Der lodzer fun patterson, New Jersey," Autobiography 108, pp. 23–26.

76. A. Gumner, Autobiography 1, n.p. Gumner's experience is also discussed in Soyer, "Class Conscious Workers as Immigrant Entrepreneurs," p. 52.

77. Sherry Gorelick, *City College and the Jewish Poor: Education in New York, 1880–1924* (New Brunswick, N.J., 1981). This desire for higher education also explains why Russian Jews surpassed Italians, the other major immigrant group in New York at the turn of the century, in completing high school as well. Thomas Kessner, *The Golden Door: Italian and Jewish Immigrant Mobility in New York City, 1880–1915* (New York, 1977).

78. A. Beitani, Autobiography 107, p. 11.

79. Ibid., pp. 11–16.

80. Ibid., pp. 39, 42.

81. Nathans, *Beyond the Pale*.

82. On Peltzman's obsession with educating her children, both in Russia and in the United States, see Mrs. Beyle Peltzman, Autobiography 42, pp. 6–14.

83. Julius Baron, Autobiography 115, pp. 9–10.

84. Dinerstein, Autobiography 159, pp. 134–35.

85. Jose Moya, "Immigrants and Associations: A Global and Historical Perspective," *Journal of Ethnic and Migration Studies* 31, no. 5 (September 2005): 833–64.

86. In New York City alone there were an estimated fifteen hundred landsmanshaft groups. See Soyer, *Jewish Immigrant Associations*, p. 1.

87. Adele Lindenmeyr, *Poverty Is Not a Vice: Charity, Society, and the State in Imperial Russia* (Princeton, N.J., 1996), p. 204.

88. Natan Meir, "Jews, Ukrainians, and Russians in Kiev: Intergroup Relations in Late Imperial Associational Life," *Slavic Review* 65, no. 3 (Fall 2006): 476.

89. See Steven Cassedy, *To the Other Shore: The Russian Jewish Intellectuals Who Came to America* (Princeton, N.J., 1997).

90. "Record no. 1, Oct. 21, 1906 of the Bialystoker Young Men's Association," in *Forty Years of History of the Bialystoker Young Men's Association* (New York, 1946), p. 6; Cassedy, *To the Other Shore*.

91. "Record no. 1, Oct. 21, 1906," p. 5.

92. Ibid.

93. See Diner, *A Time for Gathering*, pp. 105–8, 163; Benjamin Rabinowitz, "The Young Men's Hebrew Association (1854–1913)," *Proceedings of the American Jewish Historical Society* 37 (1947): 222–47.

94. Susan Milamed, "Proskurover Landsmenshaftn: A Case Study in Jewish Communal Development," *American Jewish History* 76 (1986): 42.

95. John Higham, *Strangers in the Land: Patterns of American Nativism, 1860–1925* (Westport, Conn., 1981), pp. 234–64; Eli Lederhendler, *Jewish Responses to Modernity: New Voices in America and Eastern Europe* (New York, 1994), pp. 104–39.

96. Gary Gerstle, *American Crucible: Race and Nation in the Twentieth Century* (Princeton, N.J., 2001), pp. 2–80.

97. John Klier, *Imperial Russia's Jewish Question, 1855–1881* (Cambridge, 1995), pp. 245–64.

98. Nathans, "The Other Modern Jewish Politics," p. 27; Natan Meir, "Jews, Ukrainians, and Russians in Kiev," pp. 480–84.

99. Avraham Barkai found in his analysis of German Jewish migrants to America that they also saw migration as a means to acquire rights. See Avraham Barkai, "Migration as an Emancipation Substitute? Jewish Group Identity across the Ocean," *Studia Rosenthaliana* 23 (1989): 291–98.

100. Robert Seltzer, "Jewish Liberalism in Late Imperial Russia," *Contemporary Jewry* 9, no. 1 (1988): 50–51.

101. Engelstein, *The Keys to Happiness*, pp. 7–8.

102. Dollinger, *Quest for Inclusion*, pp. 3–4.

Chapter 17. Democracy and Assimilation

1. Those killed in the period from October 1905 to September 1906 totaled about 3,100. An additional 2,000 were seriously injured and 15,000 more sought medical help for injuries sustained. See Shlomo Lambroza, "The Pogroms of 1903–1906," in John Klier and Shlomo Lambroza, eds., *Pogroms: Anti-Jewish Violence in Modern Russian History* (Cambridge, 1992), pp. 226–31.

2. Simon Kuznets, "Immigration of Russian Jews to the United States: Background and Structure," *Perspectives in American History* 9 (1975): 39, 43. Exact figures for Russian Jewish immigration to the United States show that 92,388 entered the country in 1905, and 125,234 in 1906. In 1907 Jewish immigration leveled off (see Zosa Szajkowski, "The Impact of the Russian Revolution of 1905 on American Jewish Life," *YIVO Annual* 17 [1978]: 106–7).

3. For some standard accounts of political and cultural trends in Russian Jewry in this period, see Salo W. Baron, *The Russian Jew under Tsars and Soviets* (New York-London, 1964), chaps. 10–11; Zvi Gitelman, *Jewish Nationality and Soviet Politics* (Princeton, N.J., 1972), chaps. 1–2; Shmuel Ettinger, "The Jews in Russia at the Outbreak of the Revolution," in Lionel Kochan, ed., *The Jews in Soviet Russia since 1917* (New York-London, 1972), pp. 14–28; Binyamin Pinkus, *Yehudei rusiyah uvrit hamo'atzot* (Beersheva, 1986), pp. 133–46; cf. Christoph Gassenschmidt, *Jewish Liberal Politics in Tsarist Russia 1900–1914* (New York, 1995); Benjamin Nathans, *Beyond the Pale: The Jewish Encounter with Late Imperial Russia* (Berkeley, Calif., 2002); Yehuda Slutsky, *Ha'itonut hayehudit-rusit bereishit hameah ha'esrim* (Tel Aviv, 1988); and Elias Schulman, *A History of Jewish Education in the Soviet Union* (New York-Waltham, Mass., 1971), chap. 1.

4. Arcadius Kahan, "Economic Opportunities and Some Pilgrims' Progress: Jewish Immigrants from Eastern Europe in the United States, 1890–1914," in

Kahan, *Essays in Jewish Social and Economic History*, ed. Roger Weiss, introd. Jonathan Frankel (Chicago-London, 1986), pp. 110, 112–14; cf. Thomas Kessner, *The Golden Door: Italian and Jewish Immigrant Mobility in New York City, 1880–1915* (New York, 1977).

5. See Priscilla Wald, "Of Crucibles and Grandfathers: The East European Immigrants"; David G. Roskies, "Coney Island, USA: America in the Yiddish Literary Imagination"; Hana Wirth-Nesher, "Traces of the Past: Multilingual Jewish American Writing"; and Ruth Wisse, "Jewish American Renaissance," all in Michael P. Kramer and Hana Wirth-Nesher, eds., *The Cambridge Companion to Jewish American Literature* (Cambridge, 2003).

6. This has been noted by a number of scholars. See, for example, Steven J. Zipperstein, *Imagining Russian Jewry* (Seattle-London, 1999), chap. 1; cf. Ewa Morawska, "Changing Images of the Old Country in the Development of Ethnic Identity among East European Immigrants, 1880–1930s: A Comparison of Jewish and Slavic Representations," *YIVO Annual* 21 (1993): 273–341.

7. Jonathan Frankel, *Prophecy and Politics: Socialism, Nationalism, and the Russian Jews, 1862–1917* (Cambridge, 1981), p. 499.

8. Szajkowski, "Impact of the Russian Revolution of 1905," pp. 64–74; Frankel, *Prophecy and Politics*, pp. 484–92.

9. For the history of HIAS, see Mark Wischnitzer, *Visas to Freedom: The History of HIAS* (Cleveland-New York, 1956); Ze'ev Deutsch, "HIAS: Hahevrah hayehudit lemahaseh ve'ezrah lemehagrim, 1909–1939" (Ph.D. diss., Hebrew University of Jerusalem, 2004); cf. Eli Lederhendler, "Hard Times: HIAS under Pressure, 1925–26," *YIVO Annual* 22 (1995): 105–30.

10. Naomi W. Cohen, *Jacob H. Schiff: A Study in American Jewish Leadership* (Hanover, N.H.-London, 1999), pp. 130, 134–36.

11. Ibid., pp. 130, 134–37, 148; cf. Szajkowski, "Impact of the Russian Revolution," p. 83.

12. Cyrus Adler, ed., *The Voice of America on Kishineff* (Philadelphia, 1904); Henry L. Feingold, *Zion in America* (New York, 1974), pp. 247–48.

13. Baron Revendal in the play is a character based on the Kishinev chief of police Baron Levendall.

14. On responses to Zangwill and *The Melting Pot*, see Judah L. Magnes, "The Melting Pot," *Emanu-el Pulpit*, vol. 3 (1909), reprinted in Arthur A. Goren, ed., *Dissenter in Zion: From the Writings of Judah L. Magnes* (Cambridge, 1982), pp. 101–6.

15. Szajkowski, "Impact of the Russian Revolution of 1905"; Henrietta Szold, ed., *American Jewish Year Book 5667* (Philadelphia, 1907), pp. 34–35. The lengthy report, "From Kishineff to Bialystok," appears on pp. 34–89.

16. Peter Wiernik, *History of the Jews in America* (New York, 1912), p. 1.

17. Ibid., pp. 357–58, 366.

18. Ibid., p. 358.

19. Nina Warnke, "Of Plays and Politics: Sholem Aleichem's First Visit to America," *YIVO Annual* 20 (1991): 244.

20. Ibid., p. 249, citing *New York Times* report of October 21, 1906, p. 5.

21. Ibid., p. 251, citing interview of Sholem Aleichem in the *American Hebrew*, October 26, 1906, p. 507.

22. Cited by Chone Shmeruk, "Sholem Aleichem and America," *YIVO Annual* 20 (1991): 214; original: Sholem Aleichem, *Verk*, vol. 19, p. 64.

23. Adolph Lewisohn, quoted in Szajkowski, "Impact of the Russian Revolution of 1905," p. 82.

24. *American Jewish Year Book 5667*, p. 91.

25. The American Jewish Committee and other leading Jewish groups in the United States, following the pogroms of 1906 and continued anti-Jewish discrimination under tsarist policy, waged a high-profile campaign in the American press and in Congress to exert American pressure on the Russian regime to alleviate Jewish disabilities. The main target of the campaign—the abrogation of the trade agreement between the two countries—was achieved in 1911 (see Naomi W. Cohen, *Not Free to Desist: The American Jewish Committee, 1906–1966* [Philadelphia, 1972], chap. 4).

26. Eventually the work was published in three volumes: *History of the Jews of Russia and Poland* (Philadelphia, 1916–20).

27. Israel Friedlaender to Simon Dubnov, October 29, 1913, JTS Archives, ARC 39, Israel Friedlaender Papers, Box 9, folder 1: English translation published by Moshe Davis, "Jewry, East and West: The Correspondence of Israel Friedlaender and Simon Dubnow," *YIVO Annual* 9 (1954): 24–25. Cf. Jonathan D. Sarna, *JPS: The Americanization of Jewish Culture, 1888–1988* (Philadelphia-New York-Jerusalem, 1989), p. 67.

28. Simon Dubnov to Israel Friedlaender, December 13 (26), 1913, in Davis, "Jewry, East and West," pp. 26–27; JTS Archives, ARC 39, Israel Friedlaender Papers, Box 9, folder 1.

29. See esp. Kuznets, "Russian Jewish Immigration to America."

30. See Kuznets, "Immigration of Russian Jews," pp. 50–51, and Szajkowski, "The Impact of the Russian Revolution of 1905," p. 107.

31. Mary Antin, for example, one of the earliest East European immigrants to become involved in public American discourse (in English), personified both the utopian expectation of a new dispensation for minority groups as well as a visceral, militant American patriotism (manifested during World War I) (see her memoir *The Promised Land* [London, 1912] and her pro-immigration tract *They Who Knock at Our Gates* [New York, 1914]). Her patriotism made impossible her marriage to a German American academic, and she then entered a spiral of depression and withdrawal that lasted the rest of her life (see Evelyn Salz, ed., *Selected Letters of Mary Antin* [Syracuse, N.Y., 2000]). On Jewish resistance to the military draft in the spring and summer of 1917, mainly among radical circles in New York City and based partly on considerations of Russia's internal political situation, see Christopher M. Sterba, *Good Americans: Italian and Jewish Immigrants during the First World War* (New York, 2003), chap. 3.

32. Szajkowski, "Impact of the Russian Revolution," p. 62. On socialist Jews' accommodation to American politics, cf. Eli Lederhendler, "America: A Vision in a Jewish Mirror," in *Jewish Responses to Modernity: New Voices in America and Eastern Europe* (New York, 1994), pp. 128–37.

33. Szajkowski, "Impact of the Russian Revolution," pp. 109–10. Mark Twain's observation is quoted from *Mark Twain's Autobiography* (New York- London, 1924), 2:292–94. For a similar case, see Nina Warnke on Maxim Gorky's visit to New York in 1906, where he was greeted by crowds of Jewish well-wishers and succeeded in raising funds for the revolutionary cause in Russia (Warnke, "Of Plays and Politics," pp. 248–49; cf. Frankel, *Prophecy and Politics*, p. 492).

34. Kazin is quoted by Moses Rischin, "When the New York Savants Go Marching In," *Reviews in American History* 17 (June 1989): 297.

35. Ruth Wisse, in the essay "Drowning in the Red Sea: The Lasting Legacy of Jewish Communism," raises the question why American Jews proved disproportionally susceptible to communist rhetoric. I suggest that the answer lies at

least in part in the fact that it was *Russian* communism that was involved here and, as I outline above, Jews and Russian communism were particularly bound up in a common political incubator. Wisse's paper, presented at the conference "Imagining the American Jewish Community," March 21–23, 2004, at the Jewish Theological Seminary of America, will appear in a volume of conference papers under that title, edited by Jack Wertheimer, to be published in 2008 by the University Press of New England.

Contributors

Abraham Ascher is Distinguished Professor Emeritus, Graduate Center, City University of New York. His recent publications include *A Community Under Siege: The Jews of Breslau under Nazism* (Stanford, Calif., 2007) and *P. A. Stolypin: The Search for Stability in Late Imperial Russia* (Stanford, Calif., 2000).

Dmitrii Elyashevich is Rector of the Petersburg Institute of Jewish Studies and a professor at St. Petersburg State University and St. Petersburg State University of Culture and Art. His publications include *Evreiskaya pechat', politika i tsenzura v Rossii, 1797–1917: Ocherki istorii tsenzury* (St. Petersburg, 1999) and *Dokumental'nye materialy po istorii evreev v arkhivakh SNG i stran Baltii* (St. Petersburg, 1994).

Agnieszka Friedrich is affiliated with The Institute of Polish Philology at the University of Gdańsk, Poland. Her publications include *Bolesław Prus wobec kwestii żydowskiej* (Bolesław Prus on the Jewish Question) (Gdańsk, 2007) and "Żydzi, Niemcy i Polacy w publicystyce Bolesława Prusa i Jana Jeleńskiego do 1883 roku" (Jews, Germans, and Poles in the Journalism of Bolesław Prus and Jan Jeleński until 1883), in K. Pilarczyk, ed., *Żydzi i judaizm we współczesnych badaniach polskich* (Cracow, 2003), 3:199–213.

Semion Goldin holds a doctorate from the Hebrew University of Jerusalem. He is Academic Director of the Chais Center for Jewish Studies in Russian at the Hebrew University. His publications include "Jews in the Documentation of Russian Army Counter-Espionage Corps and Russian Military Courts during World War I," in Wolf Moskovich and Leonid Finberg, eds., *Jews and Slavs*, vol. 17 (in Russian, forthcoming), and "The Russian High Command and the Jews during World War I: The Roots of the Negative Stereotype," in Oleg Budnitskii, ed., *The World Crisis of 1914–1920 and the Fate of East European Jewry* (in Russian) (Moscow, 2005), pp. 29–46.

Hannan Hever is a professor in the Department of Hebrew Literature, The Hebrew University of Jerusalem. Recent publications include *Pro-*

ducing the Modern Hebrew Canon: Nation Building and Minority Discourse (New York, 2002) and *Toward the Longed-for Shore: The Sea in Hebrew Culture and Modern Hebrew Literature* (in Hebrew) (Tel Aviv, 2007).

Brian Horowitz is the Sizeler Chair Professor of Jewish Studies at Tulane University. His book *Empire Jews: Jewish Nationalism and Acculturation in Late Nineteenth and Early Twentieth Century Russia* will be published in 2008 in the Slavica series. Among his recent publications are "Poet and Nation: Fame and Amnesia in Shimon Frug's Literary Reputation," *Russko-evreiskaia kul'tura* (2006), and "Integration and Its Discontents: Mikhail Morgulis and the Ideology of Jewish Integration in Russia," *Polin* (forthcoming, 2008).

Rebecca Kobrin is an assistant professor in the Department of History, Columbia University. Her recent publications include "Rewriting the Diaspora: Images of Eastern Europe in the Bialystok Landsmanshaft Press," *Jewish Social Studies* 12, no.3 (Spring/Summer 2006): 1–38, and *Between Exile and Empire: Jewish Bialystok and Its Diaspora* (Bloomington, Ind., forthcoming).

Mikhail Krutikov is Assistant Professor of Slavic and Judaic Studies at the University of Michigan, Ann Arbor. He has published *Yiddish Fiction and the Crisis of Modernity, 1905–1914* (Stanford, Calif., 2001) and "A Yiddish Author as a Cultural Mediator: Meir Wiener's Unpublished Novel," in Ritchie Robertson and Joseph Sherman, eds., *The Yiddish Presence in European Literature: Inspiration and Interaction* (Oxford, 2005).

Eli Lederhendler, the Stephen S. Wise Professor of American Jewish History and Institutions at the Hebrew University of Jerusalem, is the author of *The Road to Modern Jewish Politics* (New York, 1989) and *New York Jews and the Decline of Urban Ethnicity, 1950–1970* (Syracuse, N.Y., 2001).

Vladimir Levin is a post-doctoral fellow at the Kreitman Foundation, the Ben-Gurion University of the Negev, Beersheva. His latest publications are "Russian Jewry and the Duma Elections, 1906–1907," in W. Moskovich, L. Finberg, and M. Feller, eds., *Jews and Slavs: Essays on Intercultural Relations*, vol. 7, *Jews and Eastern Slavs* (Jerusalem-Kiev, 2000), pp. 233–64, and "Politics at the Crossroads—Jewish Parties and the Second Duma Elections 1907," *Leipziger Beiträge zur jüdischen Geschichte und Kultur* 2 (2004): 129–46.

Kenneth B. Moss is Assistant Professor, Felix Posen Chair of Modern Jewish History, Department of History, The Johns Hopkins University. His recent publications include "Bringing Culture to the Nation: Hebraism, Yiddishism, and the Dilemmas of Dissemination, 1917–1919," *Jewish History* (forthcoming in 2008), and "Not *The Dybbuk* but *Don Quixote*: Translation, Deparochialization, and Nationalism in Jewish Culture," in Benjamin Nathans and Gabriella Safran, eds., *Culture Front: Representing Jews in Eastern Europe* (forthcoming in 2008).

Benjamin Nathans is Ronald S. Lauder Endowed Term Associate Professor of History at the University of Pennsylvania. He is the author of *Beyond the Pale: The Jewish Encounter with Late Imperial Russia* (2002) and co-editor (with Gabriella Safran) of *Culture Front: Representing Jews in Eastern Europe* (forthcoming in 2008).

Barry Trachtenberg is Assistant Professor of European Jewish studies at the University at Albany (SUNY). Recent publications include "Ber Borochov and the Task of Yiddish Philology," *Science in Context* 20, no. 2 (June 2007): 341–52, and "From Edification to Commemoration: *Di Algemeyne Entsiklopedye*, the Holocaust, and the Collapse of Eastern European Jewish Life," *Journal of Modern Jewish Studies* 5, no. 3 (November 2006): 285–300.

Scott Ury received his doctorate from the Hebrew University of Jerusalem. He is a post-doctoral fellow in the Department of Jewish History at Tel Aviv University. His publications include "Zionism and Zionist Parties in Eastern Europe," in Gershon David Hundert, ed., *Jews in Eastern Europe: The YIVO Encyclopedia* (forthcoming, 2008), and "Noble Advocate or Unbridled Opportunist? The *Shtadlan* of the Polish-Lithuanian Commonwealth," *Polin* 15 (2002): 267–99.

Jeffrey Veidlinger is Associate Professor in the Department of History and Associate Director of the Jewish Studies Program at Indiana University. He is currently working on a book about Jewish public culture in the late Russian Empire, particularly after 1905. His publications include *The Moscow State Yiddish Theater: Jewish Culture on the Soviet Stage* (Bloomington, Ind., 2000) and ". . . Even beyond Pinsk: *Yizker Bikher* [Memorial Books] and Jewish Cultural Life in the Shtetl," in *Studies in Jewish Civilization*, vol. 16, *The Jews of Eastern Europe* (2005), pp. 175–89.

Theodore R. Weeks is professor in the History Department, Southern Illinois University, Carbondale. His most recent publications include *From Assimilation to Antisemitism: The "Polish Question" in Poland, 1850–1914* (DeKalb, Ill., 2006) and "Managing Empire: Tsarist Nationalities

Policy," in Dominic Lieven, ed., *The Cambridge History of Russia*, vol. 2, *Imperial Russia, 1689–1917* (Cambridge, 2006), pp. 27–44.

Robert Weinberg is Professor of History at Swarthmore College. His recent publications include *The Russian Revolution: A History in Documents* (New York, 2008) and, with Laurie Bernstein, "Biology and the Jewish Question after the Revolution: One Soviet Approach to the Productivization of Jewish Labor," *Jewish History* (forthcoming).

Richard Wortman is James Bryce Professor of History at Columbia University. Recent works include *Scenarios of Power: Myth and Ceremony in Russian Monarchy,* volume 1: *From Peter the Great to the Death of Nicholas I* (Princeton, N.J., 1995) (Russian translation, OGI Press, 2002), and volume 2: *From Alexander II to the Abdication of Nicholas II* (Princeton, N.J., 2000) (Russian translation, OGI Press, 2004).

Index

Acknowledgments

This volume derived from a conference held at the Hebrew University in the spring of 2004 and was made possible by the combined efforts of the Mayrock Center for Russian, Eurasian, and East European Research, the Leonid Nevzlin Research Center for Russian and East European Jewry, the Department of Russian and Slavic Studies, and the Avraham Harman Institute of Contemporary Jewry. Its subject was the Russian Revolution of 1905 and its political, social, and cultural impact on Russian Jewry and on the emerging Jewish communities of Russian origin in the New World and in Palestine/Eretz Yisrael. The conference honored Professor Jonathan Frankel of the Hebrew University, who has served there with great distinction for nearly forty years. As Benjamin Nathans notes in his introduction, the common starting point for all presentations was a reconsideration of Jonathan Frankel's influential work in the field of East European Jewish history. Indeed, a number of conference participants, young scholars who represent the future of East European Jewish studies, are former students of Jonathan Frankel. It was an honor to have Jonathan present throughout, and we thank him for his contributions to the conference as well as for his scholarly leadership, warm friendship, and support over the years.

We would like to express our gratitude to a number of individuals and institutions that were instrumental in convening the conference and in the publication of this volume. First, we thank the members of the conference planning committee: Mordechai Altshuler, Israel Bartal, Eli Lederhendler, Wolf Moskovich, Gideon Shimoni, and Steven Zipperstein. Funding for the conference was provided by the Avraham Harman Institute of Contemporary Jewry, the Nevzlin Center, the Tamara and Saveli Grinberg Chair for Russian Studies, the Marjorie Mayrock endowment, and the Jay and Leonie Darwin Fund. The following individuals played an essential role in ensuring the successful running of the conference: Nitza Genuth, administrative director of the Institute of Contemporary Jewry; Rachel Nathan, director of finances at the Institute; Anastasia Cherniavski, administrative secretary of the Mayrock Center; and Jonathan Dekel-Chen, director, and Avital Dubinsky, administrative director, of the Nevzlin Center. Special thanks go to Maria Paluy, who took over as administrative secretary at the Mayrock Center at a critical time. Our thanks also go to Ro'i Doron for technical assistance.

We owe a debt of gratitude to Jerome Singerman, senior humanities editor at the University of Pennsylvania Press, for his unflagging support of this project. Dalia Ofer, head of the Institute for Contemporary Jewry from 2004 to the end of 2006, was particularly helpful in guiding this project to its successful completion.

Among those whose financial assistance has made possible the editing and publication of this volume are the Leonid Nevzlin Research Center for Russian and East European Jewry and the Lucius N. Littauer Foundation.

Stefani Hoffman
Ezra Mendelsohn